DATE DUE

Carnegie Commission on Higher Education
Sponsored Research Studies

ANY PERSON, ANY STUDY:
AN ESSAY ON HIGHER EDUCATION IN THE
UNITED STATES
Eric Ashby

THE NEW DEPRESSION IN HIGHER
EDUCATION:
A STUDY OF FINANCIAL CONDITIONS AT 41
COLLEGES AND UNIVERSITIES
Earl F. Cheit

FINANCING MEDICAL EDUCATION:
AN ANALYSIS OF ALTERNATIVE POLICIES
AND MECHANISMS
Rashi Fein and Gerald I. Weber

HIGHER EDUCATION IN NINE COUNTRIES:
A COMPARATIVE STUDY OF COLLEGES AND
UNIVERSITIES ABROAD
Barbara B. Burn, Philip G. Altbach, Clark Kerr,
and James A. Perkins

BRIDGES TO UNDERSTANDING:
INTERNATIONAL PROGRAMS OF AMERICAN
COLLEGES AND UNIVERSITIES
Irwin T. Sanders and Jennifer C. Ward

GRADUATE AND PROFESSIONAL EDUCATION,
1980:
A SURVEY OF INSTITUTIONAL PLANS
Lewis B. Mayhew

THE AMERICAN COLLEGE AND AMERICAN
CULTURE:
SOCIALIZATION AS A FUNCTION OF HIGHER
EDUCATION
Oscar Handlin and Mary F. Handlin

RECENT ALUMNI AND HIGHER EDUCATION:
A SURVEY OF COLLEGE GRADUATES
Joe L. Spaeth and Andrew M. Greeley

CHANGE IN EDUCATIONAL POLICY:
SELF-STUDIES IN SELECTED COLLEGES AND
UNIVERSITIES
Dwight R. Ladd

STATE OFFICIALS AND HIGHER EDUCATION:
A SURVEY OF THE OPINIONS AND
EXPECTATIONS OF POLICY MAKERS IN NINE
STATES
Heinz Eulau and Harold Quinley

ACADEMIC DEGREE STRUCTURES:
INNOVATIVE APPROACHES
PRINCIPLES OF REFORM IN DEGREE
STRUCTURES IN THE UNITED STATES
Stephen H. Spurr

COLLEGES OF THE FORGOTTEN AMERICANS:
A PROFILE OF STATE COLLEGES AND
REGIONAL UNIVERSITIES
E. Alden Dunham

FROM BACKWATER TO MAINSTREAM:
A PROFILE OF CATHOLIC HIGHER
EDUCATION
Andrew M. Greeley

THE ECONOMICS OF THE MAJOR PRIVATE
UNIVERSITIES
William G. Bowen
(Out of print, but available from University Microfilms.)

THE FINANCE OF HIGHER EDUCATION
Howard R. Bowen
(Out of print, but available from University Microfilms.)

ALTERNATIVE METHODS OF FEDERAL
FUNDING FOR HIGHER EDUCATION
Ron Wolk
(Out of print, but available from University Microfilms.)

INVENTORY OF CURRENT RESEARCH ON
HIGHER EDUCATION 1968
Dale M. Heckman and Warren Bryan Martin
(Out of print, but available from University Microfilms.)

The following technical reports are available from the Carnegie Commission on Higher Education, 1947
Center Street, Berkeley, California 94704.

RESOURCE USE IN HIGHER EDUCATION:
TRENDS IN OUTPUT AND INPUTS, 1930–1967
June O'Neill

TRENDS AND PROJECTIONS OF PHYSICIANS
IN THE UNITED STATES 1967–2002
Mark S. Blumberg

MENTAL ABILITY AND HIGHER EDUCATIONAL
ATTAINMENT IN THE 20TH CENTURY
Paul Taubman and Terence Wales

AMERICAN COLLEGE AND UNIVERSITY
ENROLLMENT TRENDS IN 1971
Richard E. Peterson

MAY 1970:
THE CAMPUS AFTERMATH OF CAMBODIA
AND KENT STATE
Richard E. Peterson and John A. Bilorusky

PAPERS ON EFFICIENCY IN THE
MANAGEMENT OF HIGHER EDUCATION
Alexander M. Mood, Colin Bell,
Lawrence Bogard, Helen Brownlee,
and Joseph McCloskey

The following reprints are available from the Carnegie Commission on Higher Education, 1947 Center Street, Berkeley, California 94704.

ACCELERATED PROGRAMS OF MEDICAL EDUCATION, *by Mark S. Blumberg, reprinted from* JOURNAL OF MEDICAL EDUCATION, *vol. 46, no. 8, August 1971.**

SCIENTIFIC MANPOWER FOR 1970–1985, *by Allan M. Cartter, reprinted from* SCIENCE, *vol. 172, no. 3979, pp. 132–140, April 9, 1971.*

A NEW METHOD OF MEASURING STATES' HIGHER EDUCATION BURDEN, *by Neil Timm, reprinted from* THE JOURNAL OF HIGHER EDUCATION, *vol. 42, no. 1, pp. 27–33, January 1971.**

REGENT WATCHING, *by Earl F. Cheit, reprinted from* AGB REPORTS, *vol. 13, no. 6, pp. 4–13, March 1971.*

COLLEGE GENERATIONS—FROM THE 1930s TO THE 1960s *by Seymour M. Lipset and Everett C. Ladd, Jr., reprinted from* THE PUBLIC INTEREST, *no. 25, Summer 1971.*

AMERICAN SOCIAL SCIENTISTS AND THE GROWTH OF CAMPUS POLITICAL ACTIVISM IN THE 1960s, *by Everett C. Ladd, Jr., and Seymour M. Lipset, reprinted from* SOCIAL SCIENCES INFORMATION, *vol. 10, no. 2, April 1971.*

THE DIVIDED PROFESSORIATE, *by Seymour M. Lipset and Everett C. Ladd, Jr., reprinted from* CHANGE, *vol. 3, no. 3, pp. 54–60, May 1971.**

THE POLITICS OF AMERICAN POLITICAL SCIENTISTS, *by Everett C. Ladd, Jr., and Seymour M. Lipset, reprinted from* PS, *vol. 4, no. 2, Spring 1971.**

JEWISH ACADEMICS IN THE UNITED STATES: THEIR ACHIEVEMENTS, CULTURE AND POLITICS, *by Seymour M. Lipset and Everett C. Ladd, Jr., reprinted from* AMERICAN JEWISH YEAR BOOK, *1971.*

THE UNHOLY ALLIANCE AGAINST THE CAMPUS, *by Kenneth Keniston and Michael Lerner, reprinted from* NEW YORK TIMES MAGAZINE, *November 8, 1970 .*

PRECARIOUS PROFESSORS: NEW PATTERNS OF REPRESENTATION, *by Joseph W. Garbarino, reprinted from* INDUSTRIAL RELATIONS, *vol. 10, no. 1, February 1971.**

. . . AND WHAT PROFESSORS THINK: ABOUT STUDENT PROTEST AND MANNERS, MORALS, POLITICS, AND CHAOS ON THE CAMPUS, *by Seymour Martin Lipset and Everett C. Ladd, Jr., reprinted from* PSYCHOLOGY TODAY, *November 1970.**

DEMAND AND SUPPLY IN U.S. HIGHER EDUCATION: A PROGRESS REPORT, *by Roy Radner and Leonard S. Miller, reprinted from* AMERICAN ECONOMIC REVIEW, *May 1970.**

RESOURCES FOR HIGHER EDUCATION: AN ECONOMIST'S VIEW, *by Theodore W. Schultz, reprinted from* JOURNAL OF POLITICAL ECONOMY, *vol. 76, no. 3, University of Chicago, May/June 1968.**

INDUSTRIAL RELATIONS AND UNIVERSITY RELATIONS, *by Clark Kerr, reprinted from* PRO-CEEDINGS OF THE 21ST ANNUAL WINTER MEETING OF THE INDUSTRIAL RELATIONS RESEARCH ASSOCIATION, *pp. 15–25.**

NEW CHALLENGES TO THE COLLEGE AND UNIVERSITY, *by Clark Kerr, reprinted from Kermit Gordon (ed.),* AGENDA FOR THE NATION, *The Brookings Institution, Washington, D.C., 1968.**

PRESIDENTIAL DISCONTENT, *by Clark Kerr, reprinted from David C. Nichols (ed.),* PERSPECTIVES ON CAMPUS TENSIONS: PAPERS PREPARED FOR THE SPECIAL COMMITTEE ON CAMPUS TENSIONS, *American Council on Education, Washington, D.C., September 1970.**

STUDENT PROTEST—AN INSTITUTIONAL AND NATIONAL PROFILE, *by Harold Hodgkinson, reprinted from* THE RECORD, *vol. 71, no. 4, May 1970.**

WHAT'S BUGGING THE STUDENTS?, *by Kenneth Keniston, reprinted from* EDUCATIONAL RECORD, *American Council on Education, Washington, D.C., Spring 1970.**

THE POLITICS OF ACADEMIA, *by Seymour Martin Lipset, reprinted from David C. Nichols (ed.),* PERSPECTIVES ON CAMPUS TENSIONS: PAPERS PREPARED FOR THE SPECIAL COMMITTEE ON CAMPUS TENSIONS, *American Council on Education, Washington, D.C., September 1970.**

INTERNATIONAL PROGRAMS OF U.S. COLLEGES AND UNIVERSITIES: PRIORITIES FOR THE SEVENTIES, *by James A. Perkins, reprinted by permission of the International Council for Educational Development, Occasional Paper no. 1, July 1971.*

FACULTY UNIONISM: FROM THEORY TO PRACTICE, *by Joseph W. Garbarino, reprinted from* INDUSTRIAL RELATIONS, *vol. 11, no. 1, pp. 1–17, February 1972.*

MORE FOR LESS: HIGHER EDUCATION'S NEW PRIORITY, *by Virginia B. Smith, reprinted from* UNIVERSAL HIGHER EDUCATION: COSTS AND BENEFITS, *American Council on Education, Washington, D.C., 1971.*

ACADEMIA AND POLITICS IN AMERICA, *by Seymour M. Lipset, reprinted from Thomas J. Nossiter (ed.),* IMAGINATION AND PRECISION IN THE SOCIAL SCIENCES, *pp. 211–289, Faber and Faber, London, 1972.*

POLITICS OF ACADEMIC NATURAL SCIENTISTS AND ENGINEERS, *by Everett C. Ladd, Jr., and Seymour M. Lipset, reprinted from* SCIENCE, *vol. 176, no. 4039, pp. 1091–1100, June 9, 1972.*

THE INTELLECTUAL AS CRITIC AND REBEL: WITH SPECIAL REFERENCE TO THE UNITED STATES AND THE SOVIET UNION, *by Seymour M. Lipset and Richard B. Dobson, reprinted from* DAEDALUS, *vol. 101, no. 3, pp. 137–198, Summer 1972.*

THE POLITICS OF AMERICAN SOCIOLOGISTS, *by Seymour M. Lipset and Everett C. Ladd, Jr., reprinted from* THE AMERICAN JOURNAL OF SOCIOLOGY, *vol. 78, no. 1, July 1972.*

THE DISTRIBUTION OF ACADEMIC TENURE IN AMERICAN HIGHER EDUCATION, *by Martin Trow, reprinted from* THE TENURE DEBATE, *Bardwell Smith (ed.), Jossey-Bass, San Francisco, 1972.*

THE NATURE AND ORIGINS OF THE CARNEGIE COMMISSION ON HIGHER EDUCATION, *by Alan Pifer, reprinted by permission of The Carnegie Foundation for the Advancement of Teaching.*

*The Commission's stock of this reprint has been exhausted.

Academic Transformation

Academic Transformation

SEVENTEEN INSTITUTIONS UNDER PRESSURE

edited by *David Riesman*
and *Verne A. Stadtman*

with chapters by
Philip G. Altbach, Burton R. Clark,
Jill Conway, John A. Dunn, Jr.,
Zelda F. Gamson, Nathan Glazer,
David R. Goddard and Linda C. Koons,
Gerald Grant, Algo D. Henderson,
Paul Mangelsdorf, Jr.,
Richard P. McCormick, Marshall Meyer,
Paul E. Sigmund, Neil J. Smelser,
Benson Snyder, Irene Tinker,
John Walsh

A Volume of Essays Sponsored by
The Carnegie Commission on Higher Education

MCGRAW-HILL BOOK COMPANY

New York   St. Louis   San Francisco   Düsseldorf
London   Sydney   Toronto   Mexico   Panama
Johannesburg   Kuala Lumpur   Montreal
New Delhi   Rio de Janeiro   Singapore

The Carnegie Commission on Higher Education,
1947 Center Street, Berkeley, California 94704
has sponsored preparation of this volume as a
part of a continuing effort to obtain and present
significant information for public discussion.
The views expressed are those of the authors.

ACADEMIC TRANSFORMATION
Seventeen Institutions under Pressure

Library of Congress Cataloging in Publication Data
Main entry under title:
Academic transformation.
"A volume of essays sponsored by the Carnegie
Commission on Higher Education."
Includes bibliographical references.
1.   Universities and colleges—United States.
2.   Education, Higher—United States—1965–
I. Riesman, David, date, ed.   II.   Stadtman, Verne
A., ed.   III.   Altbach, Philip G.   IV.   Carnegie
Commission on Higher Education.
LA227.3.A63   378.73   72-10267
ISBN 0-07-010049-7

123456789MMAM79876543

Contents

The Authors

Philip G. Altbach is associate professor in the Departments of Educational Policy Studies and Indian Studies at the University of Wisconsin, Madison. He is a member of the Madison Campus Faculty Senate and has served on various academic committees. Most recently, he has edited (with R. S. Laufer and S. McVey) a book on the University of Wisconsin entitled *Academic Supermarkets.*

Burton R. Clark is professor of sociology, Yale University, where he has taught since 1966. He was research sociologist in the Center for the Study of Higher Education and professor of education at the University of California, Berkeley, between 1958 and 1966. Among his important publications are *The Distinctive College: Antioch, Reed and Swarthmore, Educating the Expert Society,* and *The Open Door College.*

Jill Conway is associate professor of history at the University of Toronto. Born in Australia, she received her Ph.D. in American history at Harvard in 1969 and has taught at the University of Toronto since 1964. A concerned observer of attempts to restructure the government at the University of Toronto, she has been kept aware of parallel developments in the United States as a participant in conferences of the Assembly on University Goals and Governance of the American Academy of Arts and Sciences.

John A. Dunn, Jr. is the assistant to the president at Tufts University, Medford, Massachusetts, and has responsibility there for long-range institutional planning. Before 1969, he held executive positions with the Budd Company, Philadelphia, Pennsylvania.

Zelda F. Gamson is a sociologist who teaches at the University of Michigan in the Center for the Study of Higher Education and does research at the Institute for Social Research. She attended Antioch College, the University of Michigan, and Harvard University. Her major commitment is to the restructuring of undergraduate education. Her teaching and research have been in the areas of organizational theory and higher education.

Nathan Glazer is professor of education and social structure at the Harvard Graduate School of Education and a 1944 graduate of the City College of New York. In 1970–71 he assisted President R. E. Marshak in developing plans for a center for urban studies and education at City College.

David R. Goddard is university professor of biology, University of Pennsylvania. He was provost of the University of Pennsylvania from October 1961 through December 1970.

Gerald Grant is associate professor of education in the Department of Cultural Foundations of Education and a member of the faculty of the Department of Sociology at Syracuse University. Prior to his current appointment he was research fellow in the Department of Sociology in the Center for Behavior Sciences at Harvard.

Algo D. Henderson is research educator at the Center for Research and Development in Higher Education at Berkeley. He previously served as director for the Center for Study of Higher Education, University of Michigan; associate commissioner of education, University of the State of New York; and president, Antioch College.

Linda C. Koons is assistant ombudsman at the University of Pennsylvania and was an assistant to the provost from September 1967 through December 1970.

Paul Mangelsdorf, Jr. is professor of physics at Swarthmore College. He is also an alumnus of the college (and its honors program), and is a member of the Society of Friends.

Richard P. McCormick is professor of history and university historian at Rutgers College of Rutgers, the State University, and is author of *Rutgers: A Bicentennial History.*

Marshall W. Meyer teaches in the New York State School of Industrial and Labor Relations and in the Department of Sociology at Cornell University. From 1967 to 1969 he was a lecturer on sociology in the Department of Social Relations at Harvard.

David Riesman is Henry Ford II Professor of Social Sciences at Harvard University and a member of the Carnegie Commission on Higher Education.

Paul E. Sigmund is professor of politics and director of graduate studies in the Politics Department at Princeton University. A specialist in political theory and Latin American politics, he has written articles on students and politics in the United States and in Latin America. His most recent book is *The Ideologies of the Developing Nations* (2d rev. ed., 1972).

Neil J. Smelser is professor of sociology, University of California, Berkeley. He was special assistant to acting chancellor Martin Meyerson from January to July 1965, with special responsibilities in the area of student political activities; between 1966 and 1968 he was assistant chancellor for educational development and from March 1969 through July 1970, was a member of the Policy Committee of the Berkeley Division of the Academic Senate. He was chairman of that committee for the academic year 1971–72.

Benson Snyder, M.D. is a professor of psychiatry, MIT, and also serves as dean for institute relations. Formerly he held the position of psychiatrist-in-chief for 10 years at MIT. In his present capacity as a senior administrator of the institute, he is involved in internal staff relations and serves on various committees dealing with this subject. He has also done extensive educational research, culminating in the book *The Hidden Curriculum.*

Verne A. Stadtman is assistant director and editor of the Carnegie Commission on Higher Education.

Irene Tinker is director of the Comparative Urbanization Project, American University. As assistant provost for curriculum development from September 1967 to July 1969, she was one of the first staff members of the fledgling Federal City College and for five months was the only academic administrator. She was also professor of political science until she resigned in August 1971.

John Walsh is a member of the news staff of *Science* and has served in recent years as European correspondent and news editor for that magazine.

Foreword

American colleges and universities will remember the 1960s for a long time. Campus disruption, abandonment of traditions, and seemingly insatiable demands for change brought tension into the academic atmosphere, exposed serious weaknesses in campus policies and procedures, and aroused public suspicion where there had been acceptance and approval.

Because the headlines about colleges across the country were so similar, the conclusion that there were uniform causes of and solutions to crises came all too easily. But it is clear that Berkeley in 1964, Columbia in 1968, and Kent State in 1970 could not be explained in exactly the same way. There were many forces at work with variable impacts on different kinds of institutions. The Carnegie Commission on Higher Education asked the 18 authors represented in this book to prepare accounts of institutions that had experienced crises and transformations during the last half of the 1960s and the first years of the 1970s. Most of the authors have lived through the events they write about and speak from first-hand experience. Some of them write not so much from the perspective of personal involvement as with the discipline of experienced observers and reporters who draw their accounts from the evidence provided by the public record, interviews with participants in the events they describe, and visits to the institutions.

On behalf of the Carnegie Commission on Higher Education, which sponsored preparation of this volume, I want to thank all the authors for their contributions. In particular, our thanks are extended to David Riesman, Henry Ford II Professor of Social Science at Harvard University and a member of our Commission. Dr. Riesman's first-hand observations of many different colleges and universities, and his wide aquaintance with persons engaged in the study of higher education is unsurpassed. This personal knowledge, and his superb perception and analytical skill have contributed enormously to the excellence and importance of this volume. Our appreciation also goes to Verne A. Stadtman, Assistant Director and Editor for the Commission, who conscientiously and thoughtfully brought this volume together.

Clark Kerr

Chairman
Carnegie Commission on
Higher Education

January 1973

*This book was set in Vladimir by University Graphics, Inc.
It was printed on acid-free, long-life paper and bound by The
Maple Press Company. The designers were Elliot Epstein and
Edward Butler. The editors were Nancy Tressel and Janine Parson
for McGraw-Hill Book Company and Verne A. Stadtman, Terry Y.
Allen, and Karen Seriguchi for the Carnegie Commission on Higher
Education. Joe Campanella supervised the production.*

1. Constellations in a Nebulous Galaxy

by Verne A. Stadtman

On a warm May morning in 1958, Robert Frost read some of his poems to a hushed convocation of several thousand students, faculty members, and townspeople gathered in the Greek theatre on the Berkeley campus. In introducing his readings, he gently chided literary critics who tried to discern in his works strong convictions that were not there. He did not try to set forth large themes, he said; each of his poems was "like a star. One here, another there, all unrelated until, when darkness falls, they begin to constellate."

That metaphor came to mind as we attempted to devise a logical sequence for the 17 accounts in this volume. The intent of the whole enterprise was to discern, if we could, the common elements in the crises experienced by hundreds of American colleges and universities between 1964 and 1971. In choosing institutions to be included, however, we made no effort to predetermine some master theme. We were more interested in institutions that went through climactic experiences in different ways. In short, our selection was on the basis of variety and not similarities.

Still, when our darkness fell (when the reports were completed and the time came to determine what they might mean in aggregation) was it unreasonable for us to expect that significant patterns might become evident? From an event described at Harvard, to an idea expressed at Stanford, to a trend evident at Michigan should it not be possible to draw interconnections that outline some simple truth standing somehow in relief from the narratives themselves? And from such truths might one not construct a logic to organize the total effort?

Such expectations were not fully realized. A galaxy that consists of diverse colleges and universities described in different ways from different perspectives by different people yields indistinct constellations. It does not, certainly, display a grand pattern. Even so, from such continuities, convergencies, and similarities—however few and indistinct—that these reports make discernable, several interesting ideas can be traced.

THE ISSUES Four broad issues were central to the most disruptive events of the period.

1 The first of them concerned the individual and political rights of students and was the central issue at Berkeley in 1964. This issue later arose in a secondary role at certain stages of crisis at other institutions, but it was never again as central as it had been at Berkeley. The reason for this was that the battle over individual rights at Berkeley was one of the last big ones to be fought on this issue. By 1964, most institutions on the East Coast and some on the West Coast had already come to terms with the "free speech" issue and had settled it on about the same terms as were reached at Berkeley in 1965. In the 1960s, students who had recently arrived in Berkeley from other parts of the country, and especially from the East Coast, took an active role in the Free Speech Movement because, among other things, they regarded Berkeley as uniquely repressive in comparison with other institutions they had known. Berkeley lagged behind other institutions because, for the entire first half of the twentieth century, it observed a tradition, built by Benjamin Ide Wheeler and perpetuated by Robert Gordon Sproul, which had the effect of insulating students from what were considered to be the concerns only of the older generations and restrained the students from concerted action within the society around them. To a considerable extent, Berkeley's crisis involved a sharp break with that tradition.

In terms of techniques of confrontation and campus disruption, however, there is no question that the Berkeley campus instructed the entire student generation of the later 1960s.

2 The war in Vietnam and war-related issues produced demonstrations and disruptions with some regularity (usually in the fall) throughout the period. Aversion to the war was expressed in demands for an end to ROTC (Reserve Officers' Training Corps) programs, an end to armed service recruiting drives on campuses, an end to the draft and the college's cooperation with the selective service system, an end to college and university cooperation with

industries engaged in the manufacture of weapons — particularly those regarded as especially cruel and brutal, and an end to the involvement of universities in war-related research and weapons development.

3 The urge to extend opportunities for higher education to members of minority groups proved to be one of the more inflammatory causes of campus strife. By the 1960s, the time of this issue had come, not just for the country, but also for higher education. Regrettably, efforts to resolve it intelligently sometimes divided the campuses internally, sometimes disengaged the campuses from significant support from outside, and often failed to satisfy those in whose behalf the efforts were made. The ways in which colleges attempted to resolve this issue may have had more significant long-run educational impacts than any of the other major issues of the period. Doors of colleges and universities were, in fact, opened to members of minority groups in great numbers. There was considerable experimentation with flexible study arrangements to accommodate those of the new students who would not have survived in college under traditional arrangements. These and other efforts to accommodate students previously shut out of higher education could not help but loosen the hold of precedent and custom on curriculum and procedures in colleges and universities generally.

4 The issue of student participation in campus decision making is an old one. It was taken seriously, however, only after 1964 when it became clear that settlements of campus controversy were impossible without the concurrence of the dissenting or challenging students. In the 1960s, therefore, it was, first of all, a tactical issue. In attempting to resolve it, however, students (and some faculty members and administrators) developed philosophical arguments based on conceptions of the college or university campus as a social unit in which the various membership classes were entitled to representation for purposes of governance. As the reports indicate, in response to such ideas new roles for students in academic policy making have been created on many campuses. The Carnegie Commission on Higher Education has called attention to this trend in some of its reports and encourages it. But limitations on student participation are important, too; it is obvious from reading the essays that there are certain roles of decision making that are more appropriate for students than others and that, in any case, the faculty and administrators must retain and exercise certain responsibilities for decision making regardless of the degree of student participation that occurs.

Except for the issue of student participation—which was rarely the central issue of dissent—the four issues that are dominant in the campus crises of the late 1960s share one important characteristic. They are either directly or indirectly related to issues external to academic functions of colleges and universities. They concern structures and procedures, equal opportunity, and the conclusion of a war. Efforts to settle such issues may severely cut into the efforts normally expended on academic endeavor, but they are not directly related to criticism of academic activities. It is largely for this reason that we encounter throughout the turmoil, the paradox of widespread unrest on the one hand, and widely reported general satisfaction of students with their education and their colleges on the other.

There was very little that colleges and universities could do alone to stop the war or end racism in America. What they could try to do, however, was to educate the country's citizenry better. Therefore, although the students' dissatisfaction with their education was low, the colleges responded most energetically to the crises of the 1960s with educational reforms. Some of these reforms had for years been subjected to tedious discussion and debate of a sort characteristic of the American academic system. Others were generated by self-studies and blue-ribbon campus commissions given wide latitude for recommending internal educational policy changes. And it is in this kind of activity, and not in responding to the external issues, that colleges and universities are transforming themselves, perhaps slowly, but profoundly.

Several of the institutions discussed in the reports in this book began a systematic effort to solve some of their organizational and educational problems long before the fall of 1964. Massachusetts Institute of Technology and Pennsylvania are notable in this regard. So, in different ways, were Swarthmore, Princeton, and Wesleyan. On the whole, institutions that were engaged in such planning seem to have accomplished more fundamental institutional change, with relatively less disruption, than did those campuses that spent the entire period addressing each crisis as it arose. For one thing, administrators, faculty members, and institutions were able to handle some of the crisis situations by considering alternative actions from a range of possibilities that already had been under discussion in a crisis-free atmosphere. For another, because some of these institutions were so obviously making an effort to change, even before crisis, the idea of transformation was not as frightening to their faculties and students as it was at Berkeley and Wisconsin where response to crisis and change was more defensive and therefore more resistant.

THE NEW COLLEGES Two of the colleges—Old Westbury and Federal City College—are very new. But their stories have little in common except that they both involve attempts by institutions to respond to critical issues of the time. At Old Westbury, the response was to demands for radical alteration of the form and duration of the college experience and for greater attention to the student "and his concern with the modern world." It featured procedural flexibility and student independence and carried the doctrine of student governmental initiative and participation to almost suicidal limits before it was given a chance to start over again.

There is a convergence of the stories of Old Westbury and Federal City College at that juncture where students at Old Westbury demanded 50 percent representation of blacks and other nonwhites in the student body, faculty, and staff. This demand—which was not acceded to—spoke to the same general issue, equality of education for racial minorities, that put the faculty at Federal City College on a course headed for total blackness.

It is hard not to talk about Antioch as an institution susceptible to all of the problems of new institutions. In the context of the period covered in these reports, it is clear that Antioch has responded to the challenge of our era with novel, sometimes calculatedly experimental, solutions. Some of these take the form of semi-autonomous institutions that are, in fact, new.

THE DEMOGRAPHIC INFLUENCE Fortunately, some of the reports in this volume present well-developed descriptions of the impacts of shifts in the composition of campus populations. The engineering of such a shift emerges as the essential point of the report about City College of New York. In fascinating ways, another such a shift is vital to an understanding of what has happened at the University of Pennsylvania. In Toronto, where the Americanization of the faculty is a lively issue, and Wesleyan, where counteraction to opened access is noted, the impacts have still different guises.

Except as these shifts are produced deliberately as a means of providing more ready access to higher education for racial minorities, they are not likely to become issues of record. Yet it is clear from these reports that they shape the course of events on campuses and reveal college and university ties to the national culture that may not be terribly well understood by the administrators and faculty members of some of our colleges.

At the very least, the character of the student population has a bearing upon the spirit and tempo of campus life and the nature of student enthusiasms. On the basis of the reports available to us here, one suspects that student-body composition may well be a source of distinctiveness that campus planners should exploit more intelligently than they have in the past when plotting their escape from the often heralded homogeneity of American higher education.

THE ROLE OF SIZE Three large public institutions are described in this book. Two of them hold signal positions in the era under discussion—Berkeley, where large-scale protest seemed to mark the beginning of perpetual campus turmoil, and Wisconsin, where a fatal bomb blast seemed to demonstrate, finally, the ultimate ugliness and tragic absurdity of its continuation. The third, Michigan, is presented to us as the capital of the philosophical movement that generated and refined the ideology of the conflict while remaining relatively untouched by the shooting.

In retrospect, what is most impressive about these three institutions is that they seem to have transformed themselves so little in consequence of the critical events of the period. In the aftermath of the most severe of its own violent disruptions, Berkeley endeavored to seek transformation through the traditional academic conduit—the faculty committee. But the recommendations that came from that effort are still largely unimplemented.

It is, of course, difficult to change large institutions—at least from the inside. And it is harder to make less than massive changes visible in these institutions than it is in smaller ones. One suspects that some of the more interesting innovations that are prominent at smaller institutions may also be present within shadowy recesses of giant ones. There is no reason to deny, however, that at large institutions the well-established interests of diverse centers of influence and power combine more frequently to restrain general transformation than to accommodate it.

It is additionally worth noting, however, that although some of their departments may have suffered from resignations or internal dissention, none of the three large public institutions have yet suffered any widely proclaimed erosion of their national academic reputations. That observation raises an intriguing question as to whether these institutions would really be better if they were more visibly engaged in educational reforms. There is no way to prove that they would be, partly because one is rarely sure in advance whether any proposed reform will prove successful. On the other-hand, institutions that appear not to change are always in danger of losing whatever reputations they may have had for being for-ward-looking and progressive. For better or for worse, those students, donors, and others who support colleges and universities and who prefer a lively atmosphere of adventure and newness to atmospheres of apparent complacency and immutability could render the telling judgment on the question.

THE CHRONOLOGY OF CRISIS Tracing the sequence of major events of the period provides some helpful reference points. But the effort can be deceptive because the authors of the accounts do not always discuss climactic events in sufficient detail to provide precise timing for historical purposes. As we have already noted, however, the most commonly accepted "beginning" occurred at Berkeley in the fall of 1964. In the develop-ment of plans for this volume, we ourselves used that date as a beginning. It is now clear, though, that what began at Berkeley was a style of confrontation rather than a trend in the transformation of institutions. Early shots of the student rebellions (though muted and benign compared to those fired at Berkeley) are heard at Michi-gan in the early 1950s. We discover that the University of Penn-sylvania began a "hardnosed" study of itself in 1953—a decade before that exercise became the vogue at other instititutions. For Antioch, educational innovation is almost a congenital condition. Algo D. Henderson finds beginnings for San Francisco State's troubles rooted in California's Master Plan for Higher Education, adopted in 1960. Benson Snyder tells us that "MIT has been re-forming for a century." And Philip G. Altbach reminds us that "Madison was a center of student radicalism in the 1930s and was one of the few bastions of student radicalism during the apathetic 1950s." So one's notion of the beginning of the crisis subjected to review in these reports depends a great deal upon which aspects of the crisis one chooses to trace. By way of orienting the events in this volume, however, it is useful to review the following crude chronology based entirely on information available in the reports themselves.

In 1964, there was the Free Speech Movement at Berkeley. The original issue was the extent to which campus facilities could be used for personal and political expression.

In 1965, Michigan students and faculty members held a "moratorium" to protest the war in Vietnam. Opposition to university contracts with the Department of Defense found students and faculty members in unaccustomed agreement at Pennsylvania that year. (It is evident that the "war issue" was alive on many of the campuses prior to this date, but these are the first events specifically mentioned in the reports.)

In 1966, disruption was again related mainly to the war issue. At Berkeley there was an incident involving the picketing of a Marines' recruiting table. Wisconsin had its first disruptive protests—against selective service and recruiting efforts by Dow Chemical Company. At Michigan that year, students voted 2 to 1 against disclosing students' academic ranking to selective service offices. This was also the year at Michigan when an issue rooted in pre-1964 times emerged. It involved a protest of the transmission of the names of 65 students and several faculty members associated with radical groups to the House Un-American Activities Committee.

In 1967, the war continued to be the focus of campus demonstrations. At Wisconsin, police were called to remove students from the Commerce Building where a sit-in to protest recruiting by Dow Chemical Company was underway. A "small demonstration" against Dow recruiters occurred at Pennsylvania. At Rutgers, police were called to unblock the entrance to the ROTC building and in October there was a sit-in at Princeton's Institute for Defense Analysis.

At San Francisco State, the first violence associated with racial tensions occurred (although Algo D. Henderson suggests that racial tension had been building for some time prior to the incident).

In 1968, Martin Luther King was murdered and race-related incidents generated crises for several institutions represented in this volume. At Rutgers, demonstrations followed King's assassination. At Wesleyan, black students demanded that a Malcolm X and Martin Luther King "day of education" be held. A black student shot at a white student at Antioch. And at Princeton, students suggested that the university divest itself of investments in South African holdings.

In November, San Francisco State's prolonged strike occurred in which demands for black studies and improvement of the lot of black students on campus were major issues. The student strike was followed in December by a faculty strike that was apparently supportive of the dissenting students, but overtly related to working conditions and other bread-and-butter issues.

Continued concern with the war was evidenced in 1968 by a confrontation with a Navy recruiter at Wesleyan, and occupation of buildings and vigils in protest of ROTC and in behalf of sanctuary for an AWOL soldier at City College.

In 1969, the lot of the black student remained a key issue. The strike at San Francisco State continued until early spring, although there were mass arrests in January. In February, a black students' strike at Wisconsin grew to such dimensions that the police and National Guard were called in. At the University of Pennsylvania, College Hall was occupied to protest the clearing of university-owned land for a city high school and other contested uses. The protesters claimed that the demolition would destroy the homes of the poor and the blacks in the area. In April, students seized the South Campus of City College to demand, among other things, proportional representation of blacks and Puerto Ricans in the state university system. The whole college was closed as a precaution against massive violence. Building occupations and demonstrations seeking concessions for black students also occurred at Berkeley, Princeton, Rutgers, Swarthmore, and Wesleyan.

At Harvard, in October 1969, the racial issue was raised in the form of protests that a number of blacks hired for work on the campus were paid as painter's helpers although they were doing the same work as journeymen. The dispute evolved eventually into demands for a 20 percent quota of Third World representatives in the workers employed on Harvard construction sites.

On the front of campus action directed against the war in 1969, the issue of institutional involvement in defense-related research was the focus of the first severe disturbances at Harvard, Stanford, and Massachusetts Institute of Technology.

1969 was also a year for maverick issues—the bookstore sit-in at Michigan that resulted in the arrest of 107 persons, and the massive Berkeley riots that occurred when students and "street people" attempted to occupy university-owned land for a "People's Park."

1970 was a climactic year for major campus disturbances. The racial issue was critical at Michigan for the first three months of that year as the University sought to deal with demands of BAM — the Black Action Movement.

References to campus demonstrations following the Cambodian invasions in April 1970 are surprisingly subdued in these reports, either because the authors regarded them as too common as campus experiences in the country at that time to note individually, or because in contrast to the horror at Kent State and Jackson State they took nonviolent forms. The trashing of Harvard Square in April 1970 is a notable exception. Protests of university engagement in defense-related activities persisted during this year, however, notably at Harvard and most shockingly at Wisconsin where a saboteur's bomb exploded in the Army Mathematical Research Center and killed a post-doctoral fellow in physics.

Compilation of *Academic Transformation* has been a time-consuming undertaking. Work on it began in early 1971. The length of time that the work has been in progress explains why some of the accounts are devoted almost exclusively to discussions of events prior to June 1971, while a few report later developments. It also explains subtle differences in the historical perspectives from which the various authors approached their subjects.

That echoes of the late 1960s and early 1970s can still be heard on the nation's campuses — despite their apparent calmness — should not be surprising. We have experienced a period of great significance for both our colleges and for American society. Alain Touraine, the sociologist and informed French observer of American colleges and universities, has described the impact of the period vividly in an essay he has written for the Carnegie Commission on Higher Education. In it he said:

America was proud of her colleges and universities, in which she saw her preferred reflection — liberal and organized, idealistic and pragmatic. Because of this, the crisis in the university led her to doubt her values, and further still, to doubt whether it was in terms of values that she was to understand herself.

Although this observation may overstate the reaction of many Americans to the events and trends described in the accounts in this volume, it takes appropriate notice of the fact that what happened in higher education in the recent past was not only of passing, isolated, and internal importance. From the accounts provided we can also glimpse some of the interactions that are found between some of the academic institutions' self-images, the aspirations of the nation's young, the expectations of the general public, and the adequacy of machinery that is instrumental in institutional and social change. In this view, the accounts are not just case histories. They also describe forces at work as American higher education adjusts to the demands of new and different times.

2. A Network of Antiochs

by Gerald Grant

Most university and college presidents in America today are searching for stability, for a way out of a period of crisis, and for means to restore some tranquility to scholarship and learning. But at Antioch, President James Dixon, while a healer by profession, has deliberately escalated the level of conflict.

In an era of accommodation, President Dixon believes that change comes through personal confrontation, and his policies for the past decade have been designed to encourage such encounters. He is a risk-taker, a man who could make a Mississippi flatboat rock on a July day. At heart, he apparently believes the college should be in a kind of continual revolution against earlier images of itself.

"It seems to me that our social institutions may need to accept risks as normative, and to institutionalize anti-establishmentarianism and to develop policy in response to it as a form of systematic flexibility," Dixon has said. "Something needs to be done that institutionalizes what I call the 'anti-establishment' into the establishment in ways that allow concrete human encounters—which are really the only things that create change—to occur around specific behaviors and not around notions of how people might behave" (Dixon, 1969).

Thus, while Antioch is one of the older experimental colleges, it is also—for those engaged in it—one of the most lively and stressful experiments in higher education.

Antioch today is a network of several campuses, of more than a

ACKNOWLEDGMENT: This essay has benefited from thoughtful readings by Burton Clark, Thomas Cottle, Kenneth Feigenbaum, Majorie Freed, Zelda Gamson, Judith Grant, Howard Greenlee, Irwin Inman, Judson Jerome, Ruth Kaplan, Morris Keeton, Theodore Newcomb, and Albert Stewart.

Research for this essay was partially supported by grants from the Ford Foundation and the Carnegie Foundation for the Advancement of Teaching.

score of field centers, and of widespread job and foreign study linkages. The catchall term used by nearly everyone at Antioch to describe its unorthodox growth in the last decade is *systems*. To many of the faculty on the main campus in Yellow Springs, *systems* is a pejorative term for the branch stores that have grown brash enough under Dixon to think that they can tell the home office how to do business. To Dixon, *systems* is an inclusive term that describes the field centers and campuses Antioch has set up across the country constituting "a congeries of associated efforts in the interests of teaching and learning." He would no longer grant hegemony to the Yellow Springs faculty in determining the future growth of Antioch's educational ventures.

Thus, the systems, or network, issue has become the subject of a protracted and intense debate on the Yellow Springs campus centering on the question of how growth and change at Antioch will be planned, managed, and financed. Disagreement over systems was a significant factor in the firing of a widely respected dean, Howard Greenlee, who had taken a more conservative stance toward expansion of the Antioch network. Greenlee challenged the idea that there was anything very systematic in Dixon's systems other than the president's desire to reserve major initiatives for change to himself. Other issues were involved, including the dissatisfactions of a significant "Get Dixon" segment of the faculty. When it all came to a crisis in early 1971, three-fourths of the faculty backed the dean's view of Antioch over Dixon's. Subsequently, however, Greenlee left to become dean and professor of history at Windham College. The trustees stepped in and directed that a new systems-wide governance and administrative structure be developed for Antioch, recognizing that it is a "complex institution with major units in addition to the Yellow Springs campus."[1]

The degree of ambiguity that exists was underscored by Morris

---

[1] The search committee experienced some difficulty in finding a candidate to replace Greenlee. In May 1972, Peter Conn of the University of Pennsylvania was chosen and ratified by Administrative Council. A militant faction on campus sought to block the appointment in a heated Adcil meeting, charging their candidate for dean was unfairly passed over because he was Marxist and black. During a hectic week, Dixon and Conn were blocked from leaving the Antioch Inn for a period of five hours as the militants sought to force Dixon to reopen the selection process. A week later, Conn withdrew. The chairman of the search committee expressed the hope that "in due time, I suppose, when we have developed processes more adequate to the passions and complexities of the new diversities we are experiencing, the College will begin anew the search for a new dean."

Keeton, Academic Vice President and Chairman of Antioch's Self-Study Committee, in a 1971 memo to the faculty. He identified the focus of the study as being the institution "as a whole" and wrote: "We will be expected to define what this means. Since we ourselves are not agreed on the point, even sufficiently for a full working agreement, an attempt to articulate alternatives and get a working agreement by June seems important" (Benowitz, 1971).

The cover theme of a recent Antioch catalog could be Mao's phrase "Let a thousand flowers bloom." It pictures a series of Antiochs blooming on receding hills. Prospective students must be a little disoriented by a catalog that opens with the quote that "nothing can be exactly defined" and describes Antioch as "a multitude of educational sorties" that emerge as old forms fail to meet new needs.

But the catalog contradicts itself and does define more engagingly than most brochures this college in dispersion. It has four principal campuses (defined as a unit that can award the Antioch degree, though considerable turbulence surrounds that assertion) and more than 20 field centers (units that are supported by a campus though they may be quite distant physically):

1 The old campus in Yellow Springs, which doubled in size in the 1960s and now enrolls about 2,300 students, supports an undergraduate urban education center in Philadelphia and had a complicated relationship with the Portland Learning Community, the communal-style Oregon group formed by exiles from Reed College. Another center, in San Francisco, known as Antioch West, began in 1971 with a focus on psychology and the arts and enrolls about 125 students in an old warehouse. In its first year, about a third of the students came from Yellow Springs to do field work. Other students were recruited through the University Without Walls Program, a creation of the Union for Experimenting Colleges and Universities, which has its headquarters on the Yellow Springs campus. The University Without Walls, a project consisting of 19 colleges and universities in which Antioch has played a leading role, is an enterprise separate from, but as in the San Francisco center, occasionally intersecting with the new Antioch network described in this essay. Two other field centers are currently affiliating with Antioch: a center for understanding media in New York and a center concerned with the culture of American Indians in Santa Fe, New Mexico.

MAP 2-1 *Where Antioch Is*

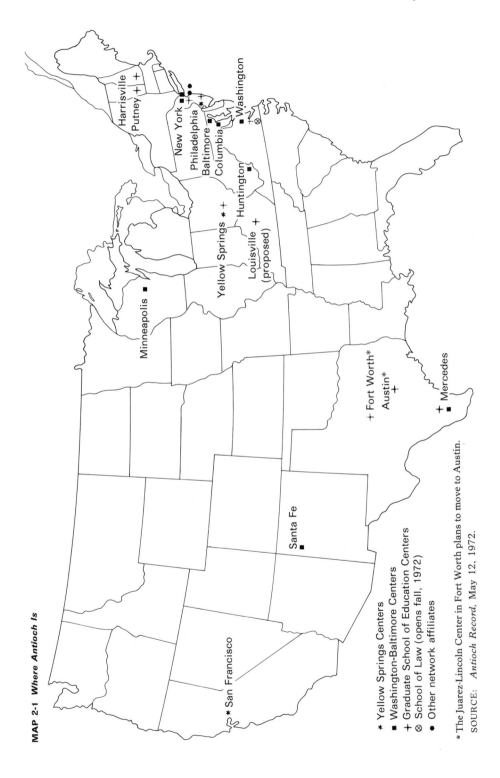

Harrisville +
Putney +
New York ■
Philadelphia +
Baltimore ■
Columbia ■
Washington ■ ⊗
Huntington ■
Yellow Springs ✱ +
Louisville (proposed) +
Minneapolis ■
Fort Worth* +
Austin* +
Mercedes + ■
Santa Fe ■
San Francisco ✱

✱ Yellow Springs Centers
■ Washington-Baltimore Centers
+ Graduate School of Education Centers
⊗ School of Law (opens fall, 1972)
● Other network affiliates

*The Juarez-Lincoln Center in Fort Worth plans to move to Austin.
SOURCE: *Antioch Record,* May 12, 1972.

2 The Antioch Graduate School of Education, formerly known as Antioch-Putney, offers the M.A.T. (Master of Arts in Teaching) and M.Ed. degrees and has centers in eight locations: Putney, Vermont; Harrisville, New Hampshire; Washington; Philadelphia; Yellow Springs; Mercedes and Fort Worth, Texas; and New York. The Mercedes unit, near the Mexican border in Texas, is a Chicano education center known as the Colegio Jacinto Trevino. Not long after it opened in 1969 in an abandoned monastery, it was attacked by the Texas press as a "revolutionary training center in disguise." Its original aim was to qualify Chicano farm workers for their high school equivalency diplomas. It now operates at both the high school and college levels, and is staffed, in part, by Antioch students who are earning their master's degrees while helping Chicano workers complete high school. After receiving their M.A.T.'s, some of the Antioch graduates stay on to join the college level staff, continuing to teach the workers whom they had prepared to become college freshmen.

3 The Washington-Baltimore campus was spawned when groups of faculty members split off from the campus that was established in 1969 in the new town of Columbia, Maryland. In rented offices in one of Columbia's shopping centers, the Columbia center continues with an emphasis on "human ecology and community planning." The Baltimore faculty, headquartered on the second floor of the old Belvedere Hotel, offer a curriculum advocating urban social change. The Washington unit serves a primarily black undergraduate enrollment in two row houses near Dupont Circle. In 1971, it offered a melange of 10 courses including Frontiers in Astronomy, Development of African Political Parties, and The Rise of Colonialism. Currently, 411 students are enrolled in the Washington-Baltimore centers. A small group of students and faculty members left in the fall of 1971 to open a center for Appalachian studies in Huntington, West Virginia. In the first year of operation, 10 students and 3 faculty members collaborated to develop courses in urban Appalachia philosophical anthropology, Appalachian history, concepts of science, and agriculture. Other units attached to the Washington-Baltimore campus include the Antioch center in Minneapolis, an evening college that grants up to two years college credit for life and work experience for 53 "bypassed adults." In New York Antioch jointly sponsors a physician associate program with Harlem Hospital. It enrolls 10 students, several of whom are former black medical corpsmen, in a program designed to train them as doctors' assistants.

4   The fourth unit designated as a campus, the Antioch School of Law, opened in the fall of 1972 in Washington with an expected enrollment of 180 students. It is an outgrowth of the Urban Law Institute founded by Jean and Edgar Cahn and is "dedicated to training lawyers to use power for the interests of the poor and the public." The unorthodox curriculum begins with an attempt to remove "perceptual blinders" to injustice by sending students to jail for a night and asking them to file for welfare benefits and food stamps. As part of a 12-months-a-year curriculum, students work in neighborhood legal centers as part of the school's teaching law firm as they study the "range of problem solving strategies available to the lawyer" (*Bulletin of the Antioch School of Law,* 1972, p. 11). George Washington University, which had formerly sponsored the Cahns' law institute, severed its relationship with the Cahns and the institute's 20 lawyers who offered their services to the urban poor explaining, "We never contemplated that the university would operate a large law firm and engage directly in the practice of law" (Statement . . . , 1971, p. 2).

The heterodox network nurtured by Dixon springs from his own style of maximum risk-taking with a built-in expectation of occasional failure. He believes that Antioch must risk criticism from the broader educational community, must risk exploring new value systems, and must risk insolvency. He says he wants to find ways to confirm "many identities . . . in operational terms instead of pre-audit kinds of judging. Can we somehow become sufficiently scientific so that we do not have to guarantee the results of an experiment in advance?"

He knows that he has introduced a new element of entrepreneurship in what used to be a collegial pattern. Parts of the system compete with each other (and even advertise for students in the *Antioch Record*). Each branch office must pay its own way and, if it does not, be "dismantleable" on short notice. Some of Dixon's critics argue that such a policy is at odds with a commitment to social change. If you announce you're temporary, your enemies will just wait you out. They also charge that such policies mean there is no development or planning time because there is no budget for it. While admitting that this style can be a "very anxiety-provoking, disturbing sort of thing," Dixon feels "the normative level of conflict can be higher in experimental colleges." It is a style that carries over into Dixon's interviews with faculty job applicants and even into his methods of fund raising. With job applicants, Dixon usually introduces some stress into the interview, probing sharply with unexpected questions. He often plants a strong opinion early in an interview and then digs it up later to see "how craven" the applicant is, how willing he is to pattern himself on Dixon's earlier comment. In fund raising, Dixon exercises an unusual combination of charm and antagonism, generally trying to arrange a direct confrontation between those who want the money and those who have it. For example, instead of trying to represent militant blacks, Dixon brought them along to speak directly to foundation officials in New York, while he mostly listened. "I enjoy fund raising," he said. But he has no taste for more traditional forms of fund raising and the parlor diplomacy it requires. He has been successful in situations that are responsive to political maneuver, but he has had difficulty raising the private venture capital Antioch's proliferating experiments need.

Dixon first arrived at Antioch as an undergraduate in the late 1930s. He was the second of six children of a tubercular chemist who had moved to Lebanon, Maine, to improve his health. As an undergraduate, he held a co-op job as a hotel night clerk and worked in a bus body factory in Indiana. He was not a political joiner but remembers keeping in touch with both the young communist and near-fascist groups on campus. "I sucked the juices," he recalled. He was active in the theater, but as a stage manager, not an actor. As an upperclassman, he stayed in Yellow Springs during work terms as a research assistant in the Kettering laboratory, but he turned away from a career in pure science because he felt he did not have the aptitude for research and because he wanted to work in "sets," and has ever since. He earned an M.D. at Harvard, was a conscientious objector during World War II, and took a degree in public health administration shortly after medical school. He was a health commissioner in Denver and then in Philadelphia, where he was active in Democratic reform politics in the 1950s. He was an Antioch trustee, and although not a very active one, was named to the committee to find a successor to Samuel Gould as president of Antioch in 1959. In the end, Dixon himself was selected. He moved slowly in the early years at Antioch and said he was tutored in the new politics by the "movement" students who came to Antioch in the sixties. He served on several White House task forces during the administrations of Presidents Kennedy and Johnson and became a trustee of the Institute for Policy Studies. Along with Marcus Raskin and Dick Gregory, he was a founder of the short-lived New Party. He was an early signer of the antiwar petitions and recently testified as a character witness for Benjamin Spock.

With mustache and beret, he has a jaunty, almost pixieish appearance. His laughter is hearty and his language is a peculiar mix of medical analogies and the argot of the organizational theorists—"sets" and "collaborative modes" and "synergies." He is a behaviorist with an intense interest in process and much less attention to substance.

Dixon's supporters see him as a visionary, and his critics, as an intensely ambitious and occasionally manipulative man bent on making a reputation as an innovator.[2] Dixon himself professes to be without aims except to create an environment in which different "sets" of people can pursue often conflicting aims. He is a president who "presides" rather than an executive who initiates an agenda and pursues specific goals. In a sense, what maddens Dixon's detractors most is that he doesn't give them a clear target at which to shoot. He refuses to set priorities. Thus, the college has become deeply politicized as competing groups attempt to establish priorities through interest group politics. One student vented his frustration at Antioch politics in the campus newspaper: "You can get anything you want on this campus if you place a rock through a pane of glass" (*Antioch Record,* February 13, 1972, p. 2). A black student leader, on the other hand, saw Antioch's style as its principal virtue: "Antioch is the only place where upper class whites and ghetto blacks have to rub together" (*Antioch Record,* January 27, 1972, p. 4).

During the second of two lengthy interviews, Dixon was perhaps most revealing of his style when he was explaining his view of national politics as a "series of complex systems. It matters more what happens at the interface of the system than at the core. One is more likely to discover that the alternative options for the social

[2] Although much of the rhetoric of innovation suggests a pervasive stodginess in higher education, it seems surprising how fast ideas do travel and that most of the rewards go to the innovator in a society that values change. Even St. John's College, one of the most traditional and unchanging in the nation, built its reputation on being a "radical experiment." Most of the traditionalists, like Robert Hutchins, have had to style themselves as reformers. An administrator who wants to be known and to move up had better be seen as an innovator.

order are at the interface of the sets than at the core. When one does that, one may find there is no core." If one thinks of this as describing Antioch systems and substitutes the Yellow Springs campus for "core," one begins to get an inkling of the nature of the conflict in which the modern Antioch is embedded. Dixon believes the "core" of the old liberal arts college is dead and its new contemporary relevance will somehow emerge out of the struggle between new sets and viable pieces of the old system.

Dixon disclaims responsibility for the form, or forms, the Antioch network assumes: "I deny even the capability to dream the wildest dreams that would result in this particular set of propositions." Perhaps his strongest guiding principle, an assertation his critics would contest, would be to minimize coercion at the institutional level. There may be no coercion in the overt sense, but as president, Dixon has clearly established an institutional environment in which the rewards go to those who push to expand the network.

CONTINUITIES AND DISCONTINUITIES Dixon may eschew responsibility for the particular constellation Antioch assumes, but he has put Antioch on a course radically different from that steered by his immediate predecessor Samuel Gould. Yet Dixon's heterodoxies are in many ways more closely allied with Antioch's authentic traditions than Gould's efforts in the fifties to elevate Antioch's scholarly reputation in a more conventional way. Those traditions began with Antioch's first president, Horace Mann, and were firmly rooted by an extraordinary educator, Arthur Morgan, who shaped the character of the modern Antioch half a century ago. Antioch's own promotional literature tends to emphasize what is new and different about the place. But this essay seeks to develop each of its major topics—work-study, social activism, faculty conflicts, and institutional growth—in a historic perspective that highlights the continuities with the Morgan era.

Horace Mann, who left Massachusetts in 1853 to head the college being founded by the Christian Church in Yellow Springs, Ohio, had high hopes for Antioch, and he moved boldly to put it in the company of those few radical colleges of the day that dared to admit women and Negroes. But, as a Unitarian with a deep aversion to sectarianism, he was dismayed when doctrinal infighting erupted over the religious identity of the college, and the assured financial backing never materialized. He soon came to feel that he had been misled about the intended character of the college. Exhausted and discouraged, Mann collapsed after the commencement in 1859 and died a few months later. Perhaps his greatest legacy to the college was an aphorism that remains near the hearts of Antioch's philosophy today: "Be ashamed to die until you have won some victory for humanity."[3]

The Unitarians joined the Christians in the sponsorship of the college in 1865, bringing it temporary financial relief. But the college did not gain a secure footing until 60 years after Mann's death. It was on the verge of bankruptcy and collapse in 1919, and the trustees tried to give it away to the YMCA. When even the "Y" balked, the trustees repossessed it.

At this watershed, Arthur Morgan, a Dayton engineer with educational ideas of his own, was placed on the Antioch board by the Unitarians to protect their interest in the college's endowment. Within six weeks of his appointment as a trustee, Morgan had presented his "Plan of Practical Industrial Education." He took control as president a few months later.

Work and Learn   Morgan had headed the Progressive Education Association before he became president of Antioch and afterwards was a director of the Tennessee Valley Authority. He was a student of utopias and saw them as essential blueprints for the betterment of human society. He had analyzed More's *Utopia* to show that it was less an imaginative construct than an actual account of Peruvian society at the time of the Incan Empire.

Morgan dreamed of a college "such as never had existed." Antioch should be "a lever to move the world . . . a great adventure, standing for radically different patterns of life." It was important to provide an "education in life as well as books" and for the student to develop "life aims and purposes." Rather than seek piecemeal reforms, Morgan totally reorganized the college by juxtaposing work and study. He originally planned short alternating cycles of two weeks of campus study followed by two weeks on a job within commuting distance of Yellow Springs. But things never worked out that way. The job market was nationalized just as the student body itself became increasingly cosmopolitan. And work-study became a three-month cycle. But the basic work-study plan—so successfully developed at Antioch, although not invented there,

---

[3] In this section, and at several other points, I have drawn heavily on Clark (1970).

as widely believed—continues to be one of the most important characteristics defining the college.[4]

One senses an unusual degree of sophistication, maturity, and political savvy among a high proportion of Antioch students. The program requires students to develop their coping capacities as they repeatedly pick up everything to begin with—to go off and tackle a new job, to find an apartment (often to share with three or four other Antiochians working in the same city), then to return to campus to resume the study of economics and music theory, and to rejoin campus picket lines.

Conversations with Antioch students are filled with references to their job experiences. And if you ask a critical upperclassman what he values most about Antioch, he will often begin with the work-study program.

I particularly remember the way a woman senior from Texas described her work experiences. Her first job as a retail clerk had seemed dull, though in retrospect its routines were a welcome shift from other tensions, and she found that talks with her coworkers were a useful corrective for most of the rhetoric she has heard about the Silent Majority. She had been challenged—perhaps too challenged for her ability at that time—by a job in Philadelphia interviewing community leaders about their attitudes toward the public schools. She had learned a good deal about interviewing, politics, and about what ethical use could be made of the material that had been gathered. She had learned, perhaps, as much off the job as when she set up house with a group of other Antioch students who worked in the Philadelphia project. She had also interned in the Washington office of the then Senator Ralph Yarborough of Texas, working long hours and gaining a whole new appreciation of the range of political constituencies he served. She remembered, with more than a touch of pride, how Yarborough had once asked her to do a letter over four times before he felt it qualified as an adequate reply to a voter's inquiry.

By the time they are seniors, 54 percent of the students at Antioch say the job program is one of the college's most appealing features, and only 17 percent speak of its academic reputation in those terms. Yet, as freshmen, students rank both equally high. This may reflect more sophisticated judgments about Antioch's academic

[4] The College of Engineering at the University of Cincinnati first adopted a work-study program in 1906. See Henderson & Hall (1946, p. 119).

status as compared with more research-oriented institutions rather than an absolute judgment about the value of its academic program. It may also reflect increased student awareness about the pressures for academic achievement among Antioch students as compared with those at other elite colleges. But it certainly constitutes a strong endorsement of the job program. When asked which persons most influenced changes in their lives, seniors are as likely to mention fellow students as they are to mention faculty members at Antioch. But when jobs are contrasted with course work, twice as many say a job experience was crucial as cite the academic program (Churchill, 1970).

At the Antioch campus in Columbia, Maryland, work is concurrent with study. In an earlier day, with another group of students, this might have been called night school, but the present ideal is that each student will have a job, such as teacher's aid or research assistant, which can be combined with study to earn both credits and pay. Actually, for a variety of reasons—restricted job opportunities in the new town development, employer resistance to lifestyles of counterculture youths, and lack of aggressiveness on the part of student job-seekers—less than half of the Columbia students have jobs at all, and perhaps only a quarter of them have jobs that fit the ideal. Interviews with both students and faculty reveal that even with the ideal jobs that are available, the academic linkages vary from minimal faculty interaction to stimulating student careers that appear profitable in both intellectual and, to a modest extent, financial terms. The most successful students tend to be transfer students who had demonstrated some work competence before they arrived.[5]

While the work-study program still wins praise from both students and faculty, some point out that the work ethic is no longer what it was. The old requirement of 100 work credits has been pared to 85 at the Yellow Springs campus, and only 60 of these must be in paid employment. Language study and travel now also qualify as a work credit. Many students refuse to compromise their counterculture values by taking on some kind of jobs, and some of those who do take such jobs have alienated organizations that have long employed Antioch students. The original meaning of "co-op," two students "cooperating" to maintain one job, has long

---

[5] Antioch officials report the job opportunities at the new campus have improved remarkably since this essay, which drew on data from the first year at Columbia, was written.

since been forgotten. At the Columbia center, students without paychecks could not pay the rent, and, to stave off evictions, the college stepped in to guarantee their leases. At the end of one semester under this arrangement, the jobless students owed the college $8,100 in overdue rent, much of which had to be written off.

The rewards that may come from Antioch-Columbia's attempts to connect work and study in ways that enrich both justify its experiment. But concurrent work-study may be best suited to adults who have already moved beyond entrance-level jobs. Here the college may play a significant role both in satisfying the adults' more clearly articulated educational needs and in serving as a credentialing agent for demonstrated achievement. For many younger students, the Yellow Springs model of alternating work and study may continue to be the most rewarding. Without the need to integrate job and study, the student may try on several occupational roles in the wider world as well as experiment with different intellectual styles on campus.

The Yellow Springs program, with its fixed cycles, also exerts healthy pressures on the students. Many at Antioch-Columbia are clearly lost. Typical of perhaps a third of the students there, was a young man who had dropped out of an experimental college on the West Coast, surfed for several months, and then enrolled at Antioch-Columbia. The previous semester he had dabbled in six different courses, including one in which he had attempted to make a film about a nude girl in a bathtub of Jell-O. He dropped out of most of the courses along the way and had not decided which, if any, he could request credit for, "because I didn't have an advisor. There was no faculty member I felt I could relate to as a friend."

There are more than a few like him. They value Antioch-Columbia for the freedom it provides, which, with a chance of a degree some day, justifies the $4,500 yearly costs. They may be afraid to "experiment" outside an institutional setting, or fear their parents would not support them if they tried.

Judson Jerome has been one of the faculty at Antioch-Columbia who have come to the conclusion that "perhaps we have to support education, in our present context, by selling freedom. If a rich kid wants to pay and split, let him do so, and use the bread to educate the poor" (Jerome, 1970, p. 202ff.). And he quotes another faculty member who argues that "Everyone has the right to slob around." But it seems critical whether the institution encourages slobbing around by some in order to bankroll the institution for others. Perhaps this question is not raised sharply enough at Antioch, although there are those who disagree with Jerome's philosophical view that "the unfettered human being has an innate drive towards the good" and that his period of dissipation and drift will be short-lived. For many, such periods may not be at all brief, and one needs to ask what responsibility the institution has to elicit sustained involvement in creative and productive work. Does it best serve the student or society in the long run to create an artificial environment in which we pretend to parents that something is happening? Why not just let American youth split, instead of demanding that they pay to split? If we are going to encourage drifting, and I would for many, let us at least have drifters who have some economic sense.[6]

Stephen Plumer, dean of the Washington-Baltimore campus, who has a background in education and social work, asked a group of students at a planning session "whether we can be satisfied with students who come here and hole up in their apartments, blowing a lot of smoke." He said he sensed more and more sentiment in the faculty to recruit students who are willing to work hard to learn the skills that are needed to move beyond mere rhetoric about social change. Plumer feared that the Washington-Baltimore recruitment message was garbled and promised too much. He said, "Our first catalogue said, let's come together and swing. The second just said let's come together, and the third said, we're here for the hippie thing. We need to get it together." But a student replied that every time they tried to state aims more clearly, some part of the community disagreed. Thus, specificity about aims was always sacrificed to generalities in order to get agreement. Plumer smiled in silent appreciation of the student's wisdom.

Governance Morgan's Dewey-like faith in learning by doing was consistent with his espousal of the participation of students in their own governance. Although he was too domineering a figure to let students or anyone else run the college, Morgan laid the groundwork for a unique system of governance in Yellow Springs. At the center of the system is an administrative council consisting of five faculty members and three students, of whom five are elected principally by the students. Three of the faculty members are elected solely by the faculty, the other five members by the entire campus. The president

[6] The 1971–72 Washington-Baltimore catalog notes: "Each student must pay the *full* tuition charge ($3,200) without deductions . . . for a year of independent study and work," although in some cases there may be a partial tuition rebate.

and the dean complete membership on the council. Under Morgan, the council was a kind of kitchen cabinet with advisory powers. But before he stepped down, it had been written into the college charter. For 30 years, it has acted as a kind of executive committee for the entire college—exercising budgetary, policy, and personnel powers. Generally, every important decision at Antioch came to Adcil, as the body is known. It has been a unique blend of faculty and administrative authority legitimated by student participation.

Now many Yellow Springs faculty are angry that Adcil's powers have eroded. They argued that Dixon did not have the authority to fire the dean independently of that body; but the board upheld Dixon despite the faculty's overwhelming censure of him. The faculty also asserted that Adcil has the authority to decide what branch campuses may be created and how they will be financed. Dixon, however, has pushed a plan in which the major units of the new Antioch would draw up budgets independently, with some central services being provided from Yellow Springs (and his critics charge he thereby siphons off funds that should be used to strengthen the home campus). One observer compared the conflict to the debates about United States island possessions in the late 1890s: "Can you preserve a participating form of government at home and also run an empire?" The whole question of Adcil's power to control the systems' expansion—and if it doesn't, who does—has resulted in the first major reassessment of Antioch's form of governance since 1940. The board has continued to back Dixon, however, and in May 1972 moved to turn many of Adcil's powers over to a network-wide Antioch College Council with representatives elected from all four campuses. Adcil, however, will have a central role in the governance of the Yellow Springs campus.

Most visitors at an Adcil meeting would have difficulty distinquishing student body members from the younger faculty. Students sit as full members, and they are unafraid to exercise initiative or to question policy in a fundamental way. During a discussion of proposed budget cuts, a faculty member suggested limits on administrative spending, but a student argued that money could be saved by giving salary increases only to the faculty at the bottom of the pay scale and scheduling pay cuts for those in the upper brackets. The proposal was seriously discussed and several weeks later adopted in a modified form: those earning least received the largest percentage increases and salaries above $20,000 were frozen.

Some students are more modest about their competence than are the faculty. During an Antioch-Columbia budget meeting, one black student on the committee interrupted a radical who had been demanding power to restructure the curriculum and fire some faculty. "We shouldn't say we know how to run this campus, or that we know all that much about the budget," the black student said. "Let's not be arrogant about making these kinds of decisions."

The student voice at Antioch became more decisive as the faculty split in disagreement over the degree to which they would support Dixon's new systems approach and its related experiments. Students tended to support Dixon's policies through the sixties, but in recent years they have sometimes joined the more conservative faculty in opposition to him.

One student member saw the president as a skillful manager of Adcil who saddled it with responsibility for unpopular decisions, such as budget cuts, but attempted to keep its agenda clear of items that might limit his initiative. Apparently one important outcome of student participation is their realization of how difficult it is to create change or govern effectively. Another is that student members, who are open but not indiscreet about decisions that Adcil takes, increase community trust in the governance process. But that trust was breaking down in the early 1970s as conflict escalated at Antioch. Decisions that were usually made at lower levels were sometimes pushed prematurely to Adcil or were jumped over Adcil to the Board of Trustees. And for the first time in memory, Adcil members caucused privately before their public meeting and voted in a bloc for a predetermined slate of nominees for the Board of Trustees.

However, Antioch has found that in some critical areas, such as faculty hiring, student participation has been erratic and of poor quality. At a time when many other colleges are rushing to catch up with the Antioch of 1968, Antioch has modified its enthusiasm in some respects. Faculty who felt students would have a significant impact on personnel policies were disappointed. A recent campus review of governance concluded that most students on the Program and Personnel Committee "lack the necessary background on both personnel policies and faculty-department-area situations for them to maintain continuous and intense interest in the Committee's affairs" (*A Study of Antioch College,* 1971, p. B-V-8). The Washington-Baltimore campus has concluded after three years of experiment with "participatory democracy" that its governance has been chaotic. A policy of encouraging any who were interested in an issue to "participate" in its solution too often meant that there was a different "solution" each week as the participants ebbed and flowed.[7]

Another distinctive element of the governance structure at Antioch is the community government, supported by fees levied on all members of the community—students, faculty, administrators, and their wives. Its budget of $170,000 finances publications, conferences, student-initiated educational experiences, rock festivals, and poetry readings. The full-time salaried student who serves as community manager functions much like the city manager of a small city, and some of Antioch's community managers have stepped into such a post after their campus experience. Acting as the executive of the community government, the community manager's responsibilities range from framing and enforcing regulations prohibiting firearms on campus to filling a sizable number of paid student jobs.

Many administrative jobs at Antioch are held by students. At first an interviewer may be surprised that the administrator of a new program of courses in social change turns out to be a student. Then he comes to expect it. One administrator I interviewed was only a sophomore, but there was nothing sophomoric about her or the Student Services Program she administered. As a result of this kind of responsibility, students acquire an extraordinary amount of knowledge about "what goes on around here" and why, and a sense that if things are not going quite right, students may be as much to blame as anybody.

Above all else perhaps, Morgan sought students and faculty with high ideals and social commitment. He personally interviewed students not only to select the most able applicants but also to identify those with a certain moral energy. Social activism and socialism ran strong in Morgan's day, with half of the faculty voting for Norman Thomas in a straw poll in 1932. Some years later, the college pastor ran for governor on the Socialist ticket, helping to stamp a national

---

[7] *A Study of Antioch College* (Antioch College, mimeographed, 1971, p. D-I-32). Participatory democracy has not been restricted to the Washington-Baltimore campus, however. In Yellow Springs, the Sociology-Anthropology Department is run by the *peopleship*, described as communal governance by all students who are majoring in the department in combination with all faculty. There is no department chairman, only a student staff administrative committee to carry out the decisions of the peopleship.

At a teacher training program in New York that Antioch conducts in collaboration with The Teachers Inc., students "get together and decide on subjects we would like to take and vote on them" (p. D-V-2).

image of Antioch as a radical college. Studies in 1958 showed that Antioch students registered higher on scales in political commitment than students at either Reed or Berkeley.[8]

In the sixties, on the campus at Yellow Springs, the wave of black nationalism ran a year or so ahead of most colleges, and Antioch found itself threatened with denial of federal funds because it allowed the establishment of an all-black Unity House. Trustees did not take a hard line against Unity House, believing that students from the ghetto, who had been brought to Antioch in sizable numbers (about 10 percent nonwhite enrollment at a time when few colleges had more than 5 percent nonwhite representation), needed a year in a protected culture in which they felt secure. But violence erupted when a black shot at a white student. The psychologist Kenneth B. Clark resigned from the board to protest Antioch's new form of segregation. Clark declined to attend the board meeting at which he resigned because of threats on his life.

In response to the demands from blacks and others, Antioch set up a New Directions Program that would increase diversity of offerings and seek even more students from nonwhite and low-income groups. This essay telescopes complex developments that began with the Antioch Program for Interracial Education in 1965 and went through progressively more militant forms including the Black Students Forum (1968), the Afro American Studies Institute (1969), and resulted in the New Directions Program in 1970. Under New Directions, Antioch committed itself to enrolling and meeting the educational needs of a significant number of poor blacks and whites. The new thrust introduced severe class and racial conflict at Antioch. As one black student administrator put it, thrusting forward her chin and pointedly shifting to a tough street accent as though she were reenacting a confrontation: "Well, man, black students didn't like coming here and not having any money, and seeing that all the whites had all the money, so they decided they'd get some, so they started ripping off stuff. And they bopped the guys up on the side of the head when they got so angry about things."

There were other reasons why many white students were hostile to the program. Under intense pressure, Adcil had voted funds for New Directions that it did not have, which meant that other programs had to be reduced. White students blamed shorter library

[8] Unpublished study of student development, Center for the Study of Higher Education, University of California, Berkeley, reported by Clark (1970, p. 62).

hours and other cutbacks on the New Directions Program. Dixon told the Board of Trustees that internal tension had been created by the "Robin Hood factor," that is, taking tuition from some to support others.[9] Two years later, a fund-raising drive was launched to provide additional funds, but it has not been very successful.

As yet, an unresolved problem is finding the kind of faculty members who are needed to serve New Directions students who need to learn basic skills. One faculty member who strongly supports the new program said he was brought up short by black students after one of his math classes: "They told me I was having a nice ego trip, doing my thing on the blackboard, but that nobody had been with me for about three weeks. I came to realize that many of these students did not know how to subtract 3 from 2." He said he had accepted the fact that for at least part of the time he had to be a high school teacher, but he was doubtful that many other faculty members would accept that definition of their role. However, a professor of physics who has supported the New Directions program even to the extent of retooling his courses has become discouraged. He questions whether it makes economic sense to pay his salary to teach precollege skills in a watered-down course in science and photography, particularly when the students walk out when he introduces some basic scientific concepts in an attempt to answer a question. Offie Wortham, a black administrator who headed Antioch's Program for Interracial Education in 1969, felt that blacks did not receive enough academic help, adequate counseling, or financial aid. He told the trustees he doubted whether most were progressing satisfactorily toward a degree.[10]

Summing up the New Directions Program in 1970, Academic Vice President Morris Keeton may have been the most prescient when he warned that "the hardest problem of all will arise if the Program succeeds and we have enough advocates of clashing ideologies. We will then have a controversial campus of a magnitude we have never known, and it may be hard to live with."[11] Less than two years later, Keeton's prophecy was played out before the board itself as representatives of Antioch's new pluralism preempted the

[9] Of course, the "Robin Hood factor" operates in a less visible way in all universities; that is, freshmen in large classes generally subsidize seniors.

[10] See "Minutes of the Annual Meeting of the Board of Trustees" (Antioch College, November 1969, p. 191).

[11] See "Minutes of the Annual Meeting of the Board of Trustees" (Antioch College, May 1970, p. 4).

board's agenda to state their grievances. There were clashes not only over ideology but also over financial aid, admissions policies, and the sharing of academic resources within the network. The following excerpt from the minutes conveys some of the conflicting pressures ("Minutes of the Board of Trustees Meeting," Antioch College, December 3–4, 1971, pp. 7–8):

After the presentation of the Huntington Field Center demands, representatives from the Graduate School of Education centers in Washington, D.C., and Mercedes, Texas, which primarily serve minority groups, were supportive, claiming similar problems at their units. Yellow Springs students and faculty split several ways. Some New Direction students (until now severely critical of the system concept since they claim it draws money from Yellow Springs that should be used to improve New Direction economic programs and financial aid packages) vigorously upheld their newly found brothers and sisters from Appalachia and demanded immediate redress of all grievances. Other Yellow Springs community members with more traditional academic aims blamed administrators for permitting Washington-Baltimore and the Graduate School to pursue the Board's mandate for cultural pluralism in their own distinctive ways—by opening centers in different sections of the country where small numbers of young people and adults can work towards Antioch degrees *in situ*. These centers, opponents declared, are draining money and manpower from Yellow Springs and undermining the academic program. Proponents of the concept said that it was not so. John Sparks, Administrative Council member, said that Trustees must recognize that their decisions have frustrated Yellow Springs. The New Directions Program, he said, was approved by the Board without consultation with the faculty; now New Directions demands for financial aid and new programs have made the Yellow Springs budget nearly impossible. Funding of New Directions, according to Mr. Sparks, is the responsibility of the Board and that responsibility has not been met. Richard Yalman, also an Adcil member, said that the needs for financial aid for New Directions students may undermine the Board's desire for cultural pluralism since "We are fast approaching the time when we may not have any white middle class students, and no intermix in the student body." The conflicting statements in frequently heated disagreements over finances led Trustees to adopt the second motion that asked the executive committee to look into the situation.

Not long after these clashes before the board, Dixon issued his first direct veto of a major demand by New Directions students. Dixon vetoed an Adcil resolution that would have granted New Directions students a large measure of control over admissions. Adcil had originally opposed giving New Directions students such power by a 5–4 vote, but one faculty member changed his vote after the students announced they would shut the place down in 15 minutes if their demands were not met.

New Directions blacks have been skillful in exploiting white liberal guilt among faculty and administrators at Antioch. They have found that if they pound hard enough and shout "racist" loud enough, votes can be swayed. One of the young radical faculty members closely associated with the New Directions Program said privately that the program needs firm curbs. Student leadership has deteriorated and program funds have been ripped off for private pleasures. But instead of forcing students to be accountable for the use of the funds, they have been allowed to draw on next year's budget.

There is less black separatism and more class consciousness at Antioch today, heightened by a move by New Directions students to define themselves as the children of nonprofessional parents who earn less than $10,000 a year.[12]

Although New Directions students follow different paths through the Antioch curriculum, the academic center for such students has become the Institute for the Solution of Social Problems (ISSP). Students teach many of the 25 courses the institute offers each quarter, ranging from carpentry for women to antimonopoly strategy. Ironically, by so doing, students who most need faculty resources sometimes receive least.[13]

---

[12] The class lines were pointed up in the struggle over admissions. One middle-class black student, who sits on the Committee on Admissions and Financial Aid, accused it of "succumbing to the crudest form of racism" when it agreed to New Directions demands for a veto power on admissions of New Directions students. He asserted that the Peoples Central Committee, a key New Directions group, was unrepresentative of minorities on campus and that it was a group of "hustlers and opportunists" who were attempting to recruit minority students who agree with them politically. A black spokesman for the Peoples Central Committee replied that its members would have more insight into the potential of the applicants because of their working class background. "If it's not the college's position to admit street niggers they should stop saying they are," he said. He was supported by an assistant professor of political science who argued that "someone with the same background isn't likely to fall for the bullshit that a white liberal is likely to fall for on an application." "Yes," said another student, "It takes a spic to know a spic" (*Antioch Record,* February 11, 1972, p. 6).

[13] However, enthusiasm for all student-taught courses—not just those offered by the ISSP—appears on the wane at Antioch. A survey showed that students rated their peer instructors lower than regular faculty in their ability to motivate students, knowledge of subject being taught, ability to organize the material, and to relate it to other fields. Student teachers received higher marks from their peers only on their enthusiasm for the subject (Sparks, 1971). Students began to criticize such courses as in a *Record* editorial that argued,

The student-run institute is now pressing for full departmental status, which would allow students to major in social change. Sponsors of the institute say its goal is revolutionary change. They wish to identify clearly with the political left, yet they seek to satisfy doubts that the institute's aims are consistent with traditional freedom of inquiry. In presenting their proposal to the community, the sponsors admitted, "It is difficult to define precisely a political position which is open and restrictive at the same time."

There is considerable evidence that, instead of radicalizing others, the students connected with the institute have taken a more moderate position as they have sought funds, drawn up syllabi, and taught and administered their program. Some now associated with it believe that if it continues as a separate, semisegregated institute, they may create less real change at Antioch than if the program were more widely disseminated to other departments.

Achievement and Judgment

Perhaps a maximum of 200 students are enrolled in the institute's courses. A number of courses in other departments could be described as radical or experimental. But in content and teaching method, many offerings at Antioch are quite traditional, although the style of interaction between students and faculty would be more casual than that in most places.

"Nor are many middle-class students as radical as they pretend to be," said an editor of the *Antioch Record*. Recalling a visit to the home of a classmate who affected a militant radical style on campus, she said: "Before we went inside his parents' big house, he turned to me and whispered, 'Listen, my mother's home. Don't tell her I smoke dope, and for Christ's sake, don't tell her I'm sleeping with Alice.'"

The "Top Ten" courses, as reported by the *Record* in 1971, include a number of standard seminar and lecture courses: Philosophy and Literature, Perspectives in Psychology, Introduction to Writing, Perception, World and Self, The Bible, Rules for Radicals, Biology of Man, Introduction to Education, Fundamentals of Music, and Participation in Music (*Antioch Record,* January 29, 1971, p. 1).

"The trend away from academic studies has reached dangerous proportions . . . college funds and facilities are still being used for courses in carpentry, automechanics and the like, courses which are not appropriate as credit offerings at an institution of higher education" ("The Budget Reconsidered," 1972, p. 2).

Grades were abolished several years ago, and a student's record shows only his credits, not his failures. And among a small minority of the faculty, there are no failures because they believe, as one said, that the "judgmental process interferes with the teaching relationship." Faculty are asked to submit written evaluations, but these are often superficial or even farcical, as the then Associate Dean Yates Hafner pointed out in an essay which stimulated a revision of evaluation procedures. Hafner (1969) reprinted these from his files:

"Five credits."

"He did fine."

"Fantastic student."

"All 60 students in this course uniformly merit the highest possible evaluation."

"Although I have never studied in this field myself, I endorse the student's own judgment that he has met the highest professional standards in his work—having been in a T-group with him, I know I can trust him."[14]

Pressure to improve evaluations also came from students, who complained about both the quantity and quality of evaluations. A number of universities notified Antioch that they would not accept its transcripts. Now, all evaluations are put on a computer, and professors are required to list in some detail the conditions for granting "credit" in their courses in terms of readings, projects, and papers required. Faculty must report a letter grade if asked by students who are unsatisfied with vagueness of written comments. Increasingly, students are requesting grades.

The new reporting methods now apply only to Yellow Springs. A wide variation in standards exists from one campus to another. A network officer who recently surveyed procedures concluded that evaluations at the Washington-Baltimore campus were "among the sloppiest I've seen." Credit there may be earned by examinations; presentation of a project or oral report to a certification board or a "panel of peers"; completion of certain tasks, such as "time served in a role, a class, or an environment"; or "the impression of the faculty member that the student should get credit." The Maryland campus takes the position that qualitative evaluation

---

[14] Hafner's humorous essay transcends the facts in some places, but he assured me that the quoted evaluations did not.

that includes some data is "stronger in terms of credentials and product-orientation than the strictly impressionistic or intuitive ones," but it does not rule out the latter. Some professors require prenegotiation before a student begins a project or task while others will grant ex post facto credit for a project they knew nothing about until a student knocked on their door. A survey of 96 courses at the Washington-Baltimore campus showed that 71 of these met on a standard basis of two hours a week. But credit for these comparable offerings of class time was awarded in 11 ways and resulted in some students earning one credit and others as many as 24 (A Study of Antioch College, 1971, p. D-I-54). A study of course enrollments at Yellow Springs turned up the surprising information that students were signing up for an average of seven courses each quarter, although only four were required. Apparently students saw this as a way of allowing for a number of "failures" or withdrawals if the going got tough in some courses while being assured of earning credit in at least four.

Antioch earned a respectable academic reputation early in the Morgan era. In 1932, Antioch won national visibility and recognition when its students achieved the second highest average scores among 205 colleges and universities on a battery of achievement and intelligence tests administered by the American Council on Education. Throughout the fifties and sixties, its graduates won an impressive share of Woodrow Wilsons and other national scholastic honors, and in Yellow Springs today, roughly 70 percent of Antioch's entrants graduate in the top quarter of their high school class. The SAT mean for the 1971 freshman was 614 on the verbal exam and 602 on the math test—a drop of 20 to 30 points in the mean scores as Antioch has sought out poor and disadvantaged students in greater numbers in recent years. In 1969, the last year in which all graduating seniors were required to take the Graduate Record Exam (GRE), the following percentile scores were achieved in subject areas in which at least 10 students took the exam (the first figure reported is Antioch's score among all graduating seniors taking the GRE; the second measures Antioch against the stiffer competition of graduate school applicants only): biology—94, 65; education—94, 74; history—85, 73; literature—69, 56; philosophy—71, 30; political science—75, 63; psychology—61, 47. If one looks at scores in which at least five seniors took the exams, Antioch was weakest in engineering—22, 15 and strongest in sociology—97, 81 (Churchill, 1969*b*). Comparable data are not available for other campuses in the systems, but they are generally less selective in traditional terms and admit great numbers of high-risk students.

Of course, standardized test data show less about the success of Antioch's teachers than they do about its admissions office. In general, Antioch students score about what one would expect on the GRE "output" exams, given the intellectual "input" they bring as freshmen. It is more difficult to ascertain changes a specific college environment may have on social and psychological attitudes.[15]

One standard attempt to get at such questions is the nationally normed Omnibus Personality Inventory (OPI), which is given to freshmen at Antioch and repeated five years later when they are seniors. In general, the OPI reveals that Antioch students score high on intellectual orientation and expressive and creative values. They are near average on people-oriented values, although somewhat above national norms on measure of altruism (and here Antioch women score higher than men) and on self-acceptance values. In addition to the OPI, Antioch has developed its own measure of the effects of an Antioch education by querying graduates on its Senior Profile. The answers Antioch seniors give on the Senior Profile show that they tend to perceive more changes in themselves than are measured by the more indirect Omnibus Personality Inventory, but there are significant changes that show up on both.

Intellectual changes   On the Senior Profile, seniors say they have grown in intellectual abilities and have acquired new skills. The OPI shows that most intellectual values tend to remain stable, with some decline in intellectual curiosity for women. But, more in line with the self-reports, the OPI also shows a decline in materialist values for both men and women.

Personal and philosophical changes   On the profile, seniors report increases in coping abilities and in acceptance of themselves, which they attribute to peer interactions and job and travel experiences. Only 42 percent felt themselves to be more tolerant and 39 percent to have less internal conflict. Only one in four felt better able to get

---

[15] For a brief yet informative survey of the conflicting literature on college impact, see Gurin (1972).

others to cooperate. Change was perceived more in terms of personal growth than in ability to work with others. In terms of basic life values, students felt Antioch had deepened and broadened values they brought to Yellow Springs rather than change those values in significant ways. The OPI shows that over a five-year freshman to senior span there is little basic change in concern for the welfare for others and a slight decline in the sociability index. On self-acceptance values, the OPI showed that Antioch students tend to be close to national averages as revealed on indices of personal integration, anxiety levels, and tendencies to have either pessimistic or inflated opinions of themselves. There is little change from freshman to senior year on any of these latter measures.

Expressiveness and Creativity Here, there is a strong congruence with what students report on the profile and what shows up on the OPI. Students say they are more aware of complexity, and the OPI shows growth on that measure and even sharper increases in autonomy and questioning attitudes toward authority. Students enter Antioch high on these measures and leave even higher, supporting the "enhancer" theories of college impact.[16]

Faculty Cultures Intellectual achievement alone has never been a source of contentment at Antioch. During his presidency, Morgan was never entirely pleased with the mere intellectual success of students who increasingly headed toward traditional graduate school and professional careers. He was disappointed that students and faculty did not generate enough "creative discontent" to break the old molds. When he retired in the early thirties, he regretted the faculty's "craving for a secure and quiet niche." Antioch's greatest defect was its "deficiency in emphasis on ethical and spiritual purpose and upon personal and social responsibility." He wished he had been more ruthless in eliminating faculty who "came here to teach my subject" and did not share his vision of Antioch as a "revolution" and "way of life." As he stepped down, Morgan said:

"Repeatedly, I have heard in our conferences a sonorous academic phrase, 'inevitability of gradualness.' That is a perfect phrase to

---

[16] *A Study of Antioch College* (1971, p. B-VII-9ff). I have attempted here to compare data from the two measures which were not designed with that intent. These are the categories partly of my own making, and while they do not lend themselves to precise comparison, they are useful in the general way outlined here.

originate in academic halls, where heroic action would be in bad form. I am told not to be impatient, that all things come slowly. . . . The question is not whether we have moved too fast, but whether we have not moved so slowly that the great prospect is lost" (Clark, 1970, p. 39).

The tensions that underlay Morgan's farewell haunt Antioch today. They are the tensions between those who seek the scholar's "quiet niche" and those who precipitate the turmoil of social reform. Since Morgan's day, these strains have reappeared through three distinct generations of Antioch faculty.

Until the years immediately following World War II, the faculty mirrored Morgan's search for mavericks and utopians who rejected specialism. They were men like the renegade Catholic priest James Horton, who headed the history department, saw the past as a lesson in ethics, and cared not whether his graduates went to Yale; or Manmatha Nath Chatterjee, a professor of sociology described by one of his disciples as a man who transcended the myopic view of the sociological researcher to teach his students to question in a fundamental way. These faculty members are gone, but they continue to exert a powerful influence through a few contemporary faculty and administrators who, like Dixon, were their students at Antioch in the thirties and forties. There is a sense in which Dixon is a "restorationist."

Dixon's core of support is drawn from a few senior men who share the ideology of the mavericks and a substantial group of radical experimenters who have gained prominence under his own administration. His major opposition comes from the middle and most numerous layer of the faculty, who might be called liberal professionals (liberal in a national setting, that is; internally they are seen as conservatives).

These were faculty members who came to Antioch after World War II and during the expansionist era of Samuel Gould's presidency in the late fifties. They were traditionally trained and respected the graduate schools, but they were personally drawn to an experimental setting in which to teach. Under Gould, they battled with the old-guard mavericks as they sought to raise intellectual standards and to cut back the work program, especially for students bound for graduate school. Now they are in opposition to the new mavericks, the radical experimenters.

The liberal professionals were characterized scathingly by one young radical faculty member who said, "They feel that coming here constituted the ultimate liberal gesture, and that no more change is necessary." The liberals do not see it that way at all. But they are aware that such opinions lie just below the surface. In general, they came to Antioch because they enjoy teaching in flexible settings. They like the opportunity for interdisciplinary work and the freedom to create new courses. While they do not see themselves primarily as researchers, a sizable minority continue to publish occasionally, to go to scholarly meetings, and to keep abreast of developments in a defined field. They worry that intellectual standards may be declining, and they want to attract bright students to Antioch and to help them into the best graduate schools.

Many also came to put down roots and to raise their children, like the senior faculty member who invited me to dinner and, with quiet pride, began a tour of his home by pointing out the foundations he poured himself. They do not want to be told, as another liberal said hotly, "That in order to be creative I've got to go off someplace else in Dixon's system to do it." They feel that community values have been eroded. "Collegiality does not exist here any more," a young scientist asserted at a faculty meeting. "We rarely talk to one another, and when we do, it's never congenial." Many are openly antagonistic toward Dixon. "I've been at Antioch since 1950," said one critic. "I think in many ways I know more about it and what it's about than Dixon."

A few of the younger radicals, disillusioned about standards, have joined the liberal professionals. One social scientist at Columbia commented: "Too many students are allowed to get by with slipshod work. It's a disorganized existence on the faculty, with no one who can respond to you in disciplinary terms. It can be very sad to realize that if you're really lousy, people don't know the difference."

The radical experimenters of the Dixon era display some internal inconsistencies. They include both political and cultural radicals, T-group enthusiasts (now rapidly fading), and educational experimenters like Judson Jerome, who "vowed never to teach courses again. . . . I would rather open a lunch stand than resume a conventional role in academia" (Jerome, 1970, p. xii). There are strong crosscurrents within this third generation. Some of the political radicals believe deeply in rigorous scholarship and more traditional teaching methods and dissociate themselves on many issues from those whom they sometimes contemptuously refer to as the "hippie trippy crowd." Most of the radicals give social change first priority, asking secondarily what intellectual skills may contribute toward that end. They may be gathered in the Institute for the Solution of Social Problems or in centers like the Colegio Jacinto. Some opposed the establishment of the Washington-Baltimore campus on the grounds that it would be irreparably tarnished by its association with the capitalist developers of the new town of Columbia. But on many issues, the radicals and experimenters form a minority coalition that represents Dixon's strongest constituency.

The cultural radicals and educational experimenters seek new forms and methods of education ranging from encounter groups to film making and broadly interpreted field work and independent study. They see themselves as resources who should adapt to changing student interests, rather than as specialists who are eager to induct students into a field of inquiry. Summarizing his differences with more traditionally inclined faculty members, one avid experimenter said: "They blame the administration for producing the kind of student who will not buy the traditional package, instead of recognizing that they ought to change to meet student demands." Among his allies are some faculty members who have become converts to the counterculture. A professor of engineering, for example, faced with dwindling classes, plunged into a whole new field of media studies. Some scoffed privately at his "hucksterism," but he now leads one of the most popular courses on campus—taught totally through films, video tapes, light shows, and slides. He sits in the audience with his students, believing that the media are the message.

Battle lines for the current conflicts were drawn in 1965 when the new experimenters pushed through the First Year Program at Antioch. Freshmen were assigned to preceptorial groups of 15 under faculty members—mostly the experimenters themselves—who volunteered as preceptors. Grades were abolished, all requirements were suspended for freshmen, and—most controversially—students received automatic credit for the year even if, as some chose, they did nothing. "I know two students who played Hearts for the entire quarter," said one disgusted opponent of the program. To its supporters, such abuses of freedom are worth the benefits that they believe will follow—freely chosen, self-directed, and hence more meaningful educational engagement. It is impossible to say who is right in the short term, and perhaps impossible under any circumstances. Individuals vary in their needs, but in at least one respect, results were clear and dramatic: the bottom dropped out of the usual freshman survey courses. In the beginning of the First Year Program, two of the most popular courses, which normally enrolled 150 or more students, drew fair-sized crowds, but by the end of the term, when students found that the promised freedoms were real, enrollment dropped to 7 students in one course and 3 in the other.

One of the drawbacks of small utopias like Antioch is that there are few niches to which one can escape. Because the faculty must choose sides in a quarrel, the First Year Program left many embittered. After five years, there are a number of faculty members who do not speak to each other. The divisions between the factions are still evident at cocktail parties.

The faculty debate tended to be centered on the concern for maintaining standards and intellectual rigor, but one senses that deep down it was a struggle over who controls the socialization process at Antioch. If these students are "converted" or "contaminated" during the first year, we won't have a chance later on, the liberals feared. The liberals began to caucus in what later became known as the "beer and pretzels" group. In the end, they tried to force Dixon out with a thinly disguised request to the Board of Trustees for a "review" of his leadership. Sixty had signed the petition. The board upheld Dixon, but a committee "more representative of the faculty as a whole" was established to oversee the First Year Program. The dean, Morris Keeton, a supporter of the program, was shifted to a vice presidency—where, ironically, he has since played a quietly effective role from the Washington-Baltimore campus in engineering the systems concept, although the First Year Program has atrophied.

SUMMARY: COSTS AND BENEFITS

An outsider can see many potential goods in Antioch's developing network. It could be a useful safety valve, providing spin-off for pressures that build up on the home campus. It could furnish a more removed and less impassioned testing ground for new ideas. It could enlarge the resources available to both students and faculty and help to overcome the limitations of a campus located in rural Ohio. It could help pull the faculty out of intellectual ruts by giving them a year or two in a different locale where they can face new challenges, do field work, and develop new interests.

It can help a small liberal arts college gain more prominence, visibility, and funds.[17]

And, in fact, to some degree the systems have served all these purposes. However, their principal flaw is that they are seen as competing, not as cooperating, systems. The liberals in Yellow Springs do not perceive recent growth as enlarging opportunities but as constituting a financial and administrative drain on the home campus. The Washington-Baltimore campus in particular is looked upon as providing a cut-rate Antioch degree, serving students who could not meet the admissions standards in Yellow Springs and who will eventually tarnish the Antioch image. Many in Yellow Springs view the systems as a threat, a goad, and a competing model of education. "Can you imagine," said one of the liberal leaders in Yellow Springs, "what people here thought when Plumer (the Washington-Baltimore dean) suggested we ought to be doing what they're doing." The system is seen as fostering competition in such sensitive areas as salary. Professors at Washington-Baltimore (and some students in administrative jobs there) receive considerably more on the average than do their counterparts in Yellow Springs. Some would defend such differentials, arguing that in an entrepreneurial system, the high-risk ventures ought to be rewarded if they succeed in attracting clients.[18]

As one might expect, there is a serious difference of opinion at Antioch about how successful the centers have been. Seven of the eight elected members of Adcil endorsed a bitter report to the board last spring, charging that the top echelon of Yellow Springs administrators had become "Network Officers," leaving Yellow Springs seriously understaffed, and eroding its budget as a result.

[17] Additional funds, of course, are one important motivation for the network. Organizations that affiliate with Antioch qualify for federal work-study and other funds. Antioch in turn will charge an overhead and management fee to the affiliates and may be able to pick up additional benefits under the provisions of recently proposed federal legislation that would aid institutions in sharing technical and administrative resources. Antioch's charges have been a sore point to some. Complaining about the $24,000 affiliation fee, James W. Wiley, president of Teachers, Inc., was quoted as saying, "One of my most vehement feelings is that I have seen little interest from the Yellow Springs Administration in our educational program. They have been much more interested in the money aspect" (*Antioch Record,* May 19, 1972).

[18] The salary mean for full professors at Washington-Baltimore in 1971 was $22,000 and at Yellow Springs, $18,100. For associates, the comparable figures were $16,200 and $14,200; for assistants, $12,800 and $10,800.

The Adcil report asserted that $585,000 had been diverted to the Washington-Baltimore campus "to balance a budget unbalanced by apparently incredible mismanagement of the collection of tuition and loans."

The trustees visited ten of the existing field centers in March. Their report indicated that they found four of them in a generally strong position, two of mixed virtues, and four in serious difficulty. The centers given the warmest endorsement were the Baltimore center, emphasizing urban social change programs (high motivation, good morale, clear goals, and strong curriculum); a teacher training center in Philadelphia (positive feelings, financially healthy, competent staff, cohesive); and the teacher training program in Washington (dedicated, purposeful, well-organized). The emerging but not yet operational law school in Washington was also seen to be highly promising. More ambiguous was the Columbia center, which was seen as having "strong motivation" as it moved toward developing ecology programs but flawed by cleavage between the professionally oriented staff and the change-oriented staff of centers which had split from it. The Yellow Springs Graduate School of Education Center was seen as generally strong but weakened by a "lack of evaluation and supervision." The most troubled centers were Antioch-West in San Francisco (marginal financial base, fuzzy relationship with Yellow Springs, inadequate planning); the Washington center for the study of basic human problems (limited courses, lack of purpose, hostility and bitterness); the Southern Appalachian Center in Huntington, West Virginia (only ten students for three faculty members, "too poor, no place to turn"); and the graduate center in Harrisville, New Hampshire (looseness, lack of critical mass, inadequate faculty leadership). These last four centers were generally characterized by inarticulate purposes and were seen as having few virtues other than "freedom and flexibility" or "opportunity for those who couldn't relate elsewhere."

The costs have been considerable. The bitterness and conflict that began with the struggles over the First Year Program are more than mere impressions. A 1968 survey by the Educational Testing Service revealed that Antioch students, faculty, and administrators had a positive view of the college in terms of its diversity, creativity, and intellectual stimulation but a negative view of it in terms of morale, conflict, and lack of cohesion that they felt characterized life there. Two-thirds of the faculty at all 37 colleges included in the survey agreed with the statement that, in general, faculty morale was high on their campuses. At Antioch, less than one-third of the faculty and only 4 percent of the administrators agreed with that statement. For all colleges in the study, an average of only 18 percent of the faculty agreed that staff infighting and backbiting seemed more the rule than the exception. At Antioch, 47 percent agreed with that pessimistic assessment of campus life (Churchill, 1969a, Peterson, 1967).

Some of Antioch's own board members have been moved to express severe misgivings about the health of the college. Alfred Marrow, chairman of the board's governance committee, presented suggestions for restructuring the administration with the comment, "This is a sick organization. It needs hospitalization in the intensive care unit to survive" (*Antioch Record,* May 12, 1972, p. 1).

There are other worrisome indicators. Withdrawal rates have increased significantly on the home campus. In 1965, about 22 percent of Antioch's students had withdrawn by the end of sophomore year. Now 35 percent have withdrawn in the first two years. The college examiner, Ruth Churchill, also concludes from interviews with seniors that at times of high conflict at Antioch in recent years many students may not leave Antioch altogether, but they withdraw into more private concerns. Conflict paradoxically led to less personal change because "instead of bringing their values out in an open system where they could be examined and perhaps changed . . . they tended to hold onto their old values. So there was less change and more polarization."

The number of Yellow Springs applicants who accept Antioch's offer of admissions has fallen sharply, from 67 percent in 1970 to 54 percent in 1971 to 49 percent in 1972. The Washington-Baltimore campus has run into financial difficulties as a result of its inability to meet enrollment projections, and the San Francisco center has had a disappointing response to its recruitment drives conducted in Yellow Springs.

The admissions office has published no study of the increase in applicant "turndown" rates, but interviews were conducted with Antioch students who have recently withdrawn from the college in great numbers. The interviews revealed that some of those who leave, citing financial reasons, truly cannot afford the increased costs. "Others do not want to pay $4,500 a year to goof off," says Mrs. Churchill. "They feel they can get the same education for less elsewhere." The dropout study also showed that another group of dissatisfied students were those who were quite successful academically in high school, where expectations were clear, but floundered in Antioch's less structured environment. Another group, one that apparently is increasing nationally, were some of the brightest students at Antioch who are "opting out of the system" to live in a commune or because they feel there are more important things to do in nonacademic settings.

Turning from symptoms to more structural difficulties, the new Antioch network presents a number of unresolved problems. One is the difficulty of establishing equity among campuses on such questions as salary, financial aid, and supportive resources. Students at branch campuses do not have access to the financial aid that is available in Yellow Springs, although their need may be as great. Libraries, laboratories, and other services are unequally distributed.

Another area of difficulty lies in deciding what work qualifies for academic credit. In several of the field centers connected with the Washington-Baltimore campus, incoming students are granted up to two years credit for "previous life and work experiences." Yet no clearly worked out guidelines have emerged for determining the basis on which such credit will or will not be granted.

The focus of most of the recent experimentation at Antioch has been at the organizational level; changing the mix of students, seeking new forms of governance, and extending credentialing powers. There has been much less attention given to the kind of teaching and program sequences that its new students need.

In a more critical context, Antioch's new network raises some difficult questions. Does the network shield fraudulent elements? Does it pretend to great virtues and goals of pluralism and social change but in reality peddle credit for life, cheapen higher education, and sell a mess of pottage to minority students who are desperate for a credential? My own view is that while there is no intent to defraud, a few of Antioch's enterprises are doubtful educational ventures. Others suffer from inflated rhetoric. Some branches of the network ought to be lopped off altogether and others severely pruned. The flaws are often serious, yet they do not invalidate what is a worthwhile and in some ways courageous, if at times reckless, experiment.[19] And there may be no more doubtful programs at Antioch than at any large state university. Experimental institutions suffer as well as profit from the extra measure of attention they gain, and Antioch has a greater willingness to offer its dirty linen to public inspection than all but a few institutions.

Basically, Antioch seeks to do with private resources what has heretofore been the function of low-cost public education. It raises the interesting question of whether the nation should allow only publicly controlled bureaucracies to create the kind of pluralistic environments that Antioch has achieved. Can we have open admissions only if we are willing to hire the bureaucracy of the City University of New York? Do we need a voucher system in higher education as much as, or more than, in primary and secondary schools? New federal legislation approaches the voucher system in its provision of basic grants for low-income students, but private institutions are not sufficiently rewarded financially to provide the high-quality programs that are needed for marginally prepared students.

Finally, one needs to look at Antioch's mode of confrontation. Conflict may provoke change, but there is no evidence that it necessarily improves learning. Perhaps, given Antioch's history of social commitment, its response to many of the pressures of the 1960s could not have been otherwise. But the pace and style of that change and the development of the field networks may be more closely related to James Dixon's style.

Antioch suffers from a need to feel itself skating far ahead of the crowd, and Dixon sometimes clings to a perverse form of courage, believing that only thin ice is worth skating on. Dixon knows that he has encouraged competition and conflict among both faculty and students, but he believes that Antioch will "be able to tolerate more contradictions and ambiguities until new understanding brings under reason and objective control what seemed irrational before." But success is not assured, and he is willing to face that. Antioch, he said some years ago, "has no obligation to pursue its own survival as an end" (Dixon, 1963).

However, it may be Dixon's own exceptional ability to tolerate

---

[19] What is difficult to judge here, as David Riesman reminded me, are the personal costs of experimentation — the degree to which experimentation can become "courageous and reckless with other people's lives."

high levels of conflict and ambiguity that shields him from the full realization of the costs of his policies for ordinary men. Hence, he makes less of an effort to rationalize his new systems and their governance than might otherwise be the case.[20]

Yet a serious question remains of whether these far-flung enterprises can be rationalized into any coherent whole. If one could construct a complexity-size ratio among institutions of higher education, Antioch would have a dangerously high rating. Perhaps the Antioch of 1992 will not be a network so much as a group of loosely connected institutions with a common midwife. And it may be as midwife that Antioch best serves American higher education—helping to bring to life or keep alive creative experiments that might otherwise die, like the Urban Law Institute that was aborted by George Washington University. And, in fact, Antioch may have more skill in spawning institutions than in managing them.

But in the short run, if the midwife herself is to be kept from faltering, Dixon must convince a larger proportion of the Yellow Springs faculty that the risks he wants to take are worth sharing. He must create an environment which supports his network of innovation while sustaining and honoring the very real accomplishments of the more traditionally minded faculty at home. This may be the crucial task facing the wider network of all colleges and universities throughout the nation.

References

Antioch Record, Jan. 29, 1971; Jan. 21, 27, Feb. 11, 13, May 12, 19, 1972.

Benowitz, Stephen: "Flaws Confirmed through Self Study," *Antioch Record,* Feb. 26, 1971.

"The Budget Reconsidered," *Antioch Record,* Feb. 4, 1972.

Bulletin of the Antioch School of Law, p. 11, 1972.

Churchill, Ruth: *The Functioning of Antioch College, Spring 1968, as Seen by Faculty, Students, and Administrators,* Antioch College Office of Education and Research, 1969a. (Mimeographed.)

[20] In this regard, a revealing comment was made about Dixon by the manager of a Yellow Springs bank who was angry that so many students had defaulted on loans. Local cosigners were required, but that didn't help, the banker said, with one exception—a delinquent student loan Dixon had cosigned. "Dixon pays without screaming, the others scream without paying," the banker said (*The Antioch Record,* January 21, 1972, p. 4).

Churchill, Ruth: "Performance of 1968–69 Graduates on the Advanced Graduate Record Examination," Testing Office Report No. 1, August 1969*b*.

Churchill, Ruth: *Changes in Attitudes and Values, 1961–66,* Antioch College Office of Educational Evaluation and Research, 1970. (Mimeographed.)

Clark, Burton R.: *The Distinctive College: Antioch, Reed, and Swarthmore,* Aldine Publishing Company, Chicago, 1970.

Dixon, James P.: "Education and Human Survival," *Antioch Notes,* January 1963.

Dixon, James P.: "The Time for Change Is Now—I," *Antioch Notes,* January 1969.

Gurin, Gerald: "The Impact of College Experience," in Stephen Withey, *A Degree and What Else: Correlates and Consequences of a College Education,* McGraw-Hill Book Company, New York, 1972.

Hafner, Yates: "Infracurriculum Notes—Springe," *Antioch Notes,* November 1969.

Henderson, Algo D., and Dorothy Hall: *Antioch College: Its Design for Liberal Education,* Harper & Brothers, New York, 1946.

Jerome, Judson: *Culture Out of Anarchy: The Reconstruction of American Higher Learning,* Herder and Herder, Inc., New York, 1970.

"Minutes of the Annual Meeting of the Board of Trustees," November 1969; May 1970; and December 3–4, 1971.

Peterson, Richard E.: "An Overview of the Institutional Functioning Inventory," Educational Testing Service, Princeton, N.J., 1967.

Sparks, Lois: *A Report on Student Initiated Courses,* Antioch College Office of Educational Evaluation and Research, August 1971. (Mimeographed.)

Statement—National Law Center of George Washington University, Feb. 24, 1971. (Mimeographed.)

A Study of Antioch College, Antioch College, p. B-V-8, 1971. (Mimeographed.)

3. Berkeley in Crisis and Change

by Neil J. Smelser

During the past eight years, the name of the University of California at Berkeley has become synonymous with crisis and change. Though its episodes of political turmoil have been surpassed in size and dramatic effect — at Columbia, Harvard, the Sorbonne, the Free University of Berlin, and Tokyo University, perhaps — Berkeley can nevertheless lay claim to number one ranking in crisis creation in the 1960s. The Berkeley campus electrified the academic world with the Free Speech Movement in 1964. Since then it has witnessed the so-called Filthy Speech Movement in the spring of 1965; the Oakland Army Terminal protest in the fall of 1965; the Navy Table incident and strike in the winter of 1966; an attempt to close the Oakland Induction Center in the fall of 1967; the controversy over Social Analysis 139X, the course taught in part by Eldridge Cleaver in the fall of 1968; the Third World Liberation Front strike over ethnic studies in the first months of 1969; the People's Park controversy in the spring of 1969; the anti-ROTC agitation and the "trashing" in the spring of 1970; and the attempt to "reconstitute" the campus in a political direction in the wake of the American intervention in Cambodia in the spring of 1970.

These and innumerable other minor crises and "near misses" have involved the university in months of intense and bitter controversy; days of physical confrontation between protesters and the police and military; thousands of arrests, many injuries, and a fatality; hundreds of thousands of man-hours in crisis-related meetings; and hundreds of altered collegial and personal relations. While the scene has cooled noticeably — and, to many, somewhat mysteriously — few predict confidently that crisis and confrontation have ended in Berkeley.

Why did these episodes erupt first at Berkeley? Why have controversies arisen over certain issues and not others? Why have the controversies been so continuous and of such great magnitude? How has the campus been changed by the turmoil? In this essay I shall reflect on these questions. Even though I have personally been in the eye of the hurricane on many occasions, and even though, like everyone else, I have seen the years of turmoil from a particular vantage point that will influence my reflections, I shall attempt to be as dispassionate as possible.

My interpretative framework is fairly simple: A number of changes were occurring in the larger society and at Berkeley itself prior to the period of turmoil. These changes modified the campus social organization and its pattern of social groups. The new social organization made previously latent issues more meaningful to more people, and the new groups were more likely than before to define these issues as controversial. From these prior changes we can understand much about the content and magnitude of the issues that gripped the campus in the 1960s. In addition, once controversy broke out, it developed a dynamic of its own, which superimposed new bases for conflict on the original issues. Finally, the political turmoil itself initiated pressures for further change; but the precise effects of the turmoil are difficult to ascertain because they were so intermingled with the effects of other, possibly independent processes of change.

PRIOR CONDITIONS AND DEVELOPMENTS The first background development, by no means specific to Berkeley, was the emergence of American society from the quiescent Eisenhower era into a period of more intense political involvement. The civil rights struggle became more intense, direct action emerged as a common political strategy, and the peace movement became stronger. The latter was augmented substantially by subsequent American involvement in a war regarded by many as illegitimate. Society as a whole was heading toward a period of political ferment.

That colleges and universities mirror and sometimes magnify the social and political conditions of the larger society is a general principle. For this reason alone we would expect an increasing preoccupation with political activity on the Berkeley campus in the 1960s. But distinctive characteristics of that campus made the principle especially applicable there. Along with institutions like Wisconsin and City College of New York, Berkeley had long been recognized as a center of student political activity. In addition, it had recently witnessed a number of episodes that had increased political consciousness on the campus—formation, in 1957, of

SLATE, a student political party composed of a number of liberal and radical political groups; protest against capital punishment, particularly against the execution of Caryl Chessman, in 1959–60; demonstrations against the House Un-American Activities Committee in 1960; and a variety of civil rights agitations directed against Bay Area restaurants, retail outlets, automobile companies, and the like in the early 1960s. Relations between the political activists and the campus administration were uneasy at best, and sometimes broke into open conflict, as in the controversy over directives limiting off-campus political stands and the demonstrations against compulsory ROTC in 1960–61. A SLATE manifesto in the summer of 1964 indicated that some of the politically active students had developed an openly hostile and even revolutionary attitude toward the Berkeley administration.

Ecologically, the Berkeley campus is conducive to the mobilization of mass protest. The south campus area has a population of indeterminate size, consisting of a shifting mixture of culturally alienated (bohemians, beatniks, hippies), politically active, and transient youthful people. Readily mobilizable by pamphlet and word of mouth, this population has moved in and out of alliance with student activists, depending on the issue at hand. Also available in times of crisis was a "floating" group of easily mobilized people around the Bay Area, most from other campuses in the urban area, some from San Francisco's enclaves of cultural and political alienation, and some from the student bodies of local high schools. Furthermore, both student and south campus life had come to be concentrated in Sproul Plaza, an open area flanked by the student union and the main administration building and, at the northern end of Telegraph Avenue, connecting the south campus area with the main campus, especially the buildings housing the social sciences and the humanities. In the natural rhythm of campus and Telegraph Avenue life, large groups of potentially mobilizable people thronged through Sproul Plaza.

The decade before 1964 also witnessed significant changes in the size and composition of the diverse groups, or "estates," constituting the university population. The campus enrollment grew from 14,927 students in 1953 to 26,939 students in 1964, a growth of about 80 percent. At the same time, trends leading to, and culminating in, the California Master Plan for Higher Education of 1960 changed the internal composition of the student body. In keeping with the trend to increase the standards for admission to the university (the master plan fixed the percentage to be admitted as the top 12½ percent of graduating high school seniors) and to divert lower-division students to junior colleges and state colleges, the number of lower-division students at Berkeley increased from 5,494 in 1953 to 7,232 in 1964, a growth of only 32 percent. In keeping with the trend to transfer highly qualified students from other sectors of California's higher education to the universities later in their college careers, the number of upper-division students grew from 5,737 in 1953 to 10,145 in 1964, an increase of about 76 percent. And in keeping with the emphasis on the University of California as the exclusive public grantor of doctoral degrees in the state, the number of graduate students increased from 3,796 in 1953 to 9,562 in 1964, a growth of 152 percent. The composition of the student body changed as follows:

	Percent in 1953	*Percent in 1964*
Lower division	37	27
Upper division	38	38
Graduate	25	35
	100	100

For the faculty, the late 1950s and the early 1960s were a kind of golden age. Leading universities were bidding aggressively with one another for top talent, and the coffers of the private foundations and the federal government were opening. Leading universities drove one another's rank and salary schedules upward; they reduced teaching loads to make their faculty positions more attractive; and they became increasingly generous in granting time to faculty to conduct research and head research institutes. Yet the need for teaching increasing numbers of undergraduates persisted. How did Berkeley respond?

Between 1953 and 1964 the number of full professors at Berkeley increased from 460 to 613, reflecting in part the campus's need to promote in order to acquire and retain qualified faculty. The number of associate professors grew only slightly, from 225 to 247. Assistant professors increased from 270 to 383. The total growth of regular faculty in this period, however, was only 18 percent, in contrast to a growth of 80 percent for the student body. In the meantime, nonfaculty research personnel, many of whom were supervised by faculty members in research institutes, increased almost eightfold, from 186 in 1953 to 1,424 in 1964.

The gap between the rate of regular faculty growth and the rate of student growth was filled mainly by appointments to nonregular faculty positions. While increases in the "instructor" and "teaching associate" categories were negligible, the number of "lecturers" (mainly visitors and temporary appointments) grew from 198 in 1953 to 279 in 1964, and the number of teaching assistants (graduate students on temporary teaching appointments) almost tripled, growing from 565 in 1953 to 1,430 in 1964. The teaching assistants' duties, moreover, were concentrated in the large undergraduate courses, especially in the lower division.

Thus Berkeley, already a prestigious university in the eyes of incoming students, appeared to be upgrading itself in several ways. The university reduced the percentage of admissible California high school graduates from the top 15 to the top 12½ percent of the graduating class; it was taking the cream of junior college and state college students as transfers; and it was becoming increasingly professionalized as a leading national center of graduate education. Yet when undergraduates arrived, they often found themselves remote from the most senior and prestigious faculty—who were teaching undergraduates less, teaching graduates more, and were more involved in research—and found themselves being serviced more by junior faculty, temporary faculty, and semifaculty. Students might well have perceived that they were being invited to an elite institution only to be educated mainly by its second-class teachers in a large, impersonal setting.

In short, under great pressures to grow and upgrade, the campus had partially fragmented its functions. It had grown at the top, but the senior professors were decreasingly involved in one of the major activities of the university, undergraduate teaching. It had also expanded greatly at the side, with the addition of nonfaculty research personnel, who were involved in one of the major activities of the campus (the generation of knowledge through research) but who did not enjoy the faculty's privileges of tenure, membership in the academic senate, or on-campus parking. It had grown rapidly at the bottom, with teaching assistants, whose roles are marginal in the sense that they are one-third faculty, one-third student, and one-third employee. By growing at the side and at the bottom, it had multiplied the number of its second-class citizens, who were, to be sure, involved in some of the central functions of the campus, but who did not receive rewards commensurate with full citizenship and whose investment of loyalty in the institution was understandably less.

The first-class citizens may have experienced great gratifications from their work, but many also experienced a vague sense of accumulated guilt for neglecting their students. (Some of the political crises of the 1960s provided an opportunity for faculty members and students to become momentarily very close to one another.) Many of the nonfaculty research personnel experienced feelings of exclusion and perhaps exploitation. (During the 1960s some of the nonfaculty research personnel exerted a low-key but persistent drive to secure privileges that would bring them closer to faculty status.) Many of the teaching assistants—and perhaps some junior faculty—felt unjustly treated and had conflicting loyalties toward the different constituencies of which they were partial members. (Teaching assistants played an important mobilizing role in many of the crises of the 1960s. In general they split into several subgroups—those who were active in campus political issues, those interested in their "employee" status, those identified with the faculty, and those who were undecided or indifferent.) All these psychological consequences suggest that when conflicts among different constituencies arose, each constituency experienced deep internal divisions, and that unexpected and volatile factions were likely to form.

One final background factor must be mentioned: the administration of Chancellor Edward W. Strong during the several years prior to 1964. From the beginning, this administration had been perceived by many faculty members as an ineffective one. Regard for Chancellor Strong was not high, and some faculty members preferred to deal directly with President Clark Kerr. This, combined with the fact that Kerr had been chancellor of the Berkeley campus previously, created a certain jurisdictional ambiguity between president and chancellor with respect to the administration of the Berkeley campus. Faculty disaffection was further crystallized around the transition from the semester system to the quarter system, which many faculty members felt was "shoved down their throats" by the statewide administration against their preferences, and the refusal of Chancellor Strong to rehire Eli Katz—a young faculty member in the German department—on grounds of his refusal to answer questions about his alleged Communist party connections. Many faculty members regarded the Katz case as an important academic freedom matter, and in the fall of 1964 the Berkeley division of the academic senate condemned the administration for its handling of it. In sum, many members of the Berkeley faculty appeared dissatisfied with the administration in 1964, and were predisposed to join in opposition to it.

THE OUTBREAK OF CONFLICT These background considerations offer some clues as to why the issue of the use of university facilities for political activity was such a lively one in 1964, and why politically active students, teaching assistants, and faculty members coalesced in numbers sufficient ultimately, in December of that year, to depose the chancellor and shatter the campus administration's authority. The conflict was magnified by two additional circumstances. At the very outset of the crisis of the fall of 1964 the administration came to be regarded as repressive, because the act that triggered the Free Speech Movement (FSM) was the administration's decision to revoke certain privileges of student groups that had been informally granted for some time. Once the confrontations began, the administration seemed to alternate between a posture of capitulation and a posture of retaliation with harsh discipline. These circumstances mobilized many who reacted against the administration not so much in terms of the substantive issues of the conflict as in response to the apparently authoritarian behavior of the administration.

The revolution of December 1964 was superficially a temporary one, in the sense that *formal* authority was quickly restored by the law-enforcement agencies and by the regents, who appointed a new acting chancellor. Crises, however, are not terminated merely by formally reestablishing authority. The very fact that a crisis of authority occurs creates new issues and escalates the bases of conflict. New groups form in the crisis period, groups which are prepared to raise previously unraised questions about the legitimizing values and goals of the institution as a whole, to rewrite history from their own perspectives, to generate new definitions of the campus situation, and to square off against other groups who do not share their perspectives. Moreover, when authority is challenged openly, groups that previously were not visibly dissatisfied may generate new expectations about their place in the institution and about their share in its authority system.

One issue—the viability of the campus administration's authority—seemed to dominate the Berkeley campus immediately after December 1964. Under stable conditions, the main question about an authority system is *how* authority is exercised—effectively, benevolently, repressively, or whatever. Once the legitimacy of authority has been successfully challenged, however, the issue becomes one of *whether* authority can be exercised at all. Under these circumstances the person who holds authority struggles to rebuild and maintain the support of the constituencies who can bolster his claims to authority, and those who have successfully challenged it continue to attempt to deny it, partly by attacking the values by which it is legitimized and partly by prodding it and testing its viability. For almost a year after December 1964 the main issue on the Berkeley campus was whether authority could be exercised. Both Martin Meyerson in his brief eight-month administration as acting chancellor and Roger Heyns in the early months of his administration fought to retain this capacity. It was of great symbolic importance that Meyerson was able to "get away with" disciplining four of those involved in the obscenity crisis without stirring a massive campus reaction. It was also significant that this discipline was exercised shortly after an enormous show of support by the faculty. It was of great symbolic importance that Heyns was able to prevent the unauthorized placing of political signs on campus in the fall of 1965 without triggering a serious challenge to his authority. In that year after FSM many of the issues appeared to be small—how many minutes after 1 P.M. could noontime political rallies continue? How large could political posters be? In reality they were very large issues, because they tested the legitimacy of the administration's authority.

After a crisis the struggle to reestablish authority is often hindered by the fact that many previously quiescent constituencies have become activated and attempt to exert influence. The students, the faculty, the alumni, the board of regents, the press, the law-enforcement agencies, the Legislature, and the Governor—all these, often themselves split into contending subgroups, emerged as political influences to be contended with on a day-to-day basis after the crisis of 1964. This activation of interests constricted the maneuverability of the chancellor, threatened to weaken his tenuous control of the campus situation, and forced him to devote more of his energy to pacifying or holding angry constituents at arm's length than to ameliorating the problems that gave rise to the crisis in the first place.

Some of these constituencies, such as the faculty and alumni, are significant primarily as political groups without whose support the campus administrator's position might be untenable. Other constituencies, such as the board of regents and law-enforcement officials, are significant both politically and legally. Various types of ultimate authority reside in them, and they have the legal right to intervene in campus affairs. When the authority of the campus administration was under fire in crisis, these constituencies rushed on the scene, sometimes on their own, sometimes under public pressure. As often as not this intervention, while perhaps necessary and justified by the logic of maintaining order, fanned the flames of crisis and intensified the political divisions on the campus. For example, the calling of police or military forces in November 1966, during the Third World Liberation Front strike in the early months of 1969, and during the People's Park crisis in May 1969, immediately heated up these situations, and precipitated new mobilization and new actions by different campus groups. Also, the regents' threat to invervene in the obscenity crisis, precipitating statements by Kerr and Meyerson that they intended to resign, produced an enormous mobilization of the faculty in their support. And while the board requested that the two continue, the entire incident revealed exactly how fragile the authority of the statewide and campus administrations was at the time. Again, the regents' intervention in denying academic credit for the Eldridge Cleaver course — which had been approved by the appropriate faculty committees — raised the whole issue of the faculty's delegated authority, inflamed many faculty members and students, and deepened the division between those who did and those who did not approve of the course. Finally, at another level, budgetary intervention by the Legislature and Governor, motivated in part by political, interventionist considerations, has had a persisting and corrosive effect on faculty morale.

One of the immediate effects of a large campus conflict is that various constituencies of the campus (students, faculty, teaching assistants, etc.) take sides and declare their loyalties. Yet as I noted earlier, the lines of polarization at Berkeley after December 1964 never followed the lines of constituency membership exactly. In fact, because the constituencies were either heterogeneous or marginal — and therefore ambivalent in their loyalties — polarized political conflict tended to split each constituency. Thus the campus was faced with a kind of "multiplier effect" whereby any serious conflict *between* constituencies (typically, between students and administration) led to the intensification of conflict *within* the various constituencies (for example, faculty members favoring the administration versus those favoring the students). Needless to say, this effect seriously undermined the system of collegial consensus, on the basis of which the campus has traditionally been governed.

Finally, reflecting the positions taken in conflict, just as the loyalty oath of the early 1950s effected a lasting realignment of loyalties and antagonisms, so the crises of the 1960s left a number of layers of scar tissue which are ready to reopen with the appearance of any new crisis.

Given this general diagnosis of the genesis and dynamics of conflict, what can be said most generally about the issues that have gripped Berkeley in the past eight years? Every issue seems traceable to the fact that the campus has been subject to enormous political pressures—agitation from the left, intervention from the right, and mousetrapping by both at once—and that these political pressures have posed a continuing crisis of legitimacy for the Berkeley administration. Thus every one of the following interrelated issues has ultimately concerned the relations between campus authority and political activity:

1 What kinds of political activity are to be authorized on campus? (FSM, Oakland Induction Center march, Navy Table incident)

2 What political uses of the campus facilities are to be authorized? (Vietnam Day Committee, Vietnam moratorium, reconstitution)

3 Should the campus become directly and officially involved in political activity—or, depending on one's point of view, become involved in different ways than it is now? (Vietnam moratorium, protest against CIA and Dow Chemical interviews on campus)

4 To what degree should others than the campus administration (faculty, students, employees) have authority on the campus? (Social Analysis 139X, Third World Liberation Front strike)

5 To what degree should delegated campus authority—of administration, faculty, and students—be protected from intervention by the board of regents, the Legislature, and the governor? (an explicit or implicit issue in almost every crisis)

6 What are the relations between campus authority and civil authority? (FSM, Oakland Induction Center crisis, the presence of police on campus during many crises)

7 What is the status of the university's authority with respect to the use, control, and disposal of its legally defined property and facilities? (People's Park issue)

EFFECTS OF THE YEARS OF TURMOIL Because of the dramatic quality of the political controversies that have occurred at Berkeley, it is tempting to overemphasize their impact by attributing all subsequent changes to political conflict. The actual causal role played by crisis, however, is more subtle. Several changes of the past few years were under way in any case, and campus crises played a minor if any role in them. I refer to the development of the new School of Journalism, the new School of Public Affairs, and the new Program of Religious Studies. In other cases, the changes were perhaps imminent, but the crises played a catalytic role, as with the liberalization of undergraduate course requirements, the modification of the grading system, and the modest efforts to break from the traditional lecture and discussion-section method of teaching. In still other cases, changes can be attributed more directly to political ferment, as with the creation of a new Department of Ethnic Studies and the increased level of student participation in affairs formerly reserved for administration and faculty. As might be said of all social change, however, no one factor, such as political turmoil, can be assigned an exclusive role; it combines and recombines in complex ways with other forces.

In many respects Berkeley in the spring of 1972 has changed very little from Berkeley in the spring of 1964. The architectural face of the campus is not dramatically different, except from some new facilities, most of which are "expected" additions to a university— a new auditorium, a new undergraduate library, and a new art museum. The campus's "table of organization" of colleges, schools, departments, research units, and service units is virtually unchanged. The course catalogs of 1964 and 1972 are very similar in content. The same research institutes pursue the same general types of research they did several years ago. The calendar of campus events reveals a similar array of scholarly and cultural activities as before. The size and composition of the student body have not changed much, with the exception that there are many more minority faces now than there were then; the proportion of graduate students has not changed radically, and, though this is difficult to document, there are probably larger proportions of students who are politically radical, who are interested in social and political issues in general, and who are involved in the "action" of hip culture. Yet the vast majority of students comes to the campus to pursue a course in academic studies, graduate, and proceed to some line of occupational endeavor.

How, then, have things changed? As might be expected, the most immediate impact of the political crises has been political. The controversies have been given heavy exposure by the mass media and have aroused widespread concern and outrage among the public and in the state government. The political repercussions of the crises on the Berkeley campus played a direct role in the demise of Strong; in the threatened resignations of Meyerson and Kerr; in the firing of Kerr in January 1967; in keeping the political position of Heyns frequently in jeopardy; and in precipitating his resignation. The disturbances have also produced direct countermeasures, such as more careful surveillance of student and nonstudent behavior by the campus administration, an increase in the number of disciplinary actions, and more police on the campus more often. Issues generated by events on the Berkeley campus were foremost in the political backlash that swept Ronald Reagan into office in 1966. The most direct effect of this backlash on the Berkeley campus has been on its budget—the most convenient and effective weapon available to the Governor and the Legislature. In addition, the Legislature has passed a few pieces of hostile legislation and initiated a few investigations, and the Governor has issued menacing statements periodically which call for "political balance" and "political tests" in recruiting faculty. It is difficult to be certain, but some evidence, mainly from the election results of 1970, indicates that the political mileage to be gained by using higher education as a whipping boy may be decreasing slightly.

The board of regents has intervened in the campus mainly in three ways: First, it has responded to crisis by passing general regulations and resolutions (for example, new disciplinary regulations) designed to prevent specific actions that occurred in the crisis immediately before. Second, it has withdrawn previously delegated power from the campuses and occasionally attempted to use that power (for example, in the areas of appointment and tenure, as in the cases of Herbert Marcuse, Angela Davis, and two Berkeley faculty members whose promotions were delayed in the summer of 1970). And third, it has attempted to strengthen the campus administrators' authority and disciplinary power over students and faculty. By and large, the regents have much more direct short-run control over the behavior of campus administrators, who are directly accountable to them, than they do over the behavior of faculty members and students. When regents have become alarmed over situations on campus, they have attempted to strengthen the hands of those campus authorities to whom they have the most direct access. Whether this strategy has been effective is questionable, however, because regental efforts to strengthen the chancellors' authority and to induce them to exercise it strictly are likely to engender further faculty and student distrust of, and opposition to, the administration.

Faculty response to each crisis has followed a typical pattern. When a crisis breaks, faculty caucuses begin to meet and hammer out positions; numerous individuals and groups spring into action, like so many Lone Rangers, each trying to ease the situation by persuading warring factions to talk with one another. Gradually faculty sentiment coalesces, usually through the mediating efforts of the Policy Committee of the Berkeley Division of the Academic Senate. Some resolution acceptable to most of the major faculty factions is drawn up and put to a vote at a mass meeting of the division. In crises primarily affecting the relations among different campus constituencies (FSM, the strike of December 1966, and the Third World Liberation Front strike), the voice of the faculty has had an important effect in calming the situation and pointing toward at least a temporary resolution. In crises when the campus was overwhelmed by external political conflicts (People's Park, reconstitution), the effect of formal faculty actions has been negligible.

Through the years of crises faculty factions have shifted continuously. At present faculty opinion appears to be broken mainly into four groups: (1) a small, conservative group whose sympathies lie with the Governor and the majority of the board of regents; (2) the majority of the faculty, who are moderate or indifferent and whose main political stance is antipathetic to the political goals of both the interventionist right and the radical left; active members in this group have formed the Council for an Academic Community, a sizable and well-organized faculty lobby; (3) a minority of liberal or radical faculty, whose sympathies lie closer to the goals of the left student movement of the 1960s; (4) a group—overlapping with the liberals and radicals—working for the unionization of the faculty; a small but fairly active chapter of the American Federation of Teachers has formed on the campus.

It is my impression that the majority of the faculty—the moderates—are caught in a dilemma. Traditionally their enemy has been the interventionist right, their struggle has been to resist intrusions on academic freedom from above, and their natural allies have been on the left. One result of the crises of the 1960s is that many faculty members find themselves also threatened by the student left and sense incursions on their traditional academic freedoms from that quarter as well. Yet they are uncomfortable fighting against the left, and especially uncomfortable when they find themselves agreeing with sentiments of the interventionist right. This dilemma goes far in indicating why many faculty members tend toward vacillation, paralysis, or withdrawal in matters of campus politics.

As indicated earlier, these divisions run deep, and have, to a degree, undermined faculty consensus on such fundamental issues as the idea of a university, appropriate authority relations within it, and appropriate conduct for a faculty member both in and out of the classroom. A few departments in the social sciences and humanities and a few professional schools are badly split, difficult to govern, and plagued by frequent, interminable, and bitter meetings. Morale has sagged in these departments, and energy for research and teaching has been drained correspondingly. The sciences and some professional schools, such as engineering, appear to have suffered much less from these effects. Faculty distrust of other faculty members is also reflected in two recent episodes in the Berkeley Division of the Academic Senate. First, the creation of a Representative Assembly to replace partially the town-meeting forum of the entire division, was motivated in part by the desire of moderate faculty members to prevent "irresponsible" resolutions from being passed at ill-attended faculty meetings dominated by extremists. Second, the recent adoption of a code of conduct for faculty—including the specification of obligations as well as the rights and the specification of sanctions and disciplinary procedures—was motivated in part by the desire of moderate faculty members to curb what they regarded as unethical behavior on the part of some of their colleagues during the reconstitution crisis, when some classes were converted into political action groups or discontinued outright. Of course, many other considerations went into the formation of the Representative Assembly and the formulation of the faculty code of conduct, but the distrust of faculty was one important ingredient.

With respect to faculty governance and academic affairs, faculty responses have been conservative. The Berkeley Division of the Academic Senate established a special student-faculty commission on governance (the Foote Commission) in the wake of the strike of December 1966, but its report, which contained numerous recommendations for campus reorganization and decentralization, went largely unheeded by both administration and faculty. Earlier, immediately after the FSM crisis, Meyerson had established a select committee on education (the Muscatine Committee), and its report, *Education at Berkeley,* issued in 1966, was a notable faculty response to both long-term curricular concerns and short-term student pressures for change. The Berkeley division adopted many of the committee's recommendations, and the Berkeley campus was one of the first to establish a major administrative-faculty unit [the Board of Educational Development (BED)]. For several years this agency sponsored programs in group tutorials, combinations of academic and fieldwork, interdisciplinary studies, and the like. These efforts were curtailed and deflected in other directions in 1968 for a variety of reasons. First, the combination of only limited faculty interest in innovation and the onset of budgetary stringency imposed inherent limitations on the magnitude of experimental programs. Also, the political crisis around Eldridge Cleaver and Social Analysis 139X discredited the BED to some extent and led to more stringent administrative controls over faculty appointments in experimental courses. Around that time experimentation seemed to degenerate into a political tug-of-war between a group of liberal and radical students on the one hand, who pressed for courses, some of which were potentially explosive politically and questionable by traditional academic standards, and faculty and administrators on the other hand, who insisted on the maintenance of standards. Also about that time the all-student Committee on Participant Education, which had been working cooperatively with the BED, broke off and proceeded independently, mainly in initiating noncredit courses and in working with individual faculty members. Finally, many departments began to incorporate experimental courses, thus further centralizing the work done previously by the BED. The movement for educational innovation must therefore be regarded as a victim of politicization in large part; its impact on the entire campus was modest, though a few valuable traces of the movement—group tutorial programs, undergraduate seminars, field study courses, and the like—can be observed from place to place on the campus.

Two main academic units that can be said to have emerged directly from the campus turmoil are the Experimental College ("the Tussman program") and the Department of Ethnic Studies. The former, a vigorous effort to expose students in their first two years to an intensive interdisciplinary education, generated considerable enthusiasm among many of the students and faculty involved, but foundered after several years for lack of faculty interest. The Department of Ethnic Studies, now apparently a permanent fixture on the campus, has enjoyed considerable popularity among minority students. During 1969–70 more than 4,000 course enrollments were counted, mainly among minority students, in the courses in the history, socioeconomic conditions, and culture of several ethnic groups. Despite this favorable start, the department faces serious ambiguities. The first has to do with the goals of the department. The administration's policy has been to regard the department as a normal academic unit whose business it is to conduct courses of instruction; many in the department prefer a more free-wheeling arrangement, with greater emphasis on serving the needs and activities of the constituent ethnic groups themselves. Thus far the administration and the department have maintained a kind of standoffish relationship with respect to this fundamental ambiguity. Second, the department faces an uncertain budgetary future. Third, the academic relations between the department and other academic units—in terms of transferability of courses to major programs in other departments, for example—are not entirely clear. In general, the department has thus far existed more or less in isolation from the mainstream of faculty and administrative activities on the campus. And finally, it is not certain whether the department can sustain sufficient interest on the part of its faculty and students to succeed in the long run.

Despite the frequent turmoil, the low morale of many faculty members, and the budgetary squeeze, Berkeley has managed to survive as a high-quality academic institution. The rate of resignations of tenured faculty since the Free Speech Movement has been about 2 percent per year, and in 1969–70 only 17 tenured members (of a total of 1,079) resigned, the lowest number in six years. I suspect that the uncertain political and economic future of the campus has presented a more severe problem for recruitment than for resignations, however, particularly among young potential recruits without the security of tenure. In the 1970 version of the American Council of Education's survey of the prestige of graduate institutions, Berkeley repeated as most distinguished in quality of graduate faculty and effectiveness of graduate programs. The same kind of standing could not be claimed for the undergraduate program, however, since it still suffers from a deficit of faculty involvement. To improve undergraduate education at Berkeley significantly—as

President Charles Hitch has asked—would require, as a minimum, the input of substantial new resources to increase the faculty-student ratio and to recruit faculty committed to the development of new programs.

How does Berkeley look to students in 1972? The typical undergraduate still has most of his fare in large lecture courses and discussions led by teaching assistants. He finds, however, that "the requirements"—language requirements, breadth requirements—have been liberalized and that some major programs demand fewer required courses. He also finds that in some quarters of the campus the classroom is somewhat more open with respect to the degree to which students may influence classroom activity. Discussions in many social science and humanities courses are more heated politically than before, and most faculty in these areas would probably agree that the level of what they used to call student manners and respect for academic authority has declined. A few classes of professors who have conducted research or taken political stands unpopular with the radical left have been disrupted by groups of intruders. In these instances most students have shown indifference or quiet resentment toward the intrusion. The faculty Committee on Academic Freedom has condemned faculty intimidation and classroom disruption and the administration has taken disciplinary action against those who indulge in it.

Undergraduates participate little in departmental governments and in the machinery of the Berkeley division. Their opportunities for participation in administrative committees are somewhat greater. Graduate students find their academic programs still primarily professional in character, though some departments have liberalized the number and kinds of requirements along the road to the Ph.D. Graduate students participate more than undergraduates in departmental affairs, and student participation in some of the professional schools is even more extensive. The success of this participation is mixed; sometimes it has increased student-faculty cooperation and led to a productive student input, and in other cases it has simply moved the adversary student-faculty stance into committees and department meetings. And despite the increase in participation, discontent about its rate of progress is voiced by some faculty and students.

Informally, student life continues to combine the principles of anomie and social pluralism. On the one hand, the student body is heterogeneous, large, and individuated by diversified housing arrangements and casual student contact in the classroom. On the other, the student finds a fantastic array of opportunities for developing social ties—in departmental clubs, in political groups, in the drug culture, in encounter groups, and in volunteer activities in the community. Political consciousness is still high among many students, and much political activity may be observed in different corners of the campus. Except for the massive attempt to "reconstitute" the campus politically after the Cambodian invasion, however, no episode of mass student political action has occurred on the campus for the past three academic years.

The campus student government, the Associated Students of the University of California (ASUC), was, like so much else at Berkeley, politicized by the Free Speech Movement and subsequent crises. It has experienced a shift from being a relatively quiescent agency concerned with student activities and services toward being a body more aggressively concerned with political issues. The student radical movement, however, has itself been divided on the issue of whether to work through ASUC channels. Some have felt this a promising avenue, largely because of the substantial financial resources of the ASUC; others have felt it useless, largely because of the considerable control over ASUC affairs exercised by the administration. In consequence, student government as a campus political issue has blown hot and cold. The campus administration, while yielding to a degree to the students' desires to interest themselves in activities such as draft counseling, community projects, and student housing, has also insisted that student funds—which are collected by compulsory fee—also be devoted to traditional activities such as band, rally committee, and extracurricular clubs. Relations between the administration and the ASUC have vacillated between harmony and conflict. One of the perennial disputes between the two has to do with the locus of legitimate authority of student government; the administration tends to view it as delegated, while some students argue that it emanates from the students and belongs to them as a right. The future of student government at Berkeley is uncertain, as it is elsewhere, but there is a distinct possibility that it will become a voluntary association, in which case a looser and more permissive relationship would likely develop between it and the campus administration.

THE FUTURE Because the past eight years at Berkeley have been so fraught with crisis and change, the future of the campus must also be regarded as fluid and unpredictable. On the one hand, if it continues to be harassed on many fronts by the left and sledgehammered politically and budgetarily from the right and above, there is no reason to believe that the long-term effects will be anything other than gloom, low morale, and institutional deterioration. On the other hand, significant shifts in a few important political forces could change the picture dramatically. If the student movement should, for whatever reasons, remain quiescent, if public antagonism toward higher education should subside, if the state's financial situation should reverse itself, if a state administration and Legislature openly favorable to higher education should appear in the next few years, and if the Berkeley campus could be protected from the intense budgetary competition with the other campuses and the other sectors of higher education—all big "ifs," to be sure—the campus might well embark on another of its historically famous golden eras characterized by opulence, goodwill, and cultural enrichment. History alone yields some grounds for optimism, for the story of the University of California has been a story of great fluctuations between gloomy crises and golden eras. But the crises of the past eight years have been so deep that one hesitates to rely on history alone as a guide.

4. City College

by Nathan Glazer

The *New York Times* reported on July 25, 1971, that the City College of the City University of New York was second only to the University of California at Berkeley in the number of undergraduates who went on to earn doctorates between 1920 and 1970. It ranked second, too, for the number receiving doctorates between 1965 and 1970. Other institutions from which particularly large numbers of students earning doctorates had come were the University of Illinois, the University of Wisconsin, Harvard, the University of Michigan, and—more recently—the Massachusetts Institute of Technology.

One wonders, reading the story, where City College will stand 10 or 20 years from now. For clearly one long-lived phase in the history of City College is coming to an end. For 70 years, City College was the school for the poorer part of the Jewish population of New York City. In a new phase now beginning, it will be in increasing measure the school of all the people of New York City, and in particular, Negroes, Puerto Ricans, and white working-class Catholics. The beginning of the new phase was marked dramatically by a traumatic strike of black and Puerto Rican students in the spring of 1969, and the beginning of open enrollment, under a new president, in the autumn of 1970. What City College has been is clear enough; what it will become now, is still obscure.

The story in the *New York Times,* by placing City College in such distinguished company, reminds one of a number of things that distinguish City College from the other large Ph.D. producers on the list.

It is, to begin with, the *only* college on the list that is not, in Jencks's and Riesman's phrase, a "university college," that is, an undergraduate school that is part of, and closely linked to, a major graduate teaching- and research-oriented university. It is true that since 1961 City College has been part of the City University of New York. But this does not really change the fact that City College is overwhelmingly a four-year *undergraduate* college. Graduate work at the college is generally restricted to the master's degree, and is given only in some departments. Doctoral work is limited to the School of Engineering and some science departments. Most university Ph.D. programs are physically located on another "campus" (the 42d Street office building that has been remodeled for CUNY). The graduate student makes almost as little impact at City College as, let us say, at Smith College, which also gives out some master's degrees.

Second: City College is the only school on the list that does not have a research-oriented faculty of distinction. The City College faculty has men who publish, even men who achieve distinction and national reputation, but they are far fewer than are to be found in the other institutions. Its regular teaching load is 9 or 12 hours, more than in university colleges. The faculty of City College is overwhelmingly a *local* faculty, to use the well-known local and cosmopolitan distinction of Robert K. Merton. Its members stay there a long time, and two-fifths were undergraduates there. The leaders in faculty affairs and discussions are old-timers who have relatively little contact with other colleges and universities and who play relatively minor roles in their disciplines. Insofar as they are men of national reputation, they are often appointed as distinguished professors, will also generally teach at the Graduate Center, and have little contact with the undergraduate college. Since the college is not the undergraduate four-year school of a university, students too have little contact with the world of graduate scholarship. City is very definitely an undergraduate teaching institution, and whatever the complaint of the students may be, it is not that the teachers lecture with briefcase at hand, ready to catch the next plane to Washington or some international conference.

Third: City College is rather smaller than most of the other institutions on the list. This may be surprising. One tends to think of it as a huge commuter college. But the full-time, day, student body at the uptown main campus has always been relatively small, compared to such giants as Illinois or Wisconsin. Thus in the fall of 1968, 10,867 students were enrolled. (Since 1970, and open enrollment, the college has become larger.)

Fourth: City College is the only school on the list without a "national" or international enrollment. Even if Illinois' under-graduates are almost entirely from within the state, they at least represent its diversity. City College's enrollment is drawn almost entirely from New York City. By law, only New York State residents and American citizens may attend. But in fact, it is only New York *City* residents who attend, though there are a few students from out of the city and even, under special regulations, a scattering of foreign students. City College is heterogeneous and includes many students whose mother tongue is not English. But these are almost uniformly immigrants who are residents and citizens or who have filed their intention to become citizens.

Fifth: It is the only one of these Ph.D.-producing undergraduate schools that has a majority of Jewish students. (Since 1970, and open enrollment, Jewish students are probably no longer a majority.)

Sixth: It is the only one that is a *city* college rather than a state university or private university.

And of course one can spell out other differences—a smaller campus, a smaller library, City's being a 100 percent commuter school in which the great majority of students live with their families, and so on. City College is an anomaly, a community or city college that has played a role in American higher education that its formal attributes in no way explain.

This can of course only be explained by its history. Yet even that is deceptive. For while it is an old school, founded in 1847, it began life as a "free academy," and it really did not become defined as an institution of higher education until the twentieth century.

THE FREE ACADEMY   New York City finally established a board of education to administer its growing number of free public schools in 1842. There was no free high school then in the city, and the board inherited a decades-old movement for, and controversy about, establishing one. In 1846, the Democratic party won an overwhelming victory in elections for the board of education and set about trying to create a free academy under the board's newly elected president, Townsend Harris (Harris's other major distinction was to serve, again through his Democratic party connections, as the first American Consul in Japan—a strange pair of achievements indeed). Harris chaired a committee of the board which, in early 1847, proposed the establishment of a free college or academy:

. . . which, while it shall be in no way inferior to any of our colleges in the character, amount, or value of the information given to the pupils; the courses of studies to be pursued will have more especial reference to the active duties of operative life, rather than those more particularly regarded as necessary for the Pulpit, Bar, or the Medical Profession. Another important feature in the proposed plan is, that the laboring class of our fellow citizens may have the opportunity of giving to their children an education that will more effectually fit them for the various departments of labor and toil by which they will earn their bread. Such an Institution, where Chemistry, Mechanics, Architecture, Agriculture, Navigation, physical as well as moral or mental science, &, &, are thoroughly and practically taught, would soon raise up a class of mechanics and artists, well skilled in their several pursuits, and eminently qualified to infuse into their fellow-workmen a spirit that would add dignity to labor—a spirit, congenial with the character of our Republican institutions, while at the same time the diffusion of correct knowledge among the working class of our population, would make them better acquainted with their inestimable value (Rudy, 1949, p. 13).[1]

The State Legislature authorized the board, after a referendum, to establish a free academy in the City of New York:

. . . for the purpose of extending the benefits of education gratuitously, to persons who have been pupils in the common schools of the said city and county of New York.

A small Gothic building, designed by James Renwick, the architect of St. Patrick's Cathedral, was put up on 23d Street (the State Legislature had limited expenditure for a building to $50,000). It remained the only college building for 60 years. Horace Webster, a graduate of West Point and professor of Geneva College, was appointed principal. A faculty was appointed, and a required curriculum was established (for the first year, mathematics, history, composition and declamation, elements of moral science, the Constitution of the United States, drawing, bookkeeping, writing, and the Latin, French, and Spanish languages were prescribed). It is not pure antiquarianism that leads to the presentation of these details. The college was not to change much for the next 60 years. Another West Pointer succeeded the first as chief officer, and thus two West Point disciplinarians reigned at the college from its founding until 1903.

[1] The historical account and all quotations are taken from Rudy (1949, p. 13).

The curriculum did not reflect any part of the elective reforms of Harvard's President Eliot until 1900. The curriculum was fixed until then, and almost completely fixed afterward. It was not until 1900 that City College was given an independent board of trustees—until then it was under the city board of education. It did not get a civilian-educated president until 1903, when John H. Finley was appointed. It did not get a campus that looked like a college until 1908, when its Gothic buildings were opened in upper Manhattan, on a height overlooking Harlem. It always included as a regular part of the college a "preparatory course" open to students just out of elementary school, which meant that students of City College were considerably younger than those of other colleges, and graduated younger. It was not until 1911 that this secondary school integrated into City College became somewhat parallel to the other secondary schools of the city and the college became, in this respect, fully parallel to other colleges. And it was also around the turn of the century that City College underwent the drastic change in the student body that was to transform it from the stodgy, conservative, undistinguished semicollege for the children of merchants of a seaport town into the very distinctive institution that it became in the twentieth century.

IMPACT OF EAST EURO- PEAN JEWISH IMMIGRANTS What happened to the City College at the beginning of the twentieth century is that its student body became overwhelmingly East European Jewish. As S. Willis Rudy, the historian of the college, writes:

When the College was first established, the bulk of its students had been either native Americans of several generations standing, or the descendants of immigrants from northern and western Europe. During the later nineteenth century, however, as the "Old" immigration gave way to the "New," the proportion of Jews, at first from Germany and Austria-Hungary, but later from Eastern Europe, and principally the Russian Empire, markedly increased. By the time that Finley assumed the Presidency [1903], this new element numbered approximately seventy-five per cent of the total student body. There also remained a few students from the older immigrant groups of the city, notably the Irish and German; also, there was a sprinkling of boys at the College from non-Jewish, Old New York families of the middle class. But, increasingly, as the percentage of Russian-Jewish boys in attendance increased, the families of Anglo-Saxon, Dutch, German, and Huguenot descent, who had been accustomed to register their boys in the College in the old days, sent them elsewhere for a college education (ibid., pp. 292–293).

The impact of the East European Jewish immigration on City College was overwhelming. In 1890, 26 percent of 57 graduates were Jewish; in 1900, 54 percent of 127; in 1910, 70 percent of 218; in 1920, 73 percent of 124. During this period the Jewish population of New York City also rose, but it never was more (according to various estimates) than about one-quarter of the population, a proportion attained in 1910. After 1920, the City College alumni office estimates, the graduates were never less than 80 percent Jewish, and at times the figure may have been as high as 95 percent.[2] The proportion of Jewish graduates did not begin to decline until the mid-sixties, even though by then the Jewish population had shifted overwhelmingly from the working class to the middle and upper middle class, and huge new populations of Negroes and Puerto Ricans had settled in the city, forming, by 1970, some 30 percent of the total population.

It is this period in the history of City College, a remarkably long one, from about 1900 to 1969, that provides the popular image of the college. We must assess the tremendous changes now taking place in the college against the background reality of an alumni body that is overwhelmingly Jewish. The alumni of City College are in one sense more important to the college than other alumni bodies. This is not because they give money particularly—they do not—or are particularly loyal to it, or highly identified with it. It is because they live in New York City and its suburbs, and thus they are a very important part of the citizenry that determines the level and kind of public support City College may depend on. In this sense, they are much closer to the alumni body of a state university than of a private university. Dominant in their minds is the sense of a college that was free, that was open to anyone with talent, that was democratic because it depended on merit alone—as given by impersonal tests, with no concern in the slightest for motivation, ancestry, leadership, alumni parents, influence, or what have you. The dilemma of City College was that this total impersonality, in which students were admitted simply on the basis of their city high school grades, with no other consideration, also seemed to inevitably produce, year after year, an overwhelmingly Jewish student body, and one which seemed impervious, except in the very long range, to the changing composition of the city.

[2] These are figures and estimates from the alumni office, made available to me, along with other unpublished material used for this essay, by Theodore M. Brown, academic assistant to the president of the college.

The alumni office, for example, has identified 41 black graduates for the decade from 1930 to 1939, 114 for 1940 to 1949, 165 for 1950 to 1954. These were remarkably modest figures for a period when the black population was increasing rapidly.

Despite the large numbers of graduates who have achieved some prominence, most of the sons of City College went on to humble if respectable pursuits, and most of them stayed in New York. Also, despite the popular image of the City College intellectual, most City College men went to the Business School, the Technology School (engineering), and the School of Education. Only 31 percent of the classes of 1940 to 1949 and less than 29 percent of the graduating classes of 1950 to 1956 graduated from the College of Liberal Arts. In both periods the largest number of graduates came from the Business School (43 percent and 38 percent), and substantial numbers from the Technology School (15 percent and 16 percent) and the School of Education (10 percent and 17 percent). Fifty-eight percent of the alumni lived in New York City, and when one adds suburbanites the figure rises to 76 percent. [Havemann and West (1952) found, in contrast, that 65 percent of those who went to college in their home state stayed in their states.] This is a stay-at-home lot, on the whole. Fewer of them (5 percent) became academics than one might expect. Fewer (5 and 1 percent) became doctors and dentists. More (6.5 percent) became lawyers. But 16 percent became engineers, 14 percent became accountants — the two largest professions by far — and 7 percent were elementary and high school teachers.[3]

THE ACA-DEMIC PRO-GRAM Nothing in the formal organization of the college responded to the great change in its student body after 1900. Nor did this student body want anything particularly different from what they were given. In 1900 five separate courses of study were set up, with very modest elective opportunities in the junior and senior years (classical, Latin-French, modern languages, scientific, and mechanical). In 1906 there was a modest extension of the allowed electives. Rudy writes:

The father of the elective system, President Eliot of Harvard, gave it his qualified approval. Speaking at the College in 1908, the famous educator said: " . . . This is a municipal college, and a strong one of its type. . . . It

[3] Podell (1960). The survey was conducted in 1956. Of 56,000 alumni, 10,000 responded.

has a characteristic policy about election of studies by the individual student. In the three four-year courses leading to the degree of Bachelor of Arts, the percentage of elective studies is twenty, mostly in the Senior year. In two of the three four-year courses leading to the degree of Bachelor of Science, the percentage of elective studies is thirty-four, altogether in the Junior and Senior years; and in the third of the science courses it is twenty-seven. These percentages are lower than in most colleges. On the other hand, every student, on entering the College, is expected to choose, out of six courses offered, the one course he will follow for four years. The consequence of this choice, made thus early, may be very far-reaching. . . " (Rudy, 1949, p. 283).

Finally, in 1913, the system of majors and electives was introduced. It would be hard to say there was much change in the decades that followed until the late 1960s. In 1919, the courses in technology and business were turned into schools of technology and business. In 1921, the courses in education became a school of education. In 1926, a board of higher education was organized as the governing body for both City College and Hunter College (the parallel free school for girls); in 1930, a coeducational Brooklyn College was added to the city system of higher education; in 1931, honors courses were introduced; in 1937, a coeducational Queens College was organized; in 1961, a City University of New York was organized to group all the colleges, and there were further foundings, particularly of two-year community colleges. Perhaps the only truly original claim that City College can make in the field of higher education is the organization of an evening session in which one could earn a bachelor's degree. This was established as early as 1909, and was fully responsive to the reality of a largely proletarian student body, most of whom had to work. The evening session has remained a powerful reality at City College since. In 1969, 1,460 students were enrolled for the bachelor's degree in the evening session, and every year hardy souls who have survived eight, ten, or more years of evening courses receive their degrees.

But if City College was not particularly innovative in education — indeed, if the truth be told it continually dragged its heels, and in educational affairs managed to stay behind the average American college and university — its distinctive student body marked it for prominence and for notoriety. Prominence was guaranteed by the East European Jewish passion for education and capacity for achievement in intellectual matters. Whatever happened or didn't happen in the classrooms, mathematicians, physicists, psychologists, critics, and sociologists poured from the school, alongside the heavier flow of businessmen, engineers, and teachers. Notoriety was guaranteed by another characteristic of East European Jews— their penchant for radical politics. In 1916, Leon Samson was expelled for leading a walkout while Maj. Gen. Leonard Wood addressed an assembly on preparedness, and in 1917 Samuel H. Friedman was suspended for defending pacifism in a college newspaper. Required or voluntary ROTC was a burning issue through the twenties and thirties. In the thirties, City College students dominated American student radical politics. Alongside the roll of distinguished alumni, one might add another roll of alumni (or near alumni) who had been expelled or suspended for political activities and who later achieved distinction, beginning with Samson and Friedman.

There are many descriptions available of the City College of the thirties and forties. They depict a college that was almost uniquely a creation of its student body, rather than its faculty, its administrators, or its educational pattern. One account, from a state investigating committee in 1944, eschews any romanticism, and strikes me as sufficiently accurate. I quote from a summary given by S. Willis Rudy:

This report stressed the fact that these students were extremely able intellectually. "Probably no group of college students of comparable size has a higher level of academic aptitude." These students averaged about a year to a year and a half younger at entrance than college students in general, indicating an extremely rapid progress through elementary and high school. Physically they tended to be less well-developed, their average weight and height being below comparable averages. The proportion of physical defects was somewhat higher than among other college populations. All of them had had to live in the City of New York and face the many pressures of metropolitan life. Many of them had been reared in small, crowded rooms, where privacy was at a premium, and their chances for building permanent friendships had sometimes been lessened by frequent moving. Many had been obliged to take long rides on the subway to travel to and from school. Few had had their perspective on social problems broadened by travel beyond the New York area.

A large majority of the students were first or second generation Americans. At City College, the committee found that only 17% of the fathers and 22% of the mothers of Freshmen who entered in 1938 were born in the United States. Parents born abroad came largely from Russia, Poland, and Austria. The committee deduced from these figures that City College students must often be torn between European and American standards, between the codes and customs of their parents and those of their own group. Since more than two-thirds of the parents of the students had been born abroad, some language other than English usually had been spoken in the home. Most of these parents seem to have had only a limited formal education. Going to college must therefore have widened still further the gap that exists so often between immigrants and their American-born sons and daughters. This also meant that few students could look to their homes for educational counsel. Moreover, at least 80% of the student population was found to be Jewish or of Jewish derivation. . . .

The committee also disclosed that fully nine-tenths of City College's student body had been educated in the New York public high schools so that they had the same general kind of academic preparation. "No higher institution of comparable size has a student body as homogeneous with respect to the character of preparatory work." At the same time, it was emphasized that these students came largely from lower income groups, and had grown up in homes where there had been a continuous and severe struggle for existence. More than three-quarters of them were found to hold some outside employment during the summer vacation, and well over half were likewise obliged to work during the regular school year, despite the lack of a tuition charge at the college. As a result, the committee found the vocational drive of these young people to be very strong. "They look upon college as an open door to financial security and social prestige, and are therefore determined to obtain whatever academic or professional training may be necessary for vocational success."

Finally, the committee turned its attention to the question of the general social adjustment of these young persons at the time of entering college. Its conclusions were that they faced unusual handicaps and that, as a result, many were poorly adjusted. The opinion of personnel counsellors was that the incidence of acute personality problems was higher than among most other student populations. Since more than 97% of these youths lived at home, parents usually continued to exercise close supervision over their time, friends, and money. They therefore lacked many of the important opportunities possessed by students in residential colleges to acquire social poise and self-responsibility. Their record of high scholastic achievement in lower schools, and the constant pressure placed on them by their parents to succeed scholastically, resulted inevitably in an over-emphasis on intellectual values, to the detriment of other vital phases of personality development. Many who had to earn money to cover their expenses and, in some cases, even to contribute to family support, had neither the time nor the money to avail themselves of social or recreational opportunities *(Report of the New York Sub-Committee. . . , 1944).*

Most of this could have been said of the student body any time between the 1920s and the 1960s.

In autumn 1966, Professor Samuel Middlebrook, associate dean of
the College of Liberal Arts and Sciences, coordinated a report on
the college for the 10-year appraisal by the Middle States Association of Colleges and Secondary Schools. Professor Middlebrook
wrote ("The State of the College," 1967, p. 4):

> By law, we keep no tabs on [the students'] race, color, or religion, as used
> to be done in the bad old days of a generation ago. Some irony is involved
> in this official ignoring of matters that have been of desperate concern in
> most eras of history and most areas of the globe. The irony may be more
> intense at the City College than elsewhere, for our main branch looks
> down like a Gothic castle or fortress from St. Nicholas Heights to the
> Harlem plain. A decade after "the revolution of Negro expectations" and
> Brown vs. Board of Education and the last Middle States evaluation, we
> do not know accurately if or why we have more or fewer non-white students
> than in 1955.

It was only 2½ years later that militant Negro and Puerto Rican
students occupied and closed part of the college and forced the
closing of the rest, demanding that 40 percent of the students be
Negro and Puerto Rican. They precipitated a political crisis in
New York City as it prepared for mayoralty elections, helped
ensure the nomination of Mario Procaccino as the Democratic
candidate for Mayor, aroused a deep emotional response from
the Jews—and, in part, the Catholics of the city—forced every
mayoralty candidate in the city (except Norman Mailer) to pro-
nounce against "quotas," forced the beginning of open enrollment—
a guarantee of college admission by the City University of New
York to every high school graduate in the city—in 1970, five years
before the master plan called for it, and ensured that no one could
ever again speak with such insouciance of the ethnic and racial
composition of the college.

In 1966, indeed, it appeared as if the college's impersonal system
of admission, which had served it so long, was no major problem.
City College, as I have suggested, had not responded in any formal
way to the fact that the great majority of its student body was
Jewish. The sequence of presidents continued in general to be
small-town Protestants who, it would appear, could not possibly
have any particular knowledge of, or empathy with, its student
body. John H. Finley was born in Grand Ridge, La Salle County,
Illinois, and attended Knox College, in Galesburg, Illinois. Sidney
E. Mezes, who succeeded him in 1914, and under whom the first

expulsions for radical political activity took place, attended the University of California in Berkeley and the University of Berlin, studied philosophy at Harvard, and eventually became, before going to the City College, president of the University of Texas. Frederick B. Robinson, who succeeded him in 1926, was, it is true, born in Brooklyn, graduated from City College in 1904, and spent his whole career at City College. Despite this background, he was totally unsympathetic to an increasingly radical student body, and was forced out as president in 1938. Harry N. Wright, who became president in 1941 after an interregnum, was born in Shelbyville, Indiana, attended Earlham College, taught at Pacific College in Newberg, Oregon, and Whittier College in California, received a Ph.D. from the University of California, and had held teaching and administrative posts at City College since 1930. His successor, in 1952, Buell G. Gallagher, was born in Rankin, Illinois, and attended Carleton College for his B.A., Union Theological Seminary for a B.D., and Columbia for a Ph.D. He was a clergyman and president of Talladega College in Alabama from 1933 to 1943, professor at the Pacific School of Religion from 1944 to 1949, and Assistant Commissioner of the U.S. Office of Education from 1949 to 1952. A pacifist and a civil rights advocate, he seemed indeed a more likely choice for the presidency of City College, but his background was radically different from that of the great majority of its student body and of its alumni.

At least he could be expected to be sympathetic to the demands of black and Puerto Rican students and the need to expand the representation of black and Puerto Rican students at the college. And yet in 1966, when the college reported to the Middle States Association, nothing indicated it was aware that this was an important problem.

In the report, other matters loom much larger. For example, the college was concerned during the 1960s, as Jews became more prosperous and more opportunities for education opened up to them, that the quality of students available to the college—who were after all its only claim to fame and prominence—was declining. The report asserts that "statistics [SATs, verbal and mathematics] indicate a remarkable degree of stability in verbal and quantitative ability over the past ten years." Nevertheless, it goes on, "many of the instructors who have been at the College for a number of years feel that the quality of the student body has declined. Ten years ago, they feel, the College was still getting the best graduates of the New York City high schools. Now those students are able to get fellowships which allow them to attend Ivy League and other first-rate out-of-town institutions" (ibid., pp. 4, 6).

Another problem was the creation of an academic community for students and faculty. No one except the president lived at the college itself. There were few and overcrowded offices, no faculty club, no faculty gathering places, few student lounges, no union. The separation of the Baruch School—the renamed School of Business—half a dozen miles downtown from the main campus, with the requirement to teach at both places, was a problem (in 1968 it was to be separated and became an independent four-year college). So was the separation between "day people" and "night people." "Recruiting new staff, especially in the sciences, is noticeably harder. In all this the creation of the City University has sharpened issues. . . " (ibid., p. 9). Actually, of course, there had never really been much of a City College community, for students or faculty, on a commuter campus in an area of the city in which very few students and faculty lived. There had of course been communities of different groups of students, drawn together by some brand of radical politics or some specific academic or non-academic interest. But the 1966 report seemed to emphasize a new malaise, and a new cause for it, and that was the creation of the City University of New York (CUNY) with its own Graduate Center building on 42d Street and its own faculty.

It would be idle to deny a persistent unease about a possible adverse impact of the "University" (i.e., the programs, ideals, teaching methods, incentives, rewards of our increased post-baccalaureate activities) on getting and keeping an undergraduate staff. A report from the Chairman of the Chemistry Department reflects this fear:

"There is a changing pattern of recruitment occasioned by a shift to the use of graduate assistants which is still incomplete. It is anticipated that most faculty departures for years to come . . . will lead to replacement not by senior staff members, but rather by graduate assistants. . . . " [Not a university, City College classes had always been taught by regular faculty.]

Sources of friction between Ph.D. graduate budget appointments and College staff teaching M.A. candidates and undergraduates are also noted in the following excerpt from a humanist's complaint. . . .

"I find it painful and demoralizing, both as a dedicated teacher and as a producing scholar, that there must be a seemingly sharp cleavage between those of us who teach graduate students in the M.A. program and hold *College* lines, and others who hold the so-called *University* lines. . . . Why cannot there be a free flow of personnel, teaching eclectically on both levels, instead of what really amounts to a mob of plebes and a sprinkling of elite among the faculty? In the long run this situation will be deleterious to students and faculty alike. . . " (ibid., pp. 11–12).

THE PRELUDE TO CRISIS The crisis that erupted in spring 1969, and in whose aftermath City College now lives, was not, however, occasioned by anxiety over the impact of the growing City University and its monopoly of Ph.D. work. The American student revolt of 1964 to 1970 (writing in 1971, one dates its end—perhaps prematurely—with the explosion at the University of Wisconsin which killed a graduate student and lists 1970–71 as the first year in which campus disorder did not escalate) had two very different roots. White radicals attacked the university because it reflected the society— first they assaulted its impersonality and bureaucracy and then, increasingly, its involvement with a society and state engaged in a terrible war. City College was not immune to disorder based on this root of the student revolt. In 1968 buildings were occupied and vigils were conducted over war-related issues such as the presence of ROTC on campus and sanctuary for an AWOL soldier.

These issues agitated black students less. They were concerned with larger numbers of black admissions, with special courses for blacks, and with control of orientation programs and of faculty teaching black students. These concerns of black students were all issues at City College during 1968–69. An ethnic census in the autumn of 1968 revealed that of 10,867 regularly enrolled undergraduate students, 565 were Negro, 431 were Puerto Rican, 26 were American Indian, and 250 were Orientals (*Undergraduate Enrollment. . .* , 1968). (The federal government insists on including Oriental students in its censuses, and the City University follows suit. As is well known, Chinese and Japanese students are represented in numbers far higher than their proportion in the population, in New York City as in California. Quotas can only reduce their numbers, because they are overrepresented groups.) While this represented substantial change over time, 5 percent black and 4 percent Puerto Rican in a city in which the proportion of both groups together approximated 30 percent (and the proportion of college-age blacks and Puerto Ricans was considerably larger) was not impressive.

This, however, is not the whole story: City College was by 1968 part of a city system of higher education, which included many institutions, and if blacks and Puerto Ricans were few at the selective four-year college level (as they were), they were far more numerous at the community college level, where the doors were wide open to those who could not make the average for entry to City College, and from which students making a modest grade average could transfer to the selective colleges after two years. New York City was in 1968 already equipped with a California-style multilevel system of higher education which offered college-level instruction to everyone.

In addition, there was a range of special programs (*Report and Recommendations . . . ,* 1969) to increase the number of black and Puerto Rican students in the selective colleges and CUNY in general that offered almost every imaginable opportunity. At City College, there was the prebaccalaureate program, in which students from low-income families who could not regularly qualify for admission were enrolled in special remedial programs—on the campus, with their own teachers—which attempted to prepare them for regular college enrollment. In summer 1966, this became a state-supported program, SEEK (Search for Education, Elevation and Knowledge). The program had grown rapidly. In 1965, 113 were enrolled (81 were still in the program at the end of the first year); by fall 1968, 700 were enrolled (3,000 overall in City University). These students received stipends for attending. Individual students were graduating from the program and being enrolled as regular students in City College.

Parallel to SEEK for the four-year city colleges, there was the College Discovery program for the two-year colleges. Seven thousand had applied for the two programs, and 2,300 were selected for admission in September 1969.

In addition, there was the One Hundred Scholars program under which the top 100 graduates in any public academic high school were guaranteed admission to a four-year CUNY college. In 1969, 9,000 were offered admission through this program, of whom 6,000 were enrolled. But only 600 would not have been eligible under "regular" admission standards. This did more for ineligible whites than it did for blacks and Puerto Ricans.

Two other programs, College Discovery and Development and Pre-Technical programs, were operated cooperatively by the university and the board of education, worked with students in high schools, and guaranteed admission to the university. There were Brooklyn and Manhattan "Urban Centers," attached to community colleges, that offered programs for those who did not qualify for regular admission to community colleges, a College Adapter program which fed into the regular college matriculated programs, and yet additional special programs at each college I have not described.

As a result of all this—and of course the regular admissions procedure—12 percent of the CUNY four-year college enrollment was black and 6.6 percent Puerto Rican in the freshman class enrolled in 1969 (which had been selected about the time of the uprising). The proportions of entering freshmen who were black and Puerto Rican were higher in the community colleges, 21 percent and 9.6 percent.

There was no great mystery to this low enrollment. Everyone knew that Negro and Puerto Rican students, even though they formed more than half of the public school enrollment in the city, and close to that in the first and second year of high school, dropped out of high school in large numbers, and of those who remained, relatively few had academic diplomas or the grades needed for regular admission to the senior city colleges. The detailed picture of just what happened emerged only after open enrollment was adopted in the autumn of 1969, and a study of graduates from New York City high schools in 1970 was undertaken. Black students constituted 21 percent of high school juniors, and Puerto Rican students 12 percent, in December 1968. But only 15 percent of the graduates in 1970 were black, and only 9 percent Puerto Rican. "Only 16 percent of all Black graduates and 24 percent of all Puerto Rican graduates received grades of 80 percent or over, compared with 50 percent of all White graduates and 53 percent of all Oriental and other graduates. . . . Only 10 percent of all high school graduates with averages of over 80 percent were Black, Latin American or Puerto Rican." Only 1,247 New York City black graduates and 1,140 Puerto Rican high school graduates scored over 80 among the graduates of New York City high schools— against 22,542 white, 1,588 Oriental, and 358 Latin Americans (Birnbaum & Goldman, 1971).

Under these circumstances, the fact that 18.6 percent of those in four-year colleges were black and Puerto Rican reflected the impact of the special programs. For under the regular system, admission to the four-year colleges was based on a required high school average of between 83 and 85, SAT scores, and a required sequence of academic courses, and from the study of the graduating high school class of 1970 somewhat fewer than 9 percent who could meet these standards were black and Puerto Rican.

But what was not clear was how one was to interpret this story, and what one was to do about it. On one side were those—most of the alumni, a majority of the faculty, and many of the students—who saw that City College's distinction came only from its highly selected student body. Studies of many colleges had more or less concluded that the quality of graduates was determined by the quality of entering students, not by what was done in college. If City College's distinction came only from its student body, how could its distinction be maintained if its student body was to be selected on nonacademic criteria? This was one argument against a radical change. Another was that the problem of low achievement of blacks and Puerto Ricans should be solved in the high schools (others of course might say in the elementary schools, and others in the family). The arguments on the other side were that City College's distinction was based on the graduates who emerged, not the students who entered; that remedial programs could solve all problems of lack of academic qualification, regardless of how severe; that in any event racism was the cause of black and Puerto Rican inadequacy and the college could not shift responsibility to the high schools or some other agency. The issue was finally decided by the distribution of power within the college, and more importantly, within the city.

The frontal attack on the whole meritocratic basis of admissions to the four-year colleges was launched, with historical justice, at City College, the oldest in the system.

THE DEMANDS The five demands of the students who seized the south campus on April 22, 1968, were:

1 A separate school of black and Puerto Rican studies, parallel to other schools, granting its own degrees

2 A separate orientation program for black and Puerto Rican freshmen controlled by black and Puerto Rican upperclassmen

3 A voice for SEEK students in setting the guidelines for the SEEK program, including the hiring and firing of personnel, regular faculty status for them, and regular student status for SEEK students

4 That the racial composition of all entering classes reflect the black and Puerto Rican population of the New York City high schools (this was

specified as 40 percent black and Puerto Rican entering classes, though
if one takes into account private and parochial schools the actual proportion
of blacks and Puerto Ricans in all New York high schools is much less than
40 percent)

5 That black and Puerto Rican history and the Spanish language be a requirement of all education majors.[4]

While all the demands aroused some opposition, the key one, it
was understood by all, was what was rapidly dubbed as a "quota"
for regular enrollments. It is scarcely necessary to detail the specific
City College variant of the standard college crisis. The faculty was
polarized and embittered between supporters of the five demands
and opponents. The administration—President Buell Gallagher—
immediately closed the college in fear of an escalation of violence
and the intervention of elements of the Harlem community and
entered into negotiations on the nonnegotiable demands. The students were also divided. A rather large fraction of students opposed
the demands. White radicals immediately seized a building in support of the blacks and Puerto Ricans (and, as had occurred elsewhere, demonstrated a weaker discipline, disdain for college
property or inability to protect it from damage, and considerable
ineffectiveness). But the engineering students in particular, who are
strongly vocationally oriented and whose classrooms and laboratories are on the older Gothic north campus, which was unaffected
by the original seizure, were angered at the fact that their school
was also closed during the endless negotiations, in accordance with
the demands of the militants. The board of higher education, prod-
ded by the mayoralty candidates (principally the conservative Dem-
ocrat Mario Procaccino and the Conservative and Republican John
Marchi, who were running against John Lindsay) and by public
opinion, finally insisted on the reopening of the campus. Violence
erupted. The liberal president thereupon resigned, and a more
conservative acting president took over to restore order.

There is nothing new in this part of the story. What was new
and unique was the one demand that, in effect, breached the City
College system of admissions on the basis of merit alone. One must
recall that the academic year 1968–69 began in New York with
a series of teachers' strikes, called to oppose the firing of teachers

[4] "The five demands" come in many forms, and I have combined elements given
in two articles surveying the City College crisis, one by Tom Ackerman in the
City College Alumnus (1969) and one by Lloyd P. Gartner in *Midstream* (1969).

by a Negro–Puerto Rican community school board. Probably a majority of the striking teachers were Jews (most of whom had attended City and its sister colleges). Charges of anti-Semitism were heard in New York City for the first time in many years. The Jewish community for the first time in two decades felt uneasy. Jews saw the positions they had attained on the basis of college entry and graduation and teacher qualification threatened. They saw the ladders of advancement to well-paid principalships and other high positions, which in New York City were based strictly on examination, now threatened because these ladders gave so few places to Negroes and Puerto Ricans. More prosperous Jews, for whom being a schoolteacher was not a big thing, and younger, more radical Jews supported the community control forces against the working-class and middle-class Jews and against the official Jewish organizations, which on the whole supported the teachers, the teachers' union, and due process. The year 1968-69, then, was a year of crisis for the Jewish community of New York. And now the bastion of City College was also under attack.

If these were the feelings on the Jewish side, feelings in the black community were as bitter. It would be a mistake, however, to conclude that the only divisions were ethnic and racial. The Harlem community was never, it appears, as aroused about the issue as either the militants insisted or the administration feared. Many of the black and Puerto Rican students themselves tried to stay out of it. Important black and Puerto Rican leaders of the city — among them A. Philip Randolph, Bayard Rustin, and Herman Badillo—had attended or graduated from City College when the meritocratic principles still stood firm, and may have been of two minds (and the politicians among them had to keep in mind the potency of the Jewish vote in the city).

The initial demand was that admissions should reflect the black and Puerto Rican proportion in the high schools. But the idea of quotas was so fiercely attacked by the mayoralty candidates and led to such a violent reaction among New York City Jews that the various negotiations all tried to get to the same objective through other mechanisms—e.g., special admissions from "poverty area" high schools.

Negotiations at the college level inevitably had to be approved by the board of higher education, and the problem of admissions gravitated to that level, taking the college off the hook. The board determined in July that it would respond to the crisis by moving the date for open admissions—the date when every high school graduate in the city would be ensured a place in one of the institutions of the City University—from 1975 to 1970. This still left the critical issue of the mechanism of admission and the degree of selectivity that would persist at City College and the other four-year colleges of the system. Would CUNY remain a California-style system, with graduates of different academic levels eligible for institutions at different levels? This would scarcely satisfy the elements that supported the five demands. A commission was established—administrators, faculty, students, SEEK representatives, and others—to struggle with the problem, and, although it issued a report, it was clear that the commission itself was radically split. It emerged with three proposals, all of which aimed to achieve "ethnic balance" at the four-year as well as the two-year colleges of the City University. It was left to the board of higher education to finally settle the delicate question of selectivity of admissions for the senior colleges.

The board of higher education settled, on November 12, 1969, on the following admission procedure: All applicants were arranged in groups determined by averages in academic high school subjects and standing in their high school graduating class. Students scoring an average of 80 in their academic high school grades, or ending in the top half of their classes, would be admitted to one of the four-year city colleges. Others would be admitted on the basis of space and their own preferences. The SATs were abandoned. Also abandoned was the requirement to take certain academic courses in high school (four years of English, three of foreign language, three of mathematics, and so on). Also abandoned for purposes of admission was the distinction between academic, commercial, and vocational diplomas. Extensive programs of counseling, remedial courses, tutoring, and financial aid would be instituted to accommodate the great increase expected in open enrollment students. Thus the open enrollment procedure opened the gates to the City College much wider but still gave preference to those with better grades.

The City College braced itself for an entering class different from any it had accommodated for decades under a new president, Robert E. Marshak, a distinguished professor of physics from the University of Rochester. Marshak was also the first president of the college drawn from the ethnic group that had contributed so large a proportion of the student body. He had himself attended City College briefly, switched to Columbia for the B.A., and then took his Ph.D at Cornell. As a very young man he was one of that galaxy of physicists who worked at Los Alamos during World War II. He went on to a brilliant career as a theoretical physicist, becoming part of a worldwide fraternity among whom a demonstrated competence was combined with great self-confidence. Marshak was committed to the open enrollment plan (appointed after the board of higher education had made its commitment he had to be), but began his work as president with a deeply divided faculty, many of whom opposed open enrollment and felt it had been shoved down their throats.

EVALUATION How does one evaluate such a radical change in the college? Masses of statistics are available, and a range of opinions to go along. Is open enrollment a success? What does being a "success" mean? And how much can one conclude in any case after one year? One can report that 1970–71 was certainly a more peaceful year than 1968–69, and even than 1969–70. How much was owing to the general peace that prevailed on campuses, how much to the heroic preparations for the first open enrollment class, how much to the work of a newly appointed, energetic, and skillful president who was well received by students and faculty it is impossible to say. But one can at least record the statistics and opinions of the first year and speculate about the future.

The entering freshman class rose from 1,752 students in 1969 to 2,450 in 1970. In addition to the regularly admitted 2,450 students, 810 new students were taken into the SEEK program. The entering freshman class at City College in 1969 was 18.8 percent black and 6.9 percent Puerto Rican. The proportions in the greatly enlarged freshman class of 1970 were 23.9 percent black and 8.2 percent Puerto Rican. The "white" percentage dropped from 77.7 to 57.8, the Oriental from 6.3 to 5.9. It was estimated that 37 percent of the entering class would not have been admitted on the basis of the old criteria.[5] A huge program of testing in English

[5] In the second year of open admissions, 1971–72, the *New York Times* (Mar. 23, 1972, p. 52) reported that "56 percent of the 2,879 [entering] students had high school averages of less than 80, according to City University records." This would suggest a rather sharp drop in the quality of entering freshmen. Conceivably the better freshmen were choosing Brooklyn and Queens, which had been less affected by open admissions, because of their location and the choices of students. The board of higher education announced in January 1972 that to prevent the concentration of the better students in Brooklyn and Queens, those with averages of over 80 would not necessarily be admitted to the colleges of their choice, and more students below this average from poor families would be admitted to the senior colleges.

composition and mathematics was undertaken. One-third of the freshman class—824 freshmen—were enrolled in remedial English courses along with 212 SEEK students. A similar remedial effort was undertaken in mathematics, and 54 remedial mathematics sections were started, for regularly enrolled freshmen and for SEEK students. All available space was pressed into service as classrooms.

A statistical picture of the freshman classes of 1969 and 1970 shows the extent of the change. The City College freshman class is still, compared to college freshmen generally, a young class— 36 percent in 1969 were 17 or under, against 22 percent in 1970 and 4.3 percent nationally in 1970. Those achieving B plus or better in high school dropped from 65 percent of the class to 46 percent— still higher than 37 percent nationally in 1970. There is only a very slight drop in the proportion with fathers and mothers who have a college education (for fathers, from 14.1 to 13.3 percent; for mothers, from 7.8 to 7.2 percent). Nationally, 28.9 percent of freshmen had college graduate fathers, and 18.7 percent college graduate mothers, in 1970. Whatever the character of the privileged classes who entered City College before 1970, it was not that they came from college-educated families, nor were they wealthier families than those of 1970 freshmen. In 1969, 38 percent of the freshmen came from families with incomes under $8,000; in 1970, 37.8 percent. (Nationally the percentage of freshmen from families with such low incomes dropped from 27.2 to 22.2 percent.) One of the largest changes was in religious composition, from 49.8 percent with a Jewish religious background in 1969 to 32.9 percent with such a background in 1970, and surprisingly a change from 28.0 percent Catholic in 1969 to 39.8 percent Catholic in 1970. Only a small part of the Catholic increase could be accounted for by the rise in Puerto Rican freshmen. Thus even at City College, where the increase in Negroes and Puerto Ricans was larger than in any other of the four-year colleges, white Catholics were among the principal gainers from open enrollment.[6]

Did the quality of students selecting City College decline, aside from the admission of large numbers of students who ordinarily would not have entered? From 1967 to 1970, there was a drop in the number of students coming in from two selective city high schools, Bronx Science and Stuyvesant (from 279 to 146 from

[6] These tabulations are from the American Council on Education Office of Research, and were made available by City College.

Bronx Science, and from 118 to 46 from Stuyvesant), and rises in numbers admitted from high schools with high proportions of blacks and Puerto Ricans (Morris, 0 to 9; Benjamin Franklin, 0 to 16; Brandeis, 6 to 31).

Overnight, open enrollment brought New York City as close to the age of universal higher education as any community has ever come. No less than 76 percent of all city high school graduates, regardless of diploma or grades, went on to higher education in 1970. The national proportion was 55 to 60 percent, and Birnbaum and Goldman's study, *The Graduates* (1971), asserts that "all the difference . . . can be attributed to Open Enrollment." In New York City, those who do not go on to college do not because they "wanted a job," "did not want college," were "tired of school," or "could not afford it." These were the only major reasons given. (There are no tuition charges in City College, students live at home, and SEEK students get stipends.) Thus in New York grades in high school do not play a role in college going. They still affect to some degree what college one goes to.

It is impossible to spell out all the varied consequences of open enrollment. A few are worth mentioning even if no full analysis is possible.

One consequence of open enrollment will be felt by the most distinctive educational program at City College. This is the evening session. Regular students who worked or found it convenient could take courses in the evening session, but most evening session students were those who had not made the average for entry into the day session (many were recent immigrants), and who could, by taking courses in the evening, and also by paying for them, get a college education. Naturally they were resentful of the mass of younger students who, having done no better than they had in high school, could now enter the regular day sessions, and attend without tuition to boot. It seems inevitable the old evening session will decline with the rise of easier alternatives, marking another stage in the decline of the Protestant ethic.

A second impact of open enrollment is being felt by the paying colleges of New York and the surrounding areas. City College and its allied four-year colleges were colleges not only for poor students but also for bright students. Now that they are colleges for all students, and there has been such a huge increase in the freshman enrollments of the City University, it seems almost inevitable that many of the private colleges of the area should feel the impact.

This combined with the general financial crisis of private colleges will have severe consequences for them.[7]

There has as yet been little discussion of a third possible consequence of open enrollment. One reason New York City retains as much of a white middle class as it does is that it has a remarkable number of specialized and selective institutions which provide opportunities for them that elsewhere are available only in the suburbs. One such institution is the system of selective high schools, most prominent among them Bronx High School of Science, which exist nowhere in the country on such a scale. (These are now also under attack because their selective system of admission on academic criteria admits few blacks and Puerto Ricans.) But another undoubtedly was the system of free colleges of high reputation. The colleges are still free, and to judge by City College, their physical resources, administration, and faculties may yet improve. But it is hardly likely the remarkable academic record and consequent reputation of the past will be maintained. In effect, one of the attractions of the city will become less attractive, and one reason for staying in it will lose some of its force.

THE NATURE OF THE CHANGE The transition is under way. City College now combines the functions of a massive remedial institution, a junior college, a four-year college, a graduate university, and a set of professional schools. While the Business School has become a separate college, the Schools of Education and Engineering have recently been joined by a School of Architecture and a School of Nursing. As in the case of many complex institutions, it is impossible to give a simple overall judgment. Even City College has different worlds. Many of the faculty teach only remedial courses, many teach courses with a mix of students, many never teach SEEK or open enrollment students. It is hard to see that admission to the Engineering School or the science majors will be much affected by open enrollment. If they are, it cannot be because standards have been lowered — they are clear and essential — but because many open enrollment students will have qualified for them. But as I write we have the experience of only one year of open enrollment, much of the work

[7] The *New York Times* (Aug. 17, 1971, p. 25) reported a plan by which CUNY would pay "part of the educational costs for up to 400 two-year community college graduates" enrolling as business majors at Long Island University and Pace College. "Both institutions have suffered sharp losses of freshman enrollment due to . . . the City University's free open admissions program." While the plan has not been put into effect, the problem remains.

the less qualified students have taken is remedial, and insofar as they have taken regular courses they cannot have been those for which mathematics prerequisites are imposed. The social sciences and humanities will show a much larger impact.

Ironically, while the undergraduate student body became less selective academically, the new president undertook steps to strengthen the City College academically. President Marshak — for the first time in City College history, as far as anyone knows — enlisted academically distinguished alumni to assist in evaluating departments and strengthening faculties. Professor S. M. Lipset of Harvard chaired a committee to evaluate the sociology department, Professor Kenneth Arrow of Harvard chaired an economics department evaluation committee. Professor Chester Rapkin of Columbia and I were asked to advise the president on the development of an urban program. Nationally distinguished scholars not connected with the college were called in to assist it. Professor Salo Baron of Columbia chaired a committee on a Department of Jewish Studies, Professor Frank Bonilla of Stanford chaired a committee on Puerto Rican studies, Professor Carl Schorske of Princeton chaired an evaluation committee for the history department, Professor Charles Hamilton of Columbia served on a black studies committee. In June 1971 President Marshak was able to announce the largest single gift in City College's history — $2.5 million — for an arts center. The idea of an arts center was as new for City College as the idea of a large personal gift. An Oceanographical Institute was launched, a Center for Urban and Environmental Problems emphasizing consultation with city departments and research was announced, a number of new distinguished faculty were appointed.

All this was quite unprecedented. City College under its previous presidents had had little contact with its academic alumni or with other distinguished academicians. With its high salaries and emphasis on teaching, it did not have the kind of faculty that was lured away to other schools, nor on the other hand — despite the high salaries — was it in a good position to lure other faculty away because of high teaching loads. Those of distinction who did come generally made arrangements to teach only graduate students, or were attracted by the city, played little role in their departments, and spent little time on the campus. In any case, it is not the sort of campus on which one can spend much time, outside of class, in view of crowded office conditions and an urban milieu which more and more approximates a slum without any attractions. Nor was it the sort of campus that other scholars visited. There are few lectures or lecture series, and thus few occasions when scholars from other colleges may lecture. When they do, the local culture is such that not many faculty or students come. When classes are over, they leave.

Around the issues of faculty upgrading, as well as the overriding issues of open enrollment, would come, it was safe to predict, the severest tests of President Marshak's term. For in accepting the presidency, he accepted not only the burden of implementing the open enrollment decision but also the burden of operating under the most elaborate and comprehensive union contract governing faculty that had ever been signed. City College faculty not only had close to the highest salaries in the country; they also had the fullest possible union protection. The combination was devastating. A City College job was not one given up easily, particularly in a declining job market. Nor need it be given up when under the terms of the union contract almost every denial of tenure or promotion could be challenged, and with a good chance of success. City College thus was threatened not only by a flood of students needing remedial work but also by a tidal wave of procedural disputes. And in a city like New York, with its strong civil service and trade-union traditions, there was a strong presumption in many quarters that a person who had held a job for a number of years had a right to it. It is scarcely possible to analyze in a brief article the complicated issues raised by the strong union contract that protects City College faculty, but it makes the task of upgrading the faculty far more difficult than it otherwise would be. Against this, however, one must place the attractions of high salaries and the fact that City College, unlike many institutions in the country, is still rapidly expanding, and does have a claim to more faculty positions.

City College, in terms of student body, was in 1971 perhaps developing a mix similar to that of some nonselective Middle Western universities which had generally been open to all high school graduating seniors (except that City reached even farther down, and farther up), while at the same time it was improving at the faculty and facilities level. Its distinction in the future, it seemed safe to predict, would depend less on a highly selective student body, more on its faculty and a range of facilities and research institutes.

Would this, in the City of New York, work? There were serious dangers.

What happened when open enrollment students were flunked out? This was a very different group from the one that was flunked out of Midwestern open enrollment universities. They did not have father's businesses or farms or filling stations to go back to, and from which they would recall fondly their year at "State."[8]

The open enrollment students wanted degrees, and the jobs that went with them. Could one have that much faith in remedial work at the college level? And if not, did it not inevitably mean that standards for graduation would drop?

How did City College maintain its capacity to get a share of the better students? Perhaps the new distinguished faculty appointments and special research institutes would help there.

If there were more disturbances as open enrollment students demanded the right to a degree as well as entry, would the damaged relationship with the alumni, and the city voters, continue to mend?

Could alumni who had gone through one kind of college adapt to the support of this rather different institution?

Could faculty who had developed their practices and skills working with one student body adapt them to one that had undergone such substantial change?

Aside from the problems every college faced, these were the special problems of City College, and it remained a question, even after President Marshak's successful first year, how they could be managed in the future.

---

[8] For CUNY four-year colleges as a whole, entering freshmen in 1970 with high school averages of over 80 had an attrition rate of 13.6 percent; entering freshmen with high school averages below 80 had an attrition rate of 29.6 percent. "Few, if any, freshmen have been forced to leave the university for academic reasons since the start of open admissions. . . . The university gave all freshmen more than a one-year 'grace period'" (*New York Times,* Nov. 18, 1971, p. 61). Since this attrition is voluntary, there is as yet no strong demand that the City University do something to keep the dropouts. But another story in the *New York Times* (Feb. 13, 1972, p. 34) reports, "Hunter College has given 61 students who failed a major clinical nursing course a chance to repeat this course this summer to enable them to enter the third year of a four-year program. . . . Of the 61 students failing, 14 were in the SEEK program. . . , 21 entered with high-school averages below 80, and 26 had high school records that might have gotten them into Hunter prior to the open-admissions program."

References

Ackerman, Tom: "The South Campus Seizure," *City College Alumnus,* vol. 65, no. 1, pp. 3–30, October 1969.

Birnbaum, Robert, and Joseph Goldman: *The Graduates: A Follow-up Study of New York City High School Graduates of 1970,* The City University of New York, Center for Social Research and Office for Research in Higher Education, May 1971.

Gartner, Lloyd P.: "Five Demands at City College," *Midstream,* vol. 15, no. 8, pp. 15–35, October 1969.

Havemann, Ernest, and Patricia S. West: *They Went to College,* Harcourt, Brace, and Company, New York, 1952, cited in Podell, 1960, p. 17.

New York Times, July 25, 1971; Aug. 17, 1971; Nov. 18, 1971; Feb. 13, 1972; Mar. 23, 1972.

Podell, Lawrence: *The Opened Door: The Report of the Survey of Alumni of the City College of New York,* Alumni Association of City College of New York, Inc., 1960.

Report of the New York City Sub-Committee Concerning Administration and Financing of the Public Education System of the City of New York, George D. Strayer, director, New York State Legislative Document no. 60, New York, 1944, cited in Rudy, 1949, pp. 396–398.

Report and Recommendations to the Board of Higher Education of the City of New York, City University of New York, University Commission on Admissions, Oct. 7, 1969.

Rudy, S. Willis: *The College of the City of New York: A History, 1847–1947,* The City College Press, New York, 1949.

"The State of the College," *The City College Alumnus,* June 1967.

Undergraduate Enrollment by Ethnic Group in Federally Funded Institutions of Higher Education, U.S. Office of Education, Research Data Analysis Branch, Fall 1968. (Mimeographed.)

5. Federal City College: How Black?

by Irene Tinker

At eight o'clock in the morning of September 1,1968, Federal City College began its first classes. Some 98 percent of its first 2,000 students were black. The local press had been gentle with the new college and had praised its policies of open admission and selection by lottery. Thus on November 12 of that year, David Dickson, the provost and academic vice-president of the college and a black scholar of English and classical literature, confounded the city by revealing that the college was in turmoil over race.

Racial tension, racial suspicion, and racial polarization have almost blasted our lovely spring buds. . . . Our meetings display passion quite as much as reason, intimidation rather than discussion. The black or white moderates, shocked at the flight of reason, are supine while the well-disciplined and intense cadre of white radicals and black separatists neglect academic principles for revolutionary ends (Dickson, 1970).[1]

In response to the speech, the chairman of the faculty organization, a white historian, tried to institute impeachment proceedings against Dickson. Some students issued a peremptory summons to all faculty and students to attend an interrogation of the administration; the notice was unsigned except for an upraised black fist. Even faculty who agreed to some of the charges felt the public recital of them was wrong and that Dickson should have kept criticism "in house." On the other hand, the college's white president, Frank Farner, played down the tensions within the faculty by describing them as "similar to what every college has." He blunted the impact of the talk by telling reporters that Dickson "overstated

[1] This paper was read by Dickson at the general meeting of the National Association of State Universities and Land-Grant Colleges, Nov. 12, 1968, and was reported and quoted in both the *Washington Post* and the *Evening Star* on Nov. 13.

the case in almost every regard. Things are just not as bleak as he describes it" (*Washington Post,* Nov. 13, 1968). Thus Dickson was left exposed, with few open supporters, for daring to speak the truth as he saw it.

This incident was a minor skirmish in a series of battles for power and of efforts to obtain a clear sense of direction which culminated six months later with the resignation of both Farner and Dickson at the request of the District of Columbia Board of Higher Education. They were not the only college administrators who were forced out of their positions in 1969, but the crises at Federal City College were unique for other reasons. First, the college itself is unique as a black, urban, land-grant institution and as the first comprehensive public college in the nation's capital. Second, impetus for campus unrest there came from within the faculty and administration; students were occasionally used as accessories, but they did not initiate action. Further, the newness and fragileness of the college exacerbated all conflict because there were not yet any established stabilizing structures or procedures.

The issues behind the decision-making struggle dealt with fundamentals: who shall run the college? who shall teach? and what shall be taught? From the beginning, the common theme of these issues was that the administrators, the faculty, and the curriculum were too white and therefore that change must be in the direction of black. This general proposition received little challenge. The problem was in definition. What is black? How black is black?

A NEW COLLEGE   Before the establishment of Federal City College (FCC) and its sister institution, the Washington Technical Institute, citizens of the District of Columbia had no other public opportunity for higher education except for the District of Columbia Teachers College. Few attended the five private universities within the District: only Howard, with perhaps one-fourth of its student body drawn locally, and Catholic, with about 10 percent of its students from the District, made any effort to recruit locally. Despite the fact that a legacy for a proposed federal university was included in George Washington's will,[2] Congress did not get around to setting up a college in its "colony" until November 1966.[3]

---

[2] Washington left 50 shares of the Potomac River Company to the United States for such a university. See Biderman (1966).

[3] See Public Law 89-791 (1966).

To District residents, the description of their city as a colony is merely a statement of fact. Bumper stickers proclaiming "D.C. Last Colony" are sold by the League of Women Voters. The District's new nonvoting delegate has joined Puerto Rico's delegate as a second-class congressman. But in Puerto Rico they at least elect their own legislature. The legislature for the District is still Congress, or more particularly, the House and Senate District of Columbia committees. Money for the college is included in the overall District of Columbia budget, which is scrutinized by the Bureau of the Budget before presentation to the District of Columbia subcommittees of the appropriations committees in both the House and the Senate, which hold hearings before recommending the budget to their respective houses for passage. The final answer to the question of who runs the college must be "Congress" until such time as home rule becomes a reality.[4] Indeed much complaint against Dickson's speech concerned the possible effect it might have on Congress.[5] Pressure from the District committees of both the Senate and the House finally forced the board of higher education to act in the black studies crisis.[6]

The board itself is a political body, responsive, particularly in the first years, more to federal than to city concerns. Technically appointed by the District mayor-commissioner,[7] the first board was named directly by the White House. Charles Horsky, board member from the beginning and chairman of the board for its first four years, was then White House adviser on District affairs. The

[4] Myers (1970, p. 7) writing on "What It's Like When Congress Runs a College," quotes the then board chairman, E. C. Sylvester, Jr., as answering that question, "In four letters, it's hell." M. C. Mapes, Jr. (1970, p. 5) in his study *The Congressional Relations of the Federal City College,* comments that during its first year, FCC's "administrative leadership and faculty were acting in a manner which appeared to ignore the existence of Congress."

[5] See Barnard Upshur (1968) in the *Spectrum,* Federal City College student newspaper; see also Rapoport and Kirschbaum (1969, p. 101).

[6] Senator Joseph Tydings has been mentioned as the person who finally decided Farner, and perhaps Dickson, must go. Wallace Roberts (1969, p. 51) says Tydings pressured for the firing of both, but other evidence suggests that the pressure was aimed primarily at Farner but that the board felt a complete change was in order.

[7] In February 1967, when the first board was appointed, the older system of three commissioners, instead of one, was still in effect, though enfeebled. Charles Horsky, long-time chairman of the board, was then the Presidential advisor on District of Columbia affairs and the logical person to select the board. Joseph Califano, Presidential adviser, actually made the contract on Horsky's advice with several Presidential changes.

role appropriate to a board of a new college probably should differ from the distant benevolence of many boards of trustees; but to attempt to govern, as the board of higher education did in the spring of 1969, was neither feasible nor felicitous.[8]

In 1968, however, until Provost Dickson gave his speech, both Congress and the board seemed remote to the power struggle at FCC. Even board members were unaware of the escalation of conflict that prompted the president, Frank Farner, increasingly to adopt a style of nonleadership.[9] Few seemed to understand the implications of Farner's early decisions concerning open admissions, low tuition, and immediate expansion both as to size and to level, although the majority of the board seemed to follow Horsky's lead in supporting Farner and urging rapid growth. These decisions altered the character of the college from what many assumed would be a relatively small, excellent city college in the model of the old City College of New York,[10] one that might attract out-of-state students of all colors by the depth of its urban commitment (*Demonstration College . . .* , 1967) to what one observer has called "the common college" (Roberts, 1969). Rather than apply open admissions only to the two-year Washington Technical Institute created by the same bill, Farner chose to admit to the liberal arts college any person with a high school degree or its equivalent with no limit on the type of training or, for a time, on the size of the student body.

The need to provide post-high school education for a variety of District students had been recognized both by various study committees and by the bill itself. In order to emphasize technical training and give it the status and dignity he felt it deserved,

[8] Only this year has the board publicly acknowledged its role in the administrative chaos at the college (*Washington Post,* Jan. 9, 1971). The current crisis concerns the demand by over half the faculty that Pres. Harland Randolph be fired. On June 23, 1972, a reconstituted board finally accepted Randolph's long-tendered resignation.

[9] Farner himself was widely quoted as saying, "I have not made any policy decisions on my own. That's probably the wrong style of administration for this situation" (*Washington Post,* Mar. 8, 1968). See the section "Administrative Nonleadership" in Mapes (1970, pp. 7–10).

[10] The District of Columbia Citizens for Better Public Education has files on various committees whose reports favor an excellent four-year college and a community college. A full history of the citizen effort of the preceding decade is contained in this organization's *Memo to the Council of Churches of Greater Washington* (1966). See also the Chase report (*A Report to the President,* 1964).

Congressman Ancher Nelson (Republican of Minnesota) had separated the practical from the academic and had written into the bill a separate institute, Washington Technical Institute, authorized to grant certificates or associate of arts degrees. Since the original bill had included a community college as well as a four-year standard liberal arts college with authority to set up a master's degree in teaching, the residual Federal City College was a multilevel college. It would have been possible to set up two separate campuses, one a junior college with open admissions or a general curriculum, the other a more selective school. To some, such preselection bore with it elements of tracking, a political anathema in the District. Further, it was argued, particularly by Board Chairman Horsky, that such a plan might lead only to the funding of the two-year college, because Congress was a notoriously fickle body, basically antagonistic to the District. Farner and the board of higher education had thus decided not to separate the college into constituent parts, but to develop it as an organic whole.

This same concern over funding led Farner to establish a master's degree program immediately. The attitude was very much one of occupying territory left unprotected by the enemy. Yet the swift establishment of beachheads at all undergraduate levels, and the graduate level as well, was to apply to the doctrine of open admissions to all students. Indeed, a bachelor's degree was not necessarily to be required for entrance into the master's program. Philosophically, desire replaced preparation as the standard for entrance.

For consistency with open opportunity there had to be a low tuition. Since the first two years of FCC were to be equated to a community college, Farner began with a comparison of fees or tuition at neighboring community colleges. On the basis of lower average income in the District, he proposed, and the board accepted, a tuition of $25 a quarter. Out-of-state students would not be charged the cost of their instruction—few colleges do that—but the incremental cost of their attendance. Nonetheless, it was decided that such students would pay 10 times the local rate, or $250 a quarter, $750 a year. Such a charge was half again as much as the annual tuition at neighboring state universities such as Virginia ($525) or Maryland ($502) and was higher even than the tuition at nearby Howard University ($618), which is subsidized through the U.S. Department of Health, Education and Welfare. Thus, even though anyone over 21 residing in the District for three months was considered a resident, and even though no check was ever really made to verify residency, this tuition differential severely limited the clientele from outside the District while extending opportunity widely within it.

Low resident tuition and open admissions at every level resulted in a flood of inquiries which were interpreted as applications. As the number of letters expressing interest in joining the college grew close to 6,000, Farner made another political calculation. He decided to ask Congress for an increase in the size of the charter class. To dramatize the need for this action as well as to solve the problem of admission priorities, Farner decided to hold a lottery among the 6,000 applicants for the spaces available.[11] Bennetta Washington, the mayor's wife, drew the first number. This was a masterpiece of public relations. FCC was featured in all the news media in the country. Pressure began to build to open more opportunities in the college for the eager students.[12]

The original funding request for the first year of teaching had called for a faculty of 60, already greater than estimates in the Chase report (*A Report to the President,* 1964). At a ratio of 1 faculty member to 16 full-time students, these instructors could teach only 960 full-time students or, it was estimated, 800 full-time and 500 part-time students for a total of 1,300 persons. Farner went to the Congress with a request for supplemental appropriations to increase the faculty size to 120 in order to accommodate 2,400 students in the initial class. Actually neither budget had in fact been passed when the school opened, but the faculty recruitment tapered off in May at slightly over 60. Although Farner had the board's backing for the larger budget, he did not finally agree to recruit more faculty until July 1968 under pressure from the faculty. This decision had a tremendous impact on the black controversy at the college, since it meant recruiting for additional

[11] Like much else in Washington, this numbers game was primarily for public relations. As applicants were processed, it became clear that many had no real intention even of applying to the college. Of the first 350 persons processed, 100 were actually traceable. Lottery numbers to 3,800 were exhausted to achieve enrollment of 2,000 heads for the first quarter, and most of the rest of the numbers were used during the winter and spring quarters to replace earlier students who dropped out.

[12] The lottery was not universally popular among potential students and was disliked by many high school counselors. Farner's own views are presented in his "Public Higher Education . . ." (1970).

faculty during the summer when most faculty would have already signed contracts.

Taken together, the decisions to combine low tuition for District residents with open admissions at all academic levels and with immediate expansion of the student body confused and complicated the curriculum thrust of the college and therefore its philosophy. The goal of quality education can be combined with open admissions at the freshman level[13] if intense efforts at "catch-up" are made for the benefit of underprepared students. Highly structured core courses with intensive skill components were originally proposed for the incoming freshmen. But rampant growth and open admissions at upper levels made quality control almost impossible and, for many, unpalatable. The social goal of educating all comers submerged vague notions of educational standards. Such was the tenor of the times that the philosophical issues implicit in Farner's decisions were never discussed at the time within the college community either by the burgeoning administration or by the faculty committee which had co-opted student representation.

THE FACULTY The confusion with the college—over curriculum, recruitment, and size of the student body—was compounded by power struggles that intensified as Farner increasingly avoided making decisions. This vacuum of leadership became clear to the faculty the first time they met together in late June 1968.

The total faculty which assembled at the June convocation included 44 whites and 18 blacks. Recruitment guidelines stressed reasonable academic preparation and experience in cross-cultural teaching. A fairly high salary scale and innovative teaching possibilities were expected to attract a highly qualified faculty. Indeed, many of the faculty came from such top graduate schools as those at Harvard, MIT, Minnesota, Chicago, Yale, and Michigan. Several young whites joined as a sort of academic VISTA experience, more ready to learn, perhaps, than to be missionaries, but certain that change was good. A small but significant group, black and white, moved over from Howard, where they had been active in challenging a conservative administration. Thus, while traditional academic preparation had been stressed, the early faculty combined with their credentials an impatience with the

---

[13] For more details of the program, see Tinker (1970).

system. Such faculty members brought with them many ideas and theories based, naturally, on their previous experiences, which had generally been at WASP[14] colleges.

A special effort had been made to recruit black professors in order to achieve parity, but the first faculty group was only 44 percent nonwhite. There were several reasons for the lack of a majority of blacks despite commitments by the recruiters to seek out black faculty. A projected recruiting trip to Negro colleges by Harland Randolph was put off. The emphasis on an academic degree in appropriate subjects limited the pool of candidates. In areas such as creative arts and drama, where a degree was not considered necessary, the percentage of blacks was higher than elsewhere. Those blacks offered jobs were often unwilling to take a chance on a new college; the refusal rate was considerably higher among blacks than whites. There was also a conscious effort to avoid widespread hiring of nonwhite foreigners, a practice widely followed in Negro colleges, mainly to avoid dialectical problems with underprepared students.

This early faculty, socially aware and generally privileged, quickly grasped the implications when Farner repeatedly informed them at the convocation that nothing about the college structure or curriculum was "writ in bronze." Instead of a planning session, the convocation became a staging ground for "doing your own thing." One of the first moves was to organize a faculty organization to take over the decision making which Farner had clearly abdicated. Student services and media staff were unwilling to let so much power pass to the faculty, with whom many had already had arguments at least partly because of status-perception conflict. There finally emerged an Interim College Committee which included representatives of every constituency at the college: media (library), student services, administration, faculty, and general employees.

Rather than a decision-making group, the ICC became an assembly where diverse views of the major constituencies were aired. About the only point of agreement was over the need for parking. At one particularly fruitless September meeting the chairman, Harland Randolph, then vice-president for development, complained

[14] The term WASP is used here as it was at the college to indicate the cultural thrust of the American mainstream as being White, Anglo-Saxon, and concerned with the celebration of the Protestant ethic as represented by unrelieved individualism and materialism.

that "everything is so amorphous. . . . I like to have my nightmares at night. . . . Misunderstanding around this place is one of the ways power shifts."

The faculty organization was much more active over the summer. Nearly 40 faculty were already working full time, and most were at first active in the organization. When Farner's decision to increase faculty size became known, a black member of the English faculty who had formerly taught at Howard offered a resolution at a meeting on July 24 stating that all new positions in the faculty or on the staff should be filled with blacks only. There was little opposition among the group of 26 faculty present; only 2 members voted against the resolution. Farner, who was present, said he would approve the motion and pass it immediately to the board. He did this without any attempt to discuss the matter with his provost, whose job it was to recruit.

A Black Committee was formed to recruit and screen new candidates. When it reported to the second convocation on August 27, it reported having recommended the hiring of 35 educational personnel, over half of whom were faculty. Many of the additional faculty hired were part-time teachers who were graduate students at nearby universities or working elsewhere. Two had started and ran a black bookstore. Another was a radio and TV announcer. Several were community organizers with the Office of Economic Opportunity. Very few came from academia, although one professor was lured from North Carolina despite the lateness of the recruiting effort. Another associate professor for a time continued to teach full time at another college in Maryland while ostensibly teaching full time at FCC. The racial tenor of this recruiting may be seen in the reaction of one black candidate who reacted to the interview process angrily. "They say I'm not black enough because I came with a tie on. I spent three years getting myself together, going to a psychiatrist. I know who I am. I'll not play their game."[15]

In September the faculty numbered 106 heads—51 black to 55 white. Anyone teaching even one course had a full vote in faculty meetings. With a quorum set at half, the faculty had constant problems with attendance. Decisions were made by 35 to 40 active

[15] One member of the committee later said that most of the recruiting was done by a few and that other members were given no real review. He felt he was never listened to: "I'd shoot a person down and they'd be appointed anyhow." Membership on the committee was technically open, and one or two white faculty did attend its meetings.

faculty. No wonder that it seemed to the provost and to many others as if the faculty were run by "the white radicals and the black separatists."[16]   When an issue was demonstrably racial, then the black-white militant coalition always won. To the question, who shall teach? the faculty had answered, black. In asserting their answer they had also, for the time, stated that they, the faculty, would run the college and determine what was to be taught. For much of the first year, they did.

Most of the issues considered by the faculty were not clearly racial, but there was usually an effort to define them as such in terms of shades of blackness. Only when an issue touched upon faculty power was there anything like unanimity. The faculty voted that no one could be fired the first year, and the administration accepted it. The faculty voted that any instructor could teach any course acceptable to its own elected Educational Policy Committee (EPC). Thus ended any attempt at curriculum structure; the administration accepted it. The faculty voted to change the organizational structure by dividing the three divisions into departments and programs. Heads of divisions as well as heads of departments and programs were elected, and changed, with no consideration of rank or experience.[17]   Privileges of having secretaries, light course loads, and space went with these elected positions. Although there were attempts to alter faculty decisions, the administration eventually accepted each change—until, as we shall see, the issue of creating a separate black program came up.

On educational or political issues, the unanimity broke down. Many white teachers felt that achievement and aptitude testing was culturally biased and should not be used at FCC. Other white faculty considered grading passé: students should be given an A the first day of class. Most blacks read this attitude as patronizing, as if the whites were saying that the blacks could not equally achieve or equally learn. Black faculty, both traditional and militant, tended to demand high standards and rigorous courses. Black students

[16] The kaleidescopic nature of the faculty makes generalizations almost impossible, yet most articles published at the time, especially Barbara Raskin's "Federal City College: Militancy in Microcosm" (1969), established typologies that then tended to be used within the college.

[17] The administrative difficulties caused by frequent and unanticipated changing of heads were much more a problem than the lack of rank, which was more of concern to the more traditional black teachers than to the administration itself.

complained that some white teachers merely liked to bull; they resented everyone getting passing grades when many did not work.

In terms of course content, the majority of the faculty in the professional and physical science divisions favored traditional curricula. In social sciences and humanities there were many faculty members interested in trying to adapt the courses to what they perceived were the experiences and needs of the student body. Some of the younger white faculty tended to hold a somewhat romantic view of the students as underprivileged rejects of society whose native intelligence was waiting to be revealed. In fact, the bulk of the students were lower-middle-class Americans with typical ideas about the upward mobility inherent in a college degree, who were in college for status and jobs, not for pure education.

Figure 5-1 gives an estimate of the teaching attitudes of the faculty by race based on a survey of courses offered and positions expressed. Faculty members preferring structure may be separated by course content into traditional and adaptive. The latter term suggests cultural, temporal, and attitudinal adaptation of the general curricula to respond to the needs of the students as perceived by the faculty members themselves. This group included those favoring the original integrated core curriculum as well as the black militants espousing black studies. Those preferring unstructured classes and free-flowing ideas were all white, although one young woman of Armenian dissent who identified herself as black could be included in this group.

On political issues faculty members were more likely to divide by race. A majority of blacks seemed to prefer avoiding any confrontation and stopped attending faculty meetings altogether. The more militant wanted to preserve their energy for their own concerns. Thus the blacks did not join whites in fighting the governmental oath required of all federal employees which eschewed union activity and queried Communist affiliation. When white faculty wished to open the college for the moratorium marches, the black students and faculty joined to countermand the offer.

The issue over Project Vault was more obscure. The black director of admissions, himself a retired army officer, originally negotiated FCC's involvement in Project Vault, a well-funded Defense Department program to help Vietnam veterans get a college degree in elementary education so they could teach in inner-city schools. Many of the white faculty objected to any affiliation

FIGURE 5-1 *Federal City College: Major faculty positions 1968–69*

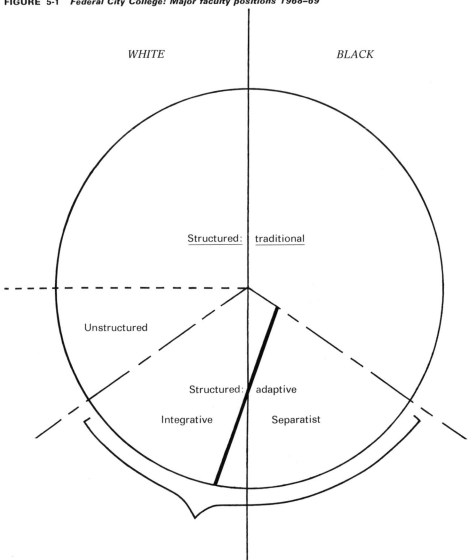

Race	Number	Curricular orientation	Percent
White	55	Structured: traditional	63
Black	51	adaptive	30
Total	106	Unstructured	7

with "the war machine and its tainted money." Other faculty of both races recognized the worth of the program both to the veterans and to the students they would teach. The militant blacks did not want to alienate these objecting whites, on whose votes they so often relied, or the moderate blacks with whom they were trying to cope. Generally they considered the war a white man's problem and unfair to black soldiers; one of their members was then in the midst of a court case over his conscientious-objector status. When the vote came, those present were mostly whites, and the project was shelved.

Depending on the subject matter, then, the faculty grouped in various ways. Of course there were individuals who fit no group, and more individuals who uncertainly swung from one group to another. The fact that most of the faculty was young and relatively inexperienced and lacked structural or behavioral alternative models exacerbated the swings. That first year at Federal City College was in many ways a continuous sensitivity session demanding exploration into the meaning of middle-classness and racism. Many black militants exalted the four-letter word as a weapon against bourgeois pretense.[18] Skin color became the most important factor in weighing opinions; the most damning thing that could be said of a black faculty member was that he was not black enough. Whites were automatically called racists if they did not acquiesce to the militant view. Race increasingly informed all decisions; the college, like the society, might be seen as institutionally racist. As this view of society and the college gained popularity, the black-white coalition against which the provost inveighed could carry the faculty, but only on racial issues which the less radical black faculty might dislike but would not dare oppose. An issue that was accepted as black would win, at least openly. The role of the silent black majority was pivotal in the defeat of black studies.

BLACK STUDIES The demand for black studies escalated through three phases, from demand for courses to demand for program to demand for a college; within the college the majority opinion switched from support to rejection. Controversy over the separatist program led

---

[18] Martin Kilson (1971) argues that this is typical of the "put-on" used by lower-class Negroes.

to a polarization between the faculty and the administration which caused the board of higher education to request the resignations of President Farner and Provost Dickson in May 1969. The board, confused and disunited, tried for a time to intervene in, and even to assume a decision-making function at, the college, tangled with the faculty, and then withdrew, leaving former Vice-President Harland Randolph as the new president.

As previously indicated, the curriculum planners assumed from the beginning that Federal City College would have courses more appropriate and more relevant to city life and to various subcultures in this country than is usual in the WASP-dominated colleges. The true test of new black subject matter is its incorporation in all courses. No one considered the short-term introduction of specifically "black" courses as contradictory to this long-term goal. During the summer hiring push for black instructors, six or seven were hired to teach courses on African antecedents, community action, and black literature, for example. Such faculty members were hired within the existing teaching divisions.

Originally the divisions were primarily to offer structured team-taught courses in their subject areas but with skills built in. Such integrated team-developed courses take much time and commitment on the part of the faculty. Instead of having two months of the summer to work on such courses, the faculty already working was obsessed with politics. The newest faculty member often had no opportunity to meet with his team, but was merely assigned a course. Further, the faculty decided to delete the teaching of skills in the divisional courses and to revert to the usual freshman English syndrome. As more and more courses were offered, the structure lost its form. Almost no one was happy with the courses thus offered the first quarter.

During that first quarter, the faculty began to move toward departmental offerings, cafeteria style. The Educational Policy Committee was charged with the enormous task of reviewing the reordering of the college's curricula. As a committee of the active faculty, it had more flexibility than the more conservative faculty condoned. Interdisciplinary programs as well as departmental offerings were encouraged. More rigid programs were criticized, and suggestions were made to make them more flexible, but, on the grounds that any program deserved a year's trial, no programs were rejected. At least two departments simply ignored the EPC suggestions and eventually bypassed the committee when the board took over curriculum review.

Such an EPC was clearly sympathetic to an interdisciplinary black studies program. The organizer of the program was James Garrett, a 25-year-old instructor of English who had already written several black plays and had helped to set up the black studies program at San Francisco State College while he worked on his bachelor's degree. In a series of memos during the fall of 1968 various faculty members, black and white, who were interested in the topic produced course outlines for a black studies department or a black studies committee. Garrett's memos as convenor of the black studies program from the beginning seemed focused upon an interdisciplinary offering. At first the subjects were all within the humanities division and included history, literature, arts, and communications; the program was to be "geared toward the isolation and specification of information in order to include the study and expression of black life with those areas of study for which Federal City was founded."[19]

A memo on black studies which Garrett sent to the provost on October 10 had added social science to the "suggested major areas of concentration." Eleven faculty, all black, were listed as giving courses. This memo was followed by an informally circulated ditto, which declared that "the Black Studies Program will be divided into four degree-granting areas: Arts, Humanities, Community Development, and Science and Technology." Under this proposal the degree would be in black studies with a concentration in one of the four areas. Students not in the degree program could take black studies courses as electives.

At this point some faculty began to wonder where such an all-embracing black studies program left the rest of the college, especially as it became clear that white faculty were not welcome to teach in the program. Then the final version of the black studies program, later renamed the black education program, ignited the controversy early in November. Garrett was now asking for an essentially separate and autonomous program with a twofold purpose of "revolution and nation-building."[20]

[19] Memo dated July 30, 1968, from James Garrett, convenor of the black studies program, to the humanities faculty.

[20] Mimeographed program that originally appeared in November 1968.

The main emphasis of Black Studies will be toward the liberation of the African world. Since education should serve to expand the minds and spheres of action of the people involved in it, Black Studies must prepare Black people for the most complete self-expression, which must, in fact, be liberation and self-determination. Black Studies will take the position that the total liberation of a people necessarily means that those people separate themselves in values, attitudes, social structure and technology from the forces which oppress them.

Students enrolled in the program were to take five mandatory courses per quarter. The first two years "have as their major focus the decolonization of the mind."[21] During the last two years the student was expected to specialize in useful skills, whether technical, political, or cultural. While there were to be a few courses open to other students, the thrust of the program was to create a cadre of black nationalists.

To mount this program, Garrett demanded that it be allotted half the total faculty and that he be named director of the program, with complete freedom to recruit. Since the college was planning to double its size for the academic year 1969–70, half the faculty meant over 100 persons. He issued a position paper on the aims and objectives of the black studies program which emphasized that "the necessity of control is vital to every level of black *endeavor.*" The issue was clearly power and revolution, not academic niceties.

As long as the black studies program was perceived as any other academic program at the college, decisions as to its cirricula could be left to the Educational Policy Committee. When the program began to demand faculty positions far beyond its programmatic size, other faculty programs were endangered. When it ideologically demanded a separation between black studies and white studies, the very philosophy of the college was in question. Yet such was the atmosphere at the college that open criticism of the program was negligible, until November 12, when Provost Dickson gave his speech.

Why did Dickson make this speech, especially since he lacked the support of any constituency at the college outside his office?

---

[21] This terminology is widely used. See, for example, Jewel Graham on *The Antioch Program for Interracial Education* (1969).

Dickson, an English scholar of Jamaican heritage and New England birth, was educated at Bowdoin and Harvard. He taught courses on Milton and the Bible at Michigan State University in East Lansing before going to Northern Michigan College as vice president for academic affairs. A sensitive man, perhaps lacking in political sophistication, Dickson became embroiled in a controversy over university expansion by supporting the rights of faculty to protect elderly residents from losing their homes to the university. This was an explosive issue for the small community, but it was played out by the rules of the game. It did not prepare Dickson for the conflicting rules, and even games, played at Federal City College.

Dickson came not merely to accept but to applaud the need for study outside his own narrowly focused Greco-Judaic classicism. He accepted the argument that black commitment might be weighed instead of academic degrees, and had agreed to hire the faculty which formed the core of the black studies program even though only one candidate held a doctorate and he was an African whose philosophical orientation soon came into conflict with Garrett's. He talked with students and ignored the expletives that offended him. When several student leaders came to his office the day after the speech, Dickson argued against hiding one's head in the sand and hoping problems will go away. He said he had given the speech because of the "paranoidal tension" at the college and hoped that putting it in the open might make it easier to deal with. Later, in response to a student reporter who asked why he had not kept his criticism "in house," Dickson replied that he thought it "very important to talk about the infancy of this youngest land grant college, this oldest perhaps of a new group of urban grant colleges." Further he stressed the importance of open discussions. "Those who deny a hearing to their fellows have no right to stay in the academic community" (Upshur, 1968).

Why did Dickson receive so little support? Farner's style of nonconfrontation meant that he played down the situation but did not attempt to deal with it. The vice-president for financial and administrative affairs was in the process of resigning; the dean of student services was being moved to a less visible post; the dean of community affairs ran an essentially separate operation. Harland Randolph, Farner's executive assistant, the vice-president for development, and later president, carefully avoided identification with either Farner or Dickson. Farner himself once commented that although he had hired Randolph, he never felt he was "staff of my staff." Among the administrators outside Dickson's immediate staff, only the new dean of student services, David Eaton, openly objected to a separate black studies program and argued this view in an open student meeting during November. Undoubtedly the racial tension at the college helped explain the lack of leadership in the administration. Whites were suspect, lumped together despite their own political perceptions as racists and exploiters. As a result, many vied with each other to acquiesce to black demands. All but the most self-confident and proved blacks were likely to be chastized as white if their stance included any criticism of black studies.

Although students had been on most faculty committees for many months, the first student government elections were held during the week following Dickson's speech. About half the student body voted and selected a relatively moderate slate from among five choices. This group, the CHOSEN FEW ("We are not a black minority, we are the chosen few"), became increasingly politicized and radicalized, so that by February, when they began to attack the administration in general but Farner and his dean of administration in particular, they were a potent force in the college.[22] The Student Government Association tended from the first to skirt the black studies issue and leave student involvement in that controversy to students enrolled in the course. A leader of this group, Leonard Brown, was also SGA vice-president, however. Those students more concerned with education than politics did not organize for another year and therefore played no role in the black studies controversy.

As the polarization of the college grew, student attacks on Dickson took on a personal tone. Typical is this open letter printed in the student newspaper and signed "enrolled citizen" (Gonzales, 1969).

[22] After two years in office, the CHOSEN FEW were deposed. At the time they gave an interview (to *Sunday Star* reporter William Delaney) which recorded various activities of the Student Government Association. They claimed to have run the college during that time. While they did not enter directly into the black studies controversy, they heightened racial tension by indicting the dean of administration and undoubtedly hastened Farner's departure (Delaney, 1970).

Mr. Dickson, you seem not to understand the nature of colonialism or to accept the fact, in the first place, that this is a colonial country and that we Black people, brown people, and yellow people are colonized. . . . The ferment you see in the world today, Mr. Dickson, on the part of colonized and oppressed people is that they are revolting against the alien culture of the colonizer, and are re-discovering their own heritage and values. Mr. Dickson, you have no identity either. It's time you re-discover yourself.

Pressure mounted among faculty members to accept the program as proposed, despite its political as well as educational implications. This memo, circulated by a white member of the Educational Policy Committee, is indicative of the psychological dilemma this program posed for many faculty:

I question the notion that Federal City College or any college can be divided in any meaningful and final sense between Black Studies and White Studies. It is my conviction that racism in America, the most pervasive and irrational racism in Western history, is itself the result of an even greater evil which afflicts our nation. . . .

The program, in its very intensity and comprehensiveness, moves away from the opening of choices and options, and toward a closed and absolute evaluation of history and society. . . .

Despite these concerns I support the Black Studies program . . . as the only realistic means for Black self-confidence, community, and ultimately, genuine intellectual freedom.[23]

Isolated within the college, the provost's office acquiesced to tacit recognition of the program by listing courses as a separate department and, after considerable negotiation, allotting 40 new slots for faculty to the program. Dickson refused adamantly to recognize Garrett as the director of the program and instituted a nationwide search for an established scholar who might head it. But Farner overruled Dickson on that issue and refused to support a search committee.

Outside the college the black studies program triggered considerable adverse comment. While some questioned the existence of black science, others objected to some of the activities listed under physical development: akido, karate, t'ai chi, kung fu,

[23] Mimeographed memo to Educational Policy Committee from Sheldon M. Stern, entitled "Some Reflections in Black and White," Dec. 16, 1968.

stick fighting, riflery, aquatics, the African hunt, gymnastics, dance. The *Post* picked up the essentials of the conflict in an editorial which began "Infanticide is easy." While the rage of blacks is understandable, that at Federal City College is wrong for two reasons, "One is that it reflects an emphasis on indoctrination at the expense of education. . . . The other is that it will bring about the certain end of public support of the college" (*Washington Post,* Nov. 20, 1968).

While the debate raged within and outside the college, black studies courses were offered during both the winter and spring quarters. Enrollment was low. Altogether 601 students enrolled in all the various black courses in the winter quarter; the number fell to 410 in the spring. Since each full-time student was expected to take four courses (black studies itself specified five courses for its majors), the actual number of full-time equivalents (FTE) students was between 100 and 150 out of a total of 1,500 students at the college. On the basis of a faculty-student ratio of 1 to 16 the black studies program already had more faculty than its students needed. For the fall the program had been granted nearly 20 percent of total faculty positions, yet it had been able to recruit only 10 percent of the students. Garrett himself complained at a faculty meeting that "black students have to be convinced of black studies."

As it became clear that the program would have difficulty in recruiting students to its rigorous course of study, the staff reversed itself on the emphasis on exclusivity and joined with the Student Government Association in a memo on April 9 which called for all students to take a minimum of 20 credit hours in black studies. A compromise might still have been possible, but Garrett kept up his vitriolic prose.

Black people are not western. They are westernized. In much the same way as one might get simonized. We are painted over with whiteness.

If you think that you can go to school and get what you call an education and feel that you will not have to pick up the gun one day to protect your life from these pigs and the rulers of the pigs and the rulers of the rulers of the pigs (those are the top pigs)—the mayors who are the rulers of those pigs, and the white businessmen who are the rulers of those pigs—stop it. It won't work. You're going to have to fight. You can't escape that. It'll be like escaping life. And this white man might let you do a whole lot of things, even marry his daughter, cause he doesn't need her anymore, but that is one part of life he will not let you escape—war.

We are trained in our educational system to be enemies of our people. . . . If we can create an atmosphere among black children in which they can understand when to pick up the gun and truly grasp that fragile line of demarcation between destruction and creation we will have fulfilled our responsibility, and this is the meaning of our lives.[24]

Further, black studies had become a symbol of the faculty in its demands for control. The active faculty argued that it had agreed to the black studies program and neither the administration nor the board had any right to object. Increasingly, the silent faculty began to approach both the board and Congress with complaints about Farner's unwillingness to confront the more radical faculty. The apparent inability of the administration to deal with its own faculty and the impact that a black studies program might have on congressional funding of the college forced the board to act. A Curriculum Committee was established in April to review all curriculum offerings in order to ascertain "(1) relevance of curriculum to the needs of adult citizens in the District of Columbia and (2) satisfaction of requirements for degree and accreditations."[25]

Each division or program prepared its statement, which was forwarded, along with comment from the provost's office, to the Curriculum Committee. An advisory panel of students and citizens heard the statements and added their comments to those of the committee and the provost. Hearings were held between May 27 and June 14 and involved over 80 community representatives and 120 students. All projected offerings were given provisional approval, with questions to be answered during the upcoming academic year. Although scheduled, the black studies program was never reviewed. First the faculty boycotted the review when the board stopped recruiting in black studies. Then the committee "was unable to clear with Mr. James Garrett a date and time for the rescheduling."[26]

In preparation for the review the board, on March 11, had announced its criteria for black studies:

[24] From a printed handout entitled "Black Power and Black Education."

[25] Memorandum from Flaxie Pinkett, chairman of the Curriculum Committee, May 7, 1969.

[26] Report to the board of higher education from the Curriculum Committee, July 1969.

- It must be academically sound.
- It must be designed to meet the needs of a student body from the District of Columbia.
- It must be consistent with legal requirements.
- It must have a proper relationship to other programs of the college.

The provost's office prepared a memorandum which said that the program "is autonomous to the point of being a separate college. . . . the methods employed by the Black Studies program stress ideological conversion rather than reasoned commitment. It is clearly outside the role of a public university to provide courses of indoctrination for True Believers."[27] This apprehension was stressed in a special report on black studies sponsored by the American Council on Education: "Programs like that Federal City College proposal will unquestionably raise serious doubts about their propriety in an academic setting." The argument was not against black studies but against separatism. [28]

The crisis reached its climax at a raucous faculty meeting on the afternoon of June 2. During the preceding weeks the active faculty had censured the board for suspending hiring for the black studies program. [29] The vote was 38 to 1; the faculty total at that time was 106. Moderates continued to absent themselves. The faculty then demanded that the board meet with them, since on May 26 the resignations of Farner and Dickson had been announced.

On June 2, five board members were present, as were some 60 faculty and 20 students. At last there was a quorum, but no votes were taken. Garrett reiterated statements he had made the week before that the black studies program would be withdrawn if the board did not cease and desist discriminatory action. "We will not accept that b —— s —— in good faith. They don't have to be faithful because they have the arms." Some faculty had proposed that they all resign if the black studies program were not fully supported,

---

[27] "Provost's Statement on Black Studies," May 21, 1969.

[28] Prepared by W. Todd Furniss (1969).

[29] Actually Garrett had not put forward any candidates for hiring, although he was allotted 40 slots, until the last week of April. By June, 39 candidates had been interviewed and 5 new faculty had been hired in black studies. It is possible that if the program had continued, all 39 would have been hired. Many thought this laxness about candidates indicated that Garrett never expected the program to be accepted.

but no resolution was presented. Board Chairman Horsky announced that he had rescinded the prohibition against hiring for black studies. This did not satisfy the faculty. They kept closing in on Horsky demanding to know whether the board could veto curriculum, and if so, how had they the competence? Horsky was accused of "not giving one clear answer on one single question." Asked whether the board was responsible to the community or Congress, Horsky answered, "Both. If in conflict, then the board must decide." Great hooting and calling followed this remark, along with much oratory on congressional colonialism. The meeting dissolved inconclusively; the faculty was unable to focus on any positive action to solve the dilemma: either to force the board to support the program or to convince Garrett to compromise. Garrett decided against retreat. On June 9 he circulated a statement on "The Fight for Black Education" which heralded the departure of the black studies program to the community.

> The Black Education Program can no longer remain on this plantation. It must no longer submit to the condition of dependency forced upon it. . . . As long as we are confined in Federal City College Plantation, the existence, or non-existence, or modification of Black Education will always be in the hands of the Congress of the United States.

Nine of the black studies faculty, then numbering nineteen, resigned along with Garrett and followed him to the Center for Black Education which he set up in the heart of the inner city.[30] Those faculty remaining at the college were distributed among the existing divisions. Many taught a course at the center and were expected to contribute a tenth of their salaries to sustain it. At Federal City no degree in black studies has yet been proposed. While most courses in social science and humanities have substantial non-white materials, there is some attempt now to be less repetitive. At first, it seemed to the students that they studied the same classics, like Malcom X's *Autobiography,* in every class. The result of the year-long controversy was to leave course content up to the individual faculty. Perhaps more importantly, the controversy gave the faculty a sense of power over the administration and involved

---

[30] Most of those who left were part-time faculty with jobs elsewhere. Of fifteen FTE faculty, five left with Garrett. The African left town. Two faculty joined the language department, three went back to English, the others joined the community development program in social sciences.

the board much too deeply in the affairs of the college, thus setting the stage for continuing conflict.

SUMMARY The first year of Federal City College [31] was full of tension as the faculty and staff undertook to answer the three fundamental questions who shall teach? what shall be taught? and who shall run the college? That first year the debate was couched primarily in terms of black ideology, and in all cases black was the answer.

Blacks shall teach The faculty hired in 1969 was with few exceptions black; almost no faculty was hired in 1970 because of budget cuts. The ability of any white to teach at the college was questioned during the Black Awareness weeks following the Jackson State College shooting in May 1970. Student government officers sat in on classes of white teachers to monitor their degree of blackness. While some white males, both faculty and students, were roughed up in the hall and several white women verbally abused, the threats of violence were not merely black-white. The militants utilized rhetoric and violence against middle-classness of any color. The life-style of the street corner penetrated the college: the drugs, the violence, the admiration of the con man. Intrablack rivalries erupted openly during the election of the social science division chairman by the black caucus of the division. The successful candidate, a West Indian, would have been automatically confirmed by the white members of the division. Instead he was severely beaten by two other faculty members, spent some weeks in the hospital, and never returned to the college. The faculty members guilty of the beating were eventually fired and later taken to court by the injured man.

Responding to the tension and chaos, many faculty left. The percentage of faculty holding doctorates fell from 42 percent the first year to 29 percent the second. Black degree holders were eagerly sought by other institutions. The result is increasingly a faculty typical of those at many Negro colleges: marginal in terms of the profession, with low status and low mobility. Such staff, lacking other teaching options, is generally compliant to administrative pressure. There are women (black and white), foreigners, and men without doctorates or with degrees from low-status institutions. Of course there are exceptions, notable ones. Nor does the degree auto-

---

[31] For a more detailed analysis of Federal City College, see the author's forthcoming book, *College in a Colony.*

matically indicate good teaching credentials. Many young faculty are stimulating and provocative, and may be much more appropriate to the student clientele than doctorate holders. But in terms of comparability to good state colleges, excellence is further away than ever.[32]

What shall be taught? With the emphasis on hiring black, a large proportion of the newer faculty was recruited from Southern Negro colleges and from the District school system, both havens of bourgeois conservatism. Once the black militants left the college, the trend toward the tried and proved accelerated. There have been several attempts to tighten standards, and students can theoretically be flunked out for not passing enough subjects. The chaos in record keeping, however, has mitigated the force of this regulation. Now in its fourth year, the college still lacks a freshman-year program and is unlikely to initiate one.

While the trend is toward traditional college courses and content, the effect of the first-year controversy was to free the faculty from administrative control and to focus faculty effort against the administration. Today the faculty are left largely alone to frame their own courses or to work in groups for general courses. Such flexibility results in greater choice for the student; but because this flexibility is tied to the individual faculty and is not policy, it may be an ephemeral characteristic.

The answer to who shall govern? has yet to be given After Farner left, his vice-president for development, Harland Randolph, was appointed acting president, and he was confirmed in that post by October 1969. In an attempt to impose management systems on the college, Randolph called an all-college meeting at a motel in Bowie, Maryland, in May 1970. Student government officers attended all meetings and threatened faculty members who would not agree to the reorganization plan. When Randolph refused to call off the students, several of whom were for a time on his payroll, the faculty walked out.

Randolph then attached provisions on faculty contracts giving

---

[32] The fact that over half the full-time faculty signed a petition against the president of the college in the spring of 1971 shows the depth of the antagonism between faculty and administration and also that FCC is resisting its slide toward traditionalism.

him almost unlimited power to fire anyone he wished. The faculty refused to sign for nearly a year, until the board intervened. In January 1971 the faculty voted 123 to 50 to censure Randolph for arbitrary actions in firing his provost. In March 1971 the faculty compiled a dossier of what they termed Randolph's arbitrary actions: over half the faculty signed the petition that he be fired. In retaliation, the faculty, except for a few with tenure, were given one-year contracts for 1971–72. The board itself voted to fire Randolph in January 1972, then reversed itself allegedly because Randolph refused to return to the college at all. The board chairman, Edward Sylvester, resigned his post over the incident and sent other board members a statement which later appeared in the press. He was quoted as writing, "Harland Randolph lacks the management capability, the administrative knowhow, and above all the integrity to produce and lead a quality educational institution. . . . His approach to the board and its members has generally lacked candor, frequently been devious and manipulative, and at times just plain lies" (*Washington Post,* Jan. 14, 1972).

The mayor's office and several congressmen are at present studying plans for reorganization of the entire higher education system within the District. Perhaps a city university will be established with various campuses serving various needs. The students have become politicized and must be given a role in any new planning. The present student government forced the resignation of those students working with Randolph and has repeatedly called for the firing of most of the present administration on the grounds of inefficiency. One group even called for the end of the intimidation of white faculty so that the few remaining might stay.

Internally, then, the struggle for black-white has been resolved at Federal City College. Rivalry within the black group tends to follow lines according to attitudes toward Randolph. Randolph's supporters tend to be found among the most conservative blacks. On the board, however, it was the white group that most consistently supported Randolph. One perceptive black member of the faculty called this a typical white guilt reaction. Five new members, appointed in March 1972, may well alter the ambiance of the interinstitutional relationships. Any reorganization of higher education in the District would call for a completely new board; meanwhile the new members have rejuvenated the old.

The fight over black studies exacerbated friction at the college and caused faculty, administration, and board to adopt roles which have proved mutually antagonistic. A change of all the major actors in this drama is probably necessary to ameliorate the situation. One decision which is unlikely to be reversed, however, is that the college will be black. The problem still is in defining what that means.

References

Biderman, Albert D.: *The Higher Learning in Washington: A 175-Year-Old Crisis,* Bureau of Social Science Research, Washington, May 1966.

Delaney, William: "Deposed Student Clique Ran Federal City College," *Washington Sunday Star,* Dec 6, 1970.

"Demonstration College for the District," Ad Hoc Committee on a D.C. University, Washington, D.C., March 1967.

Dickson, David: "Higher Education for One World or Two?" paper presented at the general meeting of the National Association of State Universities and Land-Grant Colleges, Nov. 12, 1968.

Farner, Frank: "Public Higher Education Opportunity in the District of Columbia," paper read at the UNESCO Meeting on New Models for Higher Education in Asia and America, January 1970, and, revised at the meeting of American Association of State Colleges and Universities, Washington, May 1970.

Furniss, W. Todd: American Council on Education, special report, April 8, 1969.

Gonzales, Mrs. E.: *Federal City College Spectrum,* Feb. 13, 1969.

Graham, Jewel: *The Antioch Program for Interracial Education,* Yellow Springs, Ohio, July 1, 1969. (Mimeographed.)

Kilson, Martin: Militant Rhetoric and the Bourgeoisie," *New York Times Book Review,* Feb. 21, 1971.

Mapes, M. C., Jr.: *The Congressional Relations of the Federal City College,* a report prepared for the District of Columbia Citizens for a Better Public Education, Jan. 15, 1970. (Mimeographed.)

Memo to the Council of Churches of Greater Washington, District of Columbia Citizens for Better Public Education, Jan. 10, 1966.

Myers, Phyllis: "What It's Like When Congress Runs a College," *CITY,* October–November 1970.

Public Law 89-791, 89th Cong., H.R. 16958, Nov. 7, 1966.

Rapoport, Roger, and Laurence J. Kirschbaum: *Is the Library Burning?,* Random House, Inc., New York, 1969.

Raskin, Barbara: "Federal City College: Militancy In Microcosm," *Washington Monthly,* April 1969.

A Report to the President: Public Higher Education in the District of Columbia, U.S. Government Printing Office, Washington, June 1964.

Roberts, Wallace: "Federal City: Prospects for a Common College," *Change,* November–December 1969.

Tinker, Irene: "Colleges and the Underprepared Student," *American Education,* November 1970.

Upshur, Barnard: *Federal City College Spectrum,* Nov. 20, 1968.

Washington Evening Star: Nov. 13, 1968.

Washington Post, Mar. 8, 1968; Dec. 16, 1968; Jan. 9, 1971; Nov. 13, 1971; Jan. 14, 1972.

6. After the Bust: Student Politics at Harvard, 1969-1972

by Marshall W. Meyer

Have we come the full circle? Apathy, inwardness, even individualism seem to have displaced mass political action at Harvard since 1969. Looking back, the events of that spring, or those that came soon after, appear as the climax of a political unrest that was stirred by the Vietnam War. The occupation of University Hall on April 9, 1969, and the police bust the morning after were not followed by larger and more violent incidents; quite the opposite. Indeed, in May 1970, after the Cambodia invasion and Kent State killings, one observer characterized the style of protest at Harvard as "strangely anachronistic. It [was] almost as if last spring never happened" (Lukas, 1970). But April 1969 had happened, outward appearances notwithstanding; its impact on Harvard's students and administrators was then and remains considerable. Events often engender their own contradictions, as dialecticians note fondly. Though the immediate effect of the 1969 sit-in was euphoria and exhilaration, its long-term impact was quite different: first skepticism, later cynicism—even fright— about the probable consequences of further political activism. It is important that the underlying attitudes of Harvard students were, if anything, *more* radical in 1972 than in 1969. The critical question is why the willingness to act upon beliefs had diminished so considerably. A number of answers will be suggested below. They are best understood in the context of political events at Harvard from 1969 to 1972; hence a chronology of these happenings is in order.

AFTER THE BUST: 1969–1971 Despite the faculty's pleas for total peace, and their fears for the worst, minor skirmishes took the place of massive confrontation during the fall 1969 semester.[1] The opening shot occurred on the first day of classes. A band of Weathermen invaded the Center for International Affairs (CFIA) chanting "Ho, Ho, Ho Chi Minh," and assaulted the center's advisor to Fellows, Benjamin H. Brown. Not to be outdone, the November Action Coalition (NAC), formerly the New Left Caucus of Students for a Democratic Society (SDS), marched 175 of its members into University Hall the next day. The issue was Project Cambridge, a joint Harvard-MIT program in social science methodology that was to be funded by the Department of Defense. "Total dismemberment" (!) of the study was demanded by NAC; Dean of Arts and Science Franklin Ford expressed "no strong moral feeling" about the research from which official Harvard participation was later dropped.

The October 15 moratorium occasioned no special protests at Harvard. A week before, the faculty had, by a very narrow margin, condemned the Vietnam War, asking for prompt, rapid, and complete withdrawal of United States troops. Whether this action of the faculty or the decision of SDS to switch its energies to alleged racism took the punch out of the war as a campus issue is unclear. In any case, the next spate of protests center on Harvard's alleged oppression of black and white workers. Accusations of a racist hiring policy were voiced by SDS in early November; apparently a number of slacks who were paid as painter's helpers were doing the same work as journeymen. Harvard attempted to answer the charges, but to no avail. A week later SDS staged a sit-in in University Hall and blockaded Dean Ernest May in his office for an hour. Those causing the obstruction, nearly all whites, were promptly cited by the Committee on Rights and Responsibilities (CRR), which a month later suspended 16 of them. Two were "separated" from the university, making readmission unlikely, and the others were required to withdraw for periods ranging from 6 to 18 months.[2] The penalties were to take effect imme-

[1] The language of their pleas is itself worthy of study. Adam Ulam, one of the moderates, asked for a return to "the essential function of colleges and universities, that of teaching and propagating learning." H. Stuart Hughes, somewhat to the left of Ulam, saw a need to "depoliticize connections with the right rather than repoliticize from the left" ("Universities in Trouble," 1969).

[2] Harvard's lexicon for disciplinary actions is unique and often confusing. Here are the terms: A *required withdrawal* is like a suspension, only more polite. A student is required to withdraw from the university for a stated period and is allowed to return more or less automatically. Like any jail

diately, even though less than four weeks remained in the fall semester.

Though some black students had helped Dean May escape his captors, the blacks were by no means uninterested in the workers' rights issue. Early in December, a group called the Organization of Black Unity (OBU) got the administration to abolish the painter's helper job category. Negotiations bogged down on another point, however, since OBU demanded that 20 percent of workers employed at Harvard construction sites be black or "Third World" and that compliance officers be designated to supervise hiring. Harvard would not accede to this, and the blacks conducted sit-ins at University Hall and later the Faculty Club on December 11. Those blacks who could be identified as participants were temporarily suspended, but James Q. Wilson, chairman of the CRR, announced the next day that this did not bar them from dormitory rooms or classes. Later, Dean May formally charged 40 students with harrassment arising out of the OBU incident. Toward the end of January, the CRR found that faculty legislation "was not explicit on the subject of harrassment," and handed out only mild punishments to the demonstrators (Sternhell, 1970, p 1). Wilson stated that the white students severed on December 15 had prior records of infractions whereas the blacks did not. Soon after the CRR's verdict, it should be noted, Harvard announced that future building contracts would have a clause requiring between 19 and 23 percent of workers to be from minority groups. The black students, through the OBU, claimed dissatisfaction with the arrangement because of the absence of provisions for enforcement, but there was little more discussion of workers' grievances that semester.

The most spectacular event of the 1969–70 academic year involved relatively few Harvard students. The trashing of Harvard Square on the evening of Wednesday, April 15, culminated what was to have been a full week of antiwar activities in the Boston area. Thursday the sixteenth was planned to be the big day—the

---

sentence, a required withdrawal can be suspended; sometimes the term *suspended suspension* is used in place of suspended requirement to withdraw. *Severence* from Harvard is dismissal. A student who has been severed or separated can return only after a faculty vote to readmit him. The ultimate penalty at Harvard is *expungement*. Not only is a student dismissed, but all evidence that he was ever at Harvard is destroyed. Expungement is quite rare.

advance publicity announced a march from the Cambridge Common to the Boston Common with "further activity to be determined on the spot"—but the most militant seized the opportunity to do their thing the night before. Small groups broke off from a mass rally on the Boston Common, reassembled in Harvard Square, and overturned, smashed, and attempted to burn everything in sight. The Harvard students present were mainly onlookers. Freshman residents of Wigglesworth Hall, which overlooks Massachusetts Avenue, were greeted with the accusation, "How are the nation's elite tonight?"

My sense, corroborated by several informants, is that the April trashing rendered insignificant almost all the earlier political controversies save for the bust of one year before. There was considerable embarrassment, even revulsion, at the physical damage. (The only major damage caused by the April 1969 sit-in was to the floor of the faculty room of University Hall, which could not bear the weight of so many students.) Even the *Harvard Crimson,* the student newspaper, took pause. The lead editorial on Friday the seventeenth read, "It is precisely the seriousness of the growing political oppression that compels one to oppose demonstrations like last Wednesday's. . . . Small groups using pressure tactics to end the war are engaging in the same sort of power play that today's politicians are."[3] Six months earlier, Steven Kelman's *Push Comes to Shove* (1970) had thanked the editors of the *Crimson* for making the 1969 sit-in and bust possible; the condemnation of the 1970 events reflected a change of course.[4] While the political beliefs expressed by the editors were as radical as ever, the willingness to act upon them —or act destructively—declined precipitously. The same seems to have occurred among students. Cambodia and Kent State caused not nearly the disruption at Harvard that they did elsewhere. Mass meetings and peaceful protests took place, and the faculty voted to make final examina-

[3] ("Street Fighters," 1970.) The dissenting view of a minority of editors that appeared in the *Crimson* the next day stated, "The debate over whether or not the episode was right must be subordinated to the recognition that it was inevitable, that it will happen again and again. . . " ("The Riot's Context," 1970).

[4] *Crimson's* change of course was not complete, however. A low-keyed campaign —both in the editorial columns and on the front page—was waged against the Committee on Rights and Responsibilities throughout the 1970–71 and 1971–72 academic years.

tions optional. (It refused, however, to endorse a fall recess that would allow students to go home to campaign.) But the style of protest — nonviolence, freedom songs, and the like — was very much subdued. The trashing had soured most students' taste for direct political action without leaving them ideas about what they should do. The political views of Harvard students were as much left of center in May 1970 as in 1969. As one wag put it, "In Harvard terms, conservative means somebody who has been against the war for a long time, but is still against violence in this country." But another senior observed, "People are turning away from politics except for the absurd radicals. There is a lot of resentment about the window smashing the other night. . . . We had been marching in the streets for four years. The only thing that is left is humor" (quoted in Todd, 1970).

Early in the fall 1970 semester, a small blast damaged the library of the Center for International Affairs. Little harm was done, and the incident would probably have passed unnoticed except that two suspects were young women, members of the "Proud Eagle Tribe."[5] It was the first time that women's issues had become linked to other political questions; in retrospect it is surprising that this did not occur earlier. The fall term was otherwise uneventful. There was some discussion about lettuce — Harvard decided to purchase only the union-picked kind — but the issues that had excited students the year before, those of war and racism, had become nearly dormant. The lack of political activity, ironically, concerned some faculty and students. There was talk that the class of 1974 (which had entered September 1970) had been selected for docility, and some private comments of faculty members on the Admissions Committee lent credence to this view. Toward the end of January 1971 Dean of Admissions Chase Peterson met with a faculty group to clarify matters. Peterson denied changing admissions policies at Harvard; he said that no area of the country ("docket") had had its quota reduced, though there had been some movement toward recruiting more inner-city residents. "The doughnuts around the big cities are not as successful. . . as they used to be." Peterson continued, "We have to be terribly hard on people with good grades from good suburban high

[5] It almost passed unnoticed. The *New York Times* buried the item on page 82 beneath a story on railroad negotiations. Whether the *Times* could not take women seriously or whether another campus bombing just was no longer news, I cannot tell, but I suspect the latter.

schools—good, solid, clean-nosed kids who do not have enough else going for them." One faculty member retorted, "Dr. Peterson, those aren't doughnuts; they're bagels" ("Admissions Policy . . . ," 1971).

What the *Crimson* described as an "informal check" of the freshman register seemed to confirm the bagel theory; it was reported that the proportion of Jewish students dropped from 33 percent in the class of 1972 to 25 percent among the class of 1974.[6] A poll of nearly 200 freshmen found that 57 percent called themselves liberal, socialist, or Marxist; 3 percent centrists; and 12 percent conservative. (The remainder either refused to be classified or called themselves libertarians.) Almost all agreed that their class was politically quiescent, and a majority predicted that activism would not return to campus in the foreseeable future. The comments accompanying the interviews conveyed perhaps more than the statistics. As a freshman named Craig Johnson explained, "Damn it, we know that our America has got to be restructured. We'll do it—individually—later, but first let us live for ourselves" (Frazier, 1971). These sentiments, a reporter commented, were not unique to freshmen. Changes in admissions policies could not account for shifting political currents among sophomores, juniors, and seniors.

The quiet could not last indefinitely. But when political activity resumed, it had a disparate, disconnected quality. There was no single issue or set of issues that could attract and hold large numbers of students. Just after Christmas vacation, SDS attempted to resurrect the issue of racist employment policies at Harvard. A black electrician's helper claimed he was denied a twenty-cent raise due him, and SDS staged several "confrontations" with members of the personnel department to highlight the issue. Black students, however, showed little interest in allying themselves with SDS or any group of whites. On January 19, a number of whites were forcibly excluded from a talk given by Shirley Graham Du Bois, widow of W. E. B. Du Bois. The Committee on Rights and Responsibilities received no complaints, hence there were neither citations nor disciplinary actions. And in early March, a group of women (with children) seized an old building on Memorial Drive that Harvard had scheduled for demolition. They demanded that the property be used for a women's center and that low-cost housing be provided for the Riverside community of Cambridge. The building was held

---

[6] Ibid. My own data do not support this; see table on p. 144.

for nine days. Only the imminent arrival of the Cambridge police persuaded the women to relent. Again, there was no disciplinary action.

A number of teach-ins were also held during the spring 1971 semester and contributed to the sense of anachronism, even *déja vu*. The largest, at which Eugene McCarthy was the main speaker, was held on February 22 and attracted only 1,200 students. One commentator, noting the rows of empty seats in Sander Theater, wrote "Somewhere along the line . . . the novelty was lost" ("Old Excitement Is Missing . . . ," 1971). And conservative students' groups became active for the first time in this spring term. An offshoot of Young Americans for Freedom called Students for a Just Peace (SJP) attempted to hold a prowar teach-in on March 26, but was prevented from doing so. At least half of the audience of 1,000 was hostile and sat clapping, chanting, and booing for 45 minutes before the teach-in was dissolved. Charges of criminal trespass were filed against the organizers of the disruption, mainly SDS members, by both the administration and SJP. The Committee of Rights and Responsibilities heard 16 cases and announced verdicts on June 1. Nine were found guilty, of whom four were required to withdraw, three received suspended suspensions, and two were warned. A second counter–teach-in scheduled for the first of May was canceled, according to SJP, because many of the invited speakers, including Henry Kissinger, could not make it. The mood of the Harvard campus was uneven at the close of the 1970–71 academic year. Just as in 1970, some found cause for optimism in the new political style of students.[7] Michael Kinsley, a junior, wrote:

We all succumb for a while to the glamorous idea that huge marches and other manifestations of the politics of catharsis might bring significant results, but those who were in it merely for the catharsis and the glamour have given up, now that the marching has failed. These few perhaps have packed up their consciousness three and gone home, turned to cynicism or "inner-revolution". . . . But they will not be missed, because all over Washington and to a lesser extent in other cities there are little cockroached cubbyholes filled with an incredible assortment of young lawyers and high school students. . . . Their hero is not Jerry Rubin but Ralph Nader. It is consciousness one, the pioneer spirit, and the bureaucrats are the Indians (Kinsley, 1971).

[7] See, for example, James Reston's column in the *New York Times*, June 12, 1970, ". . . there is at least a new and hopeful tone to the campus debate at the end of this academic year."

But Nathan Pusey, who could never quite mask his aversion to campus activists, was less than sanguine. In 1969, he had labeled student radicals "the Walter Mittys of the left"; his 1970 report to the overseers called the previous year "dismal." Now stepping down as president of Harvard, Pusey sounded a sour note in his valedictory. Revolutionaries he found "grievously, even malignantly, deluded."

In recent years campus revolutionaries here and elsewhere have held that a debilitating and dehumanizing contagion allegedly springing from the interests and arrangements of the world outside has so deeply penetrated and widely infected the activities and structures of academic society and so controlled them, has made them so thoroughly deceitful and corrupt that the only acceptable attitude toward them must also be one of hatred, denigration, and attack. This has disturbed me more than any other development during the recent years. . . . If they are to be believed, the world, unready as yet to be set right by them, is totally corrupt—governed, controlled, and manipulated by schemers of whom I suppose at least in a minor way I must be considered one (Reinhold, 1971a).

THE CURRENT SCENE: 1971-1972 The 1971–72 academic year marked a number of changes at Harvard. Derek Bok took over the presidency and installed a group of "professional" top administrators, including Charles Daly, a White House aide in the sixties; S. J. Hall, a former Sheraton Hotel executive; Hale Champion, once California's director of finance and a political operative for former governor Edmund "Pat" Brown; and Steven Farber, age 29, who had been executive assistant to Governor Richard J. Hughes of New Jersey. One might expect considerable political savvy from this group. Another change—or what was believed to be a change—was the new political climate among students. Stanley Hoffmann called it "student demobilization." Thomas Pettigrew professed being mystified: "I thought I understood it until the late sixties—the turn-back is just too fast for me" (quoted in Reinhold, 1971). One issue however, arose at the beginning of the term and caused the faculty considerable consternation. This was Richard Herrnstein's article on IQ in the September 1971 *Atlantic Monthly.* Herrnstein was the target of a year-long SDS campaign, ostensibly because of the article's racist implications.

The essay on IQ triggered so much rhetoric that it might be useful to review what Herrnstein actually wrote. Relatively little was said directly about race other than noting the 15-point black-white difference in mean IQ scores. Herrnstein spoke approvingly of Arthur Jensen's research: "Jensen's two papers leave little doubt about the heritability of IQ among North American and Western European whites" (Herrnstein, 1971, p. 15). But he was cautious about generalizing this to racial differences:

Although there are scraps of evidence for a genetic component in the black-white difference, the overwhelming case is for believing that American blacks have been at an environmental disadvantage. To the extent that variations in the American social environment can promote or retard I.Q., blacks have probably been held back. But a neutral commentator (a rarity in these days) would have to say that the case is simply not settled, given our present stage of knowledge (ibid., p. 57).

Herrnstein made a further point whose implications were overlooked in the furor that followed publication of "I.Q." No matter what the heritability of intelligence, attempts to diminish environmental variation would have the effect of increasing heritibility. Programs of social amelioration, to the extent to which they render environments of the advantaged and disadvantaged equal, will make social-class divisions more rigid rather than less so since success and social standing are functions of largely inherited differences in mental abilities. "A virtually hereditary meritocracy will arise out of successful realization of contemporary political and social goals. . . . The one even plausible hope is to . . . [prevent] earnings and prestige from depending upon successful achievement" (ibid., pp. 63–64).

At the first meeting of Herrnstein's Social Science 115, SDS pickets were present. "A course is being given here that SDS doesn't believe should be given," the leaflets read. During the first weeks of the course, members of SDS attended the class to interrogate Herrnstein about his views whenever they could seize the opportunity. Herrnstein soon declared that he had grown tired of the repetitious accusations by SDS, but to little avail. The article on IQ was described as "criminal" in a public debate held on November 14. "Herrnstein is as much of a social menace as the guy who goes around punching black school children" said a member of the University Action Group (UAG), an SDS offshoot ("Forum Debate . . . ," 1971). A week later, 107 faculty members signed a petition condemning personal attacks on Herrnstein. (The fact that only 107 signed indicated that faculty sentiment was far from unanimous.) Some one hundred members of Dunster House replied in a public letter: "Do the professors believe that Herrnstein's article in the *Atlantic Monthly* is an example of legitimate scholarship?

Is it legitimate to discuss the political responses to the article as brutish, intolerable and unforgivable because 'they affront Herrnstein's personality'?" ("Six Dunster Faculty . . . ," 1971). A UAG poster depicted Herrnstein as "armed with the prestige of Harvard, trumped-up statistics, and non sequiturs. He should be considered extremely dangerous to all working people." The 107 faculty members did not convince the *Crimson* either. "We uphold Herrnstein's right to publish his theory. . . . [But] Herrnstein's ideas also have potentially dangerous implications. . . . The threat of Herrnstein's ideas is more dangerous than the imagined threat of SDS and UAG to intellectual freedom" ("Intelligence/Heredity," 1971).[8]

The baiting of Herrnstein began anew in the spring semester. Toward the end of February a second public debate blasted the article on IQ, and on March 1, a group of protesters disrupted a talk given by Herrnstein at the Eliot House science table. Five days later, members of SDS and UAG burst into Burr lecture hall, surrounded Herrnstein, and trailed him back to William James Hall where a brief scuffle ensued. Herrnstein complained of "intense personal harassment" to the Committee on Rights and Responsibilities, which summoned several students but punished none of them because of a deadlock on the question of their penalty. After the March 6 incident, the anti-Herrnstein campaign subsided somewhat. SDS had applied for permission to hold its National Convention Against Racism at Harvard during the spring recess, but Dean Dunlop withheld consent because of his concern that SDS was responsible for "interference with the academic freedom and right to speak of a member of the Harvard faculty" (Shapiro, 1972). Whether this or boredom with the issue led SDS to relent is not clear. The bulk of students, though not faculty, were unconcerned with the question, and there were other things for the militants to do.

Two other issues arose in the spring of 1972 that diverted attention from the Herrnstein question and other matters with which SDS had been concerned.[9] One was the question of financial support for graduate students; the other concerned Harvard's investment in a large bloc of Gulf Oil shares. Because the two issues were

---

[8] Michael Kinsley, in a dissent, labeled SDS "coercive."

[9] SDS had not completely relented on the question of workers' rights. In the fall the Harvard Club of Boston was picketed to protest the firing of a cook, Richard Scolard. The chant was "Cook Harvard bosses, rehire Scolard."

never linked together, they will have to be treated separately. We shall consider the matter of student aid first. Throughout the 1971–72 year, there had been discussion of financial stringencies in the Graduate School of Arts and Sciences (GSAS), and the announcement in early March that Staff Tuition Scholarships for Teaching Fellows would be eliminated came as no surprise. The reasoning of the Graduate School was as follows: The cutback in direct federal support to graduate students meant that the general scholarship fund of GSAS had to be augmented for Harvard to continue to attract the best graduate students. Since additional unrestricted monies were not available, the funds had to be sought somewhere else. A convenient source was the Staff Tuition Scholarships that had previously been granted automatically to teaching fellows. By allocating scholarships on the basis of need (and presumably merit) it was argued, more students might benefit from them.

There was swift response to the proposal that would compel at least some graduate students to pay $3,000 tuition for three years. The Graduate Students and Teaching Fellows Union (GSTFU) was formed to bargain with the administration. Their case was best articulated in an issue of *Upstart,* a journal published by radical socialists in the Harvard community. It was argued, first, that Harvard's operating deficit was largely illusory; whatever the over spending of unrestricted income, it was less than the surpluses accumulated from unspent income from restricted funds. Second, the graduate students claimed that the increasing cost of Staff Tuition Scholarships was a matter of paperwork. "The Deans agree: the pay of teaching fellows is getting out of hand. . . . But in commenting on the rising pay, the University is simply congratulating itself on raising tuition" ("Teaching fellows'. . .", 1972, pp. 17–18). The GSTFU called a one-day class boycott for March 28 that was not altogether successful despite support from the *Crimson,* which asked for "full disclosure of Harvard's operating budget," and women's groups, which added an antisexism clause to the graduate students' list of demands. The unenthusiastic response to the strike reflected, in part, divisions among the graduate students themselves. A teaching fellow in economics, James Weltzer (1972), wrote, "In my opinion, improving the financial position of most graduate students, who rank in the top two percent of the country in social class, race, education, IQ, and other determinants of earn-

ing potential, is a low priority item." Indeed, a call for a two-day
strike in the middle of April was defeated by a vote of members of
the GSTFU.[10]

The second major issue of the spring 1972 term, Harvard's
680,000 shares of Gulf Oil, had been simmering for a long time. In
the fall, Randall Robinson and James Winston of the Pan-African
Liberation Committee (PALC) went to President Bok asking that
Harvard dispose of its holdings in Gulf. Their argument was that
Portuguese colonial rule of Angola could not be sustained without
massive foreign investment that helped finance the colonial regime.
Large royalties were paid to the Portuguese government by Gulf,
and quantities of petroleum products were made available for military use. Harvard's divestiture of Gulf stock, the two claimed, might
make United States corporations cautious about further investment
in Angola. Bok promised a report on the situation and delegated its
responsibility to Steven Farber, who apparently put the task aside
for the time being. Farber's report, when it came, was too little (13
pages) and too late (March 6). It recommended that Harvard sell its
Gulf stock because this might induce other Gulf shareholders to
sell, perhaps forcing the company to reconsider its position in Africa. Farber's advice ran contrary to the Austin Report, which had a
year earlier laid down maximum return on all monies as the guiding rule for Harvard's investments.[11] Despite the recommendation
of divestiture, some of Farber's recommendations were disputed by
PALC. More important, perhaps, the frustrations of black students
had grown so intense by the end of March—a press conference
called by PALC to air its views on Gulf attracted only two reporters
—that more direct action was taken. An Afro-PALC rally was held
on March 28, and on April 4 representatives of PALC met with the
Harvard Corporation to reiterate their demand that the Gulf stock
be sold.

Harvard's decision to keep its Gulf shares was announced April
19. The next day at dawn, some two dozen black students took over

---

[10] Negotiations of a sort between the GSTFU and the administration continue
through June. In most departments, the suspension of Staff Tuition Scholarships affected only students entering the Graduate School of Arts and Science
in September 1972.

[11] "Committee on University Relations with Corporate Enterprises," *Harvard
University Gazette,* March 5, 1971. The committee did recommend consideration of whether a corporation's activities were "contrary to fundamental an
widely shared ethical principles."

Massachusetts Hall where the offices of the President and the Harvard Corporation were located. A statement issued by Afro-PALC said, "Gulf Oil Company, with the blessings of the Portuguese and the U.S. government, NATO, and Harvard University, daily facilitates the slaughter of our African brothers, oppresses them and rapes the natural resources of their land." Bok replied that for Harvard to sell the shares would be to forgo the possibility of persuading Gulf to take action that might benefit black Angolans. He also pledged to send a representative to investigate conditions in Angola. Informally, Bok let it be known that there would be no police bust. "I would never do anything to hurt a student in this university," he said.[12] And Charles Daly, who had weathered a month-long sit-in at the University of Chicago, echoed the same sentiments, "We don't want anyone hurt." A meeting of 2,000 students the evening of the twentieth voted a five-day strike to protest United States involvement in Indochina and support PALC's demands. What was most notable was the group's rejection of an SDS proposal to abolish the Committee on Rights and Responsibilities and to take "militant action" against Harvard. A second "mass" meeting on the twenty-fifth, which attracted only 650 students, initially rejected a proposal to continue the strike, but the proposal was reconsidered and passed after enough people had drifted off so that the militants had a majority.

The blacks vacated Massachusetts Hall a week after occupying it, perhaps because they sensed diminished support from other students, perhaps out of boredom, perhaps out of concern about possible penalties. "Jail sentences . . . would remove us from the struggle," one of the occupiers said. "The issue is Harvard out of Gulf and not Mass Hall" ("Blacks Leave . . . ," 1972). One other issue remained, however. The Committee on Rights and Responsibilities had to decide on disciplinary action for the 34 blacks who had participated in the takeover. There was some feeling that suspension of the black students was in order. Chase Peterson, for example, said publicly but unofficially that he would favor one-year required withdrawals. But the CRR acted leniently and voted required withdrawals that were then suspended. Possibly, the CRR misread signals from the administration, but it is more likely that they were simply ignored. As soon as the decision was announced, President

---

[12] Bok, it should be noted, was one of the few deans to oppose the April 1969 bust of students occupying University Hall.

Bok in effect criticized it. "A particularly serious problem," he said, "is whether the orderly function of the University is adequately protected by an apparent precedent that building seizures . . . will not result in substantial disciplinary action" ("CRR Rules Not to Require . . . ," 1972).

Two other incidents illustrate the tone of the Harvard campus in the spring of 1972. On April 18, a group of 100 to 150 demonstrators tore up the Center for International Affairs. "The Attica Brigade," part of the People's Coalition for Peace and Justice rally, had practically no Harvard students in its ranks; the chant was, "Harvard, MIT, smash the schools of the bourgeoisie." David Landau's account described the efforts of the few Harvard students present to stop the destruction:

As the vanguard reached the foot of Divinity Ave., their march broke into a run. In seconds, they were in front of their target, and rocks flew through the Center's first-floor window. A number of Harvard student radicals, sensing what was about to happen, stepped in front and yelled at the crowd, begging them to stop. Among those who had been most active in past student campaigns against the CFIA, they vividly remember the mistakes of 1970, the inefficacy of trashing as a method of protest, the futility of the Center, or even the University, as a target.

But their pleas were useless . . . (Landau, 1972).

The most militant of Harvard students had apparently turned away from tactics of confrontation and violence; we shall have more to say about this later. The second incident occurred in May after the United States mined North Vietnamese harbors. About 40 students sat in the Littauer Center offices of the Government Department, pressing for an omnibus list of demands—"severance" of all ties between Harvard and Henry Kissinger, termination of military recruitment on campus, divestiture of the Gulf stock, amnesty for the students who had occupied Massachusetts Hall, and retention of some Marxist professors in the Economics Department. It was a bit reminiscent of the eight demands that had been voiced three years earlier. Neither the issues nor the sit-in drew much student support at this time, so the protesters went home for supper. The Committee on Rights and Responsibilities heard the case of five students identified as participants in the Littauer sit-in, and it lost patience with one of them, a Radcliffe senior, who had appeared before the CRR several other times, charged, among other things, with harassing Professor Herrnstein and shouting down speakers at the 1971 prowar teach-in. This student was required to withdraw from Harvard for one year, only three days before she was to have received her degree.

WHY NOT AN-OTHER 1969? Despite the high level of political activity at Harvard in the last three years, there has been no repeat of April 1969. A number of explanations have been proferred, but the one most frequently voiced is that students are simply not as radical as they used to be. This feeling is widely shared among Harvard faculty. My analysis of the events of 1969 identified the left-of-center political beliefs of students as one of the causal factors in the sequence of events that led to the occupation of University Hall, the police bust, and the 10-day strike that followed. Clearly the hypothesis that Harvard students are less radical than they used to be ought to be explored. The 1969 study, however, identified several other causal factors. Participation in the antiwar movement was a strong correlate of political attitudes and it was hypothesized that the left-of-center beliefs of students, which may have attracted them to antiwar activities, were stimulated, reinforced, and pushed further to the left by these activities (Meyer, 1973). Hence the Vietnam War, because of the opposition it provoked, had to be counted as a cause. The content, or structure, of student beliefs was also important. The militants, it will be remembered, had a list of eight demands that encompassed the aims of diverse radical groups. In 1969, Harvard students tended to accept, or, as a minority did, reject these demands in toto. Attitudes toward one issue predicted attitudes toward all other issues; one could speak of the existence of belief systems or ideologies. A further factor in 1969, perhaps more important than the others, was the use of police to clear University Hall. If nothing else, the appearance of outside force antagonized the moderate students who were otherwise unsympathetic to building takeovers (Meyer, 1971). We shall, then, review some forces that were operating in 1969 and that may have shaped the political scene at Harvard in 1972—the political beliefs of students and their connection to antiwar efforts, the structure of these beliefs and the relationship of this structure to the demands of various political groups, and the administration's responses to events. Two other factors require consideration: one I can only label the dialectical element. I sense that the excesses of the most radical students have had the effect of muting the behavior of others. The second factor is the reaction of the faculty.

Political beliefs of Harvard students in 1972   As far as I can tell, and there is little solid evidence to the contrary, the overall political beliefs of Harvard students were somewhat more radical—that is, further to the left—in 1972 than in 1969. Several indications support this, the best being a recent poll of Harvard-Radcliffe undergraduates and students registered in the Graduate School of Arts and Sciences.[13] In 1969, students placed themselves at a mean of 1.3 points left of center on the political spectrum illustrated below; the mean in 1972 was about −1.7.

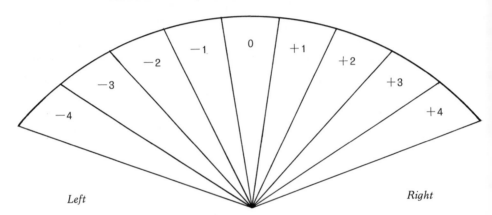

Left   Right

Put somewhat differently, 76 percent of students placed themselves at the left of the spectrum in 1969 whereas 86 percent did in 1972. Attitudes toward building takeovers had changed even more. Whereas only 17 percent of Harvard students had initially approved of the April 1969 seizure of University Hall before the police bust and 29 percent did afterwards, 69 percent of the 1972 sample thought the Afro-PALC takeover of Massachusetts Hall justified. The 1969 study linked the left-of-center political beliefs of students to participation in the antiwar movement; 34 percent of Harvard students had at that time been in various demonstrations. By 1972, this proportion had more than doubled to 69 percent.

There has been considerable speculation that admissions deci-

[13] Some 150 students registered in Harvard, Radcliffe, and GSAS *for the 1971–72 academic year* were sent questionnaires in July 1972. Because of the difficulty of reaching students during the summer, the return rate was quite low—42 percent—but not disastrous. We have good reason to believe that even this small number of returns *is* fairly representative of Harvard students, and the reader is asked to suspend his disbelief until the concluding section of this chapter.

sions have been made with an eye toward weeding out potential radicals. Perhaps the most appropriate retort came from Herrick McCulper, retired director of studies at Exeter: "I would say that Harvard has taken some of our prime troublemakers in recent years ("Admissions Policy . . . ," 1971). Information supplied by the Harvard admissions staff suggests strongly that there has been almost no change in the makeup of classes, save for increasing the numbers of minority students. Geographic quotas have not been altered significantly. If anything, student unrest may have discouraged the most conservative high school students from applying to Harvard. The table below shows the number of applications from two areas for the classes of 1972 through 1975. The first area is the Long Island and Westchester suburbs of New York City, New Jersey, and metropolitan Philadelphia; the second is the states of Ohio and Kentucky.

Class of	N.Y. suburbs, N.J., and Philadelphia	Ohio and Kentucky
1972	757	326
1973	836	410
1974	859	305
1975	665	227

The events of spring 1969, if they had an impact, would have affected applications for the class of 1974. The New York City suburbs, New Jersey, and Philadelphia had a modest increase that year; Ohio and Kentucky suffered a precipitous drop. The ratio of the New York area to Ohio and Kentucky applications was 2.3 to 1 for class of 1972 and 2.0 to 1 for 1973; it shot up to 2.8 to 1 for the class of 1974 and to 2.9 to 1 for the 1975 class. Assuming that New Yorkers are likely radicals and Ohioans conservatives, the notion that radical high school students are postponing or foregoing college—at least Harvard College—is not supported. Similar evidence comes from the 1969 and 1972 surveys. If the estimates are correct—*and it should be noted that the 1972 data are based on a very small sample*—there has been little change in the religious background of Harvard students; only the number of students reporting no religion for their parents has increased. Here, too, there is no evidence of discrimination against those thought to be radicals or potential radicals—that is, the children of Jewish or nonreligious parents.

Father's religion	1969	1972
Protestant	41%	36%
Catholic	17	16
Jewish	20	19
Other	6	5
None	16	24
TOTAL	100	100

The simplest conclusion seems to be that in terms of background variables, geographic spread, religion, even social class, Harvard students are now little different from those of the late sixties. Students' overall political beliefs have, however, moved leftward as participation in antiwar activities has increased. Clearly, political beliefs alone cannot account for the quiet mood on the Harvard campus.

The structure of beliefs The pattern of protest from September 1969 to May 1972 may have led students to compartmentalize their attitude toward various issues in 1972, whereas this had not been the case in April 1969. Most of the incidents after 1969 were single-issue affairs. Questions concerning the CFIA, Project Cambridge, minority workers' rights, women's liberation, Herrnstein, Kissinger, Staff Tuition Scholarships, and Gulf Oil never got intertwined with one another except during the abortive Littauer sit-in in May 1972. This was in sharp contrast to April 1969, when a panoply of issues was linked together in the eight demands—among them abolition of ROTC, rent rollbacks, housing for workers displaced by Harvard's expansion, a Black Studies program, and amnesty.

The issue-specific character of protests reflected as much as anything else division within the radical community. Harvard SDS had split in half during the summer of 1969—the same split was to happen nationally a year later—the Progressive Labor faction retaining the SDS title. (The more moderate group became the November Action Coalition.) At the same time, the black students dissociated themselves from SDS. It may be that the various SDS demonstrations over minority workers' rights were intended to patch up the alliance. If so, they were unsuccessful. In each case the blacks either staged separate protests (for example, the issue of minority representation on construction sites in 1969) or dropped the question altogether (for example, the firing of cook Scolard). The factionalism within SDS was described in an article "Is PL Killing SDS?" by David Landau (1971).

Many SDS now feel that PL has emerged as the most intolerant faction in a movement which cannot stand the added burden of continuous in-fighting. Within SDS, PL and its sympathizers now control *New Left Notes,*dominate the debates of national meetings, and hold overwhelming majorities on the national committees. But if there is now only minimal opposition within SDS to PL's leadership, it is because hundreds of students have privately quit SDS and old chapters have bailed out, because they no longer have an influence on the national organization. The Worker-Student Alliance which PL pushed hard and continuously with SDS sapped the organization of so much energy that it did no work on the issue of the war during the period of the moratorium. SDS had rendered itself powerless by the time Cambodia rolled around last May. SDS condemned all the moratoriums. Even if the SDS refusal to participate in liberal anti-war demonstrations was vaguely understandable, its empty denunciations of radical groups supporting the NLF was not.

Relations between SDS and other radical groups deteriorated even further after Landau's piece was published. In May 1971 it was reported that a number of checks written by PL members of SDS for transportation to the April march on Washington were worthless. The National Peace Action Coalition was left short $1,350 because payment was stopped on some checks, and others were drawn on new accounts in which very little had been deposited.

The split among radical groups is reflected in the way issues have become dissociated in students' minds. Data from the 1969 survey of Harvard students showed that students' attitudes could be reduced to a single dimension—the left-right continuum—through factor analysis. No such unidimensionality is evident in the 1972 data; correlations among opinion terms are lower than in 1969. Paradoxical as it may seem, the leftism of Harvard students in 1972 was more intense but less focused than three years before. My sense, though no data support this conjecture, is that the frustration and inwardness reported among students reflects this disconnectedness of opinions. Their leftism signals fundamental discontent with United States society, but the willingness to package all the issues together in search of a panacea has diminished considerably.

The response to student protest The Harvard administration's response to student protest changed considerably after April 1969, and disciplinary procedures have changed somewhat. In place of the Administrative Board and the temporary Committee of Fifteen, the Committee on Rights and Responsibilities, an elected group of faculty, was charged with enforcing the code of conduct. (Students were meant to serve on the CRR, but the elections were never held in some Harvard Houses while in others candidates promised to disrupt or resign from the committee. This made the legitimacy of the CRR a minor issue throughout the 1969–1972 period.) More important, perhaps, in dealing with students charged with misconduct, the CRR acted leniently in many cases and not at all in others (e.g., the Shirley Graham Du Bois talk, the occupation of 888 Memorial Drive) because there were no formal complaints. Students brought before the CRR in connection with the December 1969 University Hall sit-in, harassment of Professor Herrnstein, and the takeover of Massachusetts Hall in April 1972 were neither severed nor required to withdraw from the university. Stiffer penalties were reserved for members of SDS who had appeared before the CRR repeatedly. Required withdrawals and severances were handed out to some students found guilty of the November 1969 SDS action in University Hall, the disruption of the prowar teach-in, and the May 1972 Littauer sit-in.

Whether or not this reflected a policy of strategic lenience on the part of the CRR or the administration is unclear. The statement accompanying the decision to suspend the suspensions of the blacks who had occupied Massachusetts Hall noted "the long peculiar history of racial frustration at Harvard." Recognizing that the occupation was nonviolent and that the students cited had no previous disciplinary record, the CRR added that the blacks had "documented and explained their viewpoint with a high degree of rationality, order and patience. . . prepared position papers on the role of Gulf in Angola, explored proper administrative channels, and made appropriate effort to use acceptable forms of public debate" ("CRR Rules Not to Require . . . ." 1972). Neither President Bok nor the overseers could quite swallow this, and both issued statements indicating disappointment at the outcome.

The absence of outside force from the Harvard campus helped cool things considerably during the 1969–1972 period. The

1969 survey showed that the decision to call the police mobilized moderate students to support the strike that followed the evacuation of University Hall. The most militant students went on strike in support of the eight demands, but those at the center of the political spectrum were much more upset over the bloodied heads and bruised limbs than over the radical platform. The decision not to use force to remove students from Massachusetts Hall in April 1972 was most certainly made with the memory of 1969 in mind. Had police been called in 1972—and this is practically inconceivable since President Bok was opposed to the use of force and was never pressured on the subject by the overseers or alumni—the outcome would have been very different.

One more factor that must be labeled as administrative style distinguished 1972 from 1969. Nathan Pusey was outspoken; Bok was cautious, even indecisive. Pusey was given to taking a stand; Bok preferred to let controversy run its course. The "Parting Shot" of Garrett Epps, retiring editor of the *Crimson,* was exaggerated, but it caught the essential differences between the two men.

[Bok's] only discernible goal as President is to avoid risk to his institution and to minimize conflict which might threaten it. . . . But neither will he make a profitless stand on principle. Instead he adjusts Harvard just enough to take the initiative away from those demanding changes, makes the minimum effort necessary to blur the issue. . . . Nathan Pusey was a nasty old man obsessed with reactionary beliefs and values. Yet for all that he was more human than Bok. He [was] . . . willing to fight to the death with any weapon he had to preserve his principles (Epps, 1972, p. 2).

The dialectical element, or outright embarrassment   Any political belief when taken to an extreme eventually generates revulsion and hence loses support. The April 1970 trashing of Harvard Square cost the radical movement many followers; even fewer were left, at least at Harvard, after the 1972 attack on the Center for International Affairs. This the *Crimson* called a "rampage . . . that served no purpose." An editorial the day after the attack on the CFIA noted that

The 1970 student strike achieved real success. . . . But faced with a demand for immediate action, many activists stopped asking the questions which had shaped the movement and given it strength; questions of internal democracy, broad organizing strategy, and purposeful tactics of protest. The rush to action—any action—proved irresistible. The result, in Cambridge, was a pair of window-breaking sprees in the Square and a confused strike, centered around grades and examinations; in the nation at large, it was a succession of adventurist and terrorist acts. . . .

Yesterday's action represents almost every mistake of the 1970 strike; as in 1970, similar actions will forfeit our chance of building a broad coalition of Americans who share our views, and will leave us with only temporary success ("The Price of 1970," 1972).

The People's Coalition for Peace and Justice (PCPJ), part of the larger Cambridge Movement, was generally credited with the CFIA trashing, and did not deny (though it refused to admit) responsibility for it. PCPJ was itself a mass of contradictions. It was meant to unite workers and students, yet its leadership was composed mainly of Harvard and MIT graduates who by 1972 had had six to eight years experience in radical politics. A sense of ingroupness dominated the People's Coalition, and this, together with the defensive posture of the organization, may have intimidated undergraduates who wanted to join. The exclusiveness of the extreme left—which was present, but to a much lesser extent in 1969—may have helped undermine its base of support.

The faculty's reaction From 1967 through 1969, Harvard's Faculty of Arts and Sciences had not been unsympathetic toward the views, if not the actions, of radical students. It will be remembered that the Administrative Board had placed a number of students on probation for their participation in the October 1967 occupation of Mallinckrodt Hall in which a recruiter from the Dow Chemical company was held captive. Some of those who had participated in the Mallinckrodt sit-in were present when, on December 1968, a faculty meeting in Paine Hall was disrupted by a large group of students who had gotten there first and refused to leave. Five who had been put on probation in 1967 were ordered suspended by the Administration Board because of the Paine Hall incident, but the faculty at its next meeting rejected the required withdrawals. ("Faculty Saves Everyone," the headline read.) And at its February 1969 meeting the faculty bowed to student demands by stripping ROTC of academic credit, professorial titles, and free use of academic facilities. President Pusey and Dean Ford helped rekindle the ROTC issue later by taking strong exception to the faculty's stand. After the University Hall sit-in and police bust, the faculty moved even further toward the radical position by barring any contractual relationship with ROTC, reducing it to an extracurricular activity. A Black Studies program in which students had a voice in selecting faculty was approved. And of the nine faculty members of the Committee of Fifteen, six were elected from the slate of the liberal caucus.

By 1972, the sentiments of the faculty had shifted considerably. In part, this was because a mood of apathy replaced involvement. Some faculty meetings in the fall of 1971 had to be canceled for lack of business. More important, however, was the SDS attack on Richard Herrnstein. Though there was not unanimity, the prevailing sentiment was that a question of academic freedom was involved in the harassment of Herrnstein. President Bok personally deplored the incidents, and most statements by individual faculty members supported his view. My own feeling was that until this time most faculty members had identified with the goals of student dissenters but not their tactics. Students sensed this and used the attitude to some advantage; the "no other means were available" argument was used as justification for the various sit-ins and demonstrations. The Herrnstein controversy exposed important differences in goals, thus diminishing faculty support for student demands. The only formal indication of the faculty's attitude toward students came on May 6, 1972, when Stanley Cavell and Everett Mendelsohn together proposed to restore automatic Staff Tuition Scholarships to Teaching Fellows. The motion was defeated.

CONCLUSION (A NOTE ON STUDENT POLITICS AND EDUCATIONAL REFORM AND SOME PROGNOSTICATIONS) In the aftermath of campus unrest, there has been much talk of needed educational reforms. The most common complaint has been that the size and impersonality of the university, coupled with an often absent and overly professionalized faculty, have cut students adrift from adult control. Implicit in this is the notion that lack of supportive contact with faculty renders young people available for mobilization into radical movements. Renewed attention to undergraduate teaching, it is argued, might diminish the level of political unrest in colleges and universities.

No research evidence of which I am aware supports this assertion. A consistent finding is that no association exists between students' feelings about their education and their political beliefs. This was true of Harvard students in 1969, and it is again true in 1972. More remarkable, perhaps, is that the changes in the political climate at Harvard between 1969 and 1972 have had no effect on faculty-student contact or on students' satisfaction with their education. In 1969, 82 percent agreed that "Harvard education is very valuable"; 78 percent do now. Equally high proportions in 1969 and 1972 were friendly with one or more faculty members, spoke regularly with their professors outside of class, and felt that faculty were concerned with personal problems of students. The results of the two surveys are summarized below.

	1969	1972
Percent agreeing that "a Harvard education is very valuable"	82	78
Percent who are friendly with one or more faculty members	78	73
Percent who talk with faculty outside of class once a week or more	76	75
Percent saying that junior (nontenured) faculty are concerned with personal *problems of students*	80	77
Percent saying that senior (tenured) faculty are concerned with personal *problems of students*	48	50

The absence of an association between political beliefs and faculty-student relationships, and the stability of the latter over time, suggest that the kind of faculty and students recruited to Harvard—which have changed little since 1969—rather than labile political currents determine how much contact students have with their instructors and how satisfied they are with it. Educational reforms that attempt to promote intimacy between faculty and students are thus inappropriate as ad hoc responses to political unrest on college campuses. This is not to say that such reforms are undesirable or unnecessary for other reasons, but their impact on the political climate of colleges and universities is likely to be nil.

Administrative reform is a different matter. Depending on one's point of view, there was considerably more flexibility—or lenience—in Harvard's reaction to political protest after the lesson of April 1969. It will be remembered that the decision to call the police then was made primarily by President Pusey in the belief that Harvard had to "hold the line" against student radicals. (See Eichel et al, 1970, pp. 115–117.) Various deans were consulted, but no attempt was made to co-opt more moderate student or faculty elements. Beginning in the fall of 1969, the Committee on Rights and Responsibilities, and later the Bok administration, acted with an eye toward the political consequences of their decisions. Some students, most often SDS militants, were dealt with severely, whereas others, especially blacks and women, got off more easily. To be sure, there was some reaction to the pattern of selective discipline, but it came only in June of 1972. Whatever the intention, the effect of this pattern was to isolate the most extreme of the activists. The bulk of Harvard students were sympathetic to the demands of the blacks but repulsed by the destructiveness of the very radical fringe; amnesty for the latter could never become an issue.

If the above analysis is correct, there is little chance of another spring like 1969 at Harvard. It is true that the political views of Harvard students are now as radical or more radical than three years ago; we have not come the full circle. But the Left has splintered and may further disintegrate, depending on the outcome of the 1972 elections; protest that unites all factions is unlikely. More important, administrators have begun to respond politically— though they rarely admit it—to political demands of students; hence the blunders of three years ago are rarely repeated. The leftism of Harvard students reflects their disaffection with United States society in general and with the Vietnam War in particular. There is little that could be done about it other than to recruit an entirely different kind of student body, which Harvard is not about to do. One may therefore expect a continued high level of political activity at Harvard because of student frustrations, but one may also expect that demands will be met with negotiation and strategic compromise rather than confrontation.

References

"Admissions Policy: From Dollars to Doughnuts," *Crimson*, Jan. 27, 1971, p. 1.

"Blacks Leave Mass Hall After a Week," *Crimson*, April 27, 1972, p. 1.

"Committee on University Relations with Corporate Enterprises," *Harvard University Gazette*, March 5, 1971.

"CRR Rules not to Require Gulf Protesters' Withdrawal," *Crimson*, June 12, 1972, p. 1.

Eichel, Lawrence E., Kenneth W. Jost, Robert D. Luskin, and Richard M. Neustadt: *The Harvard Strike,* Houghton Mifflin Company, Boston, 1970.

Epps, Garrett: "Parting Shot," *Crimson,* Feb. 12, 1972, p. 2.

Epps, Garrett: "Forum Debate Centers on IQ Article," *Crimson,* Nov. 15, 1971, p. 1.

Frazier, Mark C.: "Freshman Class Survey Shows Decreasing Activism," *Crimson,* Feb. 13, 1971, p. 1.

Herrnstein, Richard: "I.Q.," *Atlantic Monthly,* September 1971, pp. 43–64.

Hernstein, Richard: "Intelligence/Heredity," *Crimson,* Dec. 8, 1971, p. 2.

Kelman, Steven: *Push Comes to Shove,* Houghton Mifflin Company, Boston, 1970.

Kinsley, Michael: "Daniel Boone on Campus," *New York Times,* Feb. 27, 1971, p. 27.

Landau, David: "Is PL Killing SDS?" *Crimson,* March 8, 1971, p. 1.

Landau, David: "CFIA Trashing: Marching With the Attica Brigade," *Crimson,* April 19, 1972, p. 1.

Lukas, Anthony: "Dissent at Harvard Reverts from College to Antiwar Protests," *New York Times,* May 20, 1970, p. 58.

Meyer, Marshall W.: "Harvard Students in the Midst of Crisis," *Sociology of Education,* vol. 44, pp. 245–269, Summer 1971.

Meyer, Marshall W.: "Harvard Students in the Midst of Crisis: A Note on the Sources of Leftism," *Sociology of Education,* vol. 46, Winter 1973.

"Old Excitement Is Missing at McCarthy's Conference," *Crimson,* Feb. 23, 1971, p. 1.

"The Price of 1970," *Crimson,* April 19, 1972, p. 2.

Reinhold, Robert: "Pusey Calls Revolutionaries 'Deluded'," *New York Times,* June 16, 1971*a*, p. 29.

Reinhold, Robert: "New Leader's Vigor Calms Harvard," *New York Times,* Nov. 29, 1971*b*, p. 35.

Reston, James: "Cambridge, Mass.: The Changing Campus Mood," *New York Times,* June 12, 1970, p. 38.

"The Riot's Context," *Crimson,* April 18, 1970, p. 2.

Shapiro, Peter: "Epps Links Herrnstein to SDS Convention," *Crimson,* March 11, 1972, p. 1.

"Six Dunster Faculty Members Challenge Herrnstein Petition," *Crimson,* Dec. 6, 1971, p. 1.

Sternhell, Carol R.: "CRR Votes No Punishment for All Students Charged with Harrassing Dean May," *Crimson,* Feb. 7, 1970, p. 1.

"Street Fighters," *Crimson,* April 17, 1970, p. 2.

"Teaching Fellows' Unions and Spring Events at Harvard," *Upstart,* special issue, no. 4, Cambridge, Mass., April 1972.

Todd, Richard: "Voices of Harvard '70—," *New York Times Magazine,* June 7, 1970, pp. 28, 54–56.

"Universities in Trouble," *Crimson,* Sept. 25, 1969, p. 2.

Weltzer, James: letter to the editor, *Crimson,* March 29, 1972, p. 2.

7. Change despite Turmoil at MIT

by Benson Snyder

At dawn on Thursday, November 7, 1969, some 320 students from the Massachusetts Institute of Technology, students from other area schools, some nonstudents, and three or four faculty members from MIT marched in a cold drizzle three blocks to the west of campus. On Webster Street they formed a tight, chanting picket line blocking the entrance to one of the Draper Laboratories. This was to be the climax of the "November action." MIT students as well as young people from the Boston area had been protesting by rallies, marches, mock trials since Monday, November 4, the institute's involvement in military research. The Draper Laboratory was their prime target, specifically for its contract to produce high-accuracy guidance systems for the Poseidon (a submarine-launched missile intended to be a Multiple Independent Re-entry Vehicle, or MIRV). This same Draper-produced system helped put the Apollo's astronauts on the moon.

Despite two hours of sometimes desperate pleading by a small group of faculty, students, and deans, the protesters refused to open up their picket line and let the day shift enter or the night shift leave. Cambridge authorities (who had jurisdiction) called in the riot police at 9 A.M. Slightly over 200 police marched at half step across the width of and down Webster Street. The pickets retreated slowly before this phalanx, shouting obscenities and slogans at the helmeted, plexiglass-visored men. The street was cleared in less than half an hour. There were 10 minor injuries, all released from hospital emergency wards by early afternoon. One protester was arrested, but charges were dropped the following day. In terms of arrests or injuries, the toll was small, as such confrontations go; but the day had inflicted deep psychic wounds.

Half an hour after this police action, some 40 of the faculty, students, and administrators who had been involved since dawn trying to avoid or minimize the confrontation in the streets came together in a large campus classroom to assess the event. We were members of advisory groups of faculty, students, and administrators. One of our assignments had been to consult with the president and others on the appropriate responses to the dissent.

We stood around in clusters, drying out and drinking hot coffee, and began to reconstruct the morning's actions. We were upset; some were close to tears; others were afraid or angry. These tensions, which underlay the rational discussion, showed through in sudden laughter, in angry disagreements over the accuracy of relatively minor details. Fatigue was evident on every face. The long efforts to first talk about the issues with the November action group and then fend off their threatened violence meant that we had had only a few hours' sleep in the preceding three days.

Out of the crisis talk, the discussion took a surprising turn. One professor began to seriously engage the question of how we had come to this point. A student asked what this told us about the nature of the modern university. A dean raised two questions: What were reliable processes for change? How could we reach consensus on what changes were in order? A graduate student insistently pursued technology's probable impact on man. Did technology have to dehumanize us, he kept asking. He didn't think so. Some of his classmates called him "pig," even as he talked out his still tentative thoughts.

A number of models of the university and of education emerged in the discussion. They ranged from simple to complex—from essentially educational notions to political ones. There were faculty members who held that their academic disciplines defined the appropriate questions for study, for research. They said the university's main function was the care and support of the discipline's representative on campus, that is, the academic department. There were students and a few faculty who said that they, rather than the discipline or the department, should define their own questions. The university did not deserve their loyalty unless it sustained their search for answers to the questions they had posed. The group that morning began to recognize that its members held dramatically divergent assumptions about the university. Further, most of us saw that these assumptions led to very different readings of the "proper" response to confrontation, to change, to governance, to grading, and to education.

The discussion became more specific when it shifted to the president's handling of the immediate threat. It was generally applauded. His use of humor at a crucial point in a faculty meeting the day before, for example, was approved by most, though a few had been put off by it. This smaller group was suspicious of the president, it seemed to me, precisely because he was so effective as a leader. Their tendency that day, because of its latent and overt tensions, was to look for the leader who, like a high-wire acrobat, would do wild gyrations in the air without a net below. During the performance they sat as spectators privately assessing his ability to balance and perform. This was a special brand of scapegoating, relying as it did so heavily on one person's skill, and ignoring as it did the inherent complexity and interrelatedness of the unfolding events.

To hear the talk that day, all the institution's efforts at change were suspended on his balance arm. Neither time nor serious thought was likely to be focused that morning on developing institutional and interpersonal processes for change that did not rely for their effectiveness on individuals inhabiting particular roles: the role of president, of provost, of dean, of professor, or of student. The danger, that morning, was that most were ignoring the context and focusing on one actor at stage center: the university on the president, the November action group on their leader. This situation made it simple for most everyone to label issues instead of comprehending them.

A high wire is not the place for thinking about long-term consequences. The premium up there is on the next step, not on conceptualizing the crisis. This context was not set by the president, but by the nature of confrontation politics, by the changes in the world around us. A most serious casualty was time for reflection. So these events had a profound impact on the university.

Several major strands of change can be described. The first, developing over the past 30 years, is the major shift in the context and the form of engineering and science education. As our knowledge has increased at an exponential rate, most faculty have responded by packing more and more content into the same number of lectures. The demands on the students' ability to deal with complexity, with abstract concepts have also escalated. This expansion of the fields would have presented serious problems for higher education even without the attendant political and social changes which have occurred during the same period.

The second strand developed from the first. The experience of growing up in a university 30 years ago was different from what it is today. The students themselves have changed. Even though they physically mature earlier, they are far more uncertain about playing the success game and ask with more urgency than before whether the degree really matters. They question, with bitterness, our present course. They are children of the apocalypse. Far more values are fighting for recognition than in the period before World War II. The proscience mood has shifted to antiscience. Consumerism, for the present, replaces technology, and a concern for the environment is coupled with a reaction against the machine. The student's definition of excellence is often made in the context of a turbulence almost unknown to the student three decades ago.

And a third strand grows from the second. We are in a world today where political goals are more furiously challenged than in the recent past. Both faculty and students are fiercely divided on a number of issues—that is, doubts about the United States' role in Southeast Asia and, beyond that, doubts about the United States' ability to run its own internal affairs. All these strands have been present on most campuses and were certainly part of the growing crises at MIT three years ago. Research at MIT, begun 10 years before, suddenly became the subject of simplified indictments by an angry and impatient group who held that the research itself was evil.

Such challenge split the academic community at many universities and has led to civil conflict both on and off campus. MIT was, as a matter of fact, heavily involved in government contracts for research and had maintained its deep ties with industry for a century. The demonstration outside the Draper Laboratory clearly was an expression of concern over this circumstance. Such conflicts, such divergence raised serious internal questions for the institution. It was wholly proper that MIT should examine its relationships to government and industry funding in the light of its educational commitments. The Pounds Panel, appointed by the president more than eight months before the November action, had done just that. However, the situation was inherently unstable for several reasons. First, there was not general consensus internally on the impact of the source of funds on educational or research activity. Second, a situation developed where the apparently excluded norms would inevitably demand recognition.

There were a number of debates raging before, during, and after the November 1969 confrontation. Two particular debates arose internally: one was primarily political and was directly related to the war in Vietnam; the other was educational and related to the role of science and engineering in public policy on a national level. It is crucial to distinguish between these two. While related, they are separable issues. Another crucial issue surfaced during this period. Many faculty and even more students asked who should decide what is to be considered relevant for study and research in a rapidly changing world. Who should define the terms of reference for that judgment? In intensely personal terms, primarily the students were asking how they could know their own worth as individuals. This was more than simply an assertion that they should do their "own thing."

ENHANCING COMMUNICA- TIONS In response to the November crisis, a number of new procedures did emerge, all directed at supporting a quality of communication where rational language would find some chance of being used and being heard, where serious issues could be engaged. For example, three days before the confrontations, a group of students had set up a communications center that sought out rumors and facts, sifted them, discriminated one from the other, and disseminated accurate information on what was going on day and night during the entire week. The immediate effect of this enterprise was to reinforce reason and subvert the rumors and the slogans, irrespective of their source. This constituted a major defense of language and thus of the university.

Another innovation of the period was the formation of a group of faculty (one from each department and not a member of a canonical few) and a group of students (asked to join because of their leadership in a variety of activities) to constantly communicate with administrators.[1] Participants basically spoke for themselves. Most were not bound or blinded by their view of their constituencies. They met frequently and for hours at a time with senior administrators and with department heads and subjected all perspectives of the crisis to a continuous review.

---

[1] Most of the administration and many among the faculty and the students spent much energy and effort dealing with the situation. All this activity took resources away from other tasks, preempting most other priorities.

At MIT now, there has been time for reflection and for examining the issues raised by the events of November 1969. Three themes emerge. First, the educational consequences of gradual versus sudden reform. Second, dehumanization, which leads to the use of reason without humility and thus to irrationality in discourse. Third, the need for new processes, new modes of education, and their probable effects on administrators, faculty, and students.

Underlying problems preceded the current unrest and have been partially responsible for its development. Many universities were unprepared for unrest or confrontation in the 1960s. Most universities, while physically surviving the immediate threat, had been sapped of energy; their ability to move ahead was largely spent. Their vulnerability may reflect a deficiency in their response to stress and change. Grown fat on expanding annual growth rates, the organizational corpus had become sluggish. There are historical precedents: The University of Córdoba and the University of Bologna in the fifteenth century are two early examples of open, lively universities that within a few decades drastically declined. Even then, their budgets played a role in their vulnerability.

As the demands on the faculty's time and attention increased dramatically over the past 15 years, the numbers of students in higher education went from 3 million to 7.5 million. Distraction became institutionalized. One professor at MIT shifted his schedule to working nights, where his interaction was with the employees who cleaned the halls and those students who, like the professor, had made a similar switch from day to night. At many universities, the faculty came to rely more and more on teaching assistants to protect them from the many undergraduates clamoring for their attention. Both responses on the personal level may have saved the professor's sanity and ability to work, but on the institutional level the normal channels of communication were severely strained.

As a counterpoint to crisis, MIT has been reforming for a century. As courses or curriculum became no longer relevant, they were dropped, and new ones emerged. Often the subject titles remained constant while the content of the courses underwent major and rapid revision. In 1971, the required freshman calculus shifted from the traditional sequence of lectures, recitation, and exams to self-paced mastery of six "modules" each semester. Quizzes can be taken whenever the student feels ready and repeated until the modules have been mastered. Civil engineering and architecture are dramatic recent examples of curriculum-content revision. Drops in the enrollment in these courses since 1870 typically have been followed within a year or two by shifts in the content of the courses. With the introduction of a new curriculum, the enrollment then characteristically increased. This is evidence that the students voted with their feet, and the faculty (and thus the curriculum) responded. The students, of course, were not the only cause for change. Most faculty have been at the edge of their field and themselves have been actively engaged in redefining their disciplines. The "half-life" of a course in 1900 was 20 years; today, for some, it is less than 5. This is now our educational context.

The classroom experience for most students in 1940 provided the setting for mastering a far more proscribed, circumspect, and stable curriculum. Even as students came to know their faculty and their peers as people, the ordering of these students' and their faculty's intellectual life (as reflected in the tightly proscribed formal curriculum) served, in itself, supportive as well as educational functions. Students in the then required mechanical drawing or machine shop worked and talked together throughout a semester in part because their assignments were not overwhelming in intellectual or time demands. Students, therefore, had time to come to know each other in the classroom in ways impossible for 300 students in a lecture course or in the competitive climate of the physics or mathematics recitation section of the early 1960s.

For students living in dormitories 30 years ago, there were informal "helping resources." The janitors knew the times and days the examinations were given in physics or in math and waited for their students to return from "the scene of battle." They had been like corpsmen tending the injured with compassionate kidding. The student, diminished by failure, would be chided by the janitor on science's inability to stop the setting of the sun. Today, such help has become more sophisticated but also further removed in time and place from "the battlefield." The student in most instances must make a decision to talk about his pain with any one of a number of sensitive members of the "helping" groups.

The academic disciplines themselves were more circumscribed in 1940, and the rate of change was presumed slow enough to keep a faculty member from intellectual obsolescence during the time of his tenure. Ironically, however, it was largely during this period that the conditions were set that 15 years later became the institutional basis for the even more intense competition among the students for grades and among the younger faculty for tenure. Cognitive obsolescence suddenly became a fact of academic life. In this past year, we have begun to examine the educational and financial implications of retirement at 60 or even 55.

World War II brought with it the rapid growth of large laboratories serving the public interest: the Radiation Laboratory, collaboration on the Manhattan Project—from which a number of highly effective faculty members were recruited. The institute in effect became a national institution in the process. Overhead from contracts from federal grants (most, but not all, bore a close relationship to the academic disciplines) provided high-risk capital and gave impetus and funds for new directions. The fiscal officers were entrepreneurs, and the central administration shifted its role in this same direction as the new context emerged.

Beginning in 1957, Sputnik and the space age altered the orbits of many universities and raised the career aspirations of high school students and the fiscal appropriations of congressional committees for science education and research. MIT—and in particular, the Instrumentation Laboratory—also rode high.

By the early 1960s, MIT had clearly become an international as well as national leader in the education of engineers and scientists. Norbert Wiener's cybernetics profoundly influenced the curriculum of the electrical engineering department. Enrollment tripled over a 10-year period, and the courses offered in 1965 were significantly different from those in the catalog five years before. The computer has had a major impact on the department and the discipline. In 1962 the mechanical engineering department developed laboratories that involved student-initiated projects, and six years later the civil engineering department founded the Urban Systems Laboratory—both examples of new approaches to education that derived from radically different definitions of these fields. The physics department during this period shifted its previous emphasis on providing "service" and became more heavily engaged in research and graduate education.

While all this was occurring in the academic disciplines and in the laboratories, the curriculum for the first two years remained essentially unchanged from 1950 to 1960. First- and second-year students had few choices. All freshmen took the same basic subjects in math, in physics, in chemistry, in the humanities.[2]

---

[2] An important exception would be the changes in the content and form of presentation of the introductory physics courses, but these and other efforts were directed at the content of courses rather than at the context of the entire curriculum.

A hidden curriculum developed in which students learned early, as a matter of sheer survival, to selectively neglect a significant amount of what they were asked to master.[3] There was the risk during this period that the competition for highest competence would become the goal of the students' education and would be achieved for many at the expense of their creativity. With the fields developing so fast, the meaning of competence itself was constantly subject to revision. The risk of obsolescence became increasingly high for faculty and students. The irony is that the institution was in this precarious position in part because it had come to do so very well the job of training a decade of professionals. The forms of examination and the reward structures suitable for immediate survival were no longer certain to be even useful, let alone helpful, for the students' future.

These problems and their solutions have a life separate from the strand of events leading up to and away from the November action. Major changes in the curriculum of the first two years began five years ago. These gradual changes were the result of much close work in and out of academic committees, of votes at faculty meetings, of reallocation of the provost's resources. Yet the diversity that now faces the students presents new problems. The janitors, their numbers greatly reduced, their role redefined, no longer function directly as helpers. A wider range of helping resources has developed. Faculty advisers, deans, and psychiatrists have taken the janitors' place.

RECENT INNOVATIONS Now the students have pass-fail in their first year. The intent of this change from letter grades to evaluation forms was to increase the feedback to the student on his understanding of the content of his course, while diminishing the possible negative effects of competition. (In a recent study, two-thirds of the pass-fail evaluation forms were found to contain more information for the students on their progress than had been conveyed by letter grades.)

Many departments are currently undergoing the kind of reevaluation that began in the department of electrical engineering 15 years ago. Faculty and students from planning and architecture were involved in a summer study last year. They developed a new curriculum which emphasized the relationship between the physical and the human environment and on finding meaningful ways to

---

[3] Benson R. Snyder, *The Hidden Curriculum,* Alfred A. Knopf, Inc., New York, January 1971, 203 pp.

teach this to students. A coherent program for black and other minority students was started in 1968. It has begun to open up the MIT educational experience to many who, for varied reasons, had no significant presence in the past. The number of black students has gone from 10 to over 200 in four years. Of the entering class last year, 10 percent were women, compared to 4 percent a decade ago. Obviously, these are only headlines and do not deal with either the successes or failures inherent in such complex educational efforts.

In September 1961 the Committee on Curriculum Content Planning was appointed by the president. This group of 12 distinguished faculty in effect went back to school. Its members read the undergraduate texts, sat in on lectures, did problem sets for many of the courses. Their final report, in the form of a Socratic dialogue, presented the faculty with an educational problem on a different, deeper level than in the past. Their report focused primarily on content but did not ignore context. Faculty response was mixed.

But this group did create an awareness of issues, even though some of its important recommendations were put on the shelf. One outcome of this extensive report was the creation of the position of a professor of undergraduate planning, a constructive though controversial post. The suggestion for this post was in part motivated by an effort at political compromise to ensure that at least some of the curriculum-content planning would be accepted by the faculty at large.

In 1963 an engineering professor began quietly improving the education of the students' first two years. First collaborating with the dean for student affairs, he strengthened the counseling and advising for the freshmen. Three years later, together with the provost, the undergraduate planning professor, and several others, he gave direction and support to educational innovation. This group monitored and husbanded the programs like growing plants. While the senior faculty committee (on educational policy) approved essentially all educational experiments that involved less than 10 percent of the students, the more informal group, augmented at times by others, worked hard to make the resources available for incremental educational change. It has been important to the process that this same professor served as chairman of the Task Force on Educational Opportunity, which developed, with full involvement of students, a program for blacks and other minorities that was meaningful to them and to the institute.

By 1965 the Committee on Academic Performance had begun to move away from its reliance on rigid rules for disqualification of students to their counseled withdrawal when in academic difficulty. Two years later the committee had developed a process which allowed faculty and students far more information than was previously available about each other's position, and, as a result, itself had a more reliable basis for deciding on academic withdrawal. This reform, occurring over three years, attests to the power of a shift in consensus in a faculty committee.

During this same period, the policy for allocating financial aid to students underwent a major shift. Scholarships were no longer linked directly to a student's grade-point average. Once a student was admitted, he was assured of financial support in the form either of scholarship, loan, or work. The importance of this change needs to be emphasized, for, in the past, some of the competition in the classroom has been, in the eyes of students, the result of a direct connection between scholarship support and grade-point average. This connection contributed to a sense of shame and much anxiety, among both average and outstanding students. Looking back at this and other experiences, it appears that a generalized dehumanization of the educational experience slowly increased during the preceding decade. The student and the professor had both come to judge intellectual and even personal worth by a grade-point average carried to the second decimal point. Many participants had limited their frames of reference. This is less the case today.

Five years ago no students were members of faculty committees. The faculty committees moved through their agendas largely uninformed by input from the students whom they presumably were trying to serve. In 1966 several students critically examined the grading system, joined the Student Committee on Educational Policy, and then brought their questions to the Faculty Committee on Educational Policy. Within a matter of months there were joint meetings between the student and faculty committees. The meetings were fruitful, and the students were asked to stay on for the rest of the year. Early the following fall, the students were given the vote by the faculty membership and thus became full working members of the group.

Those students initially had a tenuous connection with their own constituency. They had been deeply concerned about education at the institute and had done their homework on MIT's education. As a result of having become informed, they became an integral part of the process.

A meeting of elected representatives speaking for constituencies may be, in practice, an unreliable procedure for sound educational change. The hazard is greatest if the electorate has not taken the time to adequately inform itself about the issues at hand. Slogans are no substitute for subtlety. It has been my experience over these past few years that there is more chance that individuals on a task force, in contrast to members of a constituent assembly, will be judged by their colleagues, whether student or faculty, on their power to illuminate a question and to answer it insightfully. A constituent assembly, by its nature, focuses more on the size of the back-home vote. A student who significantly affected the Committee on Educational Policy was on a faculty-student task force one year later. The faculty members of this group were talking about grades and ignored his input for the better part of the afternoon. However, he kept asking questions which they could not answer. By 5 P.M., they were listening attentively to his thoughtful answers to what by then had become their questions.

As might be expected, this period of relatively calm innovation based on expanding communication between faculty and students, on more effective and more rapid feedback on educational issues, and on reallocating both human and financial resources was almost eclipsed during the highly visible, highly dramatic events of November 1969 and their bitter aftermath of disciplinary hearings and suspensions.

Universities, we know, are fragile institutions. At MIT for a time, the slow progress that had been achieved was threatened. Language was also a casualty in the back streets of Cambridge. Fear, distrust, polarization all but precluded rational discourse. Slogans, inflated and imprecise, obscured subtle distinctions and forced the most gross generalizations. Moreover, the fact that police were finally called in (though not at the institute's instigation) signaled at least a partial failure of procedures and processes for conflict resolution. Developed for earlier decades, these procedures were not designed to cope with such confrontation without, at the same time, posing a grave threat to the university's ability to remain open to divergent ideas.

The threat has become useful in a wider range of situations — as smaller groups have greater power to hurt their neighbors. At MIT this meant that "the situation" was subject to constant revision by all participants. Universities were neither intended nor designed to deal with such a shift in rules, with such disparity in so short a time. In this country, in the last half century, most universities have defended themselves against the majority and against "know-nothing Luddities" and not against minorities within.

In the face of the polarization and distrust, new processes of communication and even decision making were developed at MIT within a few weeks that brought our situation into sharper focus. Our interventions served us well in crises. Differences in assumptions about MIT's role could at least be related to specific prescriptions and plans for action by almost all participants.

DEHUMAN-IZATION Dehumanization, a basic threat that faced us, can come from the classroom as well as from confrontation. In both, the explicit intent may be to "humanize" the individual.

It is more than ironic that an educational encounter can dehumanize students, depersonalize them by routinized and bureaucratic procedures. A grading system linked to certification can become a wall between professor and student, constructed from the professor's scorn and the student's shame. Such walls can lead one individual to regard the other as an object to be manipulated or dealt with as instrumentally as by confrontation politics. This only suggests that psychological exploitation in the classroom is more subtle than that practiced in the streets and usually extends over a far longer time.

Our educational ideal had been the student working closely with his professor in a real—not contrived—shared experience in which they could come to know the expectations and assumptions each held about the other. Many have worked hard on dealing with this issue in the education at MIT. Some of the changes that occurred in the late 1960s and early 1970s have been headlined. Our education worked best where this had been or continued to be possible (in project laboratories, for example). The institute needed then, as now, more opportunities for faculty and students to appreciate the complexity of their classroom education. The danger of dehumanization was highest where we failed to develop rapid and reliable educational interaction between students and faculty.

Even before November 1969, the dehumanization had begun in earnest. One student leader in the November events who had seriously talked with me about MIT's education called me "pig" as he passed me in the halls two months later. This was an important learning experience for a physician turned dean. My role, or so it seemed, had stereotyped me.

The dehumanization took some unexpected forms. During the first of several November demonstrations, rallies, and actions, a crowd of about 500 had begun to move on a particular building to hold a "trial" there of some professors for their "crimes against the people." Slogans and chants amplified by bullhorns filled the air. As the crowd moved across the open plaza toward the portico, a voice drowning out their shouts and easily heard a half mile away began to read a court injunction prohibiting their access. Two special, finely tuned, and powerful loudspeakers had been installed quietly on the roof the night before. The crowd hesitated; then, like the tide turning, slowly receded to the street. Words again were ripped from familiar context and amplified. The speaker's accountability was lost even while the words themselves took on a new power to persuade, rather than inform. The voices, both in the street and from the roof, were anonymous.

During this period the advisory groups, the committee structure, the faculty meetings themselves, and the communications center contributed to maintaining rational discourse and meaningful human contact, but at some cost in time. What troubled me then was the move toward modes of communication that excluded so much of the subtlety, the caring that I consider crucial for an educational experience. Grossly simplified issues that personally involved me, for example, were redefined without my being asked where I stood with respect to them. Someone else assumed that he knew with certainty my motivation and my thoughts, so the problem became not education, or even politics per se, but the labeling of an issue, of a feeling, of an interaction by those who sought advantage, not understanding, by the label they assigned. An angry militant leader or an equally angry dean could create a setting where the righteousness of rage simplified all situations.

Throughout this period, the president presided at faculty meetings that grew in attendance from 60 to 600. The tension increased geometrically, and labeling became the order of the day. As noted, humor served to return some balance. Throughout the period the senior administration had to take time away from other issues. Short- and long-term financial, educational, and organizational planning was set back some by the interruptions of the moment. Those programs that did develop—several education experiments for example—went ahead in spite of, not because of, the protests.

The rate of educational and institutional change was, in sum, slowed down rather than accelerated by the turmoil. Dehumanization increased to the point where the faculty and students could scarcely communicate effectively with one another. However, significant reforms had been made in the past few years (freshman pass-fail, change in financial aid, developing programs for admitting minority students).

CHANGE DESPITE TURMOIL How did effective educational and institutional change come about against this background of mounting turmoil? Those reforms which were directed at the fundamental reward structure, at reducing classroom confrontation—like pass-fail grading—began before the political crisis and have continued to be seriously considered. The change in awarding financial aid has had some effect on reducing academic competition among the undergraduates. The increase in the number of courses and the lessening of prerequisites have opened up the whole curriculum. Beyond these immediate gains, the time and effort expended in effecting these reforms have educated both faculty and students to the new conditions facing us. Most important, the process of making these changes has provided reasonably effective feedback on what works and what doesn't work.

Educational experiments that dealt with relatively superficial educational issues (reducing a recitation section from 20 to 10) are passing from the current scene. They consumed both energy and time to almost no avail. I am tempted to include the recent political turmoil as a special case in this class of superficial educational reforms. Its conceptualization as much as its rhetoric was a superficial solution to the need to link technology to an understanding of its consequences. Educational and political restructuring that does not receive serious and informed attention is very likely to leave behind a wake of disillusionment, depression, and distrust that will seriously compromise the institutions' ability to make those major changes needed next year or 10 years from now. Dehumanization can come from confrontation politics, trivial educational experimentation, or labeling a complex interaction in simple terms. All three situations affect the conditions for reading accurately the cues from one's professor or one's student. The confusion that may result can have catastrophic consequences for a university.

I have discussed the threat to one university of confrontation — the threat inherent in simple words or simple acts. There is a larger issue. In order to survive, the university must deal with the current and increasing level of distraction and resulting helplessness. The student and the faculty member must be able to comprehend his situation, to understand his context without being overwhelmed by helplessness.

At MIT we are questioning the effectiveness of many roles and are restructuring some. The new president, for example, will have his deputy in the chancellor; both will sit as members of the corporation. Information on the budget and on the institute's hiring practices (from hourly employees to professors) is far more available today than even a year ago. Thus accountability at all levels has become both more possible and more public, a fundamental break from the past. We are developing more navigational aids than were available in the past to help us fix our line of position. With the rapid rate of change, we must find even more accurate and reliable ways to determine the longer-term effects of today's solutions. These must be built into the day-to-day workings of the institute.

I began with an episode of confrontation. The dissenting act was above all else a communication directed at that often thin and tenuous consensus which, though strained, sustained the university. The web of mutual expectations that holds an academic community together is fragile but forms the basis for the regulation of that society. Without these connections the university, at least as we have come to know it, is lost. We have so far retained, I think, what the University of Córdoba lost in 1492. Within 20 years that open institution no longer had the freedom to pursue most questions because of pressures to conform to an externally defined definition of truth. The university's consensus on this point was shattered from outside. The present threat comes from both within and without.

Dissent does strain the regulation of educational systems when that dissent becomes a basic threat to that very consensus which holds the institution together. (The energy expended in dealing with *this* issue will inevitably be drawn from other central educational problems.) There is an equal danger that the consensus is achieved by simplifying issues, dehumanizing the participants by a kind of psycho-social lobotomy.

When an individual proclaims agreement on ends but communicates, by his or her acts, contempt for that consensus which holds that community together, the deceit implicit in the act poses a special threat. Many students and faculty read the communication for what it is not—simply a dissenting opinion. Rather, the act becomes a challenge to that very consensus which the dissenter holds as evil, which the majority take for granted, and which makes the dissent possible. This signals a profound difference in apperceptive systems where no processes exist, on most campuses, to adequately acknowledge the difference. One institution made some headway but still has much to learn about this issue.

It was shortly after 1 P.M. on the day of the confrontation. The cold drizzle had become a downpour. A squad car was parked in front of the granite, neo-Roman entrance of MIT. Two officers were eating their lunch from bags when a student leader who had stood next to me in tears at dawn came up to their curbside window and asked them how they felt about the early-morning confrontation on Webster Street.

The police opened the rear door to let the student in out of the rain. They talked for almost an hour. They tried to make ends meet, the police said, on a salary only slightly more than a student's tuition, room, and board. How did the students get time to protest? Why didn't they appreciate that they had it made? Concrete concerns that centered on the cost of living in Cambridge were developed, fugue-like against the student's anger at a far-off war. The student feared that his present education, while raising his expected standard of living high above that of the two policemen, would trap him in a dangerously immoral system where the individual would be engulfed and where the education he had received would seal his doom. The police, meanwhile, worried about feeding and clothing their kids next week and envied the student's affluence. Neither police nor student saw the issues as trivial.

All three, I inferred from the student's later telling, were moved by their encounter. Some learning had occurred. Two policemen and a student were less prone to caricature each other as pigs or freaks. Scapegoating had been suspended for a brief period, but this private encounter made no headlines. This small event, in retrospect, signaled a slow return to reason and humanity. It is like the crisis which occurred with patients suffering from pneumonia in the days preceding penicillin. A slight drop in body temperature was followed in hours by marked improvement in the patient's breathing. When this occurred, the patient survived: a small sign with large consequences.

8. Michigan Muddles Through: Luck, Nimbleness, and Resilience in Crisis

by Zelda F. Gamson

I first came to the University of Michigan as an undergraduate in 1956, a reluctant transfer from the cozy discomforts of Antioch College. As a graduate student in 1958–59 and finally as a staff member, faculty wife, and citizen of Ann Arbor since 1962, I have been grumbling and complaining about the place for years. But underneath the complaints—a common pastime for many who still regard themselves as displaced persons from the two coasts—there is a reluctant attachment. For those of us who have been at the University of Michigan long enough to put in some roots, this enormous institution of 33,000 students *feels* like a small place. There is a peculiar sense of connectedness to other people at the university which we all tend to take for granted. Yet, in agreeing to do this essay, I did not want to accept these feelings. Somehow, I felt that if I could understand their sources, perhaps I might be better able to understand the crises and changes we had all witnessed and been a part of during the sixties.

To get some systematic data on events and groups at the university, I talked to many people. These people did not represent anything like a random sample. I chose them because they were obvious representatives of important formal positions or roles, because I knew them to be both experienced and observant about university affairs, or because someone else recommended them to me. Because I am a sociologist, I have tended to choose social scientists more than people in the humanities or in the sciences. I have probably spoken more to people in the middle of the political spectrum than to those at the extremes. Although I was careful to choose infor-

ACKNOWLEDGMENT: I wish to thank James Heffernan, graduate student in the Center for the Study of Higher Education, for his assistance in collecting statistics and checking facts for this paper.

173

mants with different organizational and ideological perspectives, I have skewed my selection toward those who have been active in university affairs, generally in accepted roles.[1]

We have become so accustomed to a high-intensity environment that what would have been called a "crisis" in earlier years came to be taken as the order of the day. I cannot recall a single year between 1965 and 1970 when a strike, a moratorium, or some version of a sit-in has not taken place at Michigan. Each day's paper raises some critical issue. Will the regents pass a proposed new judiciary plan? Will the Gay Liberation Front be allowed to hold a convention at the university? How will the departments implement a plan for the recruitment of more women? How will the university meet its commitment to have a 10 percent black enrollment? How will the administration and departments juggle their priorities in the face of decreasing federal and state support?

The turning point was 1965, the year of the first escalation of the Vietnam war. Soon after the bombing of North Vietnam began, a group of faculty members and students met to plan some protest action. Their original plan was to call a one-day strike — euphemistically called a "moratorium" on all university activities. Eventually the action turned into the first teach-in on the Vietnam war.[2] The teach-in caught on at campuses all over the country that year and has become a format for conferences on other issues. Antiwar actions since the first teach-in make even the original notion of a moratorium seem timid by comparison.[3] Since the first teach-in, many of the issues that have been raised at Michigan and elsewhere can be traced to animus against the war: antidraft and antiranking movements, demonstrations against certain outside recruiters, classified research, and ROTC.

The organizational skills and analyses of the University of Michigan's role in the larger society that developed out of the antiwar and

---

[1] A list of the persons with whom I talked is located at the end of this chapter.

[2] For a good documentary history of the Vietnam teach-in, see Louis Menashe and Ronald Radosh, *Teach-Ins: USA, Reports, Opinions, Documents* (1967).

[3] This discussion of the first teach-in is necessarily abbreviated. The reaction to the original plan for a moratorium was vigorously opposed by many administrators and faculty members at the university — who later strongly supported the less threatening teach-in format — and by Governor Romney and members of the State Legislature. A resolution was passed in the Legislature censuring the faculty members who were involved in planning the moratorium.

civil rights movements now have been transferred to more strictly intrauniversity issues centering around the role of students in decision making, social rules, and housing; to curricular issues; and to the recruitment and treatment of blacks and women. The initiative for these issues by and large has come from student groups in recent years and, most significantly, from legitimate groups such as the Student Government Council (SGC). Confrontation politics have not been abandoned by these groups; indeed, it has been the most effective way of riveting attention on issues that otherwise would have lain dormant. But after a galvanizing incident such as a sit-in, the style of dealing with issues has increasingly involved tough negotiation and committee work extending over many months and even years.

The teach-in on March 24, 1965, and subsequent events did not take place in a vacuum, for the University of Michigan and the town of Ann Arbor for a long time had provided fertile soil for political activity of an innovative sort. In the immediate postwar era, the new American breed of academic man nurtured and supported by federal research grants began to populate research centers and departments. Cosmopolitan and national in outlook, these men, especially those in the social sciences, were effective in groups and soon appeared on various university and departmental committees. They brought with them liberal politics and an open, adaptive view of the university. Most of them drew on a consciousness shaped by heightened political awareness during the Depression. They came in large numbers, developed friendship ties with some sympathetic colleagues already at the university, and for the most part remained at Michigan. They were early supporters of the civil rights movement; a young psychologist and his wife sold their house to a Negro family in the early fifties, producing a minor cause célèbre in what was then a small, conservative town. The early National Association for the Advancement of Colored People and Congress of Racial Equality (CORE) were populated by members of this group. Others moved into the Democratic party as faculty from an earlier time had not. Some made ties with the United Auto Workers; during the strikes after World War II, these men and their wives raised money for strike funds and union causes.

This original cadre was followed by younger men recruited during the fifties who had only dim memories of the Depression but had vivid responses to the cold war and McCarthyism. The firing in 1954 of two Michigan faculty members for refusing to testify before a subcommittee of the House Un-American Activities Committee came as a shock. The dismissals flew in the face of safeguards passed a few months earlier by the university senate to protect faculty members called before congressional committees. The recommendation of two faculty committees that Mark Nickerson, a tenured professor of pharmacology in the Medical School, be censured but retained on the staff was rejected by the university administration. Immediately following the disposition of these cases, a committee of the senate drew up more stringent guidelines for handling such cases in the future. Four years later, the American Association of University Professors (AAUP) censured the university for its actions.[4] There were few heroes in this episode, although some factions within the faculty, sickened and angry over the findings, strongly opposed the administration and soon began to organize an energetic liberal caucus.

By the late fifties the liberal faculty had changed the face of the university. Around the same time, the student body—relatively inert during the fifties—showed signs of the new activism that was beginning to stir students nationally. Antiwar groups emerged; students and faculty manned picket lines in front of Woolworth's as part of the nationwide boycott called by civil rights groups; students began going south to work in the civil rights movement. Most significant of all, a small group of bright, critical students found one another and began meeting informally. Kenneth and Elise Boulding ran weekly meetings on the peace movement; the philosopher Arnold Kaufman talked about new modes of political participation, out of which came the focus on "participatory democracy." Students in this group found jobs and office facilities in some parts of the university; they ran a noncredit seminar on conflict and civil rights that attracted some hundred students.

Out of these beginnings came the June 1962 meeting in Port Huron, Michigan, which brought together students from several different chapters of a group called Students for a Democratic Society. Michigan students issued the invitations to the Port Huron meeting and were the dominant group among the 70 attending. Tom Hayden, a 1961 graduate of Michigan and one of the initiators of the meeting, had spent the previous year in the South as an SDS representative working with the Student Non-violent Coordinating

---

[4] This discussion is based on a dissertation by Sam Ralph Snyder, "Academic Freedom at the University of Michigan, 1953–58" (1970).

Committee (SNCC). He had been an editor of the *Michigan Daily,* which for years has been a source of national liberal and radical leaders, and first attracted attention in a campaign it mounted against the dean of women. Working with Hayden were Dick Flacks, then a graduate student in social psychology, and Al Haber, the son of the man who became dean of Michigan's College of Literature, Science and the Arts (LSA) and a central figure during the sixties. The intellectual caliber and intense commitment of the early members of SDS led them to form close attachments with certain faculty members in the social sciences and philosophy. A number of them won fellowships and awards of various sorts. Undoubtedly many more could have gone into dazzling scholarly careers if they had chosen to remain in the academic world.

SDS took root at Michigan before the student movement was visible on the national scene. Some SDS members, especially females, lived in cooperative student houses, where they learned and taught the skills of collective living.[5] They influenced younger students who became active during the sixties in other political activities on a campus which seemed to produce a new political organization weekly. During the 1961–62 academic year, SDS emerged as a political party, VOICE, which ran candidates for Student Government Council. At its height, VOICE had a membership of at most 300, a minuscule proportion of the student body; and of these, perhaps there were 30 or 40 consistently active members.[6] Yet if one looks at each of the major issues which have surfaced in the last decade on the Michigan campus, one sees that in every case VOICE raised it at some earlier time through a demonstration or militant action which at the beginning attracted small groups of the faithful, through carefully reasoned position papers penned by VOICE intellectuals, or through campus elections and organizing among students, faculty members, and administrators. VOICE sponsored a rally on Vietnam in 1963. In 1964, VOICE presented a list of grievances that included the need for more emphasis on teaching, for

[5] The first student cooperative was the Michigan Socialist House, founded in 1932. The Inter-Cooperative Council was founded in 1944; by 1956, there were seven cooperative houses. In 1964–65, there were eight cooperatives with 172 students living in them. By 1970, there were 21 cooperatives, with about 500 members. (Source: Intercooperative Council.)

[6] VOICE disbanded in 1968 after a split in the chapter between those who advocated working on campus issues and those who emphasized national revolutionary actions; the latter group formed the nucleus for the Weathermen.

new student housing and better student facilities, for increased wages for student employees, and for greater student participation in decision making. In 1966, four years before a student-run bookstore was finally achieved at Michigan, VOICE agitated for a student bookstore. Corporate recruiting, university policy on classified research, ROTC, even the relatively tame matter of the language requirement were all issues initiated by VOICE.

VOICE and other dissenting students formed a critical mass of "protest-prone" types in an institution which provided all the right conditions for student dissent.[7] In the Astin study (1965) of freshmen who entered 248 colleges and universities in 1961, the beginning of the decade of activism, the University of Michigan was 1½ standard deviations above the mean for all schools on the selectivity of its undergraduates (Berkeley was about the same; Harvard was 10 points higher). As at other universities in the period we are examining, student quality at Michigan was consistently rising: the median SAT verbal score for freshmen entering the university in 1969 was 573; in 1961, it was 547. The math SAT median in 1969 was 615, compared to 588 in 1961. The percentage of students receiving undergraduate honors increased from 1965 to 1968. Grades have also been rising: in 1964 the overall grade-point average for undergraduates was 2.68; by 1969, the average rose to 2.87.[8]

Michigan students are drawn overwhelmingly from upper-middle-class families. Of the seniors in 1966 and 1967, 56 percent

[7] The notion of the protest-prone personality comes from Kenneth Keniston, "The Sources of Student Dissent," *Journal of Social Issues* (1967). A study of the kinds of students who participated in a series of protests at the University of Michigan in 1966–67 in general supports Keniston's observations (cf. Zelda Gamson, Gerald Gurin, and Jeffrey Goodman, "Activists, Moderates and Bystanders During a University Protest," 1967). A number of studies in the last three years have shown that the earlier research on student activists may have been limited to the early recruits in the student movement. As the movement has broadened in its appeal with the wider acceptance of countercultural values, there no longer seems to be a standard student activist type. More recent studies of the characteristics of dissenting students can be found in James W. Clarke and Joseph Egan, "Social and Political Dimensions of Campus Protest Activity" (n.d.); Riley Dunlap, "Radical and Conservative Student Activists: A Comparison of Family Backgrounds," *Pacific Sociological Review* (1970); and Roger Kahn and William J. Bowers, "The Social Context of the Rank-and-File Student Activist: A Test of Four Hypotheses," *Sociology of Education* (1970).

[8] These statistics come from the University of Michigan Evaluation and Examinations Office and the Office of the Registrar.

reported yearly family incomes of $15,000 or more; 54 percent of their fathers were college graduates; 64 percent came from metropolitan areas of 200,000 or more. The out-of-state enrollment at Michigan has always been high, although in recent years it has been tapering off, to slightly less than one-fourth of the Ann Arbor enrollment (out-of-state enrollment in the fifties was closer to one-third).

As freshmen in 1962 and 1963, Michigan students came to the university with moderately liberal attitudes, especially on questions having to do with civil liberties and civil rights. These attitudes, and others concerning foreign affairs and domestic liberalism, were accentuated by the time students became seniors. On other measures—religious liberalism, autonomy, impulse expression—these students who spent their four years at Michigan during the most intense period of activism showed dramatic increases.[9]

At the same time, as in American higher education generally, the university was amassing more students each year. In 1964, there were 26,000 graduates and undergraduates enrolled in the various colleges in Ann Arbor. By 1970, enrollment was up to 33,000, an increase of 26 percent.[10] In the College of Literature, Science and the Arts (LSA), where most undergraduates are concentrated and from which the largest majority of active students are drawn, the increase from 1964 to 1970 was 33 percent. Although enrollments have been leveling off, conditions in the existing buildings used for LSA classes have become hopelessly crowded and instructors have had to limit class size. The situation has become ridiculous. Students who do not register during the preceding term for certain popular and/or required courses find themselves closed out even before regular registration. Those lacking in foresight, energy, or know-how wander around dazed from table to table in the large registration hall at the beginning of the term trying to find enough open courses to fill their course cards.

[9] The data for this discussion are drawn from the Michigan Student Study conducted by Gerald Gurin of the Institute for Social Research. More than 1,400 students who entered the College of Literature, Science and the Arts in 1962 and 1963 were followed through to the senior year in a series of questionnaires and interviews. The findings reported here parallel the general conclusions of Kenneth Feldman and Theodore M. Newcomb, in *The Impact of College on Students* (1969).

[10] In 1969, 61 percent of the student body were undergraduates, a slight increase over 1964.

According to a 1971 report, the overall university student-faculty ratio was around 13 to 1 and average class size ran about 32 ("How Much . . . ," 1971). But these figures are deceptive. A breakdown by student levels gives a more accurate picture of the distribution of resources. In 1968, the direct instructional salary cost for each student credit hour was $16.51 for lower-division students and 1½ times more for upper-division students. Master's students cost approximately 3⅓ times more than lower-division students, doctoral students 7 times more.[11] In this situation, upperclassmen—particularly those in the departments with large numbers of concentrators—compete with graduate students to get into the small seminars with senior professors. Part of the slack is taken up by teaching fellows in the large undergraduate courses. In 1968, 53 percent of lower-division credit hours and 25 percent of upper-division credit hours were taught by teaching fellows (an increase of 7 percent and 5 percent respectively, over 1964).

Yet Michigan students, like most students, generally accept their professors. In the Michigan Student Study, reactions to such statements as "teachers are genuinely interested in the students," "teachers dislike spending time with students," and "the faculty is less interested in teaching than research" were quite uncomplaining—if not ecstatic, students were not highly critical of their teachers either. On questions having to do with organizational impersonalism, however, ordinary students were much more rebellious. For example, 69 percent of the seniors in 1966 and 1967 agreed that "the academic bureaucracy ignores the individual"; 58 percent endorsed the statement that "individual students [do not] have a voice in the regulations that affect them."

The dry statistics are given some life by a review of the major issues which have come up at Michigan in the past five years. Those issues which gained the widest student support concerned intrauniversity issues pertaining especially to student rights in nonacademic matters. The sequence of events has been remarkably consistent: VOICE or some other radical group raises an issue and agitates for militant action to force a change; the *Michigan*

[11] These figures are from the University of Michigan Office of Institutional Research report "Credit Hours, Instructional Cost and Faculty Activity Reports" (1968). I do not mean to imply here that these ratios are unusual. Data from Michigan State University for the same year show almost the same ratios of lower-division, upper-division, master's, and Ph.D. expenditures.

Daily[12] publicizes the issue and often supports some version of the radicals' position editorially; some legitimate, less militant group carries it to the wider student body; heightened activity and a sense of crisis mobilize the university community; faculty and administration groups meet day and night to work out a response; the response is offered and usually rejected by the active student groups; a militant action, such as a sit-in, a strike, or an invasion of a closed meeting follows; police may or may not be called; negotiation ensues, with intermittent action by the students; a settlement is worked out; faculty members and administrators breathe sighs of relief; the moderate students acknowledge some modest gain; and the radicals complain of sellout and cooptation.

THE EVENTS OF 1966–67 In the summer of 1966, the university administration responded to a subpoena from the House Un-American Activities Committee by turning over the names of 65 students and several faculty sponsors of radical groups on campus. When everyone returned that fall, all hell broke loose. The radicals issued an account of how the decision to release the names had been made and appealed to student and faculty groups for support. They also held a sit-in at the office of the vice-president for academic affairs. Several faculty and student groups issued rebukes to the administration for its handling of the matter. A struggle ensued between SGC and the Office of Student Affairs over a sit-in ban issued unilaterally by the vice president for student affairs and became generalized into a struggle over SGC's autonomy. At the same time, an unprecedented 10,000 students turned out for a referendum and voted 2 to 1 against the compilation of class ranks for selective service. SGC pressed the administration unsuccessfully to take the results of the referendum as binding. Independently of the students, a small group of faculty members drew up a pledge to submit only pass-fail grades if the compilation of class ranks was continued. Support was building among moderate students, including a number of fraternities and sororities, for SGC's struggle with the

---

[12] The *Michigan Daily* is the prizewinning student newspaper run completely by students. With assets of a quarter of a million dollars and its own press, the *Daily* is separately incorporated but under the ultimate authority of the regents of the university. Complaints about the *Daily*'s "biased reporting" have been voiced for years, but there has never been a successful challenge to its autonomy.

administration.[13] An extraordinary meeting of 4,000 people chaired by the president of the SGC voted to hold a nonviolent sit-in at the Administration Building during a lunch hour (in violation of the recently promulgated sit-in ban, which was never enforced).

At this point, about 20 senior faculty members—liberal, respected members of several social science departments—got together and drew up a statement setting up three commissions to deal with the major issues raised that fall. Five of these men went to President Harlan Hatcher with the proposal, warned him that if he did not respond flexibly a major explosion would occur, and succeeded in convincing him to announce three student-faculty-administration commissions—one to focus on class rankings, one to consider the sit-in ban, and one to deal with student participation in decision making.

An immediate outcome of the events of the year was that the Office of Student Organizations dropped the requirement that student organizations submit membership lists. A longer-range and more significant result was SGC's clear commitment to focus on issues of student authority—particularly vis-à-vis the Office of Student Affairs. SGC's activism has been passed on to new cadres of students, and I think it is fair to say that the students have gradually come to dominate decision making in nonacademic matters. The Office of Student Affairs was reorganized and renamed the Office of Student Services and was directed, until the winter of 1972, by Robert Knauss, a law professor who wrote an early, sympathetic report on the role of students in decision making. The vice-president for student services works out major policy decisions with a policy board having a majority of student members. This board effectively has the power to fire him. Replacing

[13] At the beginning, the president of SGC appealed to VOICE for support. Later, as momentum grew, other student groups joined with SGC to moderate the influence of the student left. This in itself was significant, since the traditional fraternity and sorority domination of SGC had been broken three years earlier by the combined impact of VOICE and a more politicized student body. The Greeks still retain some areas of control, mainly over social events and entertainment, but these too have dwindled in the last few years. The lavish homecoming parade of yesteryear has become a string of slapdash floats and bands of mocking hippies. In 1971–72 there were 42 fraternities and 22 sororities, just a slight drop from previous years. Pledge classes, however, have been shrinking to about half the 1961 size, so that many of the houses have become quite small. The less prestigious houses have been forced to take in boarders to survive, and several have closed down completely.

the old advisers, "advocates" in the Office of Student Services work full time with student governments in colleges, with blacks, women, gay students, Chicanos, and American Indians. Parietal rules have been virtually abandoned at Michigan, and governance for student housing rests to a great degree with the student-domi-nated policy board and with elected dormitory governments — which now must cope with vandalism, thievery, and physical attacks in the more vulnerable open dormitories, in addition to the old problems of finances and housekeeping. A majority of the seven university vice presidents have student representatives on advisory committees. More recently, student representatives, in a ratio of about two faculty members to one student, are on the major committees in LSA, with the exception of the College Executive Committee. (In the School of Education, the executive committee has three nonvoting student members.) SGC also works closely with a key faculty group, the Senate Advisory Committee on University Affairs (SACUA).[14] What we have witnessed at Michi-gan is the institutionalization of student power in the nonacademic area, which has had the effect of obviating certain issues, such as women's hours, which come up chronically on other campuses. This is not to say that fundamental problems have been solved. Conflict persists and students continue to press vigorously for changes in governance and judiciary procedures and a larger voice in academic affairs. Conditions of life for ordinary students who do not become involved in university affairs are much the same as, if not worse than, when I was a student in the fifties.

THE BOOKSTORE INCIDENT A somewhat anomalous event took place in the fall of 1969. For decades before that time, various groups on the campus had pressed for a university bookstore and were rejected by the regents,

[14] The Senate Advisory Committee on University Affairs is a nine-man group elected for three-year terms by the Senate Assembly, a body of 65 faculty elected by the faculty at large within the various schools and colleges on a proportional basis. The chairman and vice-chairman of the assembly are chosen by SACUA from among its members. SACUA has become the assembly's "mobile unit" within the university in implementing its general charge "to advise and consult with the President on University policy on behalf of the Assembly" and "to act as an instrument for effecting actions of the Senate and the Assembly." SACUA members meet at least once a week and during a crisis almost every day. As the "voice" of the faculty, the chairman of the assembly has come to have as much informal influence as many of the executive officers.

who were concerned about competition with local businessmen. More recently, one faction of the SDS chapter and then SGC decided to make a major issue of the bookstore. In the spring of 1969 the administration submitted a plan which kept responsibility for control of the bookstore in the hands of the administration. This plan was rejected by SGC and other student groups. Months of negotiations ensued, shouting matches occurred at regents' meetings, and eventually students sat in at one of the university buildings. After hours of meetings and orders that the building be evacuated, President Fleming called in the police. One hundred and seven people were arrested, one of them the faculty chairman of the Student Relations Committee of the Senate Assembly; among them were members of SGC and a large proportion of younger students. The eventual compromise came from SACUA—until the sit-in, the faculty were not much interested in the bookstore issue—essentially giving control of the bookstore to a nonprofit corporation, with a board composed of students and faculty members. The victory on this issue was crucial to the prestige of SGC and to the morale of student power activists who were struggling with more radical groups over the definition of the strategic issues to press both within and outside the university.

BAM The most significant event of recent years occurred in the spring of 1970 and concerned the admission and support of black students. The major protagonists were President Robben Fleming, who succeeded Hatcher and was the main administration negotiator; a group of black undergraduates, graduates, and faculty members who constituted the Black Action Movement (BAM); a coalition of white activists in support of BAM; SACUA; and the regents. In a month as tense as anyone can recall, rumors passed through the community: that troops were bivouacked on the outskirts of town, that some blacks from out of town were arming with guns, that there were plans to sabotage the computers. As one centrally involved person told me, "It could have been Kent State, but worse."

The University of Michigan prides itself on being first in many things: among state universities, in admitting women; in hosting one of the first ecology teach-ins and developing an early ecology action group; and, with greater ambivalence, in spawning the first Vietnam teach-in, SDS, the first student tenants' union—and the first pantie raid. In 1963, on the initiative of then Vice-President for Academic Affairs Roger Heyns and Dean of the Graduate School

Stephen Spurr, the university instituted the first Opportunity Awards program, which provided scholarships and counseling for underprivileged students. It was one of the first universities to work out a cooperative agreement with a black college, Tuskegee Institute. Early in the sixties, Michigan began to hire black counselors, recruiters, and faculty members. Nevertheless, the University of Michigan had always been viewed by black groups around the state as the university for rich white kids—the hardest university to get into (and they were right). Michigan State and Wayne State, among the major state universities in Michigan, both had larger proportions of black students than the University of Michigan.

A critical mass of blacks came to Michigan in the late sixties. By and large, they have been and are moderate in their politics; indeed, less than a year before the strike of 1970, white radicals were berating the blacks for their bourgeois moderation.

The move for increased black admissions surfaced in the fall of 1969 when the Black Law Student Alliance protested the admissions policies of the Law School. In January 1970, the black demands in the university at large took shape. The *Michigan Daily* gave increasing attention to the black issue. In February, blacks, including many of the black faculty from different colleges in the university, presented their demands to the president, SGC, and, finally, the regents for a 10 percent black enrollment by 1973–74, plus various supportive services and scholarships. The regents refused to consider the demands at their February meeting. Soon after that meeting, disruptions took place in the library and several other university buildings and classrooms. Members of BAM and the white support coalition went around to dormitories and university groups presenting the list of demands.

Weeks of negotiations accompanied by organizing by BAM and its white supporters within the university ensued. At this juncture, the regents stated acceptance of the 10 percent enrollment as a goal, the funds for 7 percent to be generated internally and the remaining 3 percent to come from outside sources. The crux of the dispute was the blacks' insistence that the funds for the 10 percent be committed immediately from the university budget. After the regents' announcement of the 7 percent commitment, a confrontation took place outside the Administration Building and several arrests were made. A strike was called, and there were fresh disruptions in classes and outside buildings.

Meanwhile, faculty members were beginning to react, and some of them issued statements to the *Daily* condemning the violence on campus. There was apparently some talk of calling in the police—a move resisted both by the chief of police and the mayor of Ann Arbor (a professor from the law school)—and rumors circulated that the National Guard stood ready to move into Ann Arbor. By this time, the strike had reduced class attendance drastically.

The stand of the BAM leaders on violence was interesting: all along, they called their movement nonviolent and attacked those who engaged in disruptive tactics as "provocateurs." This stance led eventually to a rift between the blacks and the white radicals, the whites feeling they had been covertly egged on to commit disruption, the blacks feeling the whites had tried to use the black issue for their own purposes.

Negotiations were resumed between President Fleming and BAM on March 25. During this same period, the Senate Assembly of the faculty met in special session and recommended that the 10 percent goal be funded by cuts in the budgets of each academic unit. Negotiations continued through the rest of March. BAM reiterated its policy of nonviolence as the strike gained in momentum.

By this time, BAM had built a sophisticated infrastructure. While the negotiating team met with Fleming and other administrators, other members, working out of various university offices, agreed to meet with the police and administrators to develop policies governing picketing. Still another group sent out teams to talk with groups at the university and to black organizations in town. Certain other people were designated to deal with the white support groups. Informally—and later formally—BAM people and their white supporters were meeting with SACUA, which again played a crucial intermediary role between the administration and the protesting group. The essential role of the black faculty and graduate students, especially those in the Law School, in these complex negotiations cannot be stressed enough.

Toward the end of March, faculties in the several colleges met and passed resolutions supporting the 10 percent enrollment, indicating their commitment to supply some of the funds from cuts in departmental budgets. On March 31, Fleming worked out an agreement with BAM which met its main demand for an explicit funding plan for the 10 percent enrollment and supportive services. Demands for a university-funded black culture center, tuition waivers, and an amnesty agreement were, significantly, not included in the agreement.[15] In April, the regents accepted the agreement and the strike was called off.[16]

The BAM strike had wide repercussions. Public criticism of Fleming's "softness" in handling the blacks was widespread during the crisis, and Vice-President Agnew later singled out the university for attack. The faculty was split as it had never been before. Fleming's support among the core liberal faculty dropped substantially during and immediately after the strike because of what they viewed as his "indecisiveness" in dealing with violent acts, as well as his negotiation of an agreement which they feared would take funds away from the departments and lower admission standards. But the fundamental source of their concern was their sense of not being consulted during the negotiations, on matters which they felt had direct implications for the faculty. SACUA came to be seen by these faculty members as a creature easily manipulated by protesting groups and, when convenient, by the administration. (As I have indicated, I do not think this is accurate. SACUA played an essential mediating role—and suffered all of the trials of the man in the middle.) As a direct result of the BAM episode, a group of professors based in history and economics organized a pressure group, the Reform Coalition, in the fall of 1970 which, in the space of less than two months, picked up a membership of between 100 and 200 faculty members. The purpose of the Reform Coalition, divided into a series of task forces, was to monitor substantive and procedural changes in the university, particularly on questions closely touching the academic function. In just a few months, the Reform Coalition became an influential spokesman for the liberal faculty, who felt events and decisions had been slipping away from them.

WHY MICHIGAN HAS NOT EXPOLDED For all their potential for violence, the BAM events did not explode. Schisms developed, to be sure, but time softened them. The distance between left and right takes as long to transverse at Ann Arbor as it does elsewhere, but the University of Michigan remains, as

[15] Thus far, no student has ever been expelled from the university for political activity. Under legislation passed by the state and the regents in 1970, civil penalties for students convicted of disrupting university functions were increased. Students taking part in disruptive acts could also be liable for expulsion from the university.

[16] The sequence of events described here draws heavily on accounts written by Foy Cox and Chi-Chi Lawson.

it has throughout the years of activism, relatively unpolarized in its tone and atmosphere. Morale, though lower in 1971 than in 1964, was still higher than at Berkeley, Wisconsin, Harvard, or Columbia. The rancor, the public confrontations, the bitterness, the breaking of friendships which follow crises at other universities have been more muted at Michigan. Somehow, as one of my informants put it, "People have disagreed without getting mad at each other."

Why the campus has not exploded is the question that has intrigued me most in watching Michigan through the years, and I asked my informants what they thought about it. I was startled to find a large number, each of whom claimed that the group he or she represented—whether students, faculty, or administration—was *the* group crucial to understanding the recent history at Michigan. I took this one step further and asked several people to draw maps of the significant groups on the campus and to indicate their connections. A complete picture would look something like that shown in Figure 1.

The map becomes exceedingly complicated and the arrows shift somewhat over time, but the story is quite clear: superimposed on the formal structure is a fairly stable informal network of linkages both within and across each of the student, faculty, and administration groups. With the exception of student conservatives, each group is linked to at least two other groups. The crucial ties in recent years are those between liberal and radical faculty and students and their multiple connections with institutional representatives—the *Daily*, SGC, SACUA, and the executive officers (these are indicated in double lines on the chart).

The core of the network is in a large group of liberal faculty, dominated by nationally recognized figures primarily in the social sciences.[17] In a study done in the late sixties, the overall turnover of Michigan faculty was less than 3 percent, and the greatest stability has been in this senior group. These men are loyal to the university as a institution and over the years have taken on a prodigious number of functions beyond their departmental duties. They have become department chairmen, executive committee

[17] The newest American Council on Education ratings of graduate programs show that five of the social science departments at Michigan were rated among the top five in their field nationally. The remaining two social science departments were in the top 10 (Roose & Anderson, 1971).

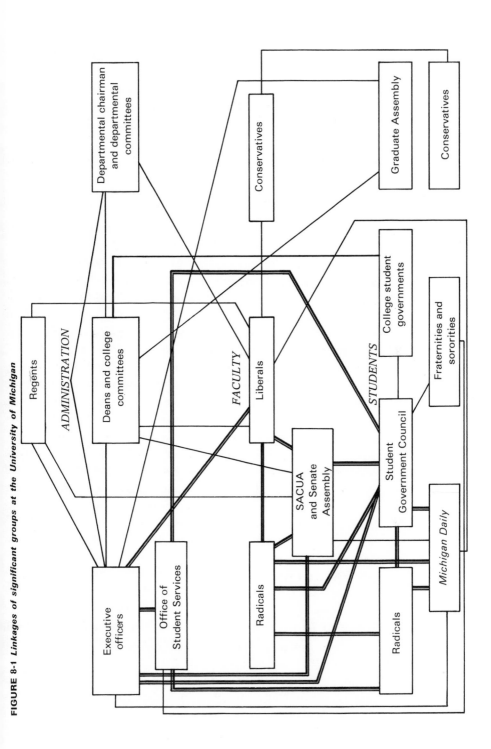

FIGURE 8-1 *Linkages of significant groups at the University of Michigan*

members and chairmen at the departmental and college level.[18] Assembly members and deans have been drawn from their ranks. They have links both with the higher administration and the regents, on the one hand, and, through their ties with the younger, radical faculty and SACUA, with student groups. The establishment at Michigan *is* the liberal establishment. When important decisions are made which circumvent what they see as procedural liberalism, as in the BAM events, they move automatically to reassert their influence.

What is the nature of these linkages? Some are strictly formal, but most are more than that. Because the university is located in a small town and quite far from competing cosmopolitan centers (Ann Arbor people do not view Detroit as a beacon of culture), people have time for one another. Most faculty and students live in Ann Arbor—where no one is more than 20 minutes away from the campus by car—and people see one another in different settings. Informal relationships develop between faculty and students in different departments, and these come into play in the daily round of activities. As one faculty leader told me, "The most effective way to get things done is through informal mechanisms."

This often means that people who find themselves on opposite sides of an issue still must live together in other situations. During a dispute over the language requirement, one of the graduate-student leaders found himself publicly disagreeing with his dissertation adviser. How, this student asked me, could he break with someone to whom he was so closely tied, someone he called by his first name? Examples abound. Linked with the younger faculty members planning the moratorium on classes in 1965, the liberal faculty members in subtle ways influenced the decision to hold the more moderate evening teach-in. The liberal faculty, in turn, were backed up by their friends in administrative positions, who assured them that university facilities would be available for the moderate alternative. An esteemed senior professor planning the university's sesquicentennial celebration was concerned about possible student disruption. He called on a young faculty radical, a former student of his, to use his considerable influence with students.

Similar things happen on the student side. The radical students may take the initiative, but they know they must get some support from their friends in other student groups and the faculty. *Daily*

18 Michigan was the first university in the country to introduce college and departmental executive committees.

students are close friends of SGC students; SGC students are on a first-name basis with SACUA members and personnel in the Office of Student Services. Active black students see black faculty regularly.

In the midst of a crisis, these networks become more transparent and exposed, as we have seen in the three major events. The networks function both to channel issues *and* to place boundaries on their form of expression and eventual outcomes. We have seen these mechanisms operating again and again. During a confrontation, members of the Senate Assembly are likely to meet in emergency session and to keep in touch with one another informally. Radical faculty will go to SACUA members to press for faculty support of the demonstrators. Both groups will talk to the demonstrators, moving in and out of an occupied building in shifts all day and night, carrying their diagnoses of the situation outside to the administration and the faculty. A radical group will decide to push a certain issue and negotiates with SGC on the terms for endorsement by student government. SGC then becomes the legitimate representative of the student position to the rest of the campus. Staff members from the Office of Student Services work with student groups, attending meetings, arguing with the protagonists, serving as liaison between administrators and students.

What has developed at Michigan over the years is a social structure which is as far from a standard bureaucratic organization as it is from a simple community. Critical groups are integrated into the system via their ties to a limited number of other groups, which in turn are tied to a series of *other* groups, and so on. (But not every group is linked with every other one, and some are not linked at all. It is important to stress that many students, faculty, and staff are not part of the picture.) In the past years, all the major constituencies have been influential on different occasions; moreover, no group has been able to keep hegemony over all areas. Thus alliances tend to be shifting and crosscutting coalitions: on some issues, students are allied with faculty and on others with the administration; on some issues faculty and administration line up together. Often, one group will not be activated at all.[19]

[19] This analysis parallels Morgan's (1970) interpretation of findings from his study of the sources, development, magnitude, and aftereffects of protests against recruiting policies at 106 schools which had experienced recruiter-related protests. In a fascinating series of tables he shows that although the initiative for the demonstrations came from students, it was the faculty who were critical to the resolution of the policy. In some schools, faculty became actively involved in mediating this issue. When the bonds of the faculty to the

Thus when student radicals agitated over language requirements in 1968, an academic issue, the administration remained on the sidelines. The radicals' demands were transmitted through a network that ran through the *Michigan Daily,* SGC, and college student governments to radical faculty, liberal faculty, deans, departments, and the faculty of LSA. The radicals demanded the complete abolition of language requirements. The network tempered this demand with a compromise: there would be a new degree alongside the regular B.A. and B.S.—the bachelor of general studies, which would have no language requirement and no subject concentration.[20]

In addition to this mix, there is an openness and flexibility in both the higher administrators and the student activists. President Fleming, who came from Wisconsin to Michigan in 1968, has an operating style which blends well with the dominant administrative style. A labor arbitrator by training, he absorbs pressure from different sides and has known whether to use the informal or formal structure during crisis.[21] For whatever reason—the strength of the labor movement in Michigan, the generally moderate political climate of the state—a strike does not shock the public as much in Michigan as it does in other states. Negotia-

students were relatively equal, the faculty acted effectively as mediators to the administrators. "The faculty in these cases achieved a high degree of impartiality . . . by becoming equally committed to the competing interests of the students and administration, and equally sympathetic to the two parties separate from their interests. In addition, an important factor in their efforts was that . . . [they] acted through the official faculty councils of their schools, and thus were able to assume an independent authority position some distance from both sides." See also Platt and Parsons (1970).

20 The bachelor of general studies (B.G.S.) began in 1969. A recent study shows that nearly 9 percent of the LSA student body is enrolled in the program ("B.G.S. Degree. . . ," 1971). The only requirement for the B.G.S. is that students elect at least 60 hours of advanced courses, with no more than 20 of these in any one department. Other recent undergraduate innovations include the Residential College, a subcollege of 680 students which opened in 1967; the Pilot Program, which houses 600 underclassmen together in one dormitory, with offerings of seminars and directed reading by graduate resident fellows; the Course Mart, a kind of internal "free university," which lists nondepartmental credit courses initiated by students and faculty; Independent Studies; and the B.A. in liberal arts.

21 During a street riot involving large numbers of young "street people" and police in the summer of 1969, Fleming, with strong encouragement from SACUA, called on each member of the assembly to bring in two additional faculty members to patrol the streets around the university. Within a couple of hours, close to 200 faculty members appeared.

tion as a way of settling conflict is built into the consciousness of warring groups. Grudgingly perhaps, but with due respect, a number of administrators commented that "our student activists" are willing to talk; rhetoric to the contrary, they will negotiate. Michigan is an unusually decentralized institution, especially on academic affairs. Whether it is because people know one another across departments or because of the intensive faculty involvement in larger university affairs, it is not too difficult to get interdepartmental programs going. Students, especially graduate students, have a great deal of freedom to move between departments and schools. Faculty meetings are open in most of the colleges. Student evaluation of courses was introduced before World War II, abandoned during the war, and then reintroduced in 1948. By now, student evaluation of courses has become just another one of those administrative trivia departments must go through at the end of each term.

These internal strengths depend on the existence of a supportive environment. Fortuitously perhaps, Michigan has been relatively protected from external attacks. Faculty and students are deeply involved in the political life of Ann Arbor, and although the sharp town-gown animosity of pre-World War II days reasserts itself on occasion, it becomes increasingly difficult to draw a firm line between town and gown. The mayoral candidates of both parties in a recent election were professors at the university. The Human Rights party, a new radical party in Ann Arbor, organized mainly by students, succeeded in electing two young candidates to the city council in the spring 1972 elections. University faculty members serve as city councilmen and as members and consultants to various local and state governmental committees.

At a time when politicians around the country have been attacking the universities, Michigan again has been relatively protected from interference. Governors of the state have traditionally taken a hands-off attitude toward the universities, and only one recent political candidate, state Senator Robert Huber, who subsequently failed to win the Republican nomination for the U.S. Senate, tried to enhance his political fortunes by making an issue of campus unrest in the 1970 campaign.

The University of Michigan was the first state university to be given independent status from legislative and executive control by a state constitution, and although legislative control over the purse has been a powerful constraint, the university's autonomy has been respected. The Michigan Supreme Court has upheld the independence of the university in case after case; the courts have ruled repeatedly that once funds have been appropriated to the university, it is the prerogative of the regents and the administration to decide how the funds will be apportioned (Hicks, 1963). Here the role of the board of regents is extremely important. Elected by the voters of Michigan, the eight regents have taken their responsibilities to the university extremely seriously. They have identified more closely with the university than with the parties that have nominated them; rarely has a regent used the position on the board as a political base. In the last two years, student and faculty groups have increasingly appealed to the board of regents directly (after the bookstore incident, an open regents meeting was instituted) and, ironically, have involved the regents to a greater extent in university affairs. The impact of this increased involvement has yet to be seen.

In a sense, the stability of the University of Michigan seems overdetermined and more than a little accidental. The picture I have drawn should not be extrapolated cavalierly; serious conflicts exist for which solutions seem exceedingly dim. Student pressure for shared power on academic matters as well as on basic university policies, such as budget decisions and classified research, implies struggle between students and new groups—the faculty on the one hand, the regents on the other. The press for a more egalitarian institution—for more blacks and women[22] throughout the ranks, for greater student involvement in curricular matters, for compensatory programs of all sorts for various groups—conflicts directly with the values of many of the faculty. Perhaps the greatest barrier to the solution of any of these problems is the budgetary crisis. Calls for tuition increases and greater faculty work loads, with inadequate provisions for reasonable salary increases, set almost insurmountable limits on meeting the old, let alone the new, commitments. Unionization becomes more attractive to a faculty that has heretofore shown little interest in collective bargaining, bringing still another set of constraints. The informal networks seem to have worked best in an expanding institution, when the

[22] In the fall of 1970, the Department of Health, Education and Welfare was instrumental in withholding funding for several government contracts after finding discrimination against women, as charged by a local women's group. The university and HEW worked out a settlement which called for hiring and advancing more women on the staff, redefinition of nepotism rules, and payment of back wages to employees who prove discrimination.

major groups were in minimal competition over financial resources. But the resilience of informal structure, like most human relationships, becomes sorely tested in times of scarcity, and it is not clear that there are formal structures with the legitimacy to mediate the scramble for funds. Add to all this the war in Indochina, the growing public mistrust of the universities, and the cleavage between the old and new cultures, and even what has appeared to be a healthy institution may turn out to be very delicate indeed.

Persons consulted in the preparation of this chapter

Robert C. Angell: Professor emeritus of sociology; longtime member of the faculty; active in countless university committees; chairman, Sociology Department, 1940–1952; director, College Honors Program, 1957–1961; codirector, Center for Research on Conflict Resolution, 1961–1965.

Fred Arnstein: Graduate student in social psychology; dissertation on the University of Michigan Tenants Union.

Robert T. Blackburn: Professor of higher education.

David Brand: Undergraduate; president, College of Literature, Science and the Arts Student Government, 1970–71.

Michael Davis: Graduate student in philosophy; administrative vice-president, Student Government Council, 1967–68.

Jerry DeGrieck: Vice-president, Student Government Council, 1970–71; elected Ann Arbor city councilman, 1972.

James I. Doi: Professor of higher education; director, Center for the Study of Higher Education, 1970–71.

Alexander Eckstein: Professor of economics; director, Center for Chinese Studies, 1967–69; cochairman and one of the founders of the Faculty Reform Coalition.

William P. Fenstemacher: Assistant to Vice-President Spurr.

Robben W. Fleming: President of the University of Michigan and professor of law.

William Haber: Professor of economics and adviser to executive officers; dean, College of Literature, Science and the Arts, 1963–1968; longtime faculty member; active in countless university committees.

Martin Hirschman: Undergraduate; editor of the *Michigan Daily,* 1970–71.

Daniel Katz: Professor of psychology; longtime member of the faculty; active in countless university committees; one of the founders of the Center for Research on Conflict Resolution.

Robert L. Knauss: Professor of law and vice-president for student services, 1970–1972; chairman, Senate Advisory Committee on University Affairs, 1970.

Chi-Chi T. Lawson: Assistant to vice-president for student services; administrative assistant to Senate Advisory Committee on University Affairs, 1966–1970.

Robert Marrone: Graduate student in the College of Engineering; president of Graduate Assembly, 1970–71.

Wilbert J. McKeachie: Professor of psychology; chairman, Psychology Department, 1961–1971; longtime faculty member active in countless university committees.

Theodore M. Newcomb: Walgreen Professor of human understanding; professor of psychology and sociology; associate director, University of Michigan Residential College; research associate, Center for Research on Learning and Teaching; longtime member of the faculty active in countless university committees; chairman, Doctoral Program in Social Psychology, 1947–1963.

Barbara W. Newell: Assistant to the president of the university and Associate professor of economics until 1971; acting vice-president for Student Affairs, 1968–1970

Joseph N. Payne: Professor of math education; chairman, Senate Advisory Committee on University Affairs, 1969–1970.

Marvin N. Peterson: Assistant professor of higher education; director of a study of governance in the university, 1968–69.

Robert J. S. Ross: Research associate, Center for Research on the Utilization of Scientific Knowledge, Institute for Social Research, until 1972; founding national secretary, New University Conference, 1968–69; national officer, SDS, 1960–1966.

Stephen H. Spurr: Vice-president, 1969–71; dean of the Graduate School, 1964–1971.

Stephen J. Tonsor: Associate professor of history.

References

Astin, Alexander: *Who Goes Where to College,* Science Research Associates, Chicago, 1965.

"B.G.S. Degree Popular, Attracts Creative Student," *University Record,* Feb. 1, 1970.

Clarke, James W., and Joseph Egan: "Social and Political Dimensions of Campus Protest Activity," unpublished manuscript, Florida State University, Institute for Social Research, n.d.

"Credit Hours, Instructional Cost and Faculty Activity Reports," unpublished report, University of Michigan, Office of Institutional Research, Fall 1968.

Derber, Charles, and Richard Flacks: "An Exploration of the Value System of Radical Student Activists and Their Parents," paper delivered at the meetings of the American Sociological Association, San Francisco, 1967.

Dunlap, Riley: "Radical and Conservative Student Activists: A Comparison of Family Backgrounds," *Pacific Sociological Review,* vol. 13, pp. 171–181, 1970.

Feldman, Kenneth, and Theodore M. Newcomb: *The Impact of College on Students,* Jossey-Bass, Inc., San Francisco, 1969.

Gamson, Zelda, Gerald Gurin, and Jeffrey Goodman: "Activists, Moderates and Bystanders During a University Protest," paper delivered at the meetings of the American Sociological Association, San Francisco, 1967.

Hicks, Fred W.: "Constitutional Independence and the State University," unpublished doctoral dissertation, University of Michigan, 1963.

"How Much Do U-M Professors Work?" *Ann Arbor News,* Feb. 21, 1971.

Kahn, Roger, and William J. Bowers: "The Social Context of the Rank-and-File Student Activist: A Test of Four Hypotheses," *Sociology of Education,* vol. 43, pp. 38–55, 1970.

Keniston, Kenneth: "The Sources of Student Dissent," *Journal of Social Issues,* vol. 3, pp. 108–137, 1967.

Menashe, Louis, and Ronald Radosh: *Teach-Ins: USA, Reports, Opinions, Documents,* Frederick A. Praeger, Inc., New York, 1967.

Morgan, William R.: "Faculty Mediation in Campus Conflict," in Julian Foster and Durward Long (eds.), *Protest! Student Activism in America,* William Morrow & Company, Inc., New York, 1970.

Platt, Gerald, and Talcott Parsons: "Decision-making in the Academic System: Influence and Power Exchange," in Carlos Kruytbosch and Sheldon L. Messinger (eds.), *The State of the University: Authority and Change,* Sage, Beverly Hills, Calif., 1970.

Roose, Kenneth D., and Charles J. Anderson: *A Rating of Graduate Programs,* American Council on Education, Washington, 1970.

Snyder, Sam Ralph: "Academic Freedom at the University of Michigan, 1953–1958," unpublished doctoral dissertation, University of Michigan, 1970.

Tygart, Clarence E., and Norman Holt: "A Research Note on Student Leftist Political Activism and Family Socioeconomic Status," *Pacific Sociological Review,* vol. 14, pp. 121–128, 1971.

9. Old Westbury I and Old Westbury II

by John A. Dunn, Jr.

MANDATE FOR A NEW COLLEGE The State University will establish in Nassau County a college that pays heed to the individual student and his concern with the modern world. . . . Specifically, this college will:

1 End the lock-step march in which one semester follows on another until four of youth's most energetic years have been consumed; to this purpose qualified students will be admitted to college without high school graduation, and those who attain competency will be granted degrees without regard to length of collegiate study.

2 Admit students to full partnership in the academic world and grant them the right to determine, in large measure, their own areas of study and research.

3 Use mechanical devices to free faculty scholars from the academic drudgery of repeated lectures, conducting classes devoted to drill, and marking many examinations, thus allowing faculty scholars to turn their full creative powers to meaningful exchange with students, to research, and to artistry.

Since the campus is to be built literally from the ground up, the president and the faculty members the president recruits will have an almost unrestricted opportunity for innovation and creativity.

From "Mandate for a New College," Master Plan of the State University of New York (1966).

In 1966, Chancellor Samuel B. Gould of the State University of New York, responding to the growing wave of student discontent at elite campuses across the country and to a desire to open up the SUNY system, launched a new experimental college on Long Island. The College at Old Westbury was to educate 5,000 students in a way which "pays heed to the individual student and his concern with the modern world."

ACKNOWLEDGMENT: The author wishes to express his appreciation to Harris Wofford, Councill Taylor, and Michael Novak from Old Westbury I and to Jon Collett and especially John Maguire and Douglas Palmer at Old Westbury II.

Much has already been written about what happened. The aspirations and troubles of the new college, reviewed here, will be familiar to some readers. Yet the story is worth retelling for its lessons and for its comparison of the first venture, now terminated, with the second just now getting under way.

Old Westbury II carries the same mandate as did Old Westbury I, but has asked for and received a second mandate as well. The new leadership has redesigned the craft and set her on a different course.

OLD WEST-BURY I You have to start with Harris Wofford, the intense, charismatic, unflappable man Chancellor Gould picked in November 1966 as the first president of Old Westbury. A lawyer by training, Wofford is a socially committed intellectual. He attended Chicago during the Great Books period and has not lost his love of ideas or his training in the Socratic method. His work as civil rights aide to President Kennedy and as associate director of the Peace Corps had given him some administrative experience, though not in an academic setting.

Wofford was and is a phrasemaker. Reactions to his style were seldom mild. One friend accused him of the arrogant omnicompetence of the lawyer; another said, "Harris never lost a discussion." He could be a strong executive, but his preference for reasoned discussion made his occasional fiats seem fits of petulance. One could not deny his attractiveness or dedication or articulateness. He deepened, sobered, and grew at Old Westbury.

In late 1966 and early 1967 Wofford gathered a group of prospective faculty members and students from other colleges and began to plan the new institution.

Our aim was a college that plans rather than a planned college, and for this a living organism, a nucleus of the real thing, with faculty and students as well as administrators and architects in dialogue with each other seemed preferable from the beginning (Wofford, 1969, p. 2).

Wofford (ibid, p. 5) explained some of his own educational predispositions this way:

I came with a long-standing special interest in designing an undergraduate liberal arts curriculum around the themes of law, medicine, and theology. . . . As lawyer and law teacher, I had been persuaded that law was a good lens through which to look at the body politic and the problems of self-government, and I had a hunch that the other ancient professions of medicine and theology, taken broadly to include psychiatry as well as physical medicine, and Eastern as well as Western religions, would be good as major undergraduate subjects unifying our knowledge about the mind, body, and soul. Some such unification of knowledge through a coherent curriculum of liberal arts rather than a scattering of elective courses, seemed to me the main object of curricular reform.

The core group talked with numerous distinguished advisers, Jacqueline Grennan, Michael Rossman, and David Riesman among them. The advice was so plentiful that it inevitably contained contradictions, so well intentioned that it often was richer in rhetoric than in concrete suggestion.

Old Westbury I was to be a "college of constituent colleges." By setting up a number of small units of contrasting styles and contents, the designers hoped to promote internal innovation, prevent bureaucratization, maintain a sense of community, and yet avoid the departmental specialization which hampers interdisciplinary programs elsewhere. The plan was to start with two or three such colleges, with a total of perhaps 1,000 students when the first set of buildings was ready in 1970. After that, one or more new colleges would be added each year until a full enrollment of 5,000 was reached.

The site for the college, in the town of Old Westbury, was the 560-acre horse-country estate of F. Ambrose Clark. The rolling, wooded estate, located on the north shore of Long Island about an hour from New York, even provided a mansion in which initial planning sessions were held.

Governor Rockefeller appointed Maitland Edey, editor of Time-Life Books, chairman of the College Council, a sort of limited board of trustees named for each SUNY institution to help it relate to its community. Edey, a brahmin and an intellectual with a social conscience, liked Wofford's search for a liberal college.

The students in the planning group pushed for a sort of one-man-one-vote equality to maximize their influence while Wofford tried to maintain some final control over the outcome. Despite such internal struggles the work progressed rapidly, and the group wanted to launch the first instructional program a full year ahead of schedule, long before the new facilities were ready. In early 1968 Wofford requested permission of the state university administration to begin a pilot program, arguing that the planning had progressed to a point where it had to be tried, and that valuable momentum would be lost if the college did not open the following fall. Overcoming official reluctance, he finally obtained permission to begin in 1968–69 with 75 students, all undergraduates.

At the urging of the student planners, the first program had an urban affairs concentration and was not at all the "College of the World" that Wofford and other ex-Peace Corps advisers had first imagined. Wofford (1969, p. 7) described it thusly:

The first main program was a work-study, education-in-action curriculum, with a practical focus on urban problems, and a continuing common humanities seminar during off-campus as well as on-campus terms, with a reading list that included a high proportion of great books. . . . About half the reading list for the year would be in common for all the seminars and agreed upon in advance, and the other half would be determined by each seminar as it went along.

Byron Youtz, academic vice president for Old Westbury I, was not able to get away from Reed College until the summer of 1968. He was the only member of the Old Westbury top group who had had academic administrative experience. A capable and respected person both as physicist and as administrator, he might have been able to shape and detail the academic planning had he been able to be on the scene earlier.

The First Year (1968-69) Some 700 applications were received for places in the initial class. Their number reflected the high expectations aroused by the considerable publicity the college had already received. Old Westbury I appealed to a special class of students who, like the faculty, were "drawn to the banner of experimental education." Most of the applicants visited the campus and were interviewed, often by student planners who, not unnaturally, tended to attract and to select students like themselves.

Far more students than anticipated accepted the offer of admission. Even after some had left for a special program in Israel, the first of many field experiences, 85 were left to begin the first program. Of these, two-thirds were freshmen and one-third were upper-division transfers from other state colleges.

The students had, in heightened form, the virtues and faults of college students of the late sixties. They came with energy, articulateness, and a fervor to reform the world. They distrusted and disliked requirements of any kind, believed in one-man-one-vote equality with faculty when any form of college governance at all was necessary, and profoundly desired to do their own thing.

The college admission planners hoped to draw from a diversity of backgrounds, and succeeded. There were no clearly disproportionate groups among the student body, though there were perhaps more Jewish students, more out-of-staters, and fewer blacks than one might have expected. Yet the students shared a quality of personality—a high moral intensity, a personal involvement. The student interviewers, rebelling against objective criteria like SAT scores and marks, had to choose subjectively, and opted for people who warmed up easily, who were affectionate and/or intense, and who shared their own convictions.

Many of the initial faculty had been outstanding teachers, educational reformers, and, often, rebels in other institutions. It wasn't easy for them to become an "establishment," to accept the rules, procedures, and coordinations which make any organization work. Nor was it easy for them to develop interdisciplinary programs, get used to new teaching techniques, or accept students as entirely equal partners. Lawrence Resnick, Michael Novak, and others were, like the students, people who need people.

When an accidental fire totally destroyed the mansion on the Clark estate, Old Westbury I moved to temporary quarters at Planting Fields, an arboretum in nearby Oyster Bay. Planting Fields, owned by the state university, had housed other planning and start-up operations. The enormous castle and spacious lush grounds there seemed to provide an ideal setting.

Some students, among them Daniel Zuckerman, whose accidental death in 1969 shook the community, responded deeply to the quietness, beauty, and order of the estate. For many from the ghetto, it presented a chance to relax, to escape the hassles. Yet as an observer commented, "Tudor castles and arboretums share a common institutional set: People are in the Way" (Hebert, 1969, p. 2). The isolation, exclusiveness, and hothouse atmosphere of the estate gave a sense of unreality to the campus during those years, heightening the intellectual animosities and the infighting.

During the first year, the educational program suffered a number of setbacks. Only half the reading list for the common humanities seminars could be agreed to by all the faculty; the students objected to anything being billed as "required" reading. Differences in styles of seminar leading and differences in readings severely disrupted the commonality of the program. The social science workshops dissolved when the faculty members responsible for them decided it was more important for each to teach his own specialty than to continue a common program. And the last third of the program elements, fieldwork assignments, which are difficult to make rigorous under any circumstances, deteriorated considerably under student pressure to keep them entirely free of requirements.

Problems of governance kept surging forward. Inordinate amounts of time were spent trying to decide how to decide what to decide. The students, in particular, insisted that any decision which affected them had to involve them. Both students and faculty members had a way of turning what should have been nuts-and-bolts administrative questions into passionate moral issues. Any issue, once resolved, could be reopened at the urging of those affected.

Two issues in particular—the proportion of nonwhites in the student body and staff and the nature of the second year's educational programs—convulsed the organism in the latter part of the first year.

Students, whose sensitivity to the plight of minorities had been heightened when they acted as substitutes during a New York City teachers' strike, demanded 50 percent representation of blacks and other nonwhites in the student body, faculty, and staff. The faculty, though in sympathy with the cause, could not accept community dictation on this issue and felt it had to act as a separate body. At Wofford's insistence that he could not buy the principle of a quota system, the faculty voted the proposal down, but recommended that the administration take steps to increase minority representation.

Given the human propensity to perpetuate what one has, Wofford and others felt that if Old Westbury I was ever to be a college of contrasting constituent colleges, it would have to be so almost from the outset. Consequently, he pushed hard for two additional college programs for the second year. After much discussion, disagreement, and a six-day sit-in by students opposed to the idea, the plan went through. The sit-in, in contrast to earlier dialogues, was civilized; the students talked quietly, sipping the sherry Wofford had left for them.

The Second Year (1969–70)   A constitutional convention labored over the summer to set up satisfactory governance machinery, realizing that the community had faced the year's problems with nothing other than the consensus politics of the planning period and a growing realization by the president of his need to retain some final authority.

The convention produced a good document. But in the fall, students and faculty fell to squabbling among themselves again, and in the end neither students nor faculty nor staff accepted the constitution. A plan was eventually agreed to, however, which recognized the powers of the president under the general policies of the state university system, and which set up a policy-recommending committee on the formula of six faculty, five students, and two administrators. This arrangement helped avoid involvement of the whole community in every issue, but in effect permitted the students to continue their de facto control.

In many ways the second year went more smoothly. The simple growth of the institution introduced diversity of interests and made things less personal. Solid new faculty members were added. The increase in student numbers from 85 to about 200 broke up the extended-family relationships of the first period. Among the new students, thanks to a vigorous recruiting drive, were substantial numbers of black and Third World students.

In addition to the Urban Studies College, a Disciplines College and a General Program were set up.

The name of the Disciplines College suggests a concentration in the usual academic specializations. Instead, it was an attempt to organize a disciplined examination of "Man's responsibility for himself, his experience, and his world (*Report on the . . . College at Old Westbury,* 1970, p. 3). Its emphasis on reflection and study provided a real contrast with the "determined activism" of Urban Studies.

General Studies offered a one-year, carefully prescribed curriculum for those students who were not ready to choose either of the other colleges; it was the only one of the three colleges to maintain the idea of common seminars.

Wofford was disappointed that only 35 students chose the two new programs. The great majority stayed with Urban Studies.

Most of the students pursued extensive independent study programs. Slowly, faculty members imposed more direction, weeding out the initial excesses, such as creative candle making. But as the academic programs were shaken down and as the moral ferment subsided a bit, some of the messianic group spirit also evaporated. While students had participated from the beginning, they had not really felt accepted as partners. Whatever trust there might have been ebbed away somewhat as students and faculty became identified more as groups and less as individuals.

Life was not easy or pleasant for many of the students. Professor Novak remembers noting on return from trips that the Old Westbury students seemed wan, troubled, and hassled. Differences in life-styles made sleep impossible in the dormitory sections of the castle. Some blacks were rowdy; some self-centered whites would do their thing by playing the stereo at top volume in the middle of the night. Social life was facilitated by setting up a coffeehouse; but the group was still too small and too diverse to find partners easily or to change without wrenches.

Transition Despite progress in the second year, a sense of dissatisfaction and precariousness persisted. This was deepened by Wofford's decision in August 1969 to accept Bryn Mawr's presidency the following June. The prevalent expectation was that a strong but conventional administrator would be named to replace him, killing off what there was left of student participation and of innovation. Wofford had his detractors among both students and faculty. Still he was "a devil they knew," and his announcement signaled the end of an era which, in retrospect, many regarded with a warmth akin to that of old soldiers reviewing their campaigns.

In December, the state university central administration instructed Old Westbury not to make new faculty appointments for 1970–71 or, except for the few to whom commitments had already been made, to admit new students.

Harris Wofford requested that he be relieved of administrative duties, and as of the middle of the year these were assumed by Byron Youtz. Wofford remained on campus through the end of the academic year but made frequent trips to Bryn Mawr.

In the spring, James Frost, vice chancellor for university colleges, asked a committee headed by Clifford Craven[1] to report on the Old Westbury experience to date. The committee found itself satisfied with such administrative functions as budgetary control and accounting; unhappy with personnel policies and academic record keeping; and distressed with more fundamental matters of curriculum development, the nature of the courses given, the absence of coherent planning, and undirected governance. It recommended "that the situation be structured by the State University so as to allow a fresh start to the maximum extent possible" (ibid., p. 17).

Evaluation The introduction of students into full partnership with faculty members in the academic world was tried at a time of mounting student discontent and activism in institutions all across the

---

[1] At the time dean of the faculty at the SUNY College at Oswego.

country. Old Westbury I attracted and selected "experimentally minded" students and faculty who had no experience at institution building. "In assembling student planners and faculty who were accustomed to the role of leaven in established institutions, we did not take into account what happens when a group is all leaven and no lump" (Wofford, 1969, p. 33).

The sensitivity, articulateness, and sense of personal mission of most of those on campus created pressures toward ideological conformity but did not result in institutional coherence. No planned sequential pattern of instruction was developed, tried, improved and tried again. "For all their thirst, [students and faculty] tended to settle for academia's dirtiest water, the ultimate irrelevance—an undisciplined and unintellectual curriculum in an unlimited version of the elective system" (ibid., p. 31). Instead of a "college that plans," there were individuals who improvised.

The institution overbilled itself. The publicity helped to attract interesting people, but it created expectations no institution could fulfill. David Riesman says somewhere that an experimental institution should allow to come only those students and faculty members whom it has to persuade to come.

The planners wanted Old Westbury I to evolve in an organic way out of the partnership of all members of the community. But they underestimated the need to make the difficult distinctions between roles, between policy formulation and execution, between planning and operation. All members may, and probably should, participate in policy decisions, at least through representatives. But successful operation of any institution depends upon acceptance of some distribution of roles and upon each individual's willingness to let those roles be played. The continued carping questioning of previously agreed-to policies greatly impeded progress. Everyone wanted to be more equal than everyone else. Wofford might even have helped the group accomplish more if he had been heavy-handed.

Given the high personal intensity of the individuals attracted to Old Westbury I, it was doubly unfortunate that it started so small. Had the planners taken more time or had the college started with a larger group of students, perhaps some of the pressure-cooker experience could have been avoided.

Wofford was a short-timer. Perhaps it was all for the best that he left when he did, for he had come to be the focus for all disagreements. But he had already lived through the worst of the crises. In general, it seems desirable for college presidents, like product engineers, to stay on the job long enough to live with and refine their designs.

It is perhaps possible to fault Maitland Edey and the College Council for being too uncritically supportive of Wofford; but there were moments like the student strike when he needed help and they provided it.

One can also report major contributions of Old Westbury I.

For perhaps the first time, an institution had honestly attempted to engage students in full partnership in planning, in governance, and in the determination of their own areas of study and research. The quality of the programs was uneven, to be sure. Professor Donald Bluestone's comment (in "Life and Death . . . ," 1971) that "on the teaching-learning level . . . the college was a 100% success" seems a bit strong given the wide variety of projects undertaken and the laxity in some areas. But it is clear that a great deal of learning did take place.

While Old Westbury's extensive publicity probably worked to the detriment of the college itself, it has assured that the lessons of the experiment received wide attention in educational circles.

Afterword: The Third Year (1970–71)

It is easy to overlook the fact that Old Westbury I had a third full academic year of operation.

In May of 1970, Councill Taylor, a black professor of anthropology, was named director of operations at Planting Fields, with the responsibility for continuing the programs during the 1970–71 year and phasing them out completely by June of 1971.

On balance, the college proceeded in a sound and orderly fashion during this period. The campus was quiet. People were tired of struggling, interested in getting an education. Since it was a terminal year, there was little future to fight over in any case. The academic programs had been fairly well shaken down. And the community had found a common enemy to unite it—the planning operations for Old Westbury II then going on at the old campus and from which they were completely excluded.

Taylor used the six-five-two policy-recommending committee in what he termed a "tribal" rather than a "parliamentary" fashion; that is, they talked through every issue until they could reach a satisfactory solution, or tabled it until they could. Under Taylor's management, the procedure worked well.

It is worth recording that almost every graduate of Old Westbury I who applied for admission to graduate school was accepted.

OLD WEST-BURY II The Craven Committee recommendation to start over was followed by the state university, but not in the repressive way some people had feared.

In May 1970, the state university invited John D. Maguire, then associate professor of religion and associate provost at Wesleyan University, to be the new president for Old Westbury. Maguire was the choice of a student-faculty search committee and apparently of Maitland Edey, who wanted a successor to Wofford who shared Wofford's aims, if not his methods.

Maguire's career hardly seemed to be that of the anticipated conventional academic. He was a scholar, to be sure, and had received the Harbison award for distinguished teaching. But he was also a civil rights activist, friend of Martin Luther King, Jr., and trustee of the Martin Luther King, Jr., Memorial Center in Atlanta. And he was a university innovator, restless with the reluctance of the private institutions he knew to experiment in a meaningful way. He shared with Wofford, who was also from the South, something of the evangelical involvement with causes.

With Councill Taylor running the operations at Planting Fields, Maguire was given a free hand, as Wofford had been, to choose his own colleagues and to devote his full-time attention to planning the academic program for Old Westbury II.

The Guiding Idea John Maguire (1971, p. 15) had advocated organizing the curriculum "around a single guiding theme or problem, one concept capable of knotting together all of the strands of inquiry, giving them coherence and visible purpose." Consequently, Maguire and his planning associates asked the state university for, and received, two challenges—to continue to work within the terms of the original mandate for Old Westbury, and to build the new academic program on what they called "the riddle of human justice."

In their "Preliminary Program Announcement" (1971, p. 1) the planners outlined to prospective students a "thorough critique of issues in society, especially in American life, that bear on the question of human justice, such as technology, institutional racism, high culture, legal structures, and environmental balance." In this critique they hoped to bring to bear most of the "liberal arts," feeling that the perspectives of history and philosophy and art are needed to understand our current situation, as much as are the tools of the social, biological, and physical sciences.

The idea of building on a central theme was not new. John Fischer (1969), among others, had proposed designing a curriculum around human survival; others had proposed using the human life cycle as a focus. The choice of the human justice theme reflected not only Maguire's personal convictions but also the planning group's desire to serve well a student body drawn from Nassau County and not served by other institutions.

The planners felt these students would also need more than intellectual analysis. Exclusive concentration on human justice could easily deteriorate into ritual condemnation or utopian dreaming. The student, they felt, needed practical training, needed to acquire skills that could put him in a position to do something about the problems he saw. The acquisition of a useful skill serves several functions: the student builds a sense of agency and of personal worth, the training experience yields practical questions for study, and the training site often provides opportunities for constructive action.

There is tension between intellectual inquiry and professional-skills training, between search for "truth" and training in techniques, between contemplation and action. But when these furies are well harnessed together, they have a mighty pull.

Briefly, then, what the planners proposed for Old Westbury II was to serve interested students from their immediate community, Nassau County, who were not well served by existing institutions, meaning particularly students from the lower-income segments of the population, regardless of age or previous education; and to offer these students a program which hopefully coupled their wants and their needs—an intensive intellectual core program focusing on human justice and American society, combined with several professional-skills training programs.

The Planning Group Each of the members of the planning group deserves description, for each contributed substantially—but only a few impressions from a visit during the planning year can be presented here.

  • *John Maguire* (president) is a robust, informal person, faintly reminiscent of Pierre Salinger, the kind who charges through the Long Island winter in an open shirt and heavy loose sweater. He animates many of the discussions but has no monopoly on ideas or verbal power. Committed to the ideal of participation but equally committed to getting things done and to retaining his legal powers, he seems apologetic sometimes in the midst of his dynamism.

  • *Jonathan Collett* (acting academic vice-president) came with Maguire from

Wesleyan, where he had been assistant professor of English. With a youthful face framed by grayish long hair and adorned with a whopping mustache, and blessed with a light smile that can put things back in perspective, he speaks thoughtfully about the academic program and the problems of consistency, quality, and evaluation.

- *Francis Mark,* a Trinidadian by birth, is an experienced social scientist who most recently taught at Federal City College in Washington. He talks precisely but openly and with great feeling.

- *Edwin Sanders* also came from Wesleyan, where, as student and recent graduate, he helped organize and run the Afro-Am program. He is in charge of field study at Old Westbury II.

- *Douglas Palmer* (vice-president) came from Harvard, and as a quiet, pipe-smoking, tweed-jacket type wearing the only necktie in sight, he seems at first glance a little out of place among these verbal, bearded, activist academicians. One senses in talking with him, however, that the implementation necessary to make it all happen will be well handled and that Old Westbury II will be thoughtfully innovative in the administrative area. He, like all the members of the planning staff, has been working 18-hour days and looks tired; still, he maintains a control and a sense of humor.

- *Benjamin McKendall* (vice-president for student affairs) draws on his experience in student affairs and admissions at Brown and Reed. He is a slim, rangy person one sees loping down the hall or slouched in a chair engaged in intense conversation.

In total there were 12 full-time members of the planning staff and almost 20 part-timers, including 5 of the faculty at Planting Fields. No students were included in the group for the first nine months. In the spring of 1971, 15 students were added—5 current students from Planting Fields (who received academic credit for their planning work) and 10 prospective students from the community.[2]

The planning group felt that it had to seal itself off from the Planting Fields operation, at least at the start. This attitude caused considerable resentment among the Old Westbury I personnel, who not unnaturally felt that they had something to contribute. But Maguire was convinced that he and his group needed time to develop their own, rather different program and to build confidence and trust in each other. As a group drawn from different backgrounds,

---

[2] Five of these prospective students came from the College Cooperative Centers, a high school–dropout training program run by ex-Old Westbury I man, Jerry Ziegler.

planning a curriculum on human justice, this group had to play out internally some of the problems of American society. There was probably an additional reason for the isolation of the planning group—a desire, given the unfavorable publicity of the early excesses of Old Westbury I, to emphasize the difference between the old and new programs.

The Students and the Admissions Process Experimental programs often convey a pervasive sense of privilege and preciousness, at least in part because they tend to be populated by intellectually bright middle- and upper-class students who, disaffected with the conventional, eagerly seek the cachet of the new. The planners at Old Westbury II avoided the word *experimental,* kept the publicity down, and specified carefully the kind of student they wanted.

President Maguire (1971, p. 17) described their aim as follows:

We did not have to look far for the kinds of students we were thinking about. . . . We discovered that less than 4 percent of the combined enrollment of the eight other colleges in the county was black and Puerto Rican (while the percent of black and Puerto Rican in the county's college-age population is far higher). A distressingly small percentage of those attending the other colleges was poor. Thus, a first principle we set up was that at least half of our student body should be from Nassau County. It also followed that we would need to find full financial aid for as many as half of our students from poor or working-class backgrounds, that half of them would be black and brown, and that we would have an older student body than is characteristic—a median age of twenty-four. [In short,] in operational terms, justice meant for us parity in faculty, administration, staff and student body; half white, half non-white, half male, half female, many with conventional academic backgrounds, many without.

McKendall and the admissions staff disliked and distrusted the usual selection procedure on the grounds that making decisions for the students inescapably involves a sort of "colonial" attitude, no matter how benign the aim. They viewed their job as that of interesting a large number of prospective students in Old Westbury II; of describing its educational program fully and frankly and getting enough feedback from the prospective student to be sure that he understood what would be expected of him; and then of letting each individual decide for himself. The only conscious weeding out the admissions staff planned on was that of clearly freaked-out kids or of those with severe psychological problems. They planned a sort of lottery-like system for selecting within categories where there were too many applicants.

The "self-selection based on good information" principle has yet to receive a complete trial. Of the 400 full-time equivalent students planned for in the fall of 1971, just over 100 were transfers from Old Westbury I. This left 300 FTE places, which were to be split between 200 full-time students and 200 part-timers, making a total enrollment of around 500. The admissions process was well advanced when, in early summer, Maguire reluctantly acceded to a new target of 30 percent black, 30 percent Puerto Rican, 30 percent white, and 10 percent other, insisted upon by vocal new faculty members who had not been in on the original planning.

Part-time status proved hard to control also. A number of students who were unsure of their ability to cope with the program signed on as part-timers, then switched to full-time status at the last minute.

Between the target change and the status switchers, Old Westbury II wound up with a fall 1971 enrollment of 571 students, with a full-time equivalency of 525 against the goal of 400.

On other dimensions, the student recruiting was more successful. "About 65% of the students come from Nassau and Suffolk counties, reflecting the commitment of the new Old Westbury to become a regional college serving greater Long Island. . . . Just under two-fifths of the student body is black and one-fifth is Puerto Rican or Spanish speaking. . . . About two-fifths of the student body is married. The median student age is 29" (Maguire, 1972, p. 2).

Financial-aid problems aggravated the confusion over numbers. Some felt that the admissions office had irresponsibly made commitments to needy students by admitting them on the grounds that justice demanded it and that somehow the aid funds just had to be forthcoming. But though the per capita aid at Old Westbury II is far higher than in most institutions, it simply could not stretch to cover all the needs.

Dropouts, transfers, financial-aid problems, and a few graduations reduced the overpopulation in the second semester, leaving about 425 FTE students enrolled, far closer to the number the staff was prepared to cope with.

Staff and Facilities Even after budget cuts, the state university allowed Old Westbury II a total of 41 full-time equivalent teaching positions the first year.

(The intended 9 to 1 student-faculty ratio was, of course, somewhat diluted by the unexpected additional students.)

The plan called for enrollment to grow slowly, permitting the faculty time to evaluate and refine programs and to start additional professional-skills sequences. Then growth was to accelerate, with the college reaching full enrollment of 5,000 students by 1980–81. During the first four or five years, the enrollment was to grow faster than the faculty size, until the college reached a more normal student-faculty ratio of 15 to 1.

These plans are now under the shadow of New York State budget difficulties. Construction delays and problems have meant that the first complex of buildings at Old Westbury II is still not ready for occupancy, and will not be until fall 1972. Some of the students have been meeting at the Old Westbury site, using converted maintenance buildings; the rest, primarily upper division and including all the transfers from Old Westbury I, meet at the SUNY Stony Brook campus, where dormitories and classrooms have been made available. Even with program coordinators and commuting faculty, the situation is awkward at best. But there is some hope: one hears the statement, "Last year we were two colleges at two campuses; this year we are one college at two campuses; next year we'll be one college at one campus."

That relief may be short-lived. If expansion plans proceed, the college will be out of space again by 1974–75, and no start at all has been made on the second complex of buildings.

A word more about the faculty. Of the 41 faculty, 10 were already on board, having participated in the planning activities; 14 more were to be transfers from Old Westbury I. These 24 were to form a nucleus of experience and familiarity with the plans around which the 17 new members could form. But 3 of the Old Westbury I people eventually resigned, and 3 more suddenly took personal leaves of absence; this reduced the nucleus to 18 and meant 23 new people had to be found. Since the recruiting program was slow getting off the ground and had to be augmented en route, the new faculty seemed to be, not unnaturally, those who could move easily and quickly—perhaps more single or divorced people than might have been expected, and certainly young. And the newcomers were in the majority.

In view of this situation, Maguire scheduled an intensive planning session in early summer 1971. The session was a painful one, as the newcomers lived out many of the conflicts the original planners had already gone through. One outcome of the session was the 30–30–30–10 racial enrollment goal already referred to; another was a similar goal for faculty and staff. (When the faculty recruiting was finished, the composition settled out about 40 percent black, 20 percent Puerto Rican, 40 percent white.) Not much educational planning got done at this session, so Maguire set back the opening of the school year till October 1 and ran yet another planning session in September.

The Educa-
tional Program The Old Westbury II Planning Group had sketched out an interesting educational program consisting of five coordinated elements:

- A core curriculum concerned with a critical analysis of issues in American life involving human justice. Its purpose is to help the students develop a skill at analysis, a language, and perceptual acuities which can thereafter be presupposed in other courses. The core program was to be "organized around . . . weekly discussion seminars and . . . central presentations in the form of plays, films, musical performances, lectures, and so on. From the discussion seminars will emerge more specialized classes, research, and action projects" ("Preliminary Program Announcement," 1971). All faculty members were to be involved in teaching the core program. The program was to be required of all students regardless of previous academic or non-academic experience.

- Several professional skills programs. Two were to be offered the first year, one additional in each of the next five years. A training program in health services, coordinated with Stony Brook's new Health Sciences operations, was to "prepare students with a community orientation to enter directly a number of health care professions, for example as nurses or as physician's assistants, or to enter medical school" ("A Curriculum Model," 1971). A program in education was to prepare students to meet State certificate requirements but more fundamentally (if somewhat pretentiously) was to make students "aware of what education in America is and what it might become" (ibid).

- A basic skills program using core materials to help students improve their reading, writing, computational, and perceptual skills.

- General courses to be developed in response to interests which the students and the faculty wish to pursue.

- Field study assignments of a full-time, short-term nature, for which there is specific and intensive advance preparation and which are accompanied by both supervision and reporting requirements.

President Maguire was well aware that the emphasis on human

justice and on field projects could lead to the sort of politicization of the campus which had wracked Old Westbury I. As a counterbalance, he stressed that, for all its interest in understanding current social problems and all its hopes that its graduates would be successful reformers, Old Westbury II was not to be a social service agency or an indoctrination center. It was to be an academic institution whose intellectual energies were focused on specific current problems. Its purpose was to study justice and human community in a structured way not possible while one is entirely engaged in community activity.

So far it seems that the nature of the student body at Old Westbury II has helped the college avoid some of the dangers of politicization; but the price has been, indirectly, the collapse of the intellectual core of the educational program.

To attract to college an older student from difficult economic circumstances, there has to be a clear payoff at the end of the road. Those aspects of the Old Westbury II program in which that payoff is clear seem to be doing well. The health services program is solid and developing strength. There was considerable student unhappiness when the education program, threatened by low priority for teacher training in the state, failed to develop as expected. Now refocused on early childhood and bilingual education, the program will soon be off and running. Field study experiences are going satisfactorily. And the need for strong basic skills training is more obvious than ever, to both students and faculty. Core materials are not being used in the basic skills training as had been hoped, and good substitutes have not yet been fully worked out, but the interest and the need are clear.

By contrast, the core curriculum has collapsed and has been discontinued, at least temporarily.

Intended to be common ground for all the programs, the core suffered from lack of detailed planning and from the absence of faculty members committed to it alone; it finally disintegrated in late fall 1971 when students called a four-day moratorium to protest financial-aid problems, lack of direction in the core program, and lack of development in the education program.

The absence of the core does not mean there are no intellectual courses, though it does indicate a lack of single focus. From the summer planning sessions emerged three sets of general courses. The first, emphasizing comparative history and comparative cultures, came out a truly multicultural endeavor involving almost half the faculty. The second, called "Politics, Economics, and Society," has a Third World emphasis. The third—American studies—stresses interest in white ethnic populations in this country. The faculty now list as degree requirements a major concentration in one of the above fields; competence in English and a second "language" which could be art or mathematics; field study; and a demonstrated ability to analyze and evaluate the fabric of American life. Maguire feels that in that last requirement the faculty reaffirmed the essence of the core idea and that, with time and an academic vice-president, some form of core program will again emerge.

Evaluation   The planning group at Old Westbury II recognized the need for perceptive evaluation not only of the college's programs but also of its people.

Everyone—individual faculty members, faculty or faculty-student committees, the academic vice-president, the regional accrediting agency, and representatives from the state university system—will participate in curricular evaluation.

Evaluation of faculty and staff is given high priority. Every faculty or staff member, tenured or not, agrees when he signs his contract to subject himself to an annual evaluation. Such an evaluation is designed to provide guidance and feedback, and will consist of several parts. A faculty member's teaching performance will be rated by his peers and his students, his professional scholarly work by his colleagues both inside and outside the institution, and his role in the program with which he is involved by the program head, dean, or president. (Junior faculty members in other institutions who get no feedback until the moment they are considered for a tenured position can appreciate the value of this arrangement.)

Evaluation of students is of particular concern. How is the faculty to judge when a student is ready to receive a degree, given the variety of experiences the students bring with them? Present policy is to recognize "experiences which [students] have had in their lives which materially contributed toward their education but were not accredited through any previous formal system of accreditation. It should be understood that this policy is not intended to accredit years of living or years of working. Rather, it is an attempt to factor out the educational content of life experiences" ("Accreditation Program . . . ," 1971). Students may earn up to one-fourth of total graduation credits in this manner.

Many of the planners wanted to use a "pass or work longer in the area" marking system, but here, as with the core curriculum, pragmatic interests overruled the theoretical values. Federal financial-aid eligibility requirements dictate a clear expression of academic status and a maximum period of eight semesters of aid. In consequence, a pass-fail system is used.

Governance   Knowing that governance was perhaps the biggest stumbling block in the Old Westbury I experience, President Maguire and his associates gave considerable thought to the principles of a system which could expedite the business of the college and yet avoid rigidity.[3]

They started with these principles: that the responsibilities and powers of the College Council, of the president, and of the officers in the state university system must be recognized; that those persons most affected by the decisions of the college should have a voice in framing those decisions; and that information about the college should be freely available to all its members, to the greatest extent possible.

The details of the governance structure are still being thrashed out, but the broad outlines can be sketched. The basic unit is the College Assembly, to which students will elect 15 members, faculty 10, and staff 5..Committees with members from each constituency will recommend policy in areas such as academic policy, finance, student affairs, and appointments. A steering committee, composed of the chairmen of these committees, the president, and other members elected by the assembly at large, will serve as the executive arm of the assembly. The steering committee will be convened and chaired by the president. Finally, since no formal machinery can be expected to deal adequately with all types of situations, provision is made for a town meeting to be called whenever any constituency feels that a problem deserves special hearing.

To maintain flexibility and responsiveness in committees and other administrative units, terms of office will be limited and chairmanships rotated.

Contrary to the Old Westbury I experience, the students have seemed to find no problems with this structure. But the faculty has taken until late winter 1972 to begin organizing itself seriously.

There remain a number of issues to be worked out in practice. Collective bargaining limits the openness of information on campus,

[3] This discussion of governance is based on Maguire et al. (1971).

especially in the area of personnel evaluations. There is generally a lack of administrative experience; will there be enough good people to permit continued rotation of chairmanships? In other situations, an assembly with more than one-third of its members from the student body seems to work out to have a student majority; how will a group in which half of the members are students turn out? How much control over curricula and related matters will the faculty be able to maintain? How much should they?

Old Westbury II: Comments, Caveats, Questions The architect's master plan for the physical facilities at Old Westbury won several awards. The buildings are arranged in a series of clusters, both for pleasanter appearance and for accommodation of the once planned constituent colleges. Complex A, the first cluster of academic-living buildings, is nearing completion and will be ready for occupancy in the fall of 1972. The other clusters, running construction-cost totals well over $100 million, have been postponed for the time being, which poses questions about the extent of the college's expansion.

Complex A, a gray-concrete version of Montreal's Habitat, is breathtaking. The campus will not give the sense of remoteness and isolation that Plánting Fields did, nor will it have the latter's lushness and natural grace. It will be up to the students and the faculty, once they move in, to concoct those informal touches like coffeehouses and zany buttons and mock-serious events which turn a vast and impressive plant into a livable, warm, and lively community.

Arthur Hug, president of the Long Island Trust Company, has been appointed chairman of the College Council; Maitland Edey resigned the chairmanship because of ill health and is now acting as vice chairman. Hug is a dynamic and politically acute man who can continue the steadying and supportive role the council has played. The council's outside function as "political ploughshare" may be even more important in the future than it has been so far. Some of Nassau County's residents could conceivably misunderstand the nature and aim of the college's programs and resent its staffing and student selection policies. The college may need some protecting.

The college must not forget that as an institution it should be able to do what it wants its graduates to do — to work constructively in the community, to assess situations and deal with them. If it is to attract the students it wants, give them the programs they need, place them well, and at the same time continue to receive the support of the community, the college will need not only solid programs but considerable political astuteness.

Astuteness, both political and educational, is needed right now in planning for the future of the college. SUNY is engaged in revising its master plans to deal with reduced income and with the need for better collaboration with the state's private colleges. The primary mechanism for dealing with both problems is optimizing educational resources in each region. This puts Old Westbury II under pressure to emphasize upper-division work (thus collaborating with large community colleges in the area) at the expense of thorough basic education of its students; to open its programs to students from all parts of society, as one of only two senior colleges in the region, rather than endeavor to serve those not otherwise served; and to shorten programs, thus making room for more students, rather than deal adequately with those who may need more than the usual time.

In the academic area there remain other puzzles. One finds neither a desire for, nor a rejection of, specialized work in a discipline. What happens, for instance, to the student who in his second year decides that he wants to study chemistry? Is provision made for him at Old Westbury II or does he transfer? Most studies undertaken at Old Westbury II are interdisciplinary or transdisciplinary, and no departments exist as such; but to what extent will they be allowed to develop as the college grows? Clearly there is need for hard and insightful research in the kinds of problems with which Old Westbury II is dealing; but what of scholarly work in more esoteric areas, which may be of interest only to the faculty member pursuing it? To what extent does the college encourage or discourage this sort of work? The reward system for faculty is as yet undeveloped, and emphasis could be placed wherever desired.

A key personnel lack is that of an academic vice president. The gap in the organization is all the more poignant when one remembers Byron Youtz's absence from the scene the first year at Old Westbury I. With only a year to plan the entire curriculum, Jon Collett and his associates did well. Yet the core program collapsed and two of the three concentration programs were "captured" by ideological groups—"Politics, Economics, and Society" by the Third World group; American studies by white radicals. (Curiously, the few black nationalists have no programmatic home.) While it must be admitted that there are few if any good models for this type of program, a combination of wider academic experience, more time for planning, and greater insistence on detailed planning and execution of the plan might have avoided some of the confusion and loss of direction.

John Maguire has been forced to deal with academic detail more than he might otherwise have been, with some consequent erosion of his clout. But he has risen to the leadership challenge well, displaying a willingness to make decisions where needed, not relying so heavily as at the beginning on consensus to solve problems. While this attitude is seen in some quarters as heavy-handed, the need for leadership is clearly evident and will continue to exist even after the administration is fully manned and the governance structure operating effectively.

Maguire takes more personal interest in the administrative details of his operation than did President Wofford, but the two share a basic way of dealing with people. Both count on simple human decency and a certain amount of noblesse oblige. In the kinds of institutions both men had seen before, these attitudes worked because they were widely recognized and accepted. Maguire occasionally finds himself operating across a gap in personal styles in dealing with a student population which has been taught by experience to be skeptical, suspicious of "causes" and principles.

Finally, with relation to the student body, one wonders whether Old Westbury II will be able to stick to the self-selection admissions process. It may become difficult not to be selective. Clearly capable people may be turned down in a lottery-like process if pressure for admission increases. Conversely, it may prove difficult to do a good job with some students, no matter how much they may want to come.

And one wonders whether difficulties may arise within a student body composed principally of black and Puerto Rican and of lower-middle-class poor, between those who want to get into the system and those who want to defend their tenuous place in it.

CONCLUSION The contrasts between Old Westbury I and Old Westbury II are striking. The programs were addressed to quite different communities. The two groups of students could hardly have been more different, though it must be said that Old Westbury I was evolving toward the student mix that Old Westbury II started with. Curricula differ widely, as do forms of internal organization. The first venture had everyone doing his own thing; the second insists on common requirements, though the core experience has been foregone. What seemed most distinctive about the first program was the involvement of students, the change in form and process of education; what seems most distinctive about the second is the emphasis on the content of that education.

Yet the similarities between the programs are almost more striking. Michael Novak, responding to the question "What ever happened to Old Westbury?" answered, "They made it into a movie and it's being replayed now at the new site." Both programs tried to organize education around a single theme: in Old Westbury I, the theme was lost from sight early on; at Old Westbury II, it is still a concern. In both cases the educational unit started out as a small group, the Socratic seminar or workshop or the core seminar—and in neither case did the original concept survive. Both programs called for universal experiences; neither was able to work out a core program and stick to it. Both were honest attempts to relate education to the world outside the campus, though the world is defined slightly differently in the second case. Both programs tried to institutionalize change, the one through "organic growth," the second through mechanisms for evaluation and renewal. The demand for 50 percent nonwhite representation in the first college becomes practical reality in the second. Both colleges developed three academic concentration areas (ignoring for a moment Old Westbury II's professional-skill areas), of which one attracted a major share of students and faculty; in both cases the concentration areas became to some extent captive programs—in the first case to people with different governance models, in the second to those with different ideologies. Both presidents are articulate, idealistic, reform-minded men, and though Old Westbury II tries to appear hardheaded, there is almost as high a quotient of evangelism on campus as in the first experiment.

There were three elements in the original mandate—breaking the lockstep, a larger role for students, and the use of mechanical aids to instruction.

Perhaps, though this is oversimplification, it can be said that Old Westbury I made its major contribution by introducing students into full partnership in the academic world. Both positive and negative features of that experience resulted from intense student participation in program planning, curriculum development, student selection, and governance. Had the attempt been made in the 1950s, it might have come off.

It seems that Old Westbury II may make its major contribution with respect to the first of the mandates: to break the lockstep, to serve a different population in new ways appropriate to it, to recognize and deal constructively with both the educational disadvantages (in level of skills) and advantages (in interest, experience, and maturity) which their chosen populations presents.

Neither venture really addresses itself to the issue of faculty productivity, of freeing the faculty member to work most effectively, though such an aim is compatible with both programs. But the physical plant at Old Westbury incorporates provision for the new educational technologies, thanks to the foresight of the planners of Old Westbury I.

Old Westbury II seems, though its plans have not all come through intact, to be somewhat more controlled, less touted, more "realistic" than its predecessor. It lacks, perhaps intentionally, something of the earlier experiment's fervor and willingness to be entirely open. Old Westbury II would seem to have both the desire and the substance for an interesting, valuable, and distinctive success, though the shakedown cruise is still under way.

Yet while this paper ends with respect and admiration for the people at both colleges and with optimism about Old Westbury II, it must also end with an expression of two concerns.

On the author's last visit to Old Westbury II, no one mentioned "human justice." It is a difficult phrase, to be sure. But it is a unifying concept. Old Westbury's major danger now is one of schizophrenia between the professional-skills programs and the academic interests and between the ideologies themselves. The unifying theme is essential.

The College Council and the State University of New York merit appreciation and admiration for their imaginative and persistent search for ways to meet real educational needs. Perhaps the most important justification for the existence of a major system of higher education is that the system can, at its best, foster considerable variety of educational experience. One hopes that budget pressures and regionalization do not homogenize the system. Old Westbury II is a courageous and valuable attempt to meet one sort of educational need; it cannot meet all needs, even in its own region. If, through budget or enrollment pressure or through a failure of nerve in the system, it is forced into homogeneity, the country will have lost an experiment of character and value.

References

"Accreditation Program for Educational Experience," College at Old Westbury, Academic Policy Committee, Old Westbury, N.Y., 1971.

"A Curriculum Model," unpublished working paper, Old Westbury II Planning Group, Old Westbury, N.Y., 1971.

Fischer, John: "Survival U: Prospectus for a Really Relevant University," published as "The Easy Chair," *Harper's Magazine,* September 1969.

Hebert, Tom: *Arena, Agora, and Tober,* a study of life at the Old Westbury Planting Fields campus with limited private publication, Oyster Bay, N.Y., 1969.

"Life and Death of a Far-out College," *New York Times,* Apr. 26, 1971, p. 39.

Maguire, John D.: "Less than a Year into a Presidency; or, What's a Sober Guy Like Me Doing in a Place Like This?," *Soundings Magazine,* Spring 1971.

Maguire, John D.: "Annual Report of the New College at Old Westbury, 1970/71," Old Westbury, N.Y., January 1972.

Maguire, John D. et al.: "Statement on Governance," filed with the State University of New York Chancellor, Old Westbury, N.Y., October 1971.

"Mandate for a New College," *Master Plan,* State University of New York, Albany, N.Y., 1966.

"Preliminary Program Announcement," sent to prospective students at Old Westbury, Old Westbury Planning Group, Old Westbury, N.Y., January 1971.

Report on the State University College at Old Westbury, ad hoc committee of the State University of New York, Clifford Craven, chairman, Albany, N.Y., June 1, 1970.

Wofford, Harris: "An Experimental College with Students as Full Partners: The State University of New York, College at Old Westbury," unpublished paper provided by the author, 1969.

10. A Profile of the University of Pennsylvania

by David R. Goddard and Linda C. Koons

In the last 15 years the University of Pennsylvania has probably made greater strides forward than any other of America's older universities, largely because it had more to make up for than most. There have been changes not only in the university's physical plant but in the quality of its students, its faculty, and its academic programs. Just how far the university has come is evident when one looks back at it in an earlier time.

In a national magazine article on the University of Pennsylvania some years ago, Alfred Bester (1962, p. 88) described the campus as he had known it as a student in 1931:

> The University was the wreck of a once-proud, once-powerful Ivy League school, fiercely maintaining antiquated traditions and rigid caste systems, and practically without prestige.
>
> Liberal Arts students sneered at the Wharton Business School. Out-of-town students were contemptuous of the Philadelphia "commuters." Fraternities fought furious political battles to the indifference of the unattached. The prep-school crowd who had failed to make the Big Three for whatever reasons, kept to themselves and regarded the others as untouchables. The faculty was larded with insular descendants of the great Philadelphia families, Main Line and British Tory in their outlook and disdainful of the 20th Century.

Although Bester's description may have been an exaggerated one, certainly there was much truth in it. When D. R. G. arrived on the campus in 1946 he found Pennsylvania dull and depressing, and although it was outstanding in law, medicine, dentistry, and classical archaeology—and had a superb anthropological museum

ACKNOWLEDGMENT: This paper was prepared while the authors were in residence in the Fels Center of Government of the university, and they wish to acknowledge the support and hospitality received from the center while there.

—he didn't hold the other schools and departments of the university in very high regard. There were distinguished faculty members, but their number was small and far too many had gained their entire academic experience at Pennsylvania. The graduate schools, particularly law and medicine, attracted able students and there were many bright undergraduates, but far too many still came to Pennsylvania as a second choice. The physical facilities were inadequate and their maintenance was poor; little construction of academic buildings had occurred in the last three decades. The university campus was dissected by city streets, and trolley cars clattered by so loudly that often lecturers in College and Bennett halls had to pause to wait for the racket to subside. Old factories, hotels, and run-down houses threatened to engulf the neighboring community.

Since the 1950s, however, the university seems to have shaken itself out of its somnolent middle age. Today there is about Pennsylvania a real excitement that a visitor can grasp immediately upon approaching the campus. The placing of streetcars in a tunnel and the closing of streets to create superblocks on the campus have startlingly changed the physical setting. The construction of libraries, classrooms, faculty studies, a faculty club, student housing, dining facilities, and recreational quarters has increased the quality of academic life. Staid, gothic College Hall, the main administration building, now faces a green quad, not trolley tracks; red, turreted Furness Building stands alongside a new glass and concrete Fine Arts Building. The old Biology Building now sits beside new and distinctive research facilities designed by faculty member Louis Kahn. And antique Houston Hall, the first student union in the country, now endures the grime and noise from the construction of a new seven-story humanities building next door.

One measure of what has happened, physically, to the campus is the amount of money spent on construction over the last 19 years. Between 1952 and December 1971, $211 million went into new buildings or major renovations, and another $39 million of construction was in progress in January 1972.

While the change in the look of the university is impressive, we believe the change in its faculty and student body has been even greater.

AN INFUSION OF NEW PEOPLE   In 1957 Hayward Keniston made a study (1959) of the graduate programs at Pennsylvania and pointed out that not only was the faculty getting old, a high proportion were men with Penn graduate degrees; some departments, such as English, were almost completely staffed by Pennsylvania-trained faculty. Although the natural scientists were for the most part young men, the average age of professors in the humanities and social sciences was 57, of associate professors 44.5, and of assistant professors 39. Of the senior faculty in the social sciences and the humanities, over two-thirds had done their doctoral work at Pennsylvania, as had nearly 40 percent of the junior faculty.

Today the university makes a much more determined effort to search the country—and frequently Europe—for the ablest people. The result is a much less Pennsylvania-bred faculty. There is greater diversity among the faculty, and its members tend to be more cosmopolitan, more sophisticated, and more liberal. Though we have made no systematic study of the ages of our faculty, we do know that it is far younger than in 1957 and intellectually much livelier. Over half of our faculty have come since 1962.

Our students have changed as well. One Pennsylvania alumnus recently wrote that what had most disturbed him when he had been a student here was that only a small segment of the student population was intellectual and too large a percentage were not academically oriented. They were at Penn for one of three reasons: "to get by and get out; to go to Wharton and go into Dad's business; or to take part in sports."

When D. R. G. started teaching here in 1946, he did not feel that there was a tradition of study among the undergraduates. Far too many were either athletes or what were then described as "Tweeds" —the prep school product—and far too many came from private schools in the Northeast.

Today this has completely changed. Our undergraduates are bright, interesting, aggressive, and exciting to teach. They have high academic credentials. Like the faculty, they are diverse in origin, no longer coming largely from private schools in the Northeast: about one-third are from the state of Pennsylvania, one-third from the Middle Atlantic and New England states, and one-third from the rest of the country and abroad. They are diverse in religion: about one-third are Jewish, 28 percent are Catholic, and the remainder are Protestant or of unknown religion. And they are increasingly diverse in race: at Pennsylvania the enrollment of black undergraduates has increased sharply in recent years from an estimated 40 black students who entered as freshmen in 1966 to 140 who entered in 1969 to 170 each in 1970 and 1971.

Full-time undergraduates now number about 8,000 and graduate and graduate professional students 7,200. Of full-time undergraduate and graduate students, about 1,200 are foreign students. (Pennsylvania has traditionally attracted students from abroad; as early as the colonial period, many of its students came from the Caribbean and Latin America, and one can find sixth- and seventh-generation Penn students from these areas on campus today.)

We believe that two factors are particularly responsible for both the physical change in the university and the change in the quality of our students and faculty: the Educational Survey begun in 1953 and continued over a six-year period and the selection of Gaylord P. Harnwell as president in that same year.

THE EDUCATIONAL SURVEY Costing $700,000, its 25 separate studies filling five volumes, the Educational Survey was a hard-nosed look at the university and where it was going. Over 300 faculty members from all over the country were brought in to evaluate our schools, our departments of instruction, our financial structures and procedures, our faculty and student body, our trustees, and our educational programs — both general and professional — at all levels. Directed by Dr. Joseph H. Willits, formerly of the Rockefeller Foundation, and the late Dr. Malcolm G. Preston of our faculty, and liberally supported by foundation grants, the survey emphasized the need for excellence in the intellectual life of all the schools and departments in the university and outlined what goals the university should set and how they should be achieved. An 18-member committee composed of six trustees, six faculty members, and six senior administrators drew from the survey the "Integrated Development Plan," an outline of the future physical expansion of the university as well as eight-year projections of the size of the student body, annual budgets, tuition levels, and salaries.

In order to implement the Integrated Development Plan, substantial new funds were required. Because the university's last major capital drive (in 1942) had met with limited success, the trustees spent two years in careful planning, and it wasn't until 1964 that a new capital campaign was announced: the goal was $93 million. In fact $102 million was raised, not counting state or federal funds or annual giving. The trustees and former trustees gave $19.2 million and the faculty, through the senate, donated over $3 million.

Hard work and a concerted effort to acquaint alumni with the "new" Pennsylvania contributed to the success of the campaign.

Early in the planning stage, staff members visited 75 cities across the country in an attempt to identify potential donors; 7,000 alumni, including many who had never before been involved in the university's programs or support, were discovered. The capital campaign was largely directed at them.

A nationwide alumni information program was launched which centered around a series of seminars entitled "Inside Pennsylvania" in which faculty, students, administrators, and trustees discussed their work, the resurgence of the university, and its plans for the future. Initially, these seminars were given on the campus, and selected alumni were invited to attend them. These proved so successful, they were taken on the road under the sponsorship of two university groups: a national council headed by former Secretary of Defense Thomas S. Gates, organized to deal with a limited number of unusually influential alumni, and a Committee for Greater Pennsylvania headed by Otto W. Manz, Jr., a New York utility executive, organized to acquaint alumni with the university's programs. All told, the "Inside Pennsylvania" seminars were viewed by some 4,500 alumni in 44 cities, and speakers included not only the president, the provost, and the trustees but some 62 professors and administrative officers and 22 students. The result is that Pennsylvania is now among a group of institutions distinguished for receiving high-level support from its alumni. This has helped us with foundations and other private groups—for the last five years Penn has received an average of $22.3 million annually in gifts and grants from the private sector. Obviously these dollars are important. They have built buildings, endowed 30 professorships, and furnished $10.2 million in new scholarships and fellowship endowments.

The commonwealth of Pennsylvania has also supported the university. Since Benjamin Franklin's days, Penn, although it is a privately controlled institution, has received state grants, albeit on an irregular basis before 1903. Although this annual support—amounting to $13.08 million in 1971–72—is only 7 percent of our total budget, it is nearly 20 percent of our academic budget. In addition, through the activity of the General State Authority, the university in the past decade has received $34 million for academic buildings with the state paying the interest and principal on the bonds. This program still continues, although now the state only sells the bonds for building construction, while the university pays to the state the interest and the principal on the bonds.

Though Pennsylvania has been successful in raising funds, this does not mean that it no longer faces serious financial problems. It continues to have, for example, a smaller endowment per student than do most of our distinguished private universities: the invested funds on June 30, 1971, had a market value of over $195 million which yielded an income of some $10 million. Under these circumstances the annual grant from the commonwealth of Pennsylvania is of major importance.

It also appears that even though the university desperately needed new buildings, the rate of building may have been too great during the time of the capital campaign. Since 1969 the university has been trying instead to direct gifts to operations or endowments, though there is still a necessity to raise funds to complete some building under construction. Martin Meyerson, who became president in September of 1971, and his administration unfortunately are facing a critical situation in which new funds must be found or certain programs must be phased out unless the state can be persuaded to support some programs and schools on a contract basis.

THE LEADERSHIP OF GAYLORD HARNWELL While the Educational Survey served as an impetus for change, not only in the physical look of the campus but in the quality of its students and faculty, and while the capital campaign provided funds for effecting these changes, it was the strong leadership of Gaylord P. Harnwell that ensured that such changes occurred.

Long before the survey had pointed out the preponderance of Pennsylvania graduates on the university's faculty, President George McClelland and the dean of the college, Glen Morrow, had made a quiet effort to attract outside scholars. During his presidency, Harold Stassen in particular had worked hard at the problem. He encouraged deans to bring in outside faculty, and he even attempted to break the university's civil service-like salary structure by paying more distinguished faculty a higher salary. Unfortunately, Mr. Stassen wasn't at Penn long enough to know of the academic politics needed to produce a change in faculty composition, and thus Penn made little effort to retain faculty members who were invited to such distinguished schools as Columbia, Harvard, or Yale. Worse, too many in the administration seemed to feel that there was no point in trying.

The situation changed when Gaylord P. Harnwell became president. He saw no reason for allowing his most able faculty colleagues to leave because of higher salaries or other factors that he could control. He also urged departments to make appointments of younger persons. Several departments were reconstituted with a youthful faculty; many of these departments not only do a first-class, even inspiring, job in teaching but also hold promise of becoming distinguished scholarly departments with national reputations a few years hence. Not all such gambles will pay off, but to date this has made the university a much more interesting place, and this is recognized by the caliber of students we are getting.

Why was President Harnwell successful in retaining—and attracting—faculty and Mr. Stassen not? Mr. Harnwell's experience was no doubt one important factor; he knew the ins and outs of the academic structure at Pennsylvania, having been on its faculty for 15 years and chairman of one of its larger departments, physics. Dissatisfaction with the presidency of Harold Stassen was also a factor. Although Harold Stassen had been initially greeted by the faculty with enthusiasm—he was bright, liberal in outlook, and seemed to have a good grasp of what a university is all about—he lost their support when he became a candidate for the Republican nomination for United States President and had to be away from campus much of the time. In his absence the university was administered by a nonacademic executive vice president, and many on the faculty came to believe that business functions were given priority over educational functions. Gaylord Harnwell quickly changed that impression and gained the support of most of his faculty.

President Harnwell also provided the catalyst for improving the quality of our student body. Under his leadership, there was a deliberate tightening of admissions standards, and enrollment dropped. In fact enrollment of undergraduates in the Wharton School dropped almost 50 percent. (It is to President Harnwell's credit that he also managed to raise money during this time to make up for the lost income.) Enrollment was then increased slowly but with the admission of more able students.

Later, in the mid-1960s, a careful study of admissions was made by a faculty committee, and the result was the McGill report, named for its chairman, Dan McGill. This report stressed that the quality that should be sought above all others in a student body was "intellectual power"; academic potential, personal promise, creativity, and leadership were to be considered also, and a small segment of the class was to be allowed to gain admission because of outstanding personal attributes or backgrounds that would enrich the social and cultural environment of the campus.

All too often those applying to Pennsylvania had been the less able students from Eastern prep schools and distinguished public high schools. With the McGill report as a guide and with the support of President Harnwell and the provost, the admissions office made it clear to many headmasters and principals that Pennsylvania had no interest in their usual applicants; as a result far more able students began to apply from these schools. Greater scholarship support helped to increase the quality of our student body as did the broadening of our recruiting base. A special effort was made to enroll more black students, and we quickly discovered our own black students were our best recruiters. A search was also made for superior students from small towns in Pennsylvania who appeared likely to make good progress at Penn but who might not be considering it because they lacked financial support. Intensive recruiting was an important factor. And as the stature of the faculty increased and the look of the campus changed, many able students who couldn't get into Harvard or Yale found Pennsylvania an acceptable alternative. In addition, our location became an attraction. Students want to be where the action is and the action is now considered to be in urban universities.

CHANGES IN CAMPUS INTERESTS *Action* of course refers to problems of inner cities: racism, poverty, education, and housing. Gone are the days when Penn students were more concerned about Saturday night dates, beer blasts, and which fraternity to pledge, when they involved themselves in Rowbottoms, a Pennsylvania way of blowing off steam (sometimes developing into pantie raids), or Skimmer, the annual crew race on the Schuylkill which became an excuse for excessive drinking and such high jinks as overturning trolleys, setting cars on fire, and dunking people into the river. Rowbottoms have nearly disappeared, and one celebrates Skimmer these days by attending a rock concert. Even fraternities have almost disappeared.

Pennsylvania has always been a strong fraternity school. As late as 1953, for example, more than 70 percent of the men in the freshman class pledged fraternities. The number pledging finally stabilized at about 50 percent of the entering class each year until 1969, when that figure dropped to 30 percent; in 1970-71 it was down to 21 percent.

Sororities were strong, too. Ten years ago they had a total of 526 members; in 1970–71 membership was down to 89 with only 15 women pledging during this year.

Until 1968, the control of student government and most activities was fraternity-dominated. And until recent years many of our faculty, particularly in the Wharton School and in the engineering schools, not only were fraternity alumni but also, together with a group of trustees, strongly supported the system. In fact, when in the mid-fifties the university tried to get rid of discrimination within the fraternity system, a senior trustee made a public statement encouraging students to discriminate! The university was also handicapped in its efforts by its own office of student affairs, which was strongly biased in favor of fraternities. It was only when that office was reorganized in the mid-sixties that fraternities were treated like any other student group.

There is no doubt in our minds that the university has suffered from the fraternity system. We had Christian fraternities and Jewish fraternities and very little communication between the two. Feeling between fraternity and nonfraternity members could be bitter. Although it is to the university's credit that it had many Jewish faculty members and accepted many Jewish students when the rest of the Ivy League did not, this was vitiated in part by the fraternity system with its institutionalized intolerance. Occasionally one still meets older alumni who have not supported the university because of the discrimination they had experienced as students (though there are also many who do support the university because it accepted them when most private universities would not have done so).

The construction of high-rise apartments by the university helped to initiate the fraternity system's decline by downgrading the traditional reasons many students had for joining fraternities: the convenience of living on campus, inexpensive meals, and a decent place to sleep.

Until the high rises were built, Pennsylvania was unable to house even half of its undergraduates and housed only 9 percent of its graduate students. The rest of the student body lived off campus in rooming houses or apartments or commuted from home. Today the campus is largely residential, with over 90 percent of the freshmen and about 50 percent of the upperclassmen and 30 percent of the graduate students now living on campus.

Fraternities also lost influence because of the growing feeling among students that such organizations were no longer "relevant." As students became more interested in racial and social problems, as they worked in ghettos, tutored disadvantaged children, and registered voters in the South, their social outlook changed. That of fraternities did not.

In order to survive, fraternities are now attempting to convince their alumni—often their greatest barrier to reform—of the necessity for change. Christian houses are electing Jewish students and would gladly elect black students if such students would join. Many fraternities are abolishing pledging, some are taking in female members, and several are involving themselves in community projects. It is of interest that at the time of our College Hall sit-in in February 1969, when students were protesting the taking over of land where poor black and white families lived, fraternity and sorority members joined the other undergraduate students in support.

From a highly rigid fraternity-sorority system the university has evolved into one of the most open college societies in the country. Numerous coed residential living arrangements for upperclassmen and freshmen have been developed by students within the dormitories and the high-rise apartments. Some are centered around social activities, while others are built around intellectual and cultural programs. Stauffer, for example, is an academic "house," with subunits centered around academic seminars taught in the house for credit by resident faculty members. Hill House is also an academic community having faculty fellows, freshman seminars, speakers, and concerts. Harnwell House, though more social, does sponsor faculty dinners and colloquiums, and art and discussion evenings which might feature a chamber group one night, movies another, and poetry reading a third. Even an urban studies project is being considered for one of the high rises where classes and supper seminars can be held, fieldwork training conducted, and a library housed.

Students are given a remarkable degree of freedom and considerable responsibility. For some, however, the responsibility is overwhelming and the freedom difficult to deal with. A recent survey of student concerns indicates that they mostly worry about loneliness, birth control—or lack of it—and drugs. In order to help students handle these problems, the university has, in addition to its traditional dormitory counselors and resident faculty members, professional people from outside the university—lawyers, nurses, teachers—living in the high rises with students, attempting to diversify the experience in the dorms. Talking Point, a walk-in counseling service conducted by medical students, has proved popular. There are guidance programs giving the pros and cons of various careers; there are sex-counseling programs, marriage-counseling programs, and drug-counseling programs; there are sessions on group dynamics and weekend retreats with faculty. Many of these programs are student-originated and -run, and all have helped to fill the void the decline of fraternities has created.

CONTRIBU-TIONS OF PROFESSIONAL SCHOOLS Fraternities were not alone in their intolerance. Many of Philadelphia's distinguished families were just as guilty. D. R. G. remembers a wealthy Chestnut Hill father calling on him one evening, disturbed because his son placed Pennsylvania first in his college preference; and another father, a graduate of Harvard and of the Penn Law School, was concerned because his elder daughter transferred from Smith to Pennsylvania and his younger daughter picked Pennsylvania as her first choice.

This had not always been the case. Until the 1890s the most correct Philadelphia families sent their sons to the university as a matter of course, although the Quaker families tended to send their sons to Haverford or Swarthmore. However, from 1890 until the late 1950s, Philadelphia upper-class boys went to Harvard, Princeton, Yale, Williams, or Amherst for their undergraduate work.

And the reason? Pennsylvania lacked social prestige. It was well known, for example, that the Wharton School accepted large numbers of students from immigrant and Jewish families.

Interestingly enough, such social snobbery did not extend to Pennsylvania's graduate and graduate professional schools. It was perfectly acceptable to send one's son to the Law School or School of Medicine. Indeed, Philadelphia law firms were largely staffed by Pennsylvania law graduates, and Philadelphia medicine was dominated by Pennsylvania medical graduates.

Unlike Harvard, which derives its personality and reputation from its undergraduate college, the character of Pennsylvania seems to have been determined in large part by its professional and graduate schools. There is no doubt that this has hurt our public reputation to some extent: the public judges a school largely on its undergraduate programs and students and the success of its alumni.

Although the college is the oldest school in the university, tracing its ancestry to the founding of the Charity School in 1740 and admitting its first collegiate student in 1754, the School of Medicine, the first in North America and founded in 1765, soon came to overshadow the college not only in wealth and importance but at one time in actual numbers of students as well. The founding of the Schools of Dental Medicine and of Veterinary Medicine and the construction of a university hospital followed, as did the first school of business in the United States—the Wharton School—and the Schools of Engineering and Fine Arts. One can readily see the great weight the professional schools have played through sheer size and number; they have given a strong professional bias to the university.

Pennsylvania is one of a very few universities in this country having all its schools located on one campus. In addition to the college and the schools mentioned above, we also have Schools of Graduate Education, Nursing, Allied Medical Professions, Social Work, and Communications.

This physical environment should have been to the advantage of both our students and our faculty. But it didn't always work out that way.

Friction between schools was a serious problem. The college was quite jealous of the professional schools, and even though the college had a distinguished faculty, it lacked the national reputation of the professional schools. The campus was a confederation of separate schools, held together by a common administration and the trustees but with little of the intellectual unity one would expect of a major academic institution. As a result, some of the schools achieved great distinction while others were mediocre; development was very uneven, producing a predictable lack of communication and a rivalry among schools.

The formation of a university senate in 1951, the naming of Gaylord P. Harnwell to the presidency in 1953, and the establishment of a faculty club in 1958—and certainly the Educational Survey—resulted in a new sense of institutional responsibility. Deans and faculty now recognize that a university such as ours cannot have varying standards of excellence.

THE UNDER-GRADUATE EXPERIENCE No longer does Pennsylvania have separate sections for college and for Wharton students in the same subjects, or separate sections for men and women. Students from different schools now sit together, a fact which means that they have a common undergraduate experience.

The complete acceptance of women is relatively new on campus. Although the College for Women was established in 1933, for many years women were not permitted in many buildings on campus including the student union, Houston Hall. There were two student governments, two student union boards, two student newspapers, and two Phi Beta Kappa chapters, one for undergraduate men and the other for undergraduate women. Finally, about 1965, the two student governments merged and a girl was elected the first president of the combined body; the student newspapers also merged, and three years later the first woman editor was named; two years after that, faculty holdouts finally agreed to there being one Phi Beta Kappa chapter for all.

The undergraduate schools developed an emphasis in humanities and the social sciences. The Wharton and Engineering Schools allowed their students to take more courses in the liberal arts—and receive credit for them—while the Schools of Nursing and Allied Medical Professions markedly decreased the amount of narrow, professional training required of their students and increased the amount of work in liberal arts and in natural sciences. Most importantly, perhaps, the faculty began to concern themselves with undergraduates.

For too many years the university ignored its undergraduates and aimed its resources primarily at graduate education and the professional schools. There was a tendency to have too many of the senior faculty occupied principally with advanced undergraduate and graduate education, with the result that in some cases there was inadequate concern for undergraduate courses. Pennsylvania also had a problem persuading its senior gifted teachers that they could make a major contribution in teaching undergraduates.

If we may believe the older alumni, the university in the 1920s and 1930s had a tradition of its senior scholars actively participating in undergraduate teaching. But by the post-World War II period, this tradition was prevalent in only a few departments, most often those in the natural sciences, but even in these departments primarily in the courses for science majors. (D. R. G. recalls that he was criticized by his departmental colleagues for giving a freshman course to nonscience students; this was considered a misuse of time and energy by a senior faculty member.) All too frequently the senior faculty ignored the freshmen and sophomores, and some even refused to do any undergraduate teaching.

A senior academic dean who served a few years ago frequently referred to "the boredom of undergraduate teaching" (though he himself was a fine scholar and a distinguished teacher). This attitude soon reached the assistant professors, who concluded that a new book or research paper was the route to academic retention and promotion.

In the last 10 years, the quality of undergraduate education has markedly improved. While this has no doubt been due in part to our young faculty and in part to the administration, which has attempted to recognize teaching in its appointment and promotions, much credit must go to our more able students.

In 1966 the Student Committee on Undergraduate Education (SCUE) issued a report based on a questionnaire sent to all undergraduates, which called for a limited pass-fail system and for an individualized major in which a student could pursue a program that could not be accommodated by any of the established departments. Through student efforts, such programs were established. While there is some doubt as to whether pass-fail actually encourages students to take courses outside their field of interest (as it was claimed it would), there is enough satisfaction with the system that its usage has been expanded. The individualized major, on the other hand, is an unqualified success. Students have developed programs in such areas as medieval studies, communications and culture, and the individual and society. SCUE led the drive to change the curriculum two years ago and was helpful in getting the required course load reduced.

Students were responsible for the formation of an undergraduate program in urban studies and in 1970 established an experimental college in which about 30 students lived and studied together. The students attempted to find an alternative to the traditional lecture-examination-grade method of learning, but the unstructured, undirected system they established proved unworkable. Small study groups were soon set up with a teacher as a sponsor and the direction of course work predetermined. The college could be termed a success only in the sense that students became aware of the problems of structure, motivation, and discipline. However, its failure was not enough to deter further efforts; a second experimental college was developed—a thematic college which emphasizes seminars in a theme area, individual projects, and self-evaluation and more fully involves the faculty. This college has been so successful that it will be continued next year.

Students also pioneered for a more open curriculum with greater access to graduate and graduate professional courses. A closer relationship between undergraduate and graduate schools has resulted. The Law School, for example, is now offering a course for undergraduates; the Department of City Planning in the Graduate School of Fine Arts is allowing many undergraduates into its courses. And some of our brighter undergraduates are working simultaneously on their bachelor's and master's degrees.

The new cohesiveness of the university has also had a beneficial effect on the graduate and professional schools. Although the School of Medicine has long been intellectually close to the departments of biology, psychology, chemistry, physics, and engineering, one now sees the Wharton Graduate School and the School of Medicine jointly teaching in programs of community medicine, in the Leonard Davis Institute of Health Economics, and in the M.B.A. program in medical administration. There are also joint programs with the Department of Psychiatry and other university departments in the West Philadelphia Mental Health Consortium and joint programs—and degrees—between City Planning and several schools, including the Engineering and Law Schools, and between the Law School and the Wharton School.

While we do not favor change for change's sake, we do think there is much room for experiment and innovation within the university. We have a wide variety of students, and not all benefit by the same kinds of instruction. It is true that some demands for innovation could result in a lowering of standards, but at Penn, at least, students and faculty have worked closely together for years in the planning of curricula and degree requirements, and we think this has made our students more responsible. We have also been lucky in the kind of faculty we have. Even our so-called radical faculty have high academic standards and seem unwilling to compromise them. Indeed, the greatest threat to academic standards at Pennsylvania probably comes from sincere, well-meaning faculty who wouldn't dream of deliberately lowering academic standards but who are unable to foresee the implications of some of their tampering.

While more concern is now being given to undergraduate teaching, students are still highly critical, and much of their criticism is justified (though some of it is based on ignorance of other institutions and some is youthful exaggeration).

In his second year as president, Martin Meyerson is challenging the educational program of the university. He believes the previously mentioned reforms are just a beginning. In a statement before the trustees in January 1972, entitled "In Pursuit of Sharpened Goals" (published in the *Pennsylvania Gazette* for February 1972) he challenged the faculty to develop additional educational innovations for the undergraduates:

Many undergraduate major programs in the arts and sciences are excellent. An increasing number of undergraduates pursue course patterns that reach up to graduate offerings; some earn a combined bachelor's and master's degree. Transfer students should be encouraged to come here with that attraction in mind. Beginning students who are equipped to start a field of concentration when they enter the University should be permitted to do so readily. Students should have the opportunity to prove their mastery of a concentration not necessarily by the accumulation of course credits, but through comprehensive examinations and also through independent research or other creative work.

For many beginning undergraduates, however, we require a much more flexible and experimental curriculum. In a number of areas we have begun such programs, but our efforts must be expanded to include:

- First year seminars to allow students to work with a member of the faculty in a small group;

- A tutorial term in which a student can work with a teacher in an individual or group tutorial on problems to which they mutually agree;

- Thematic colleges, in which part of the student's work is organized around a theme or problem;

- Technological innovations such as video-cassettes (covering lectures and laboratory demonstrations) which can be played and replayed by students at will.

Our residence halls (including the high-rises) should serve as an educational asset and a basis for a "house system" for undergraduates and graduates. We require here, not a single comprehensive house plan based on quaint or Gothic or Federal quarters, but a variety of living patterns which allow students and faculty a genuine choice. The success in developing College House at Van Pelt House, in which the students and faculty have created a varied intellectual and cultural program, testifies to the possibilities of such an approach (Meyerson, 1972).

It would appear that many young faculty and students will support the president while many senior faculty are opposed to any reform or change.

In addition to reform of the undergraduate education, the president would encourage faculty from the graduate professional schools to take a more active part in undergraduate education; at present the School of Medicine and the Graduate School of Fine Arts appear to want participation, while the Graduate School of Education appears to resent the able undergraduates who need courses from that school.

Further, Mr. Meyerson places strong emphasis on strengthening able graduate (doctoral) programs even if the university must limit the number of areas in which it grants degrees. Here the president faces the opposition of the timid, the incompetent, and that small faculty segment that believes it governs the university.

Though Mr. Meyerson is motivated in part by financial pressures, we doubt that the new programs will decrease the budget, but they may well bring greater educational return for the funds spent. The educational change that would most aid the financial picture would be to increase the number of courses taught by each faculty member. In the late 1950s and particularly the decade of the 1960s, teaching loads dropped markedly at many major universities including Pennsylvania. If many of our faculty would teach one more course each semester and some, one additional course per year, the financial outlook would change drastically for the better, with little change in the quality of scholarly work. However, these reforms are difficult if one university moves alone.

TRENDS IN GOVERNANCE The participation of students in the formulation of their undergraduate program is a strong indication of the shift in governance that has been occurring in the university.

Prior to the 1950s faculty and student participation in governance was minimal. While each faculty or school governed itself and controlled its curricula, admissions, faculty selection, and academic student discipline, control of the institution as a whole was exercised by the central administration and the trustees. As in most universities, student government was a farce and student participation in real governance, nonexistent.

In 1951 a group of about 40 senior faculty members who were dissatisfied both with President Harold Stassen's frequent absence from the university for political campaigning and with the operation of the university by his executive vice-president organized a university senate.

Though not completely successful, the senate introduced democracy into the central administration of the university: it quickly appointed committees of faculty members to nominate candidates for all senior academic administrative posts and established procedures for faculty participation in the selection of the deans of faculty. At times, however, the senate became a debating society because it forbade its committees to advise the president or provost until the senate as a whole could do so.

As a result, under the presidency of Gaylord Harnwell a University Council was established as a senior advisory body to him. Of its members, 13 are designated by the senate, 27 are faculty elected by discipline areas, 4 are assistant professors appointed by the steering committee of the council, 12 are administrative officers (at least 5 of whom must be deans of faculty), and 17 are students (9 of them undergraduates and 8 of them graduate or graduate professional).

The University Council was not the first attempt to involve students in academic governance; as far back as 1950 the deans of the college and of the Wharton School had student advisory committees. In 1961 the provost began appointing student members to some of the committees he was responsible for, and students were later added to the curriculum committees of virtually all the schools of the university.

Students now participate in many departmental meetings as well. Students and faculty in the history department developed a new major program; undergraduate majors in the Department of Classical Studies participated with their faculty in an intensive study of their programs. Graduate students in the Department of Religious Thought have worked with faculty to restructure the preliminary examination and to provide for independent study. Students in the School of Medicine sit on its curriculum and admissions committees and helped to develop the new curriculum there.

In addition, students have been appointed to search committees for deans and directors and were placed on the task force, along with faculty and trustees, to study university structure and decision making and on the search committees for a new president and provost. They sit on the Academic Planning Committee, the University Budget Committee, and the all-university judiciary.

There have been problems in having students on committees: some have revealed information they should not; some haven't bothered to acquaint themselves with pertinent data; some wish to use their committee membership as a platform; and nearly all have to be educated in the ways of committee work. However, these are problems one encounters with faculty members too, and like faculty, obstructive students are rare. Certainly students have brought a viewpoint which was often ignored before. Thus while it can be true that having students on a committee can make its work more time-consuming (generally this is more true for search committees), on the whole students can stand up to any faculty member: The experiences and contributions of each are different but equally important.

NONVIOLENT
DISSENT There is no doubt that the university's first major crisis over Department of Defense contracts for a systems analysis of chemical-biological warfare agents precipitated, in 1965, the change in student-faculty relationships. For the first time a large number of students and faculty found themselves in agreement. There were student and faculty protests over the secret research (at one point students sat in the president's office for three days), and concerted efforts were made to ban not only research that was secret but any research that was defense-related. Many meetings between members of the administration and faculty-student groups took place, and by working through established channels—the senate, the council, and finally, the trustees—they resolved the problem by adopting a research policy which stipulated that the university could undertake only freely publishable research; in addition, no outside agency could control the publication of such research or determine who was to be employed on it.

Luckily the university had only a small number of secret contracts and was not involved with the operation of any major laboratories or applied programs for government or industry. It is a member of the adjacent University City Science Center, jointly owned and operated by some 20 colleges and universities in the area, but as a result of student-faculty concern, the Science Center has also agreed not to become involved in weapons development.

Although the argument over the secret contracts was at times bitter and divided the faculty, we can't help but think that Pennsylvania is a stronger and freer university for the experience. Faculty and students learned to work together; more importantly, they learned that the channels of governance worked. The administration and trustees would listen and could be influenced.

A recent letter from a former student can express the viewpoint of a student on this matter better than we: "When my brother was at Penn (62) the administration was aloof and unknown to the students, but by the time I left Penn in 1966 Gaylord P. Harnwell was well known, at least by sight, to most students. There was a feeling that the administration, while a bit stodgy, was at least reachable, that it would respond to student feelings. . . ."

When a second small demonstration occurred in 1967 protesting the presence of recruiters from Dow Chemical Company, a manufacturer of the napalm used in the Vietnam war, a faculty-student-administrative committee under Professor Robert Mundheim of the Law School was formed and the result was a document, "Guidelines to Open Expression," which recognized the right of protest but defined its limits and conditions.

The document was adopted by a universitywide referendum of students and by the University Council, senate, and trustees, enabling the university to meet the test of the largest sit-in it had ever experienced.

In mid-February of 1969 our students and many others from Temple and Villanova universities and from Haverford, Swarthmore, and Bryn Mawr colleges marched in and occupied College Hall to protest the clearing of land for a new city high school and for the expansion of the neighboring University City Science Center. The claims were made that such expansion destroyed the homes of poor whites and blacks and that the land should not be used for institutional purposes. Because the university had helped in the development of both the Science Center and the high school, it was a prime target for student anger.

The occupation lasted from Tuesday until about 2 A.M. the following Monday morning, and although there were up to 1,000 students in the building at some times, no violence occurred, no destruction of property or records took place—or was even attempted —no doorways were blocked, and there was no need to discipline any students.

This was in part due to the fact that the issues had aroused enough campuswide support that the moderates were able to maintain control. The close relationship between the senate and the administration helped in the constructive handling of demonstrations. Vice Provost for Student Affairs Jack Russell, who with his staff kept his office open around the clock, giving out coffee and doughnuts and helping maintain communications among faculty members and between faculty and students, eased everyone into positions which would result in peaceful compromise. There were trustees on campus who were willing to talk and listen to students, and no doubt we were also helped by the fact that Pennsylvania lacked a large radical fringe on either the right or the left.

The guidelines also had helped to prevent problems: students lived up to their responsibilities and made sure that outside students did so as well; and faculty met with students day and night in an attempt to resolve differences. Indeed we believe it was the obvious concern and interest the faculty displayed that helped ensure the success of the guidelines.[1]

As a result of the peaceful sit-in, a quiet pride in Pennsylvania's tradition of nonviolence has developed among our students. In addition, the faculty and administration have recognized a responsibility to the surrounding community.

COMMUNITY SERVICE Our students recognized this responsibility long before most of the faculty and the administration did. As one former student put it, "I don't think anybody who went to Penn could escape feeling the tremendous differences between the quality of one's life at home and the quality of the lives of the people living near the university."

Since 1964, students had been quietly engaged in community service projects. They have tutored public school students, helped run hospital emergency rooms, provided companionship for psychiatric patients, and worked in programs such as those at the Philadelphia Youth Study Center.

As a result, the faculty became involved, too, particularly after the sit-in, and helped develop courses which allowed students to participate in community work for credit. Law students, for example, now work in the Philadelphia Community Legal Services offices, and many have participated in the Office of the Philadelphia Voluntary Defender in defense of indigents in criminal cases. The School of Education has offered several internship programs in-

---

[1] Unfortunately, there has been a breakdown of the guidelines. In May of 1971, when the university's nonprofessional librarians were on strike, some employees (supposedly with the help of a few faculty members and students) chained the library doors. No action was taken against them largely because at that time most university employees were not aware of the guidelines and the fact that they would also be held responsible under them. In April of 1972, after President Nixon ordered the bombing of North Vietnam, students, joined by some faculty members and a student affairs officer, took possession of the administration building, barricaded its doors, destroyed some records, and copied a large number of others, all in an attempt to rid the campus of ROTC. Fortunately, those sitting in responded to a court injunction requesting the removal of the barricades. However, the tradition of orderly demonstrations had been breached. Interestingly enough, although a great majority of the students and faculty are strongly opposed to the Southeast Asian war, they did not join the sit-in. There is strong reason to believe that if the guidelines had been observed by those sitting in, they would have received much wider university support.

(At this writing the university is moving against those involved in the sit-in, bringing them up before the university judiciary.)

cluding a teacher program in urban education: during summer sessions students lived full time in the predominantly black Mantua area north of campus working with community agencies in such areas as housing, job training, neighborhood medical centers, play streets, and neighborhood development.

The faculty of the Wharton School sponsors a special evening program for members of the black community who are interested in preparing for careers in business, and the school's Center for Studies in Criminology and Criminal Law is supporting an urban leadership training program for 22 young black leaders. The Graduate School of Fine Arts sponsors the Urban Workshop, in which its students help ghetto community groups plan the redevelopment of their neighborhoods.

In addition, our faculty have donated their services in getting some needed community programs off the ground. The university is largely responsible for helping develop a community "free school" which allows students to gain part of their high school education in computer centers, banks, museums, hospital laboratories, and college classrooms. The university has also helped maintain the Walnut Street Center, an experimental preschool program; it has provided special classes in mathematics, physics, English, and history for high school youngsters; it has developed work-study programs, summer institutes, summer sports programs, and a summer tutorial skills center, and has even been concerned with minority employment in the construction trades.

Not all these programs have been unqualified successes, and there are students who believe the university has not done enough, particularly internally. They cite, for example, great difficulty experienced in setting up an undergraduate major in urban studies and the program in black studies and note that such programs still lack strong support from the faculty and administration. However, most students recognize that Pennsylvania offers unique opportunities for involvement. As one student told us, "There is so much going on around here. I think today's students are more socially aware. They are conscious of their own social roles and of social injustices around them. There is a greater awareness of the university's role in the community."

Such awareness can, of course, create problems for the university. At Pennsylvania there are many who feel the community should have a voice in the running of the university; others believe that any neighborhood youngster, regardless of interest or ability, should be admitted to the university.

It is cruel to admit those who cannot meet the university's standards or those for whom the university cannot furnish the appropriate education. Moreover, the financial support required for minority students is very high. They need extensive scholarship aid and, frequently, summer remedial programs, tutoring, and special counseling. It is dishonest for the university to accept more students than it may grant essential aid. Unfortunately, some of our students and faculty members fail to recognize this fact.

There is a concern, too, that student demands for relevance, however well intended, may lead to superficiality. Students are wrong in wanting their courses to be as up to date as the morning newspaper. Public problems and knowledge of solutions change so rapidly that this kind of relevance can quickly become irrelevance. An educated person has a need of philosophy, anthropology, history, and literature. Unfortunately, many students are so caught up in contemporary problems that they ignore the difficult process of learning, and too often we find in students—and in some faculty—an impatience with intellectual analysis and logic.

More immediately, the demand for relevance threatens Pennsylvania's primary mission as a scholarly institution. There is, for example, a growing insistence on the part of a vocal minority of students, faculty, and community that the university not only assist in the reform of public education but actually operate and fund the area's public schools, to build low-cost public housing, and indeed to fill all the gaps left by an incompetent city government.

The university cannot meet these demands, and attempts to do so could be disastrous. Largely for this reason, President Martin Meyerson has formed an ad hoc group to help prepare a university position statement on "The University and the Community" and has appointed a Committee of Community Advisors and an urban coordinator to help coordinate and respond to community needs. In addition, the trustees have established a Committee on Urban Affairs to develop a policy on the role of the university in an urban environment.

No longer can one accuse the University of Pennsylvania of being self-centered and complacent. There have been many factors contributing to this change—the strong presidency of Gaylord P. Harnwell, the Educational Survey, and the resulting Capital Campaign, the physical rebuilding of the campus. Yet we believe that a determined search for better students and faculty has been the most important factor.

When Gaylord Harnwell was appointed president, he stated that the closest things to his heart were "the quality of the faculty, the intellectual energy of the undergraduates, and a good and solvent institution."

Well, we haven't fared too well on the third goal, which puts us in good company with institutions around the country, but we have done superbly well on the first two goals. In 1969 the American Council on Education asked our freshmen why they had selected Pennsylvania. They had three reasons: a specific curriculum, its academic excellence and reputation, and its metropolitan location.

Fifteen years ago we wouldn't have had the same answers at all.

References

Bester, Alfred: "The University of Pennsylvania," *Holiday,* November 1962.

Kenniston, Hayward: *Graduate Study and Research in the Arts and Sciences at the University of Pennsylvania,* University of Pennsylvania Press, Philadelphia, 1959.

Meyerson, Martin: "In Pursuit of Sharpened Goals," *Pennsylvania Gazette,* February 1972.

11. Princeton in Crisis and Change

by Paul Sigmund

Spring 1963. The signs of change in American higher education were everywhere. The civil rights struggle in the South had aroused students and professors from their post-McCarthy torpor. In May, "Bull" Connor set his police dogs on peaceful protesters in Birmingham, Alabama, and thousands of young people resolved to dedicate the summer to civil rights activity. The first Peace Corps volunteers were applying to graduate schools as their two-year hitches ended. A new organization called the Students for a Democratic Society (SDS) was publicizing its Port Huron statement, which called for greater participatory democracy in American life. Opposition to the threat of nuclear war had spawned disarmament organizations on American campuses, and the National Student Association took a directly political stand for the first time in its history when its national congress voted to support nuclear disarmament. And at Princeton? On May 6, 1963, there was a pantie raid on a neighboring women's college, which prompted the *New York Times Magazine* to publish an article on spring fever among college students.

Spring 1970. On Thursday, April 30, President Nixon announced the Cambodian intervention. At a mass meeting held in the Princeton Chapel immediately following the speech, students and faculty in attendance voted overwhelmingly in favor of a university strike. On Saturday a "Multi-media Rite of Protest" at the chapel led 190 students to turn in their draft cards and resulted in the formation of the Princeton Union for National Draft Opposition. On Sunday, the Council of the Princeton University Community, with representatives from nearly all sectors of the university, drew up a carefully worded resolution allowing a series of options to students wishing to suspend class activity, encouraging student participation in national electoral politics through the newly organized Move-

249

ment for a New Congress, and recommending a two-week pre-election recess in the fall. The next day, the Assembly of the Princeton University Community voted 2,000 to 1,500 in favor of the council-sponsored resolution over a more radical proposal. In the succeeding weeks the Movement for a New Congress and the Union for National Draft Opposition spread nationwide, and the Princeton Plan for a preelectoral recess in the fall was widely imitated. In June, the seniors boycotted the annual alumni parade and dedicated the graduation exercises (at which songwriter Bob Dylan received an honorary degree) to various forms of antiwar activity.

How did the sleepy "preppy"-dominated conservative bastion of 1963[1] become a major center of student political upheaval in 1970? And why did this transformation take place without the violence and division that shook similar universities elsewhere? This essay will attempt to describe how, over a period of seven years, a politically inert, all-male, virtually entirely white, tradition-bound institution changed its social, educational, sexual, racial, and administrative structures to deal with the new realities in American higher education.

THE OLD REALITIES At Princeton in 1963 life went on pretty much as it had in the days of Woodrow Wilson or F. Scott Fitzgerald. As they had in Fitzgerald's *This Side of Paradise* (1920), the privately owned and selective eating clubs dominated undergraduate life, and "Bicker," the process whereby the 95 percent of the sophomore class that chose to participate received club invitations, was still a cruel and traumatic experience for many. The prestige hierarchy of the clubs was largely the same as that mentioned by Fitzgerald, whose hero had "made it" to Cottage Club because of his private school background and his extracurricular work on the *Daily Princetonian.* Despite repeated attacks on the rule, chapel attendance was still required twice a month, although only for freshmen.[2] No student

[1] Students from public high schools outnumbered those from private schools for the first time in the late 1950s, but the high school graduates tended to come from high schools like Scarsdale (Westchester County), Shaker Heights (suburban Cleveland), and New Trier (suburban Chicago), where the values, life style, and income were often indistinguishable from those at the select prep schools which had dominated entering classes earlier.

[2] The university defended this policy in its catalog by saying, "It is a principle of the educational policy at Princeton that no man can be truly educated and at the same time religiously illiterate"—a perfectly good justification for courses about religion but not for compulsory attendance at worship services.

was allowed to have a car within 35 miles of Princeton. The proctors enforced the parietal rules on the entertainment of women (7 P.M. weekdays, 10 P.M. Fridays, and midnight Saturdays) by using their passkeys to enter the rooms of suspected violators. A not uncommon student attitude toward members of the opposite sex was described thus by one undergraduate: "Women are things to be admired, seduced, or debauched. Princeton's uniqueness is the uniqueness of the locker room, the New York YMCA, and the Alaskan army barracks"[3]—and from comments by students at the time it seemed that very many of them liked it that way. The color bar at the clubs had been broken that year at all but Cottage Club—in order to admit African students attending Princeton in the African Scholarship Program of the American Universities, of which Princeton's president, Robert Goheen, was a director.[4] When charges were made of discrimination in the Bicker process, the references were to anti-Semitism, not racism. (It was not an accident that the Woodrow Wilson Society, the "alternative facility" available since 1960 to those who did not choose to join the eating clubs—or were not chosen by them in the occasional years when "100 percent Bicker" was not achieved—was heavily Jewish in its membership.) After the appointment of E. Alden Dunham as director of admissions in 1962, the admissions policy had been consciously changed from an emphasis on the well-rounded student to an effort to achieve "a well-rounded class of outstanding individuals," but in 1963, a glance at the students walking down Prospect Street, where most of the clubs are located, would have confirmed Ashley Montagu's comment at the time, "They all look alike—with faces like well-scrubbed babies' bottoms."

On the academic side, things also were as they had been, but the reforms in instruction methods carried out earlier in the century

[3] Quoted in the *Daily Princetonian* (Jan. 30, 1971).

[4] In 1963 there were five American black undergraduates at Princeton. The three upperclassmen eligible for entry into the clubs had not chosen to Bicker. Princeton had long had a reputation as "the northernmost of the southern schools," and part of the black population in the town was said to be descended from slaves who had been freed by their student masters on graduation day. The records of the First Presbyterian Church indicate that special arrangements were made for the slaves of Princeton students. Between 1912 and 1919 letters were sent out by the university to those who inquired about its racial policies stating that although "no law exists in our statutes forbidding the presence and graduation of black students, . . . Princeton has always been so strongly southern in its clientele that we do not encourage colored applicants for admission" since they would be "lonely and unhappy" ("Negroes at Princeton").

still seemed viable. Following the system established by Woodrow Wilson in 1905, nearly every course was broken down each week into eight-man preceptorials to discuss the lectures and reading—often with full professors leading the discussion. If this sometimes led to the type of gamesmanship symbolized by the student slang expression, "getting the 'cepts" (i.e., the essential concepts for a "precept"), the preceptorial system forced the student to think about the material and to express his views with a modicum of order and intelligence. Since 1923 every student had written a senior thesis as a requirement for graduation, and most of them described this afterward as the most rewarding experience of their undergraduate careers. Examinations were carried out under an honor system, a rarity at an all-male university, which by all accounts seems to have functioned well since its establishment in 1893. Violations of these and other rules were handled by a Joint Faculty-Student Discipline Committee which had included student members since 1924. Teaching undergraduates was highly valued even by senior professors, and if the form of instruction had changed little in 50 years,[5] its content on both graduate and undergraduate levels was of very high quality—as well as very expensive.

The combination of a first-rate educational system with an antiquated social system produced a rigid separation between weekday dedication to study (described as "grinding at the libe") and weekend binges at the clubs, interspersed with the occasional "big" weekend associated with the Prince-Tiger dance, the junior prom, or house parties, when dates were imported at considerable expense. Whatever its faults, Princeton education produced fanatically devoted alumni, who contributed to fund drives at a higher rate than those of any other university; but by the early 1960s many students were finding it increasingly distasteful. In its history Princeton had produced great writers, statesmen, clergymen, and scholars, but in many cases it also seemed to encourage an attitude described by one graduating senior in 1957 as "shallow tweed"—a kind of cynical opportunism which "taught that self-interest and disloyalty are valuable qualities" and produced a student who was "proficient at varying his beliefs and purported

[5] In 1963, President Goheen cited alumni opposition as a major reason for resisting the conversion of the grading system from the 1–7 scale in use since Wilson's time to the conventional A–F system.

commitments to suit the social situation at hand."[6] Princeton students were good students, far better than those of Fitzgerald's day, but many of them were not emotionally involved either in their studies or with the problems of the world around them. And a Princeton professor, complaining in 1965 of the rigid separation of emotion and intellect in "Princeton Charlie" as he knew him and of the lack of a genuine sense of community at Princeton, concluded, "Come the Class Day when the girls break their pipes on Cannon Green, while the recently fired researcher who could not teach stands quietly by, then we will know that this place is for real."[7]

That day has come six years after those words were written. In 1971–72, 750 undergraduate women were enrolled at Princeton, and the number was expected to rise to 1,200 (30 percent of the student body) by 1974. There were 283 black undergraduates and over 50 black graduate students as well as black deans, coaches, professors, and an Afro-American studies program. The chapel rule, the car rule, parietal hours, the 1–7 grading system had all been abandoned, and the university had been restructured to permit student participation and consultation on policy making, course evaluation, and the balance and content of the program of instruction in each department and in the university as a whole. The proportion of sophomores opting for the clubs had dropped to about 50 percent, and nearly a third of those entered clubs which had given up the selective Bicker principle in favor of open admissions. The Woodrow Wilson Society had become Woodrow Wilson College, with a large enrollment of undergraduate members, and several other structures had been created outside of the club system—one of them a coeducational residential community occupying what had been the Princeton Inn. Most important, the university had successfully weathered a number of serious crises in the period from the fall of 1967 until the spring of 1970 involving

[6] Quoted in Otto Butz, *The Unsilent Generation* (1958, p. 138). Symptomatically, the expression "face man," used at bicker time to describe a "smooth" good-looking candidate for admission to the clubs, was regarded as a positive evaluation rather than a term of opprobrium.

[7] Richard Turner, *The Cold Desiccated Beauty of Task-Oriented Self-Sufficiency* (1965). (The pipe-breaking reference alludes to a ceremony at the time of graduation in which seniors break clay pipes behind Nassau Hall.) The faculty group for which this paper was written had been meeting all year to diagnose what it felt was a serious state of malaise at Princeton. Its suggestions met with a generally negative response from President Goheen at the time, but by 1970 all of them had been adopted in one form or another.

issues of military research on campus, ROTC, South African investments, the Vietnam war, and the intervention in Cambodia — and in the process had fundamentally restructured the policy-making and legitimizing institutions of the university community.

MOVES TOWARD CHANGES IN STRUCTURE The beginnings were made in two of the more vestigial aspects of undergraduate life. In 1963–64 the chapel rule was abolished without evident objection from anyone, and the forbidden area for student cars was reduced to 8 miles — a process of whittling away that led to student cars on campus four years later. More important, changes began to be made in the educational system. In the spring of 1965 the faculty voted to permit students to take one course a year outside their major fields on a pass-fail basis, and in early 1967 they reduced the course load from five to four courses a term. A committee was also appointed in the fall of 1966 to develop a comprehensive system of course evaluation by students. The result of its labors was an evaluation booklet with 109 questions and space for student comments, which was introduced on an experimental basis in 1967–68 and made mandatory in all courses in 1968–69.

In retrospect, the crucial year was 1967–68. In the fall of 1967 the proctors ceased to enforce the parietal hours by use of the passkey (thus both avoiding the problem of drug "busts" — the first and last such raid took place in the fall of 1967 — and diminishing the intense student feeling on the issue of parietals in general). For the first time there were an appreciable number of black students (55) on campus and a black was elected president of the freshman class. Early in the year a committee was appointed to look into the financial and educational implications of coeducation. (Since 1963 a few undergraduate women from other universities, never more than 15, had been enrolled in the Critical Languages program for a year of study of languages not available at their home colleges. In 1961 the Graduate School had also quietly altered its policy to allow for the admission of women graduate students who could make a strong case that their areas of specialization could best be pursued at Princeton.) But more than any other developments, the shape of the future at Princeton was determined by two events in the fall of 1967 — a sit-in at the Institute for Defense Analyses and the establishment of a second alternative to the eating clubs, Stevenson Hall.

The sit-in was carried out by the Princeton chapter of the Students for a Democratic Society, the membership of which had grown in the preceding two years parallel to the increasing student opposition to the Vietnam war. In a teach-in held in April 1965 to oppose the escalation of the war, undergraduate opinion had been divided (although the faculty was largely opposed). By 1967, however, the students' antiwar feeling was much stronger, and an easy target for their opposition was provided by a secret research facility of the Institute for Defense Analyses (IDA) located in a building adjacent to the campus which was leased from the university. On October 23, 1967, a group of SDS members and sympathizers staged a sit-in at the IDA building, protesting the university's link to the institute as one of several sponsoring institutions. Although there were a few trespass arrests by the town police, the action was largely symbolic, but it focused attention on a problem which was to plague the university in the coming years and to provide the catalyst for a series of far-reaching structural changes. To deal with the status of IDA, President Goheen appointed a committee, headed by Stanley Kelley, Jr., professor of politics. After several months of investigation the committee recommended that Princeton withdraw its official sponsorship since the secret research which IDA carried on did not benefit the university as an academic institution and could not be adequately supervised by it as a sponsor. An effort by the president and trustees to replace official university sponsorship with a director named "in a personal capacity" (rather than as a representative of the university) was strongly opposed by the faculty, and the sponsoring relationship was subsequently terminated. The lease on the building, however, still had two years to run, and included an option for a five-year extension until 1975. The termination of sponsorship satisfied most of the campus radicals, and by giving a structural rather than political reason for breaking with IDA, the Kelley Committee also satisfied the moderates and liberals. In the course of the IDA controversy, however, it became apparent that the university's decision-making processes, legally concentrated in the hands of the president and the university trustees, were not sufficiently responsive to the strong feelings of the university community. A statement was circulated among the members of the faculty in late April and signed by many of its most prominent members; it argued that Princeton's decision-making processes "were devised in a different era when universities were in a different situation with regard to both their internal relations and their corporate relation to American society. It is clear that the time for a reappraisal of institutional procedures is long overdue."

This conclusion was reinforced on May 2 when an SDS-organized demonstration by 600 students in front of Nassau Hall, the administrative center of the university, denounced as "irresponsible" the decisions of the president and trustees and argued that "we must restructure the decision-making process so that those who live in the University and are most seriously affected by the decisions which control its future, are themselves the ones who make these decisions." The students presented a list of demands including the severance of the university's relationship with IDA, ending of the draft, and abolition of parietal rules.[8]

Coming as it did at the time of the occupation of Columbia University[9] and apparently enjoying the support of at least a substantial minority in the student body, the demonstration provoked an immediate response. President Goheen (who had been standing unobtrusively in the audience even chatting at times with the radical leaders) spoke briefly at the end of the demonstration and promised a "fresh and searching review of the decision-making process of the University by a properly constituted faculty-student committee." Within a month a Special Committee on the Structure of the University had been elected. It comprised eight faculty members, four undergraduates (including the newly elected president of the Undergraduate Assembly, a leading member of SDS), and three graduate students, plus President Goheen ex officio, Its chairman was Professor Kelley, who had established a universitywide reputation for his work on the IDA question. Immediately after its election, the committee began to hold hearings on reform of the structure of the university.

CHANGES IN SOCIAL ARRANGEMENTS The second major change in 1967–68 was in the area of undergraduate social arrangements. The initiative for the change came from 84 upperclassmen, including a basketball star, the presidents of the junior and sophomore classes, the president of the Chapel

---

[8] It was difficult to evaluate the relative importance of these issues in attracting the surprisingly large participation in the demonstration. The rhetoric of the speakers was concentrated on the war and the structure of the university, but some observers claimed that the parietals issue was important in accounting for the presence of many of the students.

[9] One of the leaders of the demonstration was a graduate student who had been an SDS activist at Columbia as an undergraduate and was in close touch with the situation there.

Deacons, and the chairman of the *Daily Princetonian,* who resigned from the eating clubs. Unlike earlier protests against the club system, this was a sustained drive by those who had entered the system (juniors and seniors) and those who were slated to enter it. In November 85 sophomores announced that they would not participate in the Bicker process at the end of January, and the upperclassmen proposed the university take over one of the privately owned clubs, which was about to go bankrupt, combine it with the club next to it, which had failed a few years earlier, and create a new type of institution which would be jointly run by faculty and students, and would be open to all who wished to join. This student proposal for another social alternative was reinforced by the publication of a report of the Faculty Committee on Undergraduate Life which called the club system "a hindrance to the interaction of intellectual and social life" and criticized Bicker because it "institutionalized a superficial set of status and personality values." After some initial resistance on financial grounds, the university administration acceded, and in January a new university-owned eating facility, Stevenson Hall, was born. At the same time, the Woodrow Wilson Society was reorganized as a residential college and experienced a large increase in membership. The subsequent creation of three other alternative structures meant that the stranglehold of the clubs on undergraduate social life had been broken. In the following two years, two other clubs were taken over by the university and a number of others opted out of the Bicker process, and after coeducation was introduced, several invited female students to join. It was clear that Prospect Street would never be the same.

Parallel to the structural change went a change in the content of undergraduate socializing. The big weekend and the drunken binge became less common; proms were replaced by rock and folk-song concerts, and with the relaxation of enforcement of parietal rules, students entertained in their rooms as well as in the clubs. This process was accelerated by a trustee vote in April 1969 to delegate rule-making authority over social life to the faculty, who in turn delegated it to the student residential units. What this meant was that parietal rules, which had not been enforced since 1967, no longer really existed after the spring of 1969.

STUDENT PARTICIPATION ON COMMITTES The decentralization of rule-making authority and the involvement of students in making policy which directly affected them were among the first recommendations in the preliminary report of the

Kelley Committee when it was issued in November 1968. Its conclusions ran parallel to those of a document entitled *Students and
the University* which had been approved by the faculty a month
earlier. Drawn up by the Faculty Advisory Committee on Policy in
consultation with the Undergraduate Assembly[10] and members
of the administration, *Students and the University* recommended
the establishment of student committees in all undergraduate
departments "to encourage students to participate in departmental
affairs of special interest and relevance to them, to initiate proposals, and to seek discussion of any issue of general departmental
importance." In addition the Undergraduate Assembly was to
establish committees parallel to several committees of the faculty.
By the spring of 1969 student committees existed in nearly all
departments, and student members were sitting on the committees
on admissions and undergraduate life as well as on the Discipline
Committee, where student representation was increased to equal
that of the faculty. In addition, parallel student committees met
regularly with the committees on the course of study and the library
and the Advisory Committee on Policy. In a statement which was
to have considerable significance in the controversies of the following year, *Students and the University* also declared demonstrations
permissible "unless and until they disrupt the regular and essential
operations of the University or significantly infringe the rights of
others."

The result of the involvement of students in departmental affairs
(and of the earlier establishment of a formalized system of course
evaluation) was considerable educational experimentation. In
place of the hallowed weekly preceptorial, professors experimented
with seminars, less frequent lectures, and different patterns of

[10] The Advisory Committee on Policy had been working on *Students and the
University* since early 1967. The fact that it had been already discussing the
desirability of restructuring the university helps to explain the speed with
which the president moved in this area after the May 2 demonstration.

In March 1967, Princeton's student government, the Undergraduate Council,
had been reorganized as the Undergraduate Assembly, which was larger (50
members instead of 13) and more representative of student opinion. Students
were elected by living units rather than by class. Unusually large turnouts for
assembly elections (66 percent in 1967 and 65 percent in 1968) and the high
quality of the student representatives elected gave the body greater legitimacy
as a spokesman for the students during the crises of 1967 to 1970 than many
student governments elsewhere.

instruction within or during the same course.[11] Student-initiated seminars were authorized for credit for the first time in the spring of 1969, and educational experiments such as the Semester in the Cities program in the Woodrow Wilson School were permitted. A seminar program for credit held in a social and eating facility, Stevenson Hall, was also authorized by the faculty. The existing Creative Arts program was expanded to include such courses (taken on a pass-fail basis) as stained glass, ceramics, print making, and design. Flexibility in the structure and content of courses replaced the former restricted list of courses and nearly universal pattern of two lectures and one preceptorial per week.

THE SOUTH AFRICAN INVESTMENTS ISSUE If 1967–68 was the year of the IDA controversy at Princeton, 1968–69 was the year when South African investments were the issue. SDS had provided the impetus for the IDA protest; the Association of Black Collegians (ABC) took the lead on the South African issue. That the organization could mount such an offensive was an indication both of the increasing numbers (over 100 undergraduates and graduate students) and militancy of the black students at Princeton and of the strong sympathy for their cause among many of the white students. After the death of Martin Luther King in April 1968 the university cancelled classes for a day of discussion and reflection on race relations in the United States. At that time several students proposed that the university divest itself of its investments in all companies which had any holdings in South Africa. President Goheen established a committee to examine this proposal, and in January 1969 it issued three different reports. The faculty approved the majority report recommending against divestment on the grounds that this largely symbolic act would "seriously impair Princeton's effectiveness as an educational institution" due to the financial costs involved (a $5 million initial loss and up to $3.5 million yearly losses thereafter). The faculty added, however, that the university should not hold securities in companies whose *primary* activities were in South Africa. In February, the Undergraduate Assembly took essentially the same

---

[11] A beginning was also made on the integration of the graduate and undergraduate programs, which since Woodrow Wilson's time, and against his will, had been physically, psychologically, and academically distinct. For the first time, too, graduate students began to live in undergraduate dormitories as advisers and to eat in university-sponsored undergraduate dining facilities.

position, and on March 4 the president defended the decision against divestment in a public meeting attended by 1,500 students and professors. The obscenities shouted by white radical students during the president's statement increased his support in that audience.

The obscene shouts did not come from black students because the ABC was planning a different method of protesting the university decision. On March 11, the black students occupied the new university administration building from 7 A.M. until 6 P.M. as a symbolic gesture of opposition to the university's stand on South African investments. No effort was made to dislodge the occupying students, and they observed scrupulous good order and left peacefully at the end of the day. Seven of the leaders of the occupation were placed on probation by the Discipline Committee, but in view of the character of the demonstration, no further action was taken. The Admissions Committee continued to make special efforts to recruit qualified black and underprivileged students, and the number of black undergraduates rose to 150 in 1969–70, to 230 in 1970–71, and to 283 (7 percent of the student body) in 1971–72. One of the black students who participated in the occupation was elected a trustee of the university at the time of his graduation in 1970. His election took place under a procedure adopted by the trustees in April 1969 providing for the election each year of a trustee chosen by the juniors, the seniors, and the two classes most recently graduated, from among candidates nominated by the senior class.

COEDUCATION At the April 1969 meeting the trustees also voted to give final approval to the initiation of coeducation in the following September. This decision, which had strong faculty and student support (91 percent and 82 percent respectively in polls taken in 1968), was viewed less favorably by the alumni, especially those in the earlier graduating classes. A conservative alumni pressure group, ACTION (Alumni Committee to Involve Ourselves Now) condemned "the excessive degree of untrammeled academic liberalism sweeping through Princeton" and attempted to organize alumni opposition to the move. The faculty committee which recommended the change to the trustees argued that the addition of 1,000 undergraduate women would not substantially increase instructional costs and found strong evidence that coeducation was essential if Princeton was to continue to provide high-quality education and to attract the superior student applicants it had attracted in the past. This conclusion was confirmed by a considerable increase in the quality and quantity of applications after coeducation was initiated in 1969–70.

The decisions of the April 1969 meeting of the trustees to approve coeducation, delegate parietal decisions to the students, and add younger trustees seem to have changed the attitude of many students toward the university authorities. The *Daily Princetonian* (1969, p. 1), previously a fierce critic of the trustees, rhapsodized, "The trustees showed courage and foresight and an ability to change with the times which would do credit to any deliberative body in the country."

At the graduation ceremony in June 1969, President Goheen commented upon the appearance among some of the student activists of a secularized form of the Christian heresy of antinomianism, the "passionate conviction that your relation to the deity is so intense and so perfect as to have put you in a state of grace which sets you above both the Mosaic Code and the civil law." Whether because of the content of these remarks or because of the evident skill and flexibility with which he had directed the changes of the current year (especially the move toward coeducation), the graduating seniors responded with a standing ovation.

**NEW INSTRU-
MENTS OF
EXPRESSION
AND
GOVERNANCE**

The 1969 graduation meeting of the trustees of the university approved the most important of the recommendations of the Kelley Committee, the establishment of a Council of the Princeton University Community. After stating that "practically speaking a body with the legal powers and responsibilities of a board of trustees is a necessary feature of the government of a private university," the Kelley Committee further recommended the establishment of a Council of the Princeton University Community made up of 7 senior members of the administration ex officio, 18 elected faculty members including at least 5 professors on nontenured status, 8 graduate students, 14 undergraduates, 4 representatives of the alumni, and 6 members of the various professional and administrative staffs. Its charter declared that the council was to "consider and investigate any question of University policy, and aspect of the governing of the University, and any issue related to the welfare of the University; and to make recommendations regarding such matters to the appropriate decision-making bodies of the University . . . [to] make rules regarding the conduct of resident members of the University community[12] . . . [and to] oversee the making and applying of rules regarding the conduct of resident members of the University community. . . ." Thus the council in its relation to the president and trustees is an advisory body, the influence of which depends on its capacity to express the consensus of the university — when there is one. In relation to students and employees of the university, however, it is a rule-making body or overseer of other rule-making bodies. In both roles it attempts to develop and reflect a universitywide consensus on university policy and regulations which it adopts.

The council met for the first time on October 27, 1969. It was thus in full operation well before its most severe test at the time of the Cambodian intervention in the spring. Another group that was to play an important role in the following spring, the Assembly of the Princeton University Community, also held its first meeting in the fall. Not a part of the Kelley Committee recommendations, the assembly was originally called by the faculty in response to the Vietnam moratorium observed at universities across the country in October 1969. Open to all those connected with the university, including the alumni, the assembly was to discuss and vote on resolutions embodying the sense of the university on public issues but was in no way officially binding on the faculty or the trustees of the university as a legal entity.[13] Before the meeting, suggested resolutions dealing with the Vietnam war were screened by a small committee with representation of all major points of view which attempted to combine similar resolutions and present clear-cut alternatives to the rather unwieldy audience of 3,000 which was to vote. By a large majority the meeting endorsed a resolution proposed by Sen. Charles Goodell calling for the setting of December 1970 as a deadline for final withdrawal from Vietnam. While there was criticism of the meeting from alumni letter writers to the *Princeton Alumni Weekly,* the assembly seemed to have been successful in providing for an expression of campus opinion without formally committing the university.

On November 14, 1969, the council established the Judicial

[12] "Resident members of the university community" were defined elsewhere as "all regularly enrolled students and all persons regularly employed by the University."

[13] The fact that the Harvard faculty had just taken an official position on the war — which many Princeton faculty members felt was a serious mistake — was partially responsible for the creation of the assembly.

Committee, provided for in its charter, to adjudicate the rules
governing conduct of members of the university community. The
first of the newly created bodies to be severely tested, it consisted
of a chairman, three faculty members, two undergraduates, one
graduate student, and one representative of the other groups represented on the council. The test came on March 5, 1970, when
Walter Hickel, Secretary of the Interior, at the invitation of the
Princeton University Conference, spoke on ecological problems.
To demonstrate their opposition to the administration's conduct
of the Vietnam war, members of SDS engaged in persistent and
vociferous heckling which made Hickel's speech nearly inaudible
and prevented the question period which was to follow from taking
place. Warned by the president during the speech that they were
violating stated university policy approved by the Faculty and
Undergraduate Assembly, 12 students who had been positively
identified were subsequently summoned to appear before the Judicial Committee. A lengthy open hearing ensued at which SDS
members combined frequent disruption with a highly legalistic
attack on the ground rules for the hearing. After six weeks of
meetings, the body placed nine students on probation and required
three seniors already on probation for an earlier disruption to
withdraw from the university. (On appeal, the latter sentence
was reduced by the provost to a delay of degrees until February
1971.) The hearing had several effects. It reaffirmed the commitment of the university both to freedom of speech on campus and to
due process in the treatment of violations of that freedom. It also established the basic procedures for the nascent Judicial Committee,
which conducted the hearing with fairness and rationality in the
midst of strong attempts to discredit it. Most important, it made the
university faculty and administration more sensitive to the potential
danger which irresponsible expressions of student opposition to the
Vietnam war could pose for the integrity of the university.

When the "crunch" came, therefore, in the form of President
Nixon's announcement of the Cambodian intervention, the university was able to respond quickly, and it possessed institutions and
procedures which prevented its response from being dominated by
extremist elements. The day after the chapel meeting of 2,500
students and faculty voted a university strike, the executive committee of the council met with the president to discuss Princeton's
response. Two days later, the full council held an emotion-charged
public meeting before 1,300 spectators and produced a resolution

which provided for a series of options for students wishing to dedicate themselves to opposition to the Cambodian intervention. The assembly met on May 4, and the substance of the council's resolution was adopted over a more radical proposal by a vote of 2,000 to 1,500. This in turn gave further legitimacy to the council's work and strengthened the hand of those favorable to the council on the University Strike Committee which was then being formed.

Besides the options on the completion of the year's academic work, the council and assembly also declared their opposition to the Cambodian intervention, endorsed the Movement for a New Congress and the preelection recess, and called for termination of the ROTC program and a review of the lease of the Institute for Defense Analyses with a view to its termination. By the time these resolutions came to the faculty, it was difficult for opponents of these actions (including the president of the university, who made no secret of his opposition to a political stand by the faculty, and the dean of the college, who tried in vain to moderate the ROTC proposal) to resist the psychological and political pressure that had been built up. A preamble to the resolution on the Cambodian issue affirming the exceptional nature of that instance salved the consciences of those professors who were hesitant about taking a political stand, and the faculty condemned the Cambodian intervention. It also altered the fall calendar to permit a preelection recess, voted to phase out the ROTC program on campus (it had withdrawn academic credit from the program in 1969 but on academic, not political, grounds) and endorsed the efforts of the president to seek an early termination of the IDA lease because "the presence of the Institute on university property has become disadvantageous to both parties."

Outside the faculty meeting the IDA was threatened by more direct action. Students surrounded it day and night for six days, painting graffiti on its walls, breaking a few windows, and frolicking on the grass until May 11, when a court injunction was served and they agreed to leave the grounds crossing the road to university property and pitching camp there indefinitely. On May 13 small fires broke out at the IDA and at Nassau Hall but were discovered at once. Meanwhile more moderate students, based principally in Stevenson Hall, were working for antiwar candidates in the spring primaries and the fall preelection recess (now known as the Princeton Plan) had been adopted by many universities. By the end of the month, most students had left the campus, the faculty was meeting to act on the final recommendations of the Kelley Committee, and the university seemed to have survived its most dangerous crisis without serious damage to its physical or academic structure, and indeed in many ways much stronger for having done so. This was particularly true of the president, whose firm yet flexible handling of the crisis had placed him in a very strong posicion in terms of support from the university community.[14]

SOME OBSERVABLE CONSE- QUENCES Contrary to all expectations the fall term of 1970 turned out to be an extraordinarily quiet one on the Princeton campus. An attempted confrontation with military recruiters by the SDS in November brought out more proctors than it did protesters, and a rally in December was described by one of its organizers as "the absolute nadir of radical consciousness in this university." Despite a radicalization of dress and facial adornment, students seemed to be studying harder than in the previous year (the library reported a 15 percent increase in borrowing and twice as many books taken from the reserve desk). Twenty-four percent of the student body reported engaging in political activity during the preelection recess, and eleven percent said they had devoted "substantial" time to politics, but many more used it to catch up on their studies. In December, the Undergraduate Assembly voted to invite ROTC to return in an extracurricular status, and when President Goheen announced that the Institute for Defense Analyses would remain until 1975 because of the serious financial consequences of earlier termination of its lease, there was hardly a ripple on the campus.[15]

The financial argument was a strong one in a university facing

[14] Robert Goheen's popularity with the students in 1970 was in striking contrast to his low prestige following the 1963 pantie raid, when he was hanged in effigy on campus.

[15] The IDA subsequently announced that it would move to a new location in Princeton, thus terminating the issue as far as the university was concerned. The ROTC question, however, remained a major source of controversy. In early 1971 a universitywide student referendum supported its return as a noncredit program without cost to the university. After the faculty also endorsed this compromise, a new ROTC agreement was concluded with the Army and Air Force, but in October 1971 the faculty reversed itself and came out against the return of ROTC in any form, and the Undergraduate Assembly, by a one-vote margin, took a similar position. However, the Council of the Princeton University Community, which in addition to faculty and students included representatives of the administration and university employees, continued to favor ROTC's return, and the board of trustees voted to approve the agreement in January 1972. Later in the year students and faculty reacted to the bombing of North Vietnam by voting to "defer" reinstatement of ROTC, but the board of trustees let its decision stand.

a sizable operating deficit. In late 1970 a series of cutbacks throughout the university was recommended by the Committee on Priorities, a committee of the council that now took on considerable importance in directing and legitimizing a retrenchment which, if it had come only from the administration and the trustees, might have provoked considerable opposition. Was it the financial squeeze, cold weather, the graduation of several key SDS leaders, or a retreat after the political orgy of the spring into a "privatism" not unlike that which was supposed to have characterized the "silent generation" of the 1950s that explained the new student mood? Or was it something more ominous—a sullen cynicism born of despair? (A student attempt to organize a protest against the Laos intervention in early 1971 was met with the comment "We tried that last year and where did it get us?")[16]

As the faculty met to legislate the remaining recommendations of the Committee on the Structure of the University and the many committees and subcommittees created in the preceding three years began to become part of the regular structure of the university, thoughtful members of the university community began to make some preliminary assessments upon its recent stormy history. And they concluded that, so far at least, Princeton had been fortunate—in its leadership by a president who had moved in a brief period from a relative conservatism to flexible and responsible innovation; in its administration, which had been updated, in the last half of the sixties, with the appointment of a number of dynamic new administrators, such as Provost William Bowen;[17] in its faculty, with the emergence of creative reformers like Stanley Kelley who had helped to establish new consensus-building institutions just when they were to be most needed, producing a new sense

[16] Student interest in politics increased, however, as the 1972 presidential elections approached. In early 1972 a student campaign in favor of a 10-day recess before the November elections resulted in a reversal of an earlier faculty vote against the recess. However, the failure of a university strike in April in response to President Nixon's resumption of the bombing of North Vietnam indicated that the most radical phase of student activism was over at Princeton.

[17] Between September 1966 and September 1969 the following new appointments were made: dean of the college, provost, dean of the faculty, dean of students, dean of the graduate school, and women assistant deans in both the college and the Graduate School. An entirely new team, open to change and activist in orientation, was running Princeton at the end of the sixties. In November 1971 Provost Bowen, a major architect of the recent changes, was chosen to succeed President Goheen in 1972.

of community in a university that had lost that sense in its recent expansion.[18]

As for the student body, some may claim that Princeton was fortunate that it began the sixties with a relatively conservative student body so that it was better able to weather the ensuing strains than institutions like Columbia or Harvard, with their more radical constituencies. Anyone, however, who observed the rally of May 1968 or sampled the student mood after Cambodia would hardly have called it conservative, and in some ways the continued existence of a conservative element in the mid-sixties made needed change more difficult at the time because of the danger of polarization over politics or race. The students were important, however, in initiating the pressure for change. It was the SDS-initiated IDA protest that ultimately led to the structural reforms, and the events at Columbia in April and May 1968 gave a sense of urgency to the changes which were already being contemplated at the time. But the movement for change did not come only from SDS students. Parietal reform, the alternatives to the eating clubs, substantial student contributions to the Kelley Committee, the Movement for a New Congress, and the Princeton Plan—all came from the liberal reformers rather than the radicals.

Size is another factor that may help to explain both the intensity of the crisis at Princeton and the university's relative success in responding to it. With about 5,000 undergraduate and graduate students there was a sufficient number of students to provide the "critical mass" of radicals, of which S. M. Lipset has spoken, to keep student protest at a high peak for most of the period between 1967 and 1971. (That this protest began when it did may be attributed partially to the new admissions policy initiated in 1963, which sought out more individualistic and nonconformist students, and partially to changes in the country as a whole—especially of course, the Vietnam war). At the same time, the university was small enough that its administrators and especially its president could keep informed on impending crises, could know most of the leading protesters personally, and could mobilize student and faculty opinion quickly. The graduate school is small and its faculty-student ratio very low (about 2 to 1 for those taking courses);

---

[18] As an indication of the magnitude of that expansion, the university budget rose from $14 million to $75 million between 1957, when President Goheen took office, and 1970–71, when he announced his forthcoming retirement.

nearly all undergraduates live on campus; and meetings of the entire faculty can be called in a day or two and meet comfortably in a room holding 400 people. Thus a sense of community could emerge when the university was in crisis, and an intelligent response could elicit widespread support.

But the timely emergence of institutions to give organized and legitimized expression to student and faculty desires for reform, and to anticipate grievances on which the radicals could capitalize (as they had with parietal hours in the 1968 demonstration), was also very important. It is too early to see whether those institutions will function as intended or, as has happened with similar structures elsewhere, they will become atrophied due to student and faculty disinterest and/or be used as bases for extremists of right or left to politicize the university. At the start of 1971—as yet another committee, the Commission on the Future of the College, composed of three senior administrators, ten faculty members, and six students, began a searching reevaluation of the undergraduate program (including its financial aspects, since in describing its terms of reference President Goheen commented, "I expect a distinguishing mark of this commission to be hardheaded analysis of the costs of whatever innovations and alternatives it may propose")—it was clear that the traditional Princeton of Wilson and Fitzgerald was gone forever, and that the crises and changes of 1967–1970 would have a lasting impact on the future of the university.

Whether these changes are for good or ill remains for many an open question—as perusal of any issue of the *Princeton Alumni Weekly* will reveal. Critics of the new Princeton ask whether the abolition of parietal rules, aimed at giving the students increased freedom, has not created new pressures and new conformities. They note that there has been a perceptible lowering of Princeton's high academic standards which is attributed to the increased admission of students from disadvantaged backgrounds, and to faculty compliance with student pressure for the easing of requirements. And President Goheen, in his 1971 annual report (p. 18), observed that the new structures "put inordinate demands upon the time of senior University officers, faculty members, students, staff, and alumni involved." (The Priorities Committee for example, met 25 times in the fall term of 1970–71. Its 122-page report was distributed nationally by the American Council on Education.)

Yet there is no doubt that the Princeton of the early 1970s combined more diversity of economic background, race, sex, and ideological outlook[19] with greater sense of community than had its counterpart of a decade earlier. For this author and most of his colleagues and students, Princeton is a better place to teach, to learn, and to live.

References

Butz, Otto: *The Unsilent Generation,* Rinehart & Company, Inc., New York, 1958.

Daily Princetonian, April 21, 1969; Jan. 30, 1971.

Goheen, Robert: "The President's Report, October 31, 1971," *Official Register of Princeton University,* vol. 43, no. 7, Princeton University Press, Princeton, N.J., 1971.

"Negroes at Princeton," Princeton University Archives, Firestone Library.

Students and the University, Princeton University, Faculty Advisory Committee on Policy, Princeton, N.J., 1968.

Turner, Richard: *The Cold Desiccated Beauty of Task-Oriented Self-Sufficiency,* Princeton University faculty discussion paper, 1965. (Mimeographed.)

[19] Despite the increased presence of the left on campus, the right is not dead. In response to the withdrawal by the Undergraduate Assembly (UGA) from the Council of the Princeton University Community in 1971, the conservative Undergraduates for a Stable America (USA) initiated and overwhelmingly (1,554 to 730) won a student referendum to compel the UGA to return to the council (thus neatly reversing the usual left-right student position on this issue). The faculty has suffered virtually none of the McCarthyism of the left so painfully visited upon colleagues elsewhere. And ironically, the eating clubs, once a secure bastion of "male bonding," have a renewed lease on life because their numbers are swelled by female interest in joining.

12. Rutgers, The State University

by Richard P. McCormick

If, in the early 1960s, an informed observer had ventured to predict the development of Rutgers University, he undoubtedly would have foreseen vastly increased enrollments and the attainment of maturity as a full-fledged university. He would have envisioned an institution staffed by a highly professional, discipline-oriented faculty with a strong commitment to graduate education and research. There would be a carefully selected undergraduate body, an attitude of neutrality toward social and political issues, a bland dedication to meritocratic values, and considerable confidence in the willingness of society to provide the resources to support such an enterprise. By the end of the decade, as the result of both national and local influences, he would have had cause to be hesitant about his prognostications, for the pattern of the "normal" university was being subjected to wide-ranging criticisms, questionings, and attacks.

PROGRESS TOWARD ORMALITY" What promised to be a new era for Rutgers began in 1945, when it was declared the State University of New Jersey. Prior to the war, although it had received modest state support by virtue of its designation in 1864 as the land-grant college of New Jersey, it was a small institution, essentially collegiate in character, and still exhibiting some influences of its early association with the Dutch Reformed Church. Fortified by the expectation of increased state support, by unprecedentedly large enrollments occasioned by returning veterans, and by a vastly augmented young faculty with appropriate professional credentials, Rutgers embarked on the road to university status. Consistent with its hopes to expand its student body, it acquired branches in Newark (1946) and Camden (1950) and planned for the expansion of its overtaxed facilities in New Brunswick.

For a brief period the goals seemed attainable, but by 1950 it was becoming apparent that the state authorities would not provide funds adequate for an expanded state university, and when the wave of GIs graduated, enrollments sagged. Efforts to raise private funds were all but fruitless, and by 1956 the future seemed bleak. Nevertheless, some progress had been made. A university press (1938), a Research Council (1944), and a Graduate Faculty (1932 —reorganized in 1952 as the Graduate School) gave encouragement to research and graduate training, and there were graduate professional schools of law, social work, library service, and business administration, together with a handful of research institutes.

Beginning in 1956 new influences became operative. In that year the governing structure of the university was reorganized. Control and management were vested in a board of governors, a majority of whom were appointed by the Governor of New Jersey. Then came Sputnik and sudden concern with American education at all levels. At this juncture, too, authorities became aware of the need to provide expanded facilities for the bumper crop of postwar babies, soon to reach college age. A new Governor, Richard J. Hughes, proved to be sympathetic to higher education, and in 1959 the university installed an unusually talented president, Dr. Mason W. Gross. The most tangible breakthrough was popular approval in 1959 of a bond issue that made available to the university nearly $30 million in capital funds, the first time Rutgers had been successful in such an appeal for popular endorsement. Other bond issues in 1964 and 1968 provided $19,069,000 and $62,817,000 for capital programs, which, when augmented by funds from other sources, financed a building program in New Brunswick, Newark, and Camden totaling over $200 million. With enlarged facilities and steadily mounting annual appropriations, the university nearly doubled its full-time undergraduate enrollment between 1959 and 1964 and looked forward to at least doubling it again by 1975.[1]

The sudden availability of new resources brought not only more buildings and more undergraduates but an explicit redefinition of the goals of the institution. In a major policy statement in 1960 the board of governors declared that graduate and research programs were "not to be regarded as incidental functions that have merely

[1] Full-time undergraduate enrollments increased from 6,754 in 1958–59 to 11,191 in 1963–64. Total enrollment (full- and part-time) in 1963–64 was 27,043 and by 1970–71, it was 35,256.

been added to the traditional function of educating undergraduates. Rather, Rutgers is redefining itself as a university, and in such a way that this concept should operate to influence every aspect of the institution's operation." Subsequently, two state commissions confirmed such a role for Rutgers within the state's system of higher education.

In the decade after 1959, there were many indicators that the movement toward university status was proceeding rapidly. Enrollment in the graduate and professional schools soared from 3,277 to 6,560, doctoral programs increased from 29 to 50, and the number of doctorates awarded rose from 98 to 229. Funds for research, chiefly from federal sources, mounted from $5 million to $17 million. Two disciplines, mathematics and physics, exhibited such promise and distinction that they were the recipients of coveted "Centers of Excellence" grants from the National Science Foundation. The plan to develop a two-year medical school into a four-year institution was launched in 1961 and became fully operative in 1970. Admission to the undergraduate colleges became increasingly selective. By 1967, 83 percent of the entrants ranked in the top quarter of their high school class, and in the two most prestigious units even that level was exceeded.

The years between 1959 and 1965, when the impact of those forces that were transforming Rutgers into a "normal" university was most evident, were not distinguished by educational philosophizing. The university's goals were generally accepted as self-evident. The board of governors and top administrators were necessarily involved in planning and managing vast building programs. Individual disciplines were concerned with recruiting and retaining "visible" scholars who could add prestige to their field and attract both graduate students and research funds. There was no effective institution through which the entire faculty of the university could participate in high-level formulation of plans and policies. Despite occasional signs of restiveness, the undergraduates seemed resigned or apathetic. A network television special in 1959 depicted them as a "Generation Without a Cause."

Although the drive toward university status seemed to be clear and overpowering, there were distinctive local factors that presented complications. They related essentially to geography. In New Brunswick, as of 1965, there were four campuses. On the south side of the city were Douglass College, the women's college of the university, and the academic buildings of the College of Agriculture and Environmental Science. On the opposite side of the city was the campus of Rutgers College, including residential facilities for men students in the colleges of Arts and Sciences, Engineering, and Agriculture and other educational buildings. North of the Raritan River, approximately 2 miles from the men's campus, was the Science Center at University Heights. Located here were the main buildings for chemistry, biology, physics, and engineering, the Institute of Microbiology, and—soon to be constructed—the Medical School, Medical-Science Library, College of Pharmacy, and Mathematics-Statistics-Computer Building. In Newark, there were the College of Arts and Sciences, Graduate School of Business Administration, and School of Law. There was another College of Arts and Sciences in Camden, as well as a School of Law. Thus the facilities of the university were dispersed among four distinct sites in New Brunswick and remote locations in Newark and Camden. Moreover, the strong "university" orientation was chiefly centered in Rutgers College, which provided the great majority of the members of the graduate faculty. Douglass College remained oriented toward collegiate values, and the faculties of the undergraduate colleges in Newark and Camden had limited involvement in graduate work and research. Consequently, because of geographic dispersion and the pattern of collegiate organization, the university concept could hardly "operate to influence every aspect of the institution's operation."

CHALLENGES TO "NORMALITY" Beginning in the middle 1960s, Rutgers' commitment to "normal" university values, goals, and structure met unanticipated challenges. In common with other universities, Rutgers entered a period of turbulence, the remote causes of which can scarcely be treated here. Undergraduate rebelliousness, signalized by an increasingly distinctive life-style, or counterculture, produced demands for the abolition of parietal rules, for the relaxation or elimination of meritocratic standards, and for "relevant" curricula, as well as assaults on existing authorities, insistence on student participation in decision making, and protests against the insularity or political neutrality of the institution. Black students, previously a tiny minority, were sufficiently numerous by 1968 to dramatize their support for an extensive list of demands directed toward increasing sharply the proportion of black students, faculty, and administrators and instituting courses of study appropriate to their needs.

Faculty members, sensitive to the tensions created by the Vietnam war, the civil rights movement, the student rebellion, and the general atmosphere of dissent, were inspired or compelled to re-examine values, goals, and structures that had long been accepted as given. Only partly in response to these highly visible currents, top-level decisions regarding plans for the expansion of under-graduate facilities and abrupt changes in the attitudes and policies of state authorities created added elements of change and uncertainty. Confronted with challenges from many different directions, the university responded, not in a very systematic way and often under what seemed to be conditions of crisis or threat. It may be helpful to consider how several attributes of the "normal" university were more or less effectively challenged.

Accepted criteria for selecting students were modified or set aside to favor those from "disadvantaged" segments of society. When efforts to recruit black students who fully met normal admission standards yielded poor results, a modest program of "special" admissions was instituted in 1965. In 1968, following the assassination of the Rev. Dr. Martin Luther King and again in late February 1969, well-organized demonstrations by black students forced additional concessions. The Rutgers College faculty, explicitly acknowledging the need to increase black enrollment, approved a program to admit 100 disadvantaged students each year and to offer these students substantial support as well as remedial courses and supportive services.[2]

Even more dramatic was the action of the board of governors in creating an Urban University program (UUP) in March 1969. Economically and educationally deprived graduates of high schools in Newark, New Brunswick, and Camden who lacked the conventional prerequisites for college admission were accepted into the program. They took special developmental courses, provided through an urban university department, together with one or more regular college courses, and might ultimately qualify for a regular Rutgers degree. In September 1969, more than 500 students entered the program; 70 percent of them continued through the year. In many ways, the announced principles of the UUP were in conflict with conventional university policies, but perhaps because the

[2] Between September 1968 and September 1971, the number of black students (full- and part-time) increased from about 900 to nearly 1,900 (exclusive of the Urban University Department). For Rutgers College the comparable figures would be 100 and 272. When Livingston College opened in 1969, one-quarter of the students were black or Puerto Rican.

program was viewed as experimental, and in some respects tangential, its implications for accepted university values have yet to be fully explored or confronted.

In a related endeavor, the university administration in 1968 began a determined campaign to spur the recruitment of black faculty. Departments were informed that they might obtain additional "lines," or positions, provided those lines were filled with black personnel. The effort was successful, and the number of black faculty in the university increased from 13 in 1967 to 74 in 1971.

What was involved in the adoption of special policies toward black and disadvantaged students, as well as in the efforts to recruit black faculty—and administrators—was an admission that conventional universalistic criteria incorporated class and racial biases. Meritocratic values clashed with other social values. The university was acknowledging the pertinence of these other values, but it remained to be seen whether the new programs could be reconciled with the institution's commitment to socialize, sort, and ultimately certify its students.[3]

There were many signs of discontent with customary arrangements for evaluating students. Students mounted insistent pressure to deemphasize grades, partly on the grounds that it should be the university's function to educate, rather than to certify students. Accordingly, modest provisions were made in most colleges for pass-fail courses, for the exclusion of freshman grades from a student's cumulative average, and for new grading systems that, in effect, lessened the number of categories for rating students. A reduced rate of academic failures and, in some areas, a sharp decline in low grades suggested that many faculty members were disinclined to be as rigorous in their grading practices as formerly.

There was a trend among all faculties to move away from the assumption that they best knew what constituted a proper prescription for the content of a college education. In all the undergraduate colleges between 1967 and 1970 there were extensive revisions of curricula. Although the principle of "general education" requirements was not entirely repudiated, it was modified to broaden considerably the range of available options. Students were offered

---

[3] In response to the "women's liberation" movement, and threatened federal action under Executive Order 11,375, in 1971 the university instituted efforts to increase the proportion of women faculty—which was about 20 percent—and administrative personnel. In the same year a Committee on the Status of Women at Rutgers was established by the university senate.

limited opportunities for independent study and for designing their own fields of concentration, but at the same time there was little support for the older concept of "honors" programs, restricted to students of superior attainments. There was also a movement from a five-course load to a four-course load.

Many departments, especially in the social sciences and humanities, revised their offerings in response to student demands for "relevance," and by 1970 a large number of the listed courses contained in their titles alluring words like *revolution, black, urban, radical,* and even *women.* The most obvious innovations could be related to the demands of black students, but other constituencies were also recognized. If for no other reason than to sustain enrollments in the face of interdepartmental competition, the readiness of departments to cater to what was judged to be student interest was clearly apparent and in many respects was a more significant factor in curricular revision than the actions of college faculties.

Faculties had long been aware that the collegiate experience embraced more than what took place within the classroom, but for several decades, at least, they had been disinclined to accord such activities the dignity of academic recognition. Now there were some signs that they might concede to extracurricular experiences a legitimate place in the academic scene. At Livingston College, involvement in community projects was rewarded with college credits. Proponents of the four-course load justified a reduction in formal academic responsibilities on the grounds that students could profitably devote more time to informal learning experiences. Some individual instructors were willing to convert their courses into "consciousness raising" sessions or to give tacit recognition to activities approved by the instructor as an alternative to formal requirements.

In a related area, students were accorded increased freedom in arranging their social life. By 1925, faculties had disengaged themselves from responsibility for nonacademic regulations, turning these matters over to administrative officers and student life departments. As the rebellious styles of the youth culture became more pronounced, these authorities in turn yielded and permitted students more control over their own affairs. At Rutgers College an Inter-Residence Hall Association was created and was given the privilege—among others—of determining the hours of female visitation in the dormitories. Most living groups opted for a 24-hour rule. At Douglass College there was less permissiveness. What was thought to be a significant modification of the doctrine of *in loco parentis* was the announcement in 1965 that the university would, in general, leave off-campus offenses by students entirely in the hands of the civil authorities.

In one conspicuous area, the faculty did become involved with regulations affecting the nonacademic life of students. After some earlier rumblings, the New Brunswick campus experienced its first major incident of disruption when student radicals blocked access to the ROTC building for three days in November 1967 with the avowed objective of ending military training. (Subsequently there were sit-ins, picketings, and demonstrations of various sorts at all campuses, most of them related directly or indirectly to protests against the Vietnam war and racism.) The university administration promulgated a policy that recognized the right of orderly dissent that did not interfere with the freedom of others and announced that violations of this policy would, insofar as possible, be dealt with internally. It was specified, however, that in extraordinary cases it might be necessary to call for the assistance of the civil authorities.

College faculties reacted to this policy with confusion. In general, there was strong reluctance to concede to administrative authorities the exclusive right to decide when disruptive actions required an appeal to the police. Although it was not confronted explicitly, the basic issue of whether the faculty or the administration had ultimate responsibility for maintaining order on the campuses was involved. The issue was not resolved, but in some faculties more or less elaborate arrangements were instituted to ensure that faculty opinion would be consulted whenever disruptive actions threatened to precipitate police interference. Vague though these solutions were, they did serve to minimize outside intervention.[4] The faculty also recognized the students' impulse to engage in protests and demonstrations by providing on several occasions for the suspension of classes, notably in connection with the presentation of demands by black students in February 1969, for Vietnam Day in October 1969, for Earth Day in April 1970, and for the turmoil that followed the Cambodian invasion.

Yet another area where conventional beliefs and practices were seriously challenged was that of governance. The faculty tradi

---

[4] In December 1969, 21 students were arrested after breaking into an executive session of the board of governors and refusing to leave. There was no violence and the offenders subsequently were given 90-day suspended sentences.

tionally controlled such matters as curriculum, degree requirements, and even recruitment and promotion of academic personnel.
The administration provided a range of auxiliary services, handled
student discipline, and made decisions affecting budgets and long-
range plans and general policies. The board of governors dealt
mainly with problems of physical expansion and fiscal strategies
and approved policies formulated by the administration. Undergraduates, aside from their own ineffectual student government,
had little voice in formal decision-making agencies.

Around 1967, students moved from protests against particular
rules and regulations to demands for participation in making any
decisions that affected them. The provost urged all deans to explore ways of involving students in college deliberations and announced that students would be appointed to certain university
committees that dealt with student affairs. In due course students
were added to college committees, and when the university senate
was reorganized in 1970, students from all colleges were accorded
representation. In some departments, structures were created to
elicit undergraduate opinion. Basic problems, as yet unresolved,
had to do with the "legitimacy" of student representatives and the
extent to which they should have a voice on matters related to the
selection, retention, and promotion of faculty members. Some
students were prepared to contend that the college was a "community" where distinctions of status or rank in the area of governance were inappropriate, but this sentiment found slight support
from the faculties.[5]

While the faculty was contending against demands for "student
power," it was engaged in another kind of struggle with the board
of governors. In 1970 the board rejected decisions of the Rutgers
College faculty ending academic credit for ROTC and proposing
that the college should become coeducational. The first issue,
especially, was seen as involving the faculty's prerogative of setting
academic requirements. On another front, there was the inconclu-
sive clash with the administration over the question of disciplinary
power. Further complicating the scene was the potential emergence
of a new power structure. In accordance with recent legislation

[5] In January 1971, the board of trustees, which remained in existence with
minimal powers after the creation of the board of governors, authorized the
appointment of two faculty and two student representatives to meet with the
board, without voting privileges. These representatives were appointed in
March by the university senate.

sanctioning collective bargaining by state employees, the university faculty designated the American Association of University Professors (AAUP) as its bargaining agent in 1970. The AAUP leadership announced its intention to seek not only improved economic conditions for its constituency but also a large role in the determination of university policies. There was the prospect, at least, that an "extralegal" faculty organization would develop as a new base for "faculty power." This movement held intriguing possibilities, especially because the university senate included representatives of faculty, students, and administration, and the AAUP could claim to be the sole universitywide faculty body.

Much of the ferment of these years was politically as well as educationally oriented, and consequently the highly esteemed value of "neutrality" was challenged. On one broad front there was the charge by radical students, with some faculty support, that because the university was financed and controlled by the power structure, it was, in fact, not politically neutral and used its resources to socialize students in corrupt values and to sustain the established order. Proponents of this view insisted, with some success, that the university must rid itself of all military-related research, decline a substantial benefaction from an industrialist with interests in South Africa, refuse to permit recruiters from certain industries to interview on the campus, and purge itself of white racism. The prime target of this movement was ROTC. Changed from a compulsory to a voluntary program in 1960 and brought under academic control in 1968, ROTC was under constant attack as a symbol of militarism and imperialism, and at the height of the Cambodian excitement the Rutgers College faculty resolved to eliminate the program, an action that produced an impasse with the board of governors.

There was parallel insistence that the university should commit itself to specific political positions, that it must engage positively in promoting radical change. The technique of the "teach-in," which brought teachers and students together in a quasi-academic relationship, produced some confusion as to the applicability of traditional norms of academic freedom. When Professor Eugene D. Genovese, at the first teach-in in April 1965, declared that he was a Marxist and a socialist and that he would welcome a Viet Cong victory, he created such a sensation that he was soon the major issue in the state's gubernatorial campaign. Pressures for "involvement" resulted in several "moratoriums," when classes were suspended in order that all elements of the university community might demonstrate their political convictions. The university senate sanctioned an eight-day "political recess" prior to the 1970 election so that students might work within the political system to effectuate their demands—an opportunity of which very few availed themselves. In these and numerous other ways, students and faculty members signified their growing belief that "neutrality" was a questionable ideal.

THE FEDERATED PLAN—A CASE STUDY Most of the tensions, crosscurrents, and innovations that were operative within the university can be epitomized in the story of the founding of a new college and the repercussions that it had on the entire structure of the university. Until 1963, university plans generally projected that future expansion in New Brunswick would center mainly in the vicinity of the Science Center at University Heights. Then the United States government decided to abandon Camp Kilmer, located roughly a mile from University Heights, and the Rutgers administration made application for 540 acres, which was ultimately approved in December 1964. In the meantime, various planning committees worked on the problem of how best to use this tract.

A sharp conflict developed between those who favored the establishment of several relatively small autonomous colleges there and those who, in one manner or another, wanted the new facilities to be tied in closely with existing college structures. From one perspective, the debate was between those favoring an updated version of the "special interest" college and those who adhered to the concept of the "normal" university. By late 1964 the decision was made, essentially by key administration officials, that the Kilmer area would be used to develop three or more coeducational undergraduate colleges, each with an enrollment of 3,500 students, and that the first of these—Livingston College—would open in 1967 (subsequently delayed until 1969).

A dean was appointed and in due course a small staff was assembled to shape the character of the new college. Over the next few years it was determined that Livingston would become a unique liberal arts college, with special emphasis on creating in its students an awareness of such contemporary problems as those associated with urbanization and racism. "Livingston College will have no ivory tower," proclaimed its first catalog. "It cannot; our cities are decaying, many of our fellow men are starving; social injustice and racism litter the earth; weapons of awesome destruction threaten our existence." Accordingly, studies would be oriented toward problems rather than disciplines; students would have freedom to plan their own curricular and extracurricular life-styles; off-campus activities would be integrated with the formal academic programs; students would share fully with faculty in the direction of the college; and faculty members would be encouraged to develop close relations with students through carefully planned office and residential arrangements. Particular efforts would be made to enroll disadvantaged students, toward whom the college recognized a special commitment. In essence, the college was to challenge almost every element of the "normal" university creed, and during the first two years of its existence, it conformed with remarkable fidelity to the model of its planners.

The decision that Rutgers in New Brunswick was to expand through the creation of several additional colleges, each with some distinctive emphasis, raised agonizing issues regarding the relations of all the colleges to one another and to that elusive entity, the university.[6] To resolve some of these issues, the Federated College Plan was contrived. The plan rested on the assumption that small, distinctive units were best suited to the needs of undergraduate education, but it assumed as well that as the faculties expanded, the various disciplines could be strengthened and the university's resources for graduate training and research could be proportionately augmented. Each faculty member, in effect, would have a dual identity. He would be a member of one of the college faculties and he would also be a member of a New Brunswick-wide disciplinary department. Uniform standards of appointment and promotion and comparable degree requirements would prevail among all colleges. Each college, then, would have its own dean, faculty, and budget, but there would also be disciplinary departments and a dean of the faculty of liberal arts to oversee these departments.

The Federated College Plan, which in actuality was flexible in application, was strongly opposed by the faculties of Rutgers College and the graduate school. Opponents contended that the colleges would have too much autonomy, that they would have diverse

---

[6] Although the new colleges were often referred to as liberal arts colleges, their precise character is difficult to define. For example, two additional colleges, still in the planning stage, were to emphasize, respectively, science and technology and environmental studies. No consideration was given to creating such conventional preprofessional schools as a College of Business, a College of Education, a College of Architecture, or such other units as are often associated with a state university.

standards, that the disciplines would be weakened, and that physical facilities, especially libraries and scientific laboratories, would either be fragmented or inconveniently located. The result, in brief, would be a loose affiliation of diverse undergraduate colleges rather than a "normal" university. The proponents argued that it was inappropriate to build a Berkeley-style campus with huge masses of students, that small colleges permitted highly differentiated and experimental educational programs, and that such a mode of undergraduate collegiate organization was not necessarily inconsistent with the attainment of excellence. [7]

The founding of Livingston College and the adoption of the Federated College Plan constituted an effort to reconcile "normal" university values with an identifiable set of counter values. The issues involved were fundamental, and the tensions were predictable. Livingston differed so radically from Rutgers and Douglass in its basic commitments, its curricular arrangements, and its scheme of governance, as well as in the composition of its student body and faculty, that it could hardly fit the pattern of a coordinate institution. Aggressively experimental, geographically remote, and subject to its own peculiar internal stresses, it was viewed with apprehension and even hostility by members of the more conventional faculties. In addition, those features of the Federated College Plan that had been intended to strengthen disciplinary interests were never fully implemented, and even in their mild forms they were eroded by collegiate interests, zealously defended by the college deans. For better or worse, collegiate autonomy seemed to be in the ascendant, but there are presently some signs of a counterattack against the "distinctive college" policy.[8]

[7] The New Jersey Department of Higher Education in the most recent version of its master plan (1970, p. 22) strongly endorsed the concept that "no operating undergraduate college located in a major university center have an enrollment larger than 4,000 to 5,000 students." But a report by a special evaluation team of the Middle States Association of Colleges and Secondary Schools (1967, p. 20) expressed some reservations about the Federated College Plan and suggested that all members of a discipline in New Brunswick should constitute "a single departmental group, whose primary thrust is involved in research and graduate work, and who accept responsibility for research laboratories and facilities at advanced undergraduate and graduate levels."

[8] The Federated College Plan contemplated that students in any of the undergraduate colleges would, through cross registration, have easy access to courses in all the colleges. Intercollege transportation was provided through a free bus system. Because of physical inconveniences and subtle impediments to cross registration, students continued to take approximately 90 percent of their credits in their own colleges.

Rutgers University, of course, is not completely the master of its own destiny; it is shaped in part by public policy. Within this context, the fact that New Jersey has always ranked near the bottom of all the states in per capita expenditures for higher education (forty-eighth in 1969) and sends a higher proportion of its youth out of state to college than any other state is suggestive of public policy. At all levels and by any meaningful measures, New Jersey's system of public higher education is underdeveloped. In 1966 the Legislature created the department of higher education, headed by a chancellor. The new department was empowered to engage in long-range planning and policy formulation for a state system of higher education, to coordinate the activities of individual institutions, and to maintain financial oversight of the system. Included in its jurisdiction were the state university, the Newark College of Engineering, eight state colleges, 14 recently established two-year county colleges, the College of Medicine and Dentistry, and certain other educational authorities. [9]

The State University Act of 1956 guaranteed Rutgers a "high degree of self-government" under its board of governors. As the department began to formulate plans for a coordinated system of higher education, conflicts developed because the university's own plans did not coincide with those of the department. Moreover, the university would have to compete more obviously than before for its share of the limited resources made available for public higher education. From the standpoint of the university's autonomy, the action of the Legislature in 1970 in imposing more stringent controls on the university's disposition of appropriated funds was an ominous sign. Even more disconcerting was legislation that detached the Medical School from the university and placed it under a new state board, which also controlled the College of Medicine and Dentistry in Newark. How effective the chancellor and the department will be in determining the character of Rutgers remains a subject of speculation, but there are reasons to believe that explicit public policy will be a more significant factor in the university's future than it was in the past.

No general review could enumerate all the elements of change in what was obviously a very dynamic situation. Much could be writ-

[9] The department administered several financial-aid programs, including the Educational Opportunity Fund. Instituted in 1968, this fund provided grants to over 1,600 disadvantaged students from families with incomes under $6,000. Its budget has increased since then.

ten, for example, about the manifold programs newly designed to bring the university's resources to bear on critical social problems through the University Committee on Equal Opportunity, the Center for Urban Social Science Research, the Center for Alcohol Studies, the Community Service Bureau, the Cooperative Extension Service, and other agencies. In a similar context the College of Agriculture in 1965 became the College of Agriculture and Environmental Science, in recognition of both the declining role of agriculture in New Jersey and mounting concern about threats to the environment. The amazing growth of two-year county colleges after 1966 greatly affected University College, the degree-granting evening college. Because of competition from the new institutions it suffered losses in enrollment in the first two years of its programs and was obliged to concentrate on upper-division work. The same development threatened drastic reductions in the programs of University Extension, which offered noncredit courses. The Newark and Camden units necessarily became deeply involved in the vast urban renewal projects that impinged on their plans for expansion. At the level of graduate studies and research, severe cutbacks in public funds and sudden changes in the demands for scholars trained in particular fields necessitated readjustments in priorities and programs. Many identifiable external influences, then, had immediate bearing on the university's character.

CONCLUSION In surveying broadly what has happened to Rutgers in the past few years, three developments seem most significant. First, there was the wide range of challenges to accepted notions of what were the appropriate values and goals of a university. These challenges were posed mainly by students, who, with a small segment of sympathetic allies in the faculty and administration, were able to effect, not a revolution, but substantial change. Second, there was the founding of Livingston College and the commitment to the Federated College Plan, with all that these actions signified in terms of a conflict of purposes. Third, there were the indications that the relative autonomy of the university would diminish and that public policy would become increasingly influential in shaping Rutgers. The "academic revolution" that had been strongly under way for two decades prior to 1965 was neither halted nor reversed, but its direction seemed less clear and its ultimate victory less assured.

References

New Jersey Master Plan for Higher Education, Number 2, December 1970, New Jersey Department of Higher Education, Trenton, 1970. (Mimeographed.)

A Report to Rutgers, State University by a Special Evaluation Team Appointed by the Middle States Association of Colleges and Secondary Schools, Commission on Institutions of Higher Education, 1967. (Mimeographed.)

13. San Francisco State College: A Tale of Mismanagement and Disruption

by Algo D. Henderson

A stroll across the campus and discussions with students, faculty, and administrators at San Francisco State College in the early spring of 1971 gave one an impression of peace and quiet. Just two years previously it was enduring the longest strike in American college history (Finberg, 1969; Karagueuzian, 1971). More than 700 persons were arrested during the conflicts. On one day, January 23, 1969, 454 persons (252 of them students) were arrested. Administrators at the college are now sure that this mass arrest broke the back of the strike. The people of California were greatly relieved.

The strike was the culmination of a series of disruptions at the college. These consisted of marches, sit-ins, mass meetings, brick throwing, bombings, and arson—all the tactics so familiar to the militant-disturbed campuses of the 1967-to-1969 period. San Francisco State was perhaps the college with the greatest amount of internal tension and turmoil. The agitations and the violence were the product of the frustrations of students, of youth generally, and, more specifically at this college, of black students. There was also a considerable intrusion from off-campus advocates of revolution. Meanwhile, the faculty had become polarized into power-seeking groups, and the college was suffering from weak leadership. Governor Ronald Reagan frequently inflamed the situation by his attacks on the college; indeed, he and some of the radicals were mirror images of each other, each feeding on the other.

The first act of unusual violence occurred in November 1967, when black students invaded the offices of the campus newspaper, claiming that the paper was racist. They attacked the editors and left the premises in a shambles. But, as will be seen from later discussion, tensions had been building at the college for 10 years previously.

During the ensuing months, the issues on the campus became exceedingly complex. They can best be summarized by noting the demands that eventually became the basis of the strike. The Black Students Union (BSU), taking the lead in striking, announced 10 demands. At the top of the list was a full-fledged black studies department (apparently the idea of a black studies program had been advanced for the first time at this college). The demands specified that a certain man, Nathan Hare, be made chairman, that 20 faculty positions be budgeted, that the department have full authority to hire faculty, determine its own character, and grant bachelor's degrees. Next came demands that all black students who wished admission to the college should be admitted and that the person in charge of financial aids to students be replaced by a black. A black instructor who was under investigation by the administration and the chancellor's office was to be retained on the faculty. The trustees of the state system were not to be allowed to interfere with the black programs. Finally, all participants in the strike were to be free of any discipline. The Third World Liberation Front, representing several minority groups, subsequently added five demands patterned after those of the BSU.

The student strike began on November 6, 1968. A month later, the American Federation of Teachers led a strike of a portion of the faculty. They published 13 demands, three of which were subdivided into additional items. The faculty strike leaders seemed to be motivated by a desire to join in the student effort, but as a means of getting labor-union endorsement their demands were heavily weighted toward alleviating conditions of employment.

The strike ended on March 13, 1969. Although it had dramatized the campus problems, it was merely the boil coming to a head. For example, most of the demands of both students and faculty had been in process of identification and articulation over the preceding two years. The angry speeches, the demonstrations, and the violence had been occurring almost without interruption. The invasions of the campus by radical leaders had been more or less continuous.

Following the arrest of so many persons at the January demonstration, the strike had gradually lost its momentum. Thus the leaders, both students and faculty, found their bargaining effectiveness diminished. In the meantime, the governing board had appointed an acting president, Dr. S. I. Hayakawa, a member of the faculty, who invoked firm tactics and proved to have a flair for getting public support behind him. Thus in the final negotiations for a settlement, very little ground was gained by the strikers. (Daniels, Kahn-Hut, & Associates, 1970. Appendix, give in full the documents relating to the strike. Several books and reports noted in the bibliography for this chapter describe the situation of the college from 1967 to 1970 in great detail and from several points of view.)

A black studies program had been worked out several months before the strike had begun. It remained about the same during the two years that followed. The Black Students Union did not secure control over the curriculum and the appointment of teachers. Ironically, Oriental and Chicano studies are more fully developed than black studies, even though the idea of having them was not pressed until the middle of the conflict. Ethnic studies as a whole, however, by 1971 achieved considerable vitality, offering 73 courses. The director is not black—he followed a succession of black directors—but is Japanese-American. Nationally, there is much division of opinion about the merits of ethnic studies; however, at the college the drive to launch them was insistent.

Two intensively pressed demands, retention of two faculty members who had been fired and amnesty for arrested disrupters, were not granted. The two faculty members were blacks. One, the chairman of black studies, was relieved for insubordination. The other, a recently appointed instructor in English, had been fired by the chancellor for alleged misconduct. The American Federation of Teachers, which launched the strike, enlisted 30 percent of the faculty. A year earlier, the faculty had voted to reject the AFT as a bargaining agent, and at no time did it get effective support from the faculty. The strike was ill timed. It was divisive at a moment when unity was essential to the welfare of the institution. On the other hand, teachers did strike and were continued in employment, thus demonstrating that college teachers could participate in a strike in California. (A more sympathetic view will be found in Daniels, Kahn-Hut, & Associates, 1970.)

The peace and quiet on campus today may be deceptive. The peace is a peace of defeatism. The faculty have retreated into their cubbyholes; the dynamic, irritating, and sometimes obnoxious student leaders have largely disappeared; the off-campus revolutionaries have fled to greener pastures; and the president, backed by the governing board and the Governor of California, has taken command. But few of the conditions that produced the turmoil have been alleviated. Those who have demonstrated their power over the college desire that the image of its endeavor be that of peaceful contemplation behind ivy-covered walls rather than vigorous inquiry into controversial issues. President S. I. Hayakawa, shortly after assuming office during the strike, was quoted by the press as calling for "a sanctuary for debate and scholarship uninterrupted by secular problems" ("Why Hayakawa . . . ," 1969, p. 1).

TRANSITION BACKGROUND In one respect the history of San Francisco State is typical of that of a few hundred regionally placed state colleges. Begun as a normal school in 1889, the college successively became a teachers college (a four-year program) and an institution with multiphase and master's degree programs. Growing pains in purposes, budgets, plant, admission of students, and recruitment of faculty have been felt. But the last phase—the multiphase programs of the past two decades—led to divisiveness within the faculty and between service-oriented faculty and the administration over policy. For example, should the institution remain service-oriented (as it was in training teachers) and concentrate the bulk of its energies on its highly regarded undergraduate programs? Or should it now emulate prestigious and elitist universities by investing its resources and inventiveness in graduate programs? Where should the department of psychology now be located—in the school of education, as formerly, or in a new school of social and behavioral sciences? A move would mean a shift in power within the faculty; failure to move would mean a partial defeat of objectives. To become elitist would draw the college away from its community, and many faculty opposed doing this.

In other respects, San Francisco State was (and is) unique. It was located within San Francisco, where over half of the population is composed of such cultural groups as Orientals, Negroes, and Mexican-Americans. Youth from these groups have developed a desire to rediscover the cultural heritage from which most of their ancestors came. The city was almost surrounded by water, water that was rapidly becoming grossly polluted and encroached upon by housing developments and factories. Smog was enveloping this beautiful community, which formerly enjoyed the freshest of air. Questions of city zoning to preserve its natural beauty were as much at issue as the "Manhattanization" of San Francisco, which in spite of voluble public protest, proceeded rapidly. The youth of draft age in San Francisco and the Bay Area were especially sensitive to the Vietnam war—the transport of homebound bodies past the Golden Gate added a touch of realism to the war tragedy.

San Francisco needed an institution of higher education that would be concerned with its problems. Many black students, Chinese, and Chicanos wanted to learn how to change the conditions under which their people have lived (Tape recordings . . . , 1969). They wanted to do it *now,* while they were in college. Before the violence started, the black students found an outlet for their ideas and energies in the tutorial program, tutoring blacks in the ghetto—a plan conceived by two blacks while in jail—and in Experimental College, which offered mainly noncredit courses focused on the kinds of problems about which students expressed concern. These experiences whetted their appetites for work on the problems of their own communities.

The college is also unique as a unit in a state system of colleges. The fifth of 19 regional state colleges in California, it had always been part of a system. Before 1960, the colleges were under the state board of education, and supervised by the state superintendent of public instruction. But the effect on the college was different then. The board was busy with the public schools, and the superintendent allowed and encouraged the colleges to develop individually. As a consequence each college had a large degree of autonomy. This necessitated the recruitment of strong presidents, and it also enabled each college to devote itself primarily to serving its own community.

One such president was J. Paul Leonard, who was at San Francisco State from 1945 to 1957. The development of a new campus on a beautiful site near the ocean, the beginning of the multiphase program, and the recruitment of imaginative faculty much committed to teaching were products of Leonard's administration. The college was regarded nationally as one of the best and most innovative of teachers colleges. In retrospect, this period (especially the years from 1951 to 1957) can be identified as the most creative one that the institution has experienced.

In 1960, the State Legislature gave legal sanction to a Master Plan for Higher Education. It gave to the University of California primary responsibility for research, advanced teaching, education for such professions as law and medicine, and lower-division work for elite students—the top eighth of the high school graduating classes. The state colleges were to provide for the bulk of undergraduate education for the top third of high school graduating classes and offer limited graduate work. The public junior colleges were to have open doors for two-year programs. The functional roles of the respective institutions were thus defined by law.

Defining this three-level distribution of functions seemingly was sound academic planning. The problems did not become apparent until later. One was in admissions. At San Francisco State, as the admissions standards were revised to accord with the master plan, the percentage of blacks in the student body dropped from 12 percent to 4 percent. The reason may have been the inferior education provided for blacks in ghetto high schools, but to the blacks it seemed that the establishment had deliberately erected a barrier against them. No longer could they attend the state college that was within commuting distance of their homes. Furthermore, they did not like being relegated to the junior colleges, which were regarded as providing inferior education; they had had enough of that. (A concession has recently been made to admit a limited number [427 places in 1968, but not all were filled] of unqualified students under the National Educational Opportunity Program, but the state colleges are still tied to the principle of superior academic preparation as the basis for admission rather than social demand and need.) The blacks think the existing plan is racist. This charge enlisted the support of many white persons.

Another problem resulting from the master plan lay in the shock to faculty morale. The University of California was clearly marked for the highest prestige. Salary differentials between the two types of institutions were maintained, and this implied that greater recognition was being given by the state for research rather than for teaching. And the prohibition against giving doctoral degrees at the state colleges seemed to these faculty members like a slap in the face; for it was clear that certain departments at such colleges as San Francisco State, San Diego, and San Jose were qualified to grant the doctorate, whereas some of the campuses of the university were new and still in the formative stage. The plan of allocating functions to each college within a state system has merit, but the problem of securing faculty acceptance has not been resolved.

Still another factor of crucial importance was the manner in which the system of state colleges became centralized. A single board of trustees was created for the 15 (currently 19) colleges, and the law required the trustees to *administer* them. The office of chancellor was formed, and a headquarters was authorized and located in Los Angeles. A system needs a planning and coordinating mechanism, and so the board-chancellor concept has certain merit. But in practice the central office and the one board for 19 colleges have made decision making very complex and time-consuming and have hamstrung initiative and innovation at the local institutions. This is because centralized planning and coordination were confused with centralized operation. The state mandate to the trustees for administration, implemented through the chancellor's office, has had unfortunate results. The office, called "chancellorville" on the campus, is regarded by most state college faculty as responsive only to crises, always ready to issue edicts, but characterized by delays when requests for program authorizations are made by the faculty. In addition, the board and the chancellor are regarded by most faculty as having let themselves become a tool for political maneuvering from the governor's office.

Furthermore, the state maintains detailed supervision over the finances of the colleges. The budget is of the line item type, which means that an official at the state level may pass judgment upon every proposed expenditure by the college. This is done first when the budget is constructed, a process that takes over 18 months. Then the college is left no discretion in making three kinds of changes: shifts among budgetary categories, new programs, and programs that use money that comes from sources other than the state. The effect is twofold: noneducators do much planning for education; and changes, innovations, and the meeting of emergency demands are stymied. Thus when the proposed black studies program faced the reality of implementation and it became clear that additional funds for the purpose would not be provided by the state, the 11.3 faculty positions needed to staff the new program were found by pressuring departments to release positions or portions of them. Probably the violence, which showed how intense feelings about the program were, helped with the persuasion.

COMPLEXITIES OF DECISION MAKING The manner in which the hands of the college are tied became obvious to the students when they proposed a student union building. At that time, 1968, the college had dormitory rooms for only 800 students and 72 married couples. The other 17,000 students lived off campus. Any college—and especially a commuter college such as this one—needs a place for student activities, food services, and between-class recreation. These facilities at San Francisco State were inadequate. A plan for a student union building financed with student fees was developed. Thus the students would have to pay for the space; but this had been agreed to. The students, collaborating with college staff, had worked hard to devise and refine architectural plans. In doing so, a commendable degree of student participation was being achieved, and this was an added dividend in promoting college unity and morale. Moshe Safdie, famous for his *Habitat* design at the Montreal World's Fair, provided a design which would have given a lift to an otherwise staid campus. After a negative review by the chancellor's office, it was turned down by the board of trustees. Appeals were made twice; the second appeal took the form of a petition with 6,000 signatures. The board voted 8 to 8 and thus killed the plan. The vote of one man —the vote needed to gain a favorable majority—would have enabled a design supported by 6,000 people on the campus to be adopted.

Decision making at the college is much too complex and time-consuming. The steps include the development of plans and getting the necessary clearances on the campus, submission for approvals to the chancellor's office, then action by the board of trustees. The submission of a request to the chancellor's office requires several pages of justification. But even this procedure is not always final in view of the veto power held by the state department of finance. The process takes many months. All too often, plans initiated with much enthusiasm wither or become the victim of the veto. No one is trusted to initiate and carry out programs within adopted policies and overall budgets.

POWER STRUGGLES But not all the difficulty in decision making has been in this cumbersome and negatively oriented, state-focused procedure. During the period of trauma at San Francisco State, there was no clear decision-making authority or procedure on the campus. A power vacuum had existed on the campus for several years, and there was intense rivalry in filling it. In an effort to achieve power, the faculty built up several suborganizations. And at time during the two years of crisis, student and even nonstudent leaders exercised the most power.

From 1960 to 1970, the college had five presidents and two acting presidents. One of the presidents was too old when appointed, and at least three of them were misfits for the role of leading the institution in its educational mission. Not only were the selections by the board bad, but the board did not give the presidents—with the exception of the last one—appropriate responsibility and support. Instead of threshing out policy with the president and then giving him full authority and backing, the board put each president through repeated grillings, some of them publicly televised, and used public statements to undermine him. Although an individual member of a corporate board has no legal authority—the power is in the collective board—certain members of the board, notably the ex officio ones, repeatedly made statements to the newspapers and over television and radio criticizing the conduct of affairs on the campus.

When he was president of the college, from 1957 to 1961, Chancellor Glenn S. Dumke had encouraged faculty participation in decision making but apparently failed to define clearly the location of final authority. President Paul Dodd had come from a large university where departments had considerable power. He encouraged departmentalization but failed to integrate the departments as a working part of the team. He granted to the faculty a liberal constitution but failed to retain or provide authority for the extraordinary powers required in an emergency. By the time John Summerskill became president, the faculty, divided into discrete groups rivaling one another for power, had become entrenched in their control of their own parts of the college. But no one was running the whole institution. It didn't take long for faculty and students to discover that the decisions made by the president were reversible, and as a result many of his actions were ineffective. President Robert Smith had support from the faculty and some from students, but was undercut by the chancellor and whipped by the trustees at crucial moments.

A faculty senate and a council of academic deans existed, but their roles became confused—the distinction between policy-program formation and administrative implementation was not made and adhered to. What should have been a mutually congenial relationship became a dichotomous one. The history of this chaotic period made clear that a faculty cannot function administratively and cannot be decisive or prompt in meeting a crisis.

In the meantime, unofficial faculty groups were building up pressures to gain power. These included extrainstitutional organizations such as the militant American Federation of Teachers. A rival of the AFT was the Association of California State College Professors. S. I. Hayakawa, who later was named president, became visible to the trustees through his pronouncements as a member of an informal faculty group that called itself the Faculty Renaissance.

These manifestations of campus politics are instructive not only in their relation to the decision-making process but also because of the depth of feelings aroused. A college is supposed to be a goal-oriented and directed organization, but at San Francisco State internal antagonisms became so intense that goals spun off in all directions, communication became invective, and leadership was either lacking, under some presidents, or undercut from above, under others.

MORALE ON THE CAMPUS   Bearing in mind that the first instance of gross violence was in November 1967, it is interesting to contemplate the findings of a survey of the faculty and administrators of San Francisco State in 1966. The Center for Research and Development in Higher Education of the University of California interviewed 50 and sampled by questionnaire 250 of the 1,100 faculty members. Ninety percent of the sample complained about office space, and almost as many were critical of working conditions, salaries, teaching loads, and leaves. Their concerns were about departmental growth, not about intellectual climate and educational objectives. The vested interests were opposed to anything new that might cause a displacement of budgets. Most faculty members held that much politicking was necessary to get anything done on campus. Although the normal expectation from such a sampling of faculty attitudes is statements of unmet expectations, the results in this case depicted an institution with extremely low morale. It also revealed the nature and extent of the power vacuum.

A few quotations from the answers (two years before the strike) show some of the perceptions about the mounting difficulties:

FACULTY: The state treats us as workers, not professionals.

ADMINISTRATION: President gets caught between his senate and the chancellor.

FACULTY: There is no structure to get things done, so you have to get around it. Becomes a lawless place.

ADMINISTRATION: Dissidents and AFT line up at microphone at faculty meetings; others tire and leave.

FACULTY: The faculty feel that the senate does not really represent the faculty, the president [Summerskill] doesn't really represent the college, the board doesn't really represent the people. Thus communication is permeated with suspicion.

FACULTY: Faculty are afraid of students in general and mistrust them all.

ADMINISTRATION: As a rumor factory we are number one.

ADMINISTRATION: You can't solve revolutionary problems with a reactionary legislature looking over your shoulder.

FACULTY: Trustees run the system, but it is hard to get to them.

ADMINISTRATION: I fear we are in for right wing pressures that will blow this place to smithereens.

The climate on the campus thus was conducive to violence-prone exploitation (for further evidence, see Smith, Axen, & Pentony, 1970).

THE ATTRACTIONS OF VIOLENCE During much of the postwar period in the United States, a primary goal of the student movement was to achieve student power. By 1967, the students found San Francisco State to be especially vulnerable. There was a tradition of democracy on the campus and belief in the values of student participation. This caused faculty members and administrators to feel considerable sympathy toward the students in their earlier efforts to participate. In addition, taking advantage of the power vacuum, the student leaders knew what they wanted, were successful in resolving differences among themselves, and were willing to devote untold energy to their causes. Had they not in their impatience with the hamstringing procedures resorted to violence, they might have worked out a model for participation in college governance.

However, some leaders, including off-campus nonstudents, favored violence as a means of promoting revolutionary change. In 1968, a circular bearing the imprint of the Students for a Democratic Society provided instructions for making bombs. Subsequently several bombs were exploded on the campus. As the disruptions mounted during 1968, the campus became a magnet for revolutionary-minded people. An off-campus coordinator for the Black Students Union announced at a college convocation that BSU's major objective was the seizure of power. "Until we have power, everything is bullshit," he said (Smith, Axen, & Petony, 1970, p. 155). But the dissident students were not all "creeps and bums," as characterized by a high state official (Orrick, 1969, p. 142). The struggle for Negro manhood, for example, is dynamic; its leaders are not content with the gradualism of appeasement. As more and more youth from the ghettos come to college, these institutions must be prepared for ghetto vocabulary and customs. The answer to the social problem lies in education, not in suppression.

The initial disturbance was by blacks, and the major strike in 1968–69 was led by the Black Students Union and the Third World Liberation Front (Gumas, 1969). The gutter language, the shock rhetoric, the vandalism, and the personal assaults resorted to in the actions turned many potential friends against them. The state was able finally to suppress the violence, and the blacks should have anticipated that this would be the case. Hopefully, they too may have learned that the answer lies in education, not in violence.

But the public needs also to be educated about the social problem. When people have been spit upon, they get an exhilaration from spitting back. When people feel frustrated and think they can gain by violent action, they will riot. As bad as an actual situation is, the *feelings about it* count most. Youth of college age are very knowledgeable about social ills, but there are few channels open to them to effect change. From their viewpoint, the establishment is too entrenched and concerned with self-interest to initiate or support change. They perceive rioting as a form of communication. In spite of the losses from using the strategy of violence, the blacks and other "Third World" leaders have made all of us somewhat more conscious of their problems.

PERCEPTIONS OF INSTITU-TIONAL ROLE Issues such as the above spill over onto the campus and raise a question about the central purpose of each college. Should a college, in part at least, be concerned with the relevant issues of the surrounding community, or should it become an ivy-covered institution emulating the nearby university?

San Francisco State's shift in focus away from its community began with Dumke's administration as president, and was accelerated under President Dodd. Dr. Dumke came when there was a need to convert the teachers college into a multiphase college, and his appointment was greeted favorably by those who foresaw this need. But in action he seemed to many observers as wanting also to subordinate the service role of the institution. Writing a defense of the college (in opposition to some conclusions expressed in a vignette written by David Riesman and C. Jencks, 1962; see also Riesman and Jencks, 1961), Dumke expressed pride in the events that were "gradually making people forget the college's proletarian background" (1962, p. 263) and in the fact that the institution was getting away from being a streetcar college. He pushed the college strongly toward the liberal arts tradition, and was perceived on the campus as being prejudiced against teacher education. He is, as chancellor, an advocate of the state system as a "university," a status that would be appropriate to the size and complexity of programs. But it would be most unfortunate to change the regional colleges to elitist institutions. Since the state has a strong university, staffed with distinguished research-oriented professors, the state colleges should be regionally located, emphasize undergraduate teaching, and include attention to the demands and needs of their own communities. This policy calls for diversification in programs, rather than the standardization that is the product of pressures and directives from the central office in Los Angeles.

But to achieve this result, each college must have some autonomy in curriculum planning and decision making, and the faculty must be allowed to define their own goals within the larger identification of role. Each college also should have its own operating board, for it is impossible for a central board to administer effectively so many diverse educational programs. Furthermore, it is impossible for the trustees to visit and become acquainted with the 19 campuses in any meaningful way.

RESPONDING TO CHANGE There is clearly a political and economic hazard involved in having chaos and violence on a campus. Newspapers, radio, and television had a heyday during the melees at San Francisco State (Pentony, Smith, & Axen, 1971). A radio commentator, Pat Michaels, having discovered that the Experimental College had a course on guerrilla warfare, gleefully and savagely attacked the college day after day. Although much of the reporting was balanced and fair, the effect of having the spotlight on the college continuously was to deepen the alarm felt by the public. The number of bills restrictive in purpose that flooded the California Legislature at its 1969 session is proof of public concern.

Four-letter words and pornographic pictures in the student newspaper didn't promote good public relations. This dilemma—how to bleach dirty linen without suppressing the freedoms that faculty and students prize—has not been solved. The suppression that has been invoked at San Francisco State is only a transitional expediency.

A related issue concerns academic freedom. Chancellor Dumke seems to believe that faculty members should curtail academic freedom in order to pacify the politicians. In an interview about the problems of San Francisco State, he said, "The type of public institution now developing is so big, so massive, involves so many people, that the forces of professionalism which formerly domi nated academic operations are being replaced by the typical politica forces which operate in any large group of human beings" (*Campu. Violence . . . ,"* 1968, p. 53). But progress in civilization depend on critical inquiry; and the state must be as subject to critica inquiry as are the rocks on the moon.

The right of teachers to teach and of students to attend classe has been much discussed at San Francisco State. At intervals dur ing the critical weeks of the student strike, gangs of students burs into classrooms to intimidate the occupants. In most cases, this wa one of the tactics used in trying to close the institution; in some cases, however, the attack was against a professor who was no teaching ideas acceptable to the students. Polarizations within the faculty and hysteria induced by the crisis prevented the faculty as body from rallying to the support of these professors. The attemp to stifle ideas by students who are intolerant of differing views i just as much a threat to the learning process as is off-campu political interference.

Collective bargaining and the right to strike are issues that need resolution at all colleges. Teachers believe that they need to use union tactics in their competition for funds to provide good compen sation and working conditions, and also because they are apprehen sive about the concentrated political power that threatens to take over the job of education. On the other hand, professors are no laborers; they are professionals with corresponding responsibilities to youth and to society. The answer seems to lie in an enlarged role for the American Association of University Professors; it has main tained the professional viewpoint and approaches to the problems Even so, administrators and governing boards should acquire greater skills and finesse in dealing with mass faculty actions.

One conclusion from the San Francisco State experience is that the college had insufficiently defined procedures for discipline at the time of the crisis. Infractions of behavior were not well defined, but this is not so surprising. Massive student disruption was a new phenomenon in the United States. Also, it isn't a simple matter to punish the right people, because the provokers of violence—on both sides—knew when to disappear and leave innocent people to bear the brunt. But the penalty for attempting to intimidate a teacher or a class, for example, should be defined, and the procedures for hearing a case need to be worked out in advance. Definition of infractions and procedures not only permit action with promptness but also satisfy the courts that due process is being granted to the accused.

The ambivalence toward the use of police at this college was typical of that at other colleges and universities. Decisive administrative action might have made a difference and saved much turmoil. But universities are not accustomed to using police to counter activities by their own students. In many countries, the university is a sanctuary, and seemingly the good results of that policy outweigh the bad. A complication is that a group of radical nonstudents (for a discussion of the concept *nonstudents,* see Lunsford, 1968), including a small but determined group of revolutionaries, moved in to take over. The public has a right to be on a public campus, but not to capture the institution for unauthorized purposes. From a pragmatic view, the police are called in order to make the violence so costly to its perpetrators that they will be forced to renounce it as a tactic. Calling the police is, however, costly to the public—the estimated cost of the police action at San Francisco State was over $700,000. America must select and train police by better methods. For when poorly trained police overreact, they provide an image of "fascist pigs," as they were called in this instance, and this in part is just what the brick throwers want, for it brings the middle-of-the-road believer in freedom of expression to *their* side.

PROBLEMS REMAIN Probably the worst residue of the nearly three years of conflict and 10 years of mismanagement is the polarizations that remain within the college. The faculty divisions are still there. A large portion of the faculty distrusts the president and is even more hostile than formerly to the chancellor. The president has brought order—at least in the most directly visible aspects of college operations—out of chaos, but it remains to be seen whether he can provide the educational leadership that is so urgently needed. In the meantime, he is extremely popular with conservative citizens and busies himself with speaking engagements.

The need now is leadership—and also support from the state, combined with sufficient freedom to initiate change. Recent experience demonstrates the need of fresh goals, both to revise the program of the college and to serve as a rallying point for the faculty in their mission to teach the youth of California.

References

"Campus Violence—Crackdown Coming," interview with Glenn S. Dumke, *U.S. News and World Report,* Sept. 23, 1968, p. 53.

Daniels, A. K., R. Kahn-Hut, and Associates: *Academics on the Line,* Jossey-Bass, Inc., San Francisco, 1970.

Dumke, G. S.: "The Response from San Francisco State College," *Teachers College Record,* January 1962, pp. 258–266.

Finberg, H.: *Crisis at S.F. State,* Insight Publications, San Francisco, 1969.

Gumas, N.: "Annotated Chronology of Events at San Francisco State College from September 26 to December 20, 1968," unpublished, Center for Research and Development in Higher Education, University of California, Berkeley, 1969.

Karagueuzian, D.: *Blow It Up!,* Gambit, Inc., Boston, 1971.

Lunsford, T.: "Who Are Members of the University Community?," *Denver Law Journal,* Special 1968, pp. 545–557.

Orrick, W. H., Jr.: *Shut It Down! A College in Crisis,* a staff report to the National Commission on the Causes and Prevention of Violence, U.S. Government Printing Office, Washington, June 1969.

Pentony, D., R. Smith, and R. Axen: *Unfinished Rebellions,* Jossey-Bass, Inc., San Francisco, 1971.

Riesman, D. and C. Jencks: *"The Viabilities of the American College."* in Nevitt Sanford (ed.), *The American College,* John Wiley & Sons, Inc., New York, 1961, pp. 74–192.

Riesman, D. and C. Jencks: "Case Study in Vignette: San Francisco State College," *Teachers College Record,* January 1962, pp. 233–257.

Smith, R., R. Axen, and D. Pentony: *By Any Means Necessary,* Jossey-Bass, Inc., San Francisco, 1970.

Tape Recordings of Speeches and Panel Discussions Related to San Francisco State College, KPFA, Berkeley, Calif., 1968 and 1969.

"Why Hayakawa Took the Job," interview with S. I. Hayakawa, *San Francisco Chronicle,* Jan. 2, 1969, p. 1.

14. Stanford's Search for Solutions

by John Walsh

If any major American university campus could be described as arcadian it has been Stanford's, but in the late spring of 1970 Stanford looked like a collegiate paradise lost. The reaction to the American incursion into Cambodia came as climax to weeks of conflict on other issues and brought Stanford its worse outbreak of violence and physical damage. But broken windows and other outward signs of strife and even the estimated $500,000 cost of a half year of trouble represented something less serious than the cumulative effect on students and faculty of three years of crises. The university was betraying signs of institutional anomie, and Stanford's president, Kenneth S. Pitzer, was in fact to resign that summer, barely a year after he had been inaugurated. In subsequent months there was to be a change of mood, a recovery of momentum, but in retrospect it seems that the disruptions at Stanford had a particularly dispiriting effect, because no American university, public or private, had made a more intense effort at organized self-examination and reform.

Stanford, of course, has shared the effects of the expansionary forces at work in American higher education after World War II. Until the war, it had been a regional university, essentially a college with conventional professional schools, with a good reputation that was perhaps more social than academic. In a relatively few years after the war Stanford was transformed into a full-fledged major university of national prestige and drawing power. Its transformation was an astutely conducted metamorphosis achieved through purposeful management of resources and particularly of its relations with industry and the federal government.

Stanford has always had unique advantages and special problems that trace back to its founding in 1885 by Leland Stanford and his wife as a memorial to their son, Leland Stanford, Jr., for whom the university is named. In an act of educational philanthropy perhaps matched only by Rockefeller at Chicago, Leland Stanford gave the university some 8,000 acres of prime Santa Clara County ranchland in an area south of San Francisco that was to become a land developer's Eldorado. The university's role as landowner and employer gave it more local influence than a Lateran Treaty. For example, restrictions placed on the sale of liquor in Palo Alto are only now being eased. The university's use of its land, not surprisingly, has been a sore point, and it now must defend its land against those who want it for schools, roads, parks, reservoirs, flood-control and drainage schemes, and other public and commercial purposes. Stanford is also under increasing pressure to justify its land policies in moral terms by those who say the university is perpetuating local patterns of discrimination against low-income and minority groups. But the point is that the Leland Stanford demesne, through sheer size and the possibilities it still represents, continues to influence the character of Stanford University.

Leland Stanford, a senator and railroad tycoon, was a typical product of the gilded age—Ambrose Bierce, the well-known Hearst columnist and early black humorist, habitually spelled his name £eland $tanford. And Mrs. Stanford was a nineteenth-century *grande dame* who outlived her husband, leaving a strong imprint of her own on the university, particularly on the lives of women undergraduates. But the Stanfords' aspirations for the university were equalitarian, at least as equality was then construed, and their casual California attitude toward tradition established an openness to ideas at Stanford that still persists. One tradition that took root was that of a strong administration. David Starr Jordan, the university's first president, was handpicked by Senator Stanford to to run the place. It was in this tradition that Stanford's president after World War II, Wallace Sterling, and his provost, Frederick Terman, set about transforming the university. In their own way they showed a dynamism equal to Jordan's in building Stanford, or for that matter a dynamism equal to Stanford's in building the Central Pacific Railroad.

GROWTH IN THE 1960s   The university's biggest burst of growth came in the 1960s. At the beginning of the decade, it had about 8,700 students: 5,300 undergraduates and 3,400 graduate students. By 1970, the balance had shifted toward graduate education; enrollment was approximately

11,600, with 6,300 undergraduates and 5,300 graduate students. During the same decade, the number of faculty rose from 619 to 1,200.

During the decade, the campus was also one big construction site, with academic space nearly doubling, from 1.5 million to 2.8 million square feet. Millions of dollars were spent not only for bricks, mortar, concrete, and glass but also for such things as tripling library collections from about a million volumes to 3.3 million and creating a major computer capacity. A medical school–hospital complex costing well over $20 million had been opened in 1959 on a site adjoining the main campus. The 2-mile-long Stanford Linear Accelerator (SLAC), which cost the Atomic Energy Commission some $114 million to construct and about $25 million a year to operate, was built on Stanford land, making the university a national laboratory and a world center of research in particle physics.

Standord's operating budget excluding SLAC and the hospital, rose from $40 million in 1960 to $130 million in 1970, and the portion of the budget ascribable to federal grants and contracts rose from $13 million to nearly $60 million. Federal funds were crucial to growth at Stanford, but the Stanford formula for expansion relied on an orchestration of federal funds with an increased flow of private support and income from Stanford lands. Management of this development required an administration with a strong sense of direction and a willingness to take risks. Sterling and Terman, men with complementary talents and personalities, more than adequately supplied these.

FREDERICK TERMAN— ENGINEER Terman's influence was strongest on the buildup of research and graduate education. During World War II, Stanford had been relatively unaffected by the research and development work supported by the federal government at major universities. Terman had been deeply involved in the wartime mobilization of scientists and engineers, and when he returned to Stanford after the war as dean of engineering, he foresaw that the government would seek to continue its relationship with the universities, providing a major source of funding for research and graduate education. Sterling picked Terman as provost, and when the Korean war increased government demand for university assistance in sophisticated research and development and training of technical manpower, Stanford was more than receptive.

Two policy decisions made then were to have important consequences when relations with the government came under scrutiny
15 years later. The university decided to permit classified research
on campus under certain circumstances and also to include federal
money in funds used to pay faculty salaries in engineering and
some other departments. It was axiomatic with Terman, however,
that federal work would not be accepted if it had no palpable educational value. Stanford, for example, has not operated off-campus,
contract laboratories, as, for example, have Berkeley with the Liver-
more and Los Alamos laboratories, Caltech with the Jet Propulsion
Laboratory, and MIT with the Lincoln Laboratories.

At the same time that federal research contracts and grants were
flowing in, Stanford scientists and engineers cemented relationships with high-technology industry in the area. In the 1930s, some
of Terman's prize electrical engineering and physics students had
successfully established their own firms—Hewlett-Packard and
Varian Associates are the most notable examples—and after the
war, Stanford engineers and scientists, following precedent, played
a leading part in colonizing the San Francisco peninsula for electronics, aerospace, and pharmaceutical industries. At the same
time, the presence of the Stanford laboratories provided a strong
attraction for other research firms. The synergistic relationship
between Stanford and industry was encouraged by the creation of
the Stanford Industrial Park, where many firms engaged in R&D
established laboratories and offices. For faculty at Stanford, the
implication was clear that research scientists and engineers were
expected to win the research support from government and industry
necessary to finance an expanding program of high-quality research
and graduate education.

Stanford's provost is academic vice president, and as such Terman presided over the effort to make Stanford an institution in
which excellence in the sciences and engineering was matched in
the humanities and arts. It took a little longer, but Terman (who as
an emeritus is still a prodigious worker) proved to have a talent for
finding good men across the board academically. He worked on a
"steeples-of-excellence" principle, which in practice meant concen-
trating resources successively on particular areas of teaching and
research deemed important or on faculty members of outstanding
ability and energy. Stanford is still a relatively small university with
gaps in its academic skyline, but where it is good, it tends to be very
good. Terman had his critics, and not only among those whose egos

he bruised, but there is little question that just as Sterling was the architect of a super Stanford, Terman was, in the same figurative sense, its engineer.

Sterling, who had taught history at Stanford in the 1930s and then moved to Caltech, returned to Stanford as president in 1949. When he arrived, the postwar occupation by veterans was still on, and priority had to be given to refurbishing the physical plant after the neglect of the Depression and war years. Sterling says that when he set about the necessary fund-raising effort, he was asked by corporation executives and foundation officers why Stanford's alumni weren't helping more and why the university didn't exploit its land assets to raise money. From this period date both Stanford's highly successful campaign to increase income from private gifts and its land-development program. In 1950 the university received perhaps $3 million in bequests and gifts. By 1960 private gift support, including that of foundations, was up to $20 million, and last year it was $30 million.

Land development at Stanford has been governed by the founders' prohibition against selling any of it. The university, however, leases land to developers under terms allowing it to retain planning control. Because Stanford needed larger sums of money than would have been produced under ordinary leasing arrangements, it struck on the device of requiring full payment of a lease at the beginning of the term. (The typical term is 51 years.) The industrial park, a shopping center, a professional area, apartments, and now a new financial and office center have been the main projects developed under lease.

But Stanford has also used its land to give it a competitive advantage in recruiting and retaining faculty. Land costs are high and housing is tight in the area, and the university has opened sizable tracts of land where faculty have been leased lots and allowed to build houses subject only to approval of design and the proviso that the house be sold only to eligible members of the university community. Mortgages at relatively low interest rates have made the faculty housing program attractive.

Stanford's pragmatic use of its endowment in land has often pained private developers and sometimes offended local officials, but in the 1960s a new sort of criticism began to gather force. The university was blamed, on the one hand, for contributing to the haphazard urbanization of a previously pleasantly uncrowded area and, on the other, for perpetuating, through its land-use policies, the patterns which made the mid-peninsula largely an enclave of the affluent white middle class. One result of the criticism was the commitment to a pilot plan for low- and moderate-income housing.

CRITICISMS
OF THE 1950s
AND 1960s

It would be misleading to give the impression that criticism of the Stanford administration cropped up only in recent years. For example, in the 1950s, a decision to consolidate clinical and pre-clinical training in a new medical school facility on the Stanford campus caused bitter dissension among medical school faculty and opposition from medical school alumni. Consolidation meant uprooting clinical faculty from San Francisco and cutting ties with hospitals in the city. Sterling and his allies were convinced that the medical school could develop its potential as a research-oriented school only if it could draw on university resources. The move to the campus made possible the recruiting of researchers of the caliber of Nobel Prize laureates Arthur Kornberg and Joshua Lederberg and the development of the nationally noted program in cardiac surgery associated with Norman Shumway. But it took great determination and a prodigy of fund raising to accomplish the move.

Toward the end of the 1950s momentum had been established, but there were questions about where the institution was going academically. Sterling organized an effort by a group of faculty and administrators to digest the experience of the early 1950s and to put forward minimum and maximum educational programs. The work was done in 1957 and 1958 and represented a kind of detailed academic planning that was rare in those days. Fortuitously, the so-called *Red Book* containing the results of the study was at hand when the Ford Foundation began fashioning its program of major incentive grants to universities. The *Red Book* provided the basis for the Stanford PACE (Plan for Action for a Challenging Era) program, which was aimed at matching a Ford grant of $25 million on a 3-to-1 basis. In three years PACE produced $114 million. It was probably this exploit in planning and fund raising that as much as anything fixed Stanford in the minds of government officials and foundation officers as the most enterprising and innovative university on the West Coast, perhaps in the nation.

In the early and middle 1960s, Stanford, under Sterling, also began to take steps to adapt the educational program, governance of the university, and relationships within the university to other changes in the university and in American society. These efforts were overtaken by events in the middle 1960s and by no means immunized Stanford from the turmoil that swept through the universities as the decade progressed. Yet by the end of the decade, Stanford was changed as much internally as the building program had altered it physically.

By the standards customarily applied, the record of the Sterling-Terman stewardship is an imposing one. Almost from the start, however, there were critics who felt that overexpansion in science and technology created an imbalance at the expense of the humanities and, for a time at least, of the social and behavioral sciences. The critics also complained of a lag in the growth of scholarly resources, particularly libraries, though this shortcoming seems to have been largely remedied. In the 1960s criticism increased in a new key. A revisionist view of the expansion was put forward based on assertions that Stanford's links with the federal government and industry had perverted the university and that the very growth of the institution was proof of the perversion. The radical analysis at Stanford led to insistence that the university cease not only all classified research but all "war research." The university was accused of conducting "counterinsurgency" research against people in underdeveloped nations and against minority groups in the United States. By the time of Cambodia, demands from some radicals extended to a prohibition of all government work.

THE CHANGE IN LEADERSHIP Sterling left the Stanford presidency in 1968, when there had been serious disturbances on campus, but when these disturbances still involved a relatively small minority of students. Inevitably, there was speculation as to whether subsequent events would have been moderated if Sterling had still been in the president's office. Most observers agree that in view of the strength of the tides running at the end of the decade, even Sterling would have been cast in the role of a modern King Canute.

This is not to deprecate Sterling's policies or the power of his personality. It is hard to think of a university president in the years immediately past who was so firm an administrator and phenomenal a fund raiser and, at the same time, maintained such esteem among alumni and students. He personified the university in a way that Jordan had in an age vastly less skeptical of authority figures, and preserved into an era of the impersonal university what is, in the literal sense, a personal style. The Sterling touch as president (which he still manifests as chancellor) was based on a remarkable social ease that went beyond charm or charisma. He had the energy to talk to many people and the power to communicate that he was genuinely interested in them and totally committed to his university. But it was that university, of course, which became the target in the late 1960s.

Pitzer's brief term as Stanford president coincided with a period of sharpening student militancy and a rapid shifting of issues, so that Pitzer and his associates were almost constantly engaged in crisis management. A distinguished chemist, Pitzer had come to Stanford with impeccable academic credentials and a reputation made as president of Rice for maintaining good rapport with students. He started with an a priori handicap at Stanford when students protested the process of his selection, and he never achieved a working relationship with students. It was a period when faculty members were uncertain about where their loyalties lay and when alumni were growing alarmed about the course of events on campus. Pitzer was never able to establish a style of his own at Stanford or to create a supporting constituency. In discussing his resignation, he said that flagging alumni support of his administration seemed to threaten financial damage to the university. The consensus was that he never had a chance.

PORTENTS OF MAJOR DISRUPTION Looking backward, historians of the protest decade might discern portents of what was coming on American campuses in some events at Stanford in the early 1960s. In 1962, for example, an editorial in the Stanford student daily objected to a Navy recruiting van's operating in a central campus area. At the 1963 commencement, with NATO commander Lauris Norstad scheduled as speaker, a graduating woman student tried to join the academic procession carrying a placard reading "I protest NATO not Norstad." She was not allowed to carry the placard into the ceremony. Early in 1964 a recruiting van was picketed, and that spring, at the president's review of the ROTC, signs sprouted protesting ROTC. In retrospect, those involved in later troubles at Stanford agree that these incidents were anticipatory tremors. They seem to agree that Stanford was able to avoid serious conflict because the administration dealt with the incidents with sufficient flexibility so that, as one staff member put it, "whenever the line was drawn, the line was held. That is until 1968."

Most observers date the process of "politicization" at Stanford from the involvement of students and faculty in the civil rights movement in the early 1960s. About 50 Stanford students and faculty members participated in the voter-registration drive in Mississippi in the summer of 1964. And the rise of the Free Speech Movement at Berkeley in the same year had special impact on Stanford because Berkeley is within easy commuting distance. San Francisco and the Bay Area have a rich tradition of radical politics, and there clearly has been an interaction between Bay Area radicals and Stanford's indigenous activists, but the consequences are hard to sort out. First, there have been several generations of radicals at Stanford since the early 1960s. The first group was essentially homegrown, produced by the civil rights movement and the early Vietnam war reaction. In the later sixties, a group of older activists, some of them graduate students or instructors with combat experience at Berkeley, provided tactical and ideological leadership which the Stanford left hadn't had before. For the past two or three years Stanford's battles have increasingly involved younger students who were radicalized in high school and were abetted by even younger recruits from neighboring towns. A number of veteran Stanford radicals have left the scene or gotten interested in efforts to organize minority workers or the work force of aerospace firms on the peninsula and seem to regard the university as a good recruiting ground but a less inviting primary objective. The extent of the radical interaction is interesting and important, but difficult to define. Information on the activities of radicals from faculty members, sympathetic or unsympathetic, often proves remarkably unreliable. And the radicals themselves are not disposed to confide in a stranger asking political questions.

AN UNREAL WORLD Although events on the Stanford campus have been influenced by radical political action, Stanford has been insulated by its location between middle- and upper-income residential towns and the foothills of the coastal range. Stanford faculty, the arts and sciences faculty at any rate, tend to be politically liberal and sympathetic to their students on many issues; the administration in general has tended to tolerate protest when it followed the forms of nonviolent civil disobedience. One of Pitzer's first acts after he was named to the Stanford presidency was to declare that he thought the Vietnam war was a tragic error. One young psychologist who was deeply engaged in the post-Cambodia political activities on campus finds at Stanford "a relatively apathetic pattern. The university," he says, "is virtually self-contained. We're not dependent on the community and there's not a large nonstudent group. The radicals couldn't get at the kids. The environment conspires against them. It's an unreal world, the beach and the mountains. The administration has been permissive, with coed dorms, etc. It's the good life in a sense." Whatever the reasons, militant action at Stanford has never involved more than a few hundred students. In several instances, support among students for the aims of the militants has been quite broad, but in general, the great majority seemed to be disenchanted by violence.

PROTESTS IN 1969   A major instance of a protest gaining the support of large numbers of students occurred in 1969 over the university's involvement in defense research. Stanford's relationship with the Stanford Research Institute (SRI) was the precipitating factor. SRI in Menlo Park had been established with university backing after World War II primarily as a means of stimulating economic and industrial development in the West. SRI developed along "think tank" lines, and its ties with Stanford were probably less highly developed than the university's ties to high-technology firms in the area. SRI's work for the military, nevertheless, came under increasing fire from university critics. Early demands that the trustees end Stanford's relationship with SRI were succeeded by insistence from more militant critics that SRI be bound closer to the university and converted to "socially useful" research. The issue brought the first face-to-face confrontation between militants and trustees, and the trustees were shocked not only by the aggressiveness of their critics but by the accusation that the trustees—whose links to large corporations were stressed—were using the university to implement a policy of aggrandizement carried on overseas by the government at the behest of American industry.

Since the status of SRI was the responsibility of the trustees, the Stanford faculty did not have to face the issue of military research fully until May of 1969, when the militants suddenly switched attention from SRI to the campus by occupying the Applied Electronics Laboratory (AEL) where research funded by the armed services, including the bulk of classified research on campus, was carried out. This week-long occupation attracted wide support among students, in part because militants publicized information about research on campus about which little had been known in detail and because the occupation proceeded, by and large, without violence or serious damage to property.

Subsequent to the occupation of AEL, the trustees cut the university's ties with SRI, requiring that SRI provide open-ended repayment of $25 million or more to the university and getting agreement that SRI would not engage in types of work deemed most objectionable, such as research in chemical and biological warfare. On campus, a decision was taken to phase out classified research and to tighten the screening process governing acceptance of research grants and contracts.

FACULTY REACTION

The reaction of Stanford faculty to the events of the spring gave outsiders the impression that most faculty members knew very little about the details of government research performed on campus and had not thought much about the implications of disengagement from research sponsored by the military. The question had special impact at Stanford because funds acquired through indirect-cost payments on defense research grants had helped to underwrite expansion in fields outside science and engineering. Some close observers feel that it was only at this point that many faculty members outside science and engineering began to recognize the fact that renunciation of government research support at Stanford could decisively affect them.

By the time faculty members had begun to think through the ramifications of actions being taken, not least to consider the effect on the university budget of the drying up of overhead payments from federal contracts, there was really no chance to reconsider. A salient characteristic of the troubles of the 1960s at Stanford and elsewhere was that events generated such momentum and such emotion that there was no opportunity for second thoughts.

"OFF ROTC" AND THEN CAMBODIA

In the fall of 1969, attention was deflected from the university by the Vietnam war moratorium activities, but early in 1970, an "Off ROTC" movement began to gather momentum, and it appeared that ROTC, which had been an issue at least since 1968, would give Stanford its third turbulent spring. Some observers think the matter would have remained manageable except for inept administration handling in the early stages, but the superimposition of the Cambodia crisis makes the question a moot one. At any rate, serious window breaking began late in March, and ultimately sit-ins at the Old Union Building brought police to the campus, and, after Cambodia, the first use of tear gas at Stanford, a rash of injuries and arrests, and more broken windows. Before it was over, shots were fired into the house of the ROTC commander, and arsonists had set fires causing at least $60,000 damage at the Center for Advanced Study in the Behavioral Sciences, on Stanford land.

At Stanford, the depth of the reaction to Cambodia was indicated by the involvement in protest action for the first time of a large number of professional school students, faculty, and staff. The Cambodia crisis, of course, produced massive efforts on many campuses to involve students and faculty in nonviolent political activities, and at Stanford—at the medical schools and on the campus at large—these activities were varied and ingenious. It is worth noting that at Stanford at least some of those who organized the post-Cambodia political action saw fundamental danger to the university in the "strike" spirit generated by Cambodia. The medical school, for example, was "politicized" for the first time by Cambodia. The initial response there was unprecedentedly tough—talk of a strike threatening the operations of the hospital and medical school. An action group was formed by students, medical school faculty members, and staff of the hospital, and the initiative was captured by moderates. Their aim in part seems to have been to protect the hospital and medical school from the overreaction which appeared to be in progress. This analysis held up when checked a year after the event, and in the medical school and elsewhere there appears to have been a conscious effort made to defend the university by making it a base for political action rather than a target.

A NEW STUDY OF EDUCATION AT STANFORD   It is now a commonplace that the experience of opposing the war in Vietnam and injustices in the society has made young people determined to participate effectively in decisions directly affecting their lives and the institutions to which they belong. Sterling seems to have been one of the first college presidents to sense the trend and began appointing students to presidential committees in the late 1950s, thereby foreshadowing the tripartite administration-faculty-student committees which now make many decisions at Stanford. Through much of his presidency, Sterling had been accustomed to working through a small group of student leaders, but by the middle 1960s it became clear that new forms of student government would be necessary. It was equally clear that changes in secondary education and in the society were producing a new breed of incoming student. The university undertook to revise the parietal rules that had governed dormitory regulations and social life in general. The general relaxation of rules pained some trustees and alumni acutely, but seems to have spared Stanford the pitched battles over parietals that some universities experienced.

At Stanford, a similar overhaul of the educational program took place. The last serious review had been carried out in the mid-fifties and had resulted in a revision of undergraduate education along the "general studies" lines fashionable after World War II. Sterling felt that a new look was needed, and what developed after discussion was a major effort called Study of Education at Stanford (SES), involving more than 200 students and members of the faculty and administration. The product of the study, carried out in 1967 and 1968, was a series of reports to the university on undergraduate and graduate education; university residences and campus life; undergraduate admissions and financial aid; advising and counseling; the extracurriculum; teaching, research, and the faculty; international education; and the government of the university.

Sterling seems to have envisioned a concentration on undergraduate education, but Herbert Packer, the law school professor who was chairman of the SES steering committee, was instrumental in extending the appraisal to practically every aspect of university life. Packer says he saw that bright students were getting restive and "turned off" and that the committee was trying to relax undergraduate education. He thinks the reports on undergraduate education and university government were the most important and most influential parts of SES.

The principal sources for comment on the origins and operations of SES were Packer and a number of students and faculty members who had served on the original SES committees or been involved in implementation of SES recommendations. There was a clear consensus among informants that the major aim of SES in approaching undergraduate education was to open up the curriculum for students who were different intellectually and temperamentally from students of the 1950s when the general studies program was shaped. The internal politics of the thing can be described as a power struggle between the SES reformers and the man heading the general studies program, who had become a sort of superdean, and his backers.

The SES committee found the undergraduate general studies program overloaded with requirements, the faculty approach to the program perfunctory, and the student attitude negative. SES recommendations on curriculum led to a redesign based on a general reduction of requirements. At Stanford, freshmen are now asked to undergo a two-quarter "writing experience" which may be integrated into courses outside the English department. A strong effort is made to have each freshman take at least one course in which a small group deals with a basic theme in a subject in which he is particularly interested, or a specific topic in history. Often, freshman seminars are taught by illustrious members of the faculty, but perhaps more important, those teaching are encouraged to build the courses around their academic special interests as the best way of communicating the excitement and rewards of scholarship.

The "university distribution requirement" that each student must satisfy before graduation amounts to three courses of one quarter each in three major areas: humanities; social sciences; and natural sciences, mathematics, and technology. Requirements for a major have not been altered radically, but it is possible for a student to devise his own major by working out, with consultation, a coherent program of interdepartmental study built around a single theme.

Although not without dispute and delay, the ground rules on grading and academic credit have been changed. Under a new grading system which finally went into effect in September 1970, A, B, and C are the only marks that count toward the total number of academic credits a student must accumulate to be graduated. Marks below C simply do not count for or against; in some cases a pass–no-pass option is available. The basic criterion for staying in school is progress toward a degree.

The unspoken premise of the new grading system is that Stanford's high admission standards ensure that students are capable of doing work at the level required. At the same time, it is acknowledged that the Stanford system requires considerable judgment and initiative on the part of the undergraduate and that a sophisticated advising apparatus is necessary. The university now has a centralized Academic Information Center where students get specialized advice, take vocational tests, change majors, or even change advisers. The center falls under the purview of Dean of Undergraduate Studies James L. Gibbs. The post is a new one and of strategic importance in the SES reforms. As one administrator put it, the dean's job is to counterbalance the departments. Since his constituency is the undergraduate student body, he lacks the direct authority over faculty that gives other academic deans leverage. But to enhance his power as the champion of undergraduate education, he is supposed to contribute to decisions on hiring, promotion, and pay of faculty members who teach undergraduates. His effectiveness will depend heavily on the support he gets from the administration.

Students' influence on university policy increased markedly during the 1960s, the decade that began with students limited to what Packer tartly calls "sandbox government." In the latter part of the decade, under the impetus of student leaders like David Harris, who resigned the student organization presidency halfway through his year in office and later became a national founder of the draft resistance movement, student government changed its aims and organization. A student legislature of 140 members elected by living groups was, after SES, replaced by a 40-member senate elected by academic constituencies. Perhaps more important, the executive was strengthened by creating a four-member "council of presidents" who share the burdens of the office. Roles were left undefined so the presidents could operate according to individual talents and interests, and they were provided a budget and staff, which added to their effectiveness.

Most important, students now sit on most university committees, and have voting membership on most trustee committees. The board of trustees has been enlarged and somewhat democratized with the inclusion of alumni members in the under-35 age group. There are complaints, it should be noted, that students are given inadequate roles in decisions on key areas of admissions, faculty appointments, promotion and pay, and on the budget. Whether students will maintain and expand their role in decision making is hazardous to predict.

Stanford in recent years has sought actively to recruit students from among minority groups and in the late 1960s experienced the sort of adjustment problems which occurred at a number of other universities. Perhaps because the number of minority students remains proportionally small at Stanford, most observers feel that minority groups have not had a strong impact on innovation and change there. Black students organized efficiently and won major demands, for example, for a black studies program and black student center, but student activists of both the center and left say that black students have not been deeply involved in the principal political events of recent years. There are indications that the black, Chicano, and Asian students may make effective use of classic bloc tactics in student government to press for changes in policy on minority admissions, wider employment opportunities, and other aims, but it is simply too early to be certain. Certainly many students remain totally apathetic toward involvement in university governance, and some give their attention and loyalties to such "alternative" activities as the local "Free University." But it does not seem unreasonable to suggest that the new machinery developed at Stanford was inadequate to handle the issues that erupted in the 1960s but helped make it possible to muddle through.

NEW ROLES FOR THE FACULTY Something of the same sort might be said of widening faculty involvement in university government. The faculty role at Stanford had been in the typical university pattern of formal authority vested in an academic council constituted of all regular faculty members. In practice, President Sterling relied on consultation with influential members of the faculty and the council who, in effect, ratified policy. A much stronger and more direct faculty influence on university policy is now exercised through a faculty senate created along lines conceived by Packer. The senate is made up of representatives of the various academic schools and departments elected by proportional representation. The system provides for equitable distribution between younger and older members of the faculty. Three students sit in the senate but have no voting rights. The student senate can place issues on the agenda of the faculty senate.

William Clebsch, former chairman of the faculty senate, says the reforms have opened up to the faculty decision making on all the workings of the university. As a result, he thinks, criticism of policies is more widespread, but at the same time support of university policies is more profound. Another impact, says Clebsch, is that university citizenship is becoming a factor alongside teaching, advising, and research in deciding matters of promotion and salary increases. Clebsch, along with a number of others, however, feels that wider involvement is pushing faculty close to the edge of their interest and talent.

Faculty morale is not susceptible to measurement in the way salary schedules are, but some academic visitors to Stanford in the late 1960s detected a low-grade, generalized malaise infecting a surprising number of Stanford faculty. Local pathologists ascribed the discontent variously to bad reactions to the West Coast lotusland ambience, dissatisfaction over salary and promotion prospects in a university with postexpansion problems, and (probably most important) distress over campus disruptions which seemed to be reaching a chronic state. Since Cambodia, the feelings of being beleaguered have subsided, but the new relationship between professor and student at Stanford, as elsewhere, remains unsettled and for many faculty members unsettling.

One area of continuing conflict and uncertainty is the campus judicial system. Discontent over the system caused the first Stanford sit-in with major campus support in 1968. The university operated from the start on an honor code and strong applications of the *in loco parentis* principle. By the middle 1960s, criticism of administration intervention in the judicial system was active enough to prompt serious scrutiny of the system. By 1968, the year of the sit-in, reform efforts produced a new structure based on two faculty-student committees, one charged with making rules and another with enforcing them. The results have been satisfactory to almost nobody. What has happened at Stanford and elsewhere, of course, is that university efforts to make and enforce rules of conduct on campus have collided with new kinds of political action whose manifestations range from peaceful acts of civil disobedience to serious property damage and acts of physical violence. Stanford's new president, Richard Lyman, who was provost during the troubles of recent years, says that the judicial system works satisfactorily in dealing with cases of plagiarism, cheating on exams, and other conventional campus disciplinary problems. Where students are accused of disruption or more serious acts on campus, and particularly where they are facing prosecution in regular courts, the university judicial system flags. Campus authorities, for example, are reluctant to act before the outcome of cases heard in regular courts is known. Lyman admits also that the university has been open to criticism on its performance in gathering evidence, making identification for judical cases, and preparing cases for court. Since other universities are having similar difficulties with their judicial machinery, the major justification for asking more of Stanford is that the SES reforms put such heavy emphasis on restructuring the disciplinary system up and down the line. Stanford, like other universities, is now organizing itself better to handle these problems. But universities are naturally ambivalent about taking serious action against members of their own communities, and Lyman indicates the essential dilemma when he cites "the extreme reluctance on the part of students and faculty to prosecute people whose offenses have allegedly idealistic motives."

Faculty discipline is an allied and similarly unsettled issue. By a vote of the faculty senate in 1968, faculty members involved in campus disorders are subject to penalties on the same terms as students. But while the faculty is in theory subject to penalties as serious as reduction in pay or dismissal, attempts to construct a workable system have so far been unsuccessful. A serious effort is being made to fill the gap, but so long as there is the present ambivalence, "justice" is likely to remain an intractable problem on campus.

ACADEMIC STATESMEN Although reform of the judicial system has not succeeded brilliantly at Stanford, the university developed some new mechanisms to respond to demands of the 1960s. Out of the SES effort, for example, came an "academic statesmen" program which enables a group of capable younger faculty to work half-time on innovative programs. The Ford Foundation grant which finances the program provides modest sums, thus overcoming one chronic difficulty for innovators. Judgments on the success of the program probably should wait until results show whether it can produce administrators and faculty members genuinely attuned to innovation. SES also provided the impetus for the Stanford Workshops on Political and Social Issues (SWOPSI). The idea is that students and faculty members work together to bring university skills and manpower to bear on important problems. Typical products have been critical reports on forestry planning and on the federal science advisory apparatus. One incidental point proved by the academic statesmen program and SWOPSI is that the university investment in SES led to substantial outside support of innovative programs.

FINANCIAL RETRENCH-MENT Financing change is becoming increasingly difficult at Stanford as inflationary pressures and the decline in federal support cause the university to retrench financially. Stanford ran a deficit of $600,000 in 1968–69 and a deficit of $1.3 million in 1969–70, and expects one of about $1 million for 1970–71. Efforts to bring expenditures into line with income have been organized into a Budget Adjustment Program (BAP) which contemplates cuts of $4 million from the budget over four years, reflecting a curtailed growth rate. William F. Miller, a computer applications specialist, who has been appointed provost, will be expected to preside over a retrenchment affecting both faculty and programs and to carry out a kind of planning which goes against the grain of Stanford's experience for a whole generation.

For Lyman the central question is "How does a university advance without expanding?" Universities are no longer governable in the way Stanford was under Jordan or even under Sterling. As Lyman says, "the place doesn't respond to series of orders. The president's responsibilities have grown and his powers diminished." A university president's central role as Lyman sees it is to adjudicate, mediate, and use his powers of exhortation. And these powers are likely to be fully tested, since budget realities require some redistribution of funds and this is difficult in an institution constructed to support vested interests.

CONCLUSIONS In writing this profile of Stanford, my instinct has been to emphasize the objective conditions of Stanford's postwar development. By this I mean the pressures exerted by society and the federal government toward growth of a particular kind and the choices made by the administration in responding to these pressures and opportunities. Of course it is obvious that personalities, local issues, Stanford's peculiar bohemian-bucolic atmosphere, and the general revolt against authority also influenced events. But it does seem in retrospect that the people Stanford set out to attract behaved predictably under the circumstances and that the confrontations—the word has acquired a period flavor already—over campus discipline, military research, ROTC, and Cambodia were programmed by the decisions of the 1950s.

Stanford has made big advances since World War II, and they can be attributed to the dynamism of Sterling and Terman and in varying degrees to an era of easy money in education, the Stanford patrimony, a lack of fettering traditions, good planning, and, from the standpoint of locational economics, being in the right place at the right time. By any of the ordinary indices—growth in facilities or budget, faculty distinction, the test scores of successful applicants, or the American Council on Education ratings of graduate programs—Stanford rose to a place among the best half-dozen American universities and is still, on top of it, a marvelously pleasant place.

Ironically, the means the university has used to gain its prominence—its relations with government and industry, its land-development policies, its quest for academic excellence—have been primary targets for militant critics. At this point, inevitably, the question of violence at Stanford, its origins, extent, and effects, suggests itself. As a journalist I have a conditioned interest in conflict but feel ambivalent about violence as an index. It seems to me that the degree of violence is capricious and often disproportionate to the causes. There are, in fact, few signs that more than a small minority of students and faculty approve of violence or fully accept the radical analysis which, in effect, claims that success has spoiled Stanford. But there is little question that the critics have influenced the university to redefine its educational and social responsibilities and to make far-reaching changes. Even peace in Vietnam is unlikely to guarantee peace on the campus. And to the political problems left over from the past decade may be added a new dimension of economic problems. Faced with an inexorable rise in costs, private universities like Stanford, for example, could find that only the most affluent students or most disadvantaged students on scholarships can afford the tuition.

Will the reforms of the 1960s at Stanford be adequate to the challenges of the 1970s? A lot depends on the imponderables. As Joyce Kobyashi, a member of the council of presidents at the time of Cambodia, observed of the new organizational changes at Stanford, "the structure is going to be imperfect, but when there's no trust the structure doesn't count." The boast of the SES reformers is that Stanford has institutionalized change. The test is whether the university will be able to go on finding imperfect solutions.

15. Swarthmore Knocks on Wood

by Paul Mangelsdorf, Jr.

Staunch and Gray thou stand'st before us
On the Campus fair.
Thy high spirit guarding o'er us
Who thy blessings share.

From Swarthmore's "Alma Mater"
(To the tune of "Annie Lisle")

These days the "Alma Mater" is only heard once a year, when the alumni gather at the June reunion. Nobody else on campus knows the words or would be caught dead indulging in the sentiment. Strangely, the words are probably more true now than ever. Here on her eminence Swarthmore stands, reasonably staunch and definitely gray—though whether a Quaker gray it would be hard to say.

In most respects the college has been very little altered by the waves of change that have swept through higher education during the past decade. Only in allowing some coed dormitories has Swarthmore yielded significantly, and even this, in retrospect, is more the logical culmination of a half century of gradual relaxation of social restrictions than a sharp break with the past.

In 1969–70, a year when other campuses were plagued with rioting and bombing. Swathmore's most violent outburst consisted of a militant antimilitaristic slogan painted in red on the upper facade of the du Pont Science Building. (Or was it anticapitalistic? It was difficult to be sure.) At a time when formal academic requirements are going out of fashion, the Swarthmore faculty has stood firm on its core distribution requirements and even on its physical education requirements. True, the language requirement for graduation—a tradition as old as the college itself—was abolished, but only because the department of modern languages wanted to get out from under. It is difficult to argue against a department which insists that its own course offerings, though valuable, are not essential for a liberal education.

At Swarthmore most classes continued through the several moratoria and through the Cambodia–Kent State "strike," although a number of special arrangements were made for postponing papers and final examinations. The faculty refused to commit itself, as a faculty, to specific political positions in support of protesting students. At the time of the 1969 October moratorium, the faculty adopted the Harvard resolution, then reconsidered, rescinded its action, and finally left the matter up to faculty members as individuals.

Or take the far more serious financial crisis facing higher education today: Swarthmore's Vice President Edward Cratsley, in charge of financial matters, anticipates some belt tightening but no critical problems. Last year, for the twenty-fourth consecutive year, the operating budget showed a modest surplus, although costs of fuel and insurance had risen sharply. Another slight surplus seems possible this year.

Enrollments are full. The number of applicants for admission fell off last year, completed applications running about 13 percent less than the year before but the ratio of applications to places available still stands at a substantial 7 to 1, despite annual charges (for tuition, room, board, and other financial fees) now totaling more than $3,800 per student.

Swarthmore's insulation from the fiercer stresses racking the rest of academia has been by no means perfect. Only three years ago a sit-in at the admissions office by black students triggered a campuswide "crisis" in the midst of which President Courtney Smith died suddenly of a heart attack. This tragedy left the college chastened and subdued. Although some of the bitterness and suspicion generated in the preceding controversy still lingers, there also lingers a protective atmosphere of caution and restraint.

THE HONORS PROGRAM AS A KEY TO EXCELLENCE A central fact that has to figure largely in any discussion of what Swarthmore is like, and why, is the Swarthmore honors program initiated by President Frank Aydelotte in 1922. The honors program is not only the symbol of Swarthmore's pursuit of academic excellence but also the principal mechanism by which excellence has been achieved and, over the years, sustained.

When Aydelotte took over Swarthmore from Joseph Swain in 1921, he found it a small, well-endowed, Quaker-dominated, coeducational college much better known for its power on the football field than for any academic achievement. By the time Aydelotte handed the college on to John Nason in 1940, he had turned it into an academic powerhouse with a growing national reputation. To achieve this transformation, Aydelotte applied his own personal mixture of vision, enthusiasm, luck, and ingenuity — especially ingenuity. The honors program he devised has proved to be the most ingenious mechanism one could imagine for propelling a college toward a high standard of academic excellence and keeping it there.

The beauty of the honors program is that it demands more of both students and faculty in the academically significant ways while freeing both from much of the drudgery of lectures, examinations, and grading. A junior entering honors takes no examinations and receives no grades until the end of his senior year, when he takes a full battery of honors examinations complete with orals.[1] These examinations are set, not by the Swarthmore faculty, but by scholars invited from other institutions. On the basis of these examinations, the visiting examiners recommend degrees with honors, high honors, or highest honors. Or, if no honors, they turn the student back to his major department for further examinations.

The honors instruction takes place in small honors seminars in which the instructor is supposed to be more of a moderator or consultant than a lecturer. The honors students themselves are charged with the responsibility for preparing the material for the seminar, usually in the form of written papers circulated in advance. The educational mechanism here was consciously derived by Aydelotte from the century-old Oxford tutorial, but with the clever and economical modification of shifting much of the responsibility for criticism onto the students themselves. By this means the seminar instructor is able in one weekly four-hour seminar to fill half the instructional needs of six to eight honors students, the instructional equivalent of meeting 12 to 16 students in a one-hour class three times a week. At the same time, capable and independent honors students, spending much of their time in the library, can learn much more on their own than they could in a regular class.

---

[1] The student usually takes a set of trial honors examinations at the end of his junior year for practice and to verify that all is going well. No record is made of these if he continues in honors.

Though the instructor is freed from lecture preparation and from setting and grading examinations, he has a much-expanded responsibility to know the relevant literature in his subject. He must be able to supply, on the spur of the moment, sensible, articulate comments on any aspect of his subject. He must be able to tell the honors students where to look for specific information. Because each seminar is potentially an oral examination for the instructor as well as for the students and because the final evaluation of the honors students by a visiting examiner is implicitly understood to be an evaluation of the instructor as well, there is strong pressure on the instructor to keep up with his current literature.

One purpose of the program, as Aydelotte conceived it, was to make academic achievement seem at least as challenging and prestigious to students of that period as athletic achievement, though not to the exclusion of athletic achievement. Indeed Aydelotte, himself a former Rhodes scholar and later American secretary for the Rhodes Trust, was an enthusiastic advocate of that combination of scholarship and manly virtues that Rhodes had wanted his scholars to exemplify. This Rhodesian inheritance became an important part of the Swarthmore mystique: John Nason and Courtney Smith, Aydelotte's two immediate successors, were both former Rhodes scholars; Smith was also Aydelotte's successor as American secretary. The continued emphasis on athletic achievement helped reassure the alumni from the earlier, less academic period that the college was not changing beyond all recognition. Over the years the goodwill of these older alumni has been invaluable; they have been notably generous in their support of the college.

Fortunately it did not seem to occur to Aydelotte or his associates that this educational ideal was decidedly masculine in derivation and might be inappropriate for coeduational Swarthmore. Thus it was that a Quaker-inspired system of coeducational equality "in a home setting" found itself in the late 1920s hell-bent for scholarly achievement in one of the oldest and highest masculine traditions.

Nason took over the college from Aydelotte just as World War II was spreading across Europe. The next five years were marked by year-round classes and disappearing faculty. Civilian male enrollments dwindled, to be replaced by uniformed Navy V-12 trainees. No sooner were wartime problems out of the way than the college was overwhelmed by the surge of returning veterans, packing the classrooms and overcrowding the dormitories. It says a great deal for Nason's navigation that when the upheaval finally subsided in the early fifties, the college emerged precisely on the academic course set by Aydelotte, with the honors program functioning better than ever.

Courtney Smith, who succeeded Nason in 1953, upheld the Aydelotte tradition vigorously and confidently. It was during his time that the full wave of national recognition hit Swarthmore. The college found itself showing up at the top of more and more indexes of alumni achievement. Courtney Smith had the gift to share these recognitions with the students, faculty, and alumni as their proper due and yet, at the same time, hold forth still higher ideals and nobler goals. He took Aydelotte's vision and image of the college and polished them to a new surpassing luster. He made it possible for a faculty member or student to feel that Swarthmore was the best place in the country to be and that the educational job being done here was the most important.

Swarthmore's reputation spread widely in academic circles well before the general college-going public had ever heard of the place.[2] One of the unanticipated fringe benefits of the honors program was the fact that visiting examiners, seeing the Swarthmore honors candidates at the peak of their undergraduate attainment, tended to go away mightily impressed, thus building up a big reservoir of respect for Swarthmore in the broader academic community. The applicant list began to include more and more children of college professors. In the early fifties, Swarthmore joined the Tuition Exchange program for children of college faculty members, but was compelled to withdraw in 1960 because the number of faculty children from other colleges coming to Swarthmore was running about 10 times as great as the number of Swarthmore faculty children going elsewhere.

Since a large proportion of its graduates have also gone on to careers in college teaching, Swarthmore has found itself to a remarkable degree functioning as a caste institution for the teaching caste in this society.

IMPACTS OF ACADEMIC EGALITARIAN- ISM During the sixties Swarthmore's institutional self-esteem began to wane slightly. Students who felt they had already encountered

[2] Most people still haven't. The name Swarthmore, from Swarthmoor Hall, Lancashire, England, an early center of seventeenth-century Quakerism, seems to carry some inexplicably feminine connotation. Generations of Swarthmore men have winced at the inevitable remark, "But I thought Swarthmore was a *girl's* school!"

enough challenge and had acquired enough prestige in getting admitted to Swarthmore began to be critical of the honors program. Honors students felt narrowly confined by the standard eight-seminar program which took up a full two years of their college work. They chafed at the limited choice of seminar topics, further limited by faculty requirements that students' programs be integrated and consistent. The impulse to be original and creative, which was supposed to find expression in seminar work, was showing up in curriculum planning.

Though Swarthmore had long had a pronounced streak of social egalitarianism, a new strain of academic egalitarianism (of a kind Aydelotte had often decried) was making honors students uneasy about the superior status of honors work. At the same time academically oriented students who had been attracted to Swarthmore by the honors program but hadn't made it into honors were finding difficulty in keeping up their motivation for course work.

Even from the beginning of honors, the college has had some qualms about the honors-course distinction. After the first few successful years of the program there was some expectation that the college would eventually go over entirely to honors instruction for the juniors and seniors. Instead the number of honors graduates rose to 70 in the class of 1937, amounting to just over half the senior class, and has fluctuated around 70 ever since (with the exception of the war years).[3] All this while, enrollments were increasing, the admissions were becoming more and more selective, and the academic qualifications of the entering classes were getting better and better. How and why was the further selection for honors sustained? Nobody knows. The Swarthmore faculty has certainly not been setting an arbitrary limit of 70 honors students per class. Most departments have been quite ready to welcome any number of qualified honors majors. Of course performance standards in the

[3] A few illustrative statistics:

Year	Total enrollment	Graduating seniors	
		Total	In honors
1937	695	137	70
1961–1970*	1,008	225	65
1971	1,143	228	44
1972	1,149	257†	79†

*Ten-year average.
†Estimate.
SOURCES: Figures to 1971 from annual catalogs. Estimated 1972 figures supplied by registrar's office.

first two years have drifted steadily upward over the years, so that confidence-building A's and B's have been harder to come by. On the other hand the experienced honors instructors have in mind a fairly clear picture of what a good honors student should be like, and they can often spot the desired behavior patterns during a student's first few months at the college. Perhaps the criteria used for admissions selections are different from those used for honors; perhaps the incidence of honors-type students in the general population has been slowly declining so as to offset the increasing selectivity of admissions; perhaps a student population, no matter how selected, will expand to fill all behavioral niches in a given college community, using grading cues and the like to find their position— maybe the honors-student characteristics the faculty are looking for are those associated with the top of an academic "pecking order." The question is troubling and deserves some serious research, especially since one of the explicit goals of the Swarthmore education is to encourage and reward that particular behavior pattern.

Many of the faculty have agreed with the students in finding the honors program restrictive. In those honors seminars which are open to both juniors and seniors (so that students of two vintages face the same honors examiner) the syllabus cannot change much from year to year. The opportunities for free exploration, or even for shifting the emphasis of a seminar, are not as great as they ought to be.

Some faculty members felt that new offerings in the course program were impeded by the presence of the honors program. The main faculty complaint has been that there had to be in each department a substantial degree of duplication between the offerings in course and in honors so that both groups of students should receive a balanced academic diet. The possibilities for curricular diversity were correspondingly reduced.[4]

---

[4] It should be clearly pointed out, since few faculty members anywhere are apt to see it immediately, that such duplication of offerings is not necessarily a bad thing and may well be a good thing for students. Presumably one of the attractions of Swarthmore to students is its smallness and its exceptional faculty-student ratio among coeducational colleges of its size. One thing Swarthmore is implicitly offering students in exchange for high tuitions is more individual attention, especially in the classroom. However, there is a natural faculty tendency to squander that attention on specialized advanced courses inaccessible to the average student while skimping on attention to standard offerings. Thus, paradoxically, though the Swarthmore honors program is unabashedly elitist in conception, it has had the effect of limiting the unconscious elitism of faculty specialization.

The most serious signs of faculty dissatisfaction appeared in the middle sixties when faculty mobility was at its peak throughout the nation. Swarthmore faculty members found themselves tempted by offers of higher salaries, lower teaching loads, and the chance to teach graduate students. In 1965–66, while Courtney Smith was on leave, such temptations lured away 6 of the 69 members of tenured faculty and two of the more promising untenured faculty members with unexpired contracts.

Such raiding presented an especially serious threat to Swarthmore. Courtney Smith prided himself on having a top-quality faculty, and he made a point of maintaining a good salary scale and a generous leave policy. However, the main noneconomic attractions Swarthmore offered to faculty—the opportunity to teach bright, eager undergraduates, the atmosphere of secure common-room gentility that one finds in a well-established, well-endowed institution—were much better suited to keeping the senior faculty he had than to attracting new senior faculty from elsewhere. If larger institutions continued to skim off his best faculty at the rate of 10 percent a year, a serious drop in quality was inevitable.

A SELF-EXAMINATION In the fall of 1966 Smith announced the appointment of a blue-ribbon Commission on Educational Policy (CEP) which was to make an intensive year-long study of all academic aspects of the college. At the same time he also named two special committees: one to look into ways of increasing the instructional use of the library and the other, a student-faculty-board-administration committee, to consider social rules and related aspects of student life.

All these investigative bodies researched busily for a year, consulted numerous experts, and then in November 1967 submitted their reports jointly in a single volume entitled *Critique of a College* but better known on campus as the "red book." To emphasize the solemnity of the occasion, the faculty suspended classes for a whole week (thereafter known as "Super-week") so that all members of the college community might join in the reading and discussion of the reports. This achieved the desired involvement, but set an unfortunate precedent: for several years after, Swarthmore students nominated further topics they deemed urgent enough to merit similar campuswide discussion and suspension of classes.

The CEP put forward 165 specific recommendations but later withdrew five of them. Of the remainder, the faculty eventually rejected four, modified nine more, and adopted the rest verbatim.

Very few of the proposals could be considered far-reaching or revolutionary. In particular, Aydelotte's honors program emerged very little changed in character, though somewhat reduced in scope. The standard honors program was reduced from eight seminars, followed by eight honors examinations, to six seminars and six examinations. The two seminars thus removed were to be replaced with four single-credit elective courses, to be graded pass-fail. It was already known that a six-seminar modification was safe since the department of biology had been permitting one for years to its honors students whose premed or other curricular requirements were incompatible with the full eight seminars. Swarthmore was not in any hurry to discard its trump suit.

A number of the CEP recommendations were designed to give the course program greater variety, to make it more attractive to students and more interesting to faculty. Tutorials, theses, selected-reading courses, special projects, and student-run (though faculty-examined) courses all were to be permitted and encouraged. Many of the proposals were intended to minimize the number of prerequisites and required courses. The abolition of the language requirement, finally approved by the faculty in 1970, was originally proposed by the CEP.

Another concern of the CEP was to relieve the stress of heavy work loads on the freshmen and sophomores. The normal course load for the first two years was reduced, in stages, from five courses to four. Pass-fail grading for the freshman year was introduced.

The effects of these changes have not been especially dramatic but have generally been in the expected direction. Performance of honors students in seminars remains good, though a number of honors students show a marked tendency to neglect their work in the elective courses in favor of seminar work. Others arrange to get into double-credit courses run as seminars. It appears that the seminar mode of instruction is a stable mode that will exclude regular lecture courses if permitted to do so.

The thornier problem of the honors-course distinction has not been resolved, and the general campus uneasiness on this question persists. The present year, 1971–72, has seen renewed campuswide discussion of the question.

The relief of pressure on the freshmen and sophomores has not resulted in the conspicuous deterioration of performance that loomed as the worst possible consequence. Instead, though some instructors claim to detect deterioration, others are able to report a general improvement in class levels. However, some of the side effects may be fairly drastic. Swarthmore students once rarely went off the campus, even to Philadelphia. With the reduced pressure and with the elimination of Saturday classes since 1968, students now seem to scatter all over the East Coast every weekend.[5] What effect this will have on the self-contained, self-sufficient character of the college community remains to be seen.

For a time it appeared that the level of nonacademic activity had been affected adversely by these changes. The campus was no longer bubbling over with as much creativity and organized extracurricular activity as it once was, as if the traditional plethora of feverish activity had actually represented the elaborate avoidance behavior of conscientious young intellectuals under heavy academic stress. On the other hand, this past year has seen some resurgence of the older style, so it begins to appear that widespread flooding and ebbing of counterculture attitudes were much more influential than any local academic changes.

The CEP proposals that broke most sharply with previous Swarthmore tradition concerned the creative arts. Instruction was to be offered in creative writing, theater, and the visual arts; course credit was to be given, and the instructors were to receive faculty status. For many years there had been academic programs in music, in fine arts, and in the various literatures, but actual practice of any of these art forms had been rigidly excluded from the curriculum. While the standards of extracurricular performance had risen steadily over the years, the official attitude had always been that academic credit for the arts, even at a high standard of excellence, was incompatible with the intellectual commitment of the college.[6]

---

[5] Informal classroom polls by the author indicate that something like a quarter of the students are apt to leave town on any given weekend. On the other hand, SAGA food service reports that the number of meals served on weekends is only 3 percent less than on weekdays. If this means that the weekend outflow of Swarthmore students is nearly balanced by an influx of visitors, the long-standing insularity of the Swarthmore campus is being doubly diminished.

[6] This attitude toward the arts has sometimes been traced to the Quakers, but it persisted long after other direct evidence of Quaker influence had effectively disappeared. A more likely explanation is that the college, while leaving behind the Quaker tradition in its pursuit of academic excellence, has remained a pronouncedly bourgeois institution, with a middle-class faculty training middle-class students according to middle-class ideals. The emphasis on hard work, deferred gratification, and standards of professional excellence are all parts of this pattern. So is a general distrust of the arts and, more especially, of artists. This distrust is diminishing, however, as more students, and even some faculty, are drawn from backgrounds of assured affluence.

Now the CEP thought otherwise, concluding that the likely benefits to personal development of the students outweighed the possible dangers of dilution of the college's intellectual standards. The faculty went along with this somewhat grudgingly, but the students were delighted. Art, it seems, figures largely in today's vision of the good life.

The report of the Special Committee on Library Policy, which accompanied the CEP report, proposed a number of modest improvements in the instructional use of the library which aroused no controversy and were readily endorsed by the faculty.

STUDENT LIFE   Quite the opposite reception was given the report of the Special Committee on Student Life, which was supposed to develop a general philosophy of college social rules on which future discussions of the topic could be based. This was probably a hopeless task from the outset. The college had come down to Aydelotte's day with a set of social rules such as would befit a Quaker college attempting to secure for Quaker youth "an opportunity for higher educational training under the guarded supervision and care of those of their own religious faith."[7] The subsequent history of the social rules has consisted of a steady slow erosion of the protective regulation exercised by the college. The faculty, which used to supervise all extracurricular activities, has tended more and more to confine its contacts with students to academic settings. Over the years the deans have bravely maintained a losing struggle, holding to each degree of regulation as long as possible before abandoning it, so that the college has always been as protective as the prevailing climate would permit, but, as one former dean put it, "There are no restrictions upon behavior involving cars, liquor, sex, and dress that the young intellectuals will not rationalize away."[8]

In the middle of such continued erosion it is patently impossible to stop and build some solid philosophical foundation for future conservatism. The committee tried. After long consideration it concluded that the college, simply as the operator of residential real estate, had a continuing proprietary responsibility to keep men and women students out of each other's bedrooms. The student body thought otherwise. The report was greeted with scorn and indigna-

---

[7] From a statement of religious background carried in Swarthmore catalogs during the twenties.

[8] Everett Hunt, reviewing his quarter century of experience as dean of men at Swarthmore in his book *Revolt of the College Intellectual*, Human Relations Aids, New York, 1963.

tion. The faculty postponed discussion while several student-faculty committees set to work to take the report apart and make alternative recommendations.

The issue dragged on for more than a year, generating another "Super-day" with classes suspended for collegewide discussions and lending fuel to the subsequent "crisis" of January 1969. The students were asking for dormitory autonomy amounting to complete college abdication on the bedroom question, which was further than anybody in charge wanted to go officially. Unofficially the dormitories were pretty unrestricted already because much of the dormitory supervision was by students or by young people who were sympathetic to students. Moreover the college judicial system for dealing with social rules was, and still is, a jurisdictional thicket which protected most student violators from the full force of administrative disapproval but also introduced an unfortunate element of chance into the disposition of cases.

Finally in spring of 1969 the faculty took the fatal step and recommended dormitory autonomy to the board of managers. To campuswide dismay the board overruled the faculty, which it rarely does. The following year the board came around. For the first time since its founding, Swarthmore was no longer dragging behind popular attitudes, much to the relief of the administration. When the proposals for coed dormitories came up slowly thereafter, the main problems had to do with such technical questions as dormitory security for the women; no significant changes in college policy were required.

DISSENSION AND DISAFFECTION Like all colleges these days, Swarthmore has had its internal dissensions and disaffections, and general militance. The year 1968–69 was the worst. The junior faculty began to distrust the senior faculty and set up an informal caucus for bloc voting in the faculty elections to the CEP.[9] The students were mistrustful of the faculty and administration and began demanding student power. Faculty winced at a new column in the campus newspaper, the *Phoenix,* entitled "Up Against the Wall, ——." Radical faculty members joined students in protests and demonstrations, including a protest against military recruiting on campus. The faculty voted down a proposal to permit student observers at faculty meetings. The dean

[9] The name and initials have been passed on to a permanent policy body which advises the president and faculty.

of admissions vigorously rejected criticism of the recruitment and admissions procedures for black students.

The "crisis" in January 1969 began with a sit-in in the admissions office by members of SASS—the Swarthmore Afro-American Student Society—who were protesting what they felt to be a lack of concern for increasing the numbers of black students at Swarthmore. The issues were local, although the rhetoric (e.g., "non-negotiable demands") and attitudes were widely fashionable at that time. The principal complicating factor at Swarthmore was that the rest of the students decided that this was an emergency requiring collegewide discussion and abandoned their classrooms to participate in "plenary sessions" in Clothier Auditorium. In the excitement many students were proposing, with some faculty encouragement, to make an immediate general bid for student power.

The faculty and administration agreed that Swarthmore Quaker tradition precluded the use of force or violence to eject the sitters-in, but nobody knew how far the general unrest would carry if not dealt with promptly. The faculty went into emergency marathon meetings punctuated by the exchange of clarifying communiqués with SASS and by the frequent hortatory resolutions forwarded from the students in *plenum.*

The student power bid collapsed fairly early, partly because SASS asked the rest of the student body not to confuse the issues, partly because Swarthmore students are fond of rational deliberative processes and are not easily stampeded into extreme positions. This did not, however, reflect any overwhelming confidence in the faculty. When the faculty's general acceptance of SASS demands, including an agreement that SASS should be represented on all major committees, was rejected by SASS because of differences in terminology that seemed ominous at the time, the rest of the student body was disposed to share SASS's suspicions.

The crisis ended abruptly with Courtney Smith's death. The sitters-in quietly withdrew from the admissions office. In Clothier Auditorium the plenary sessions were succeeded by solemn memorial services framed in Quaker silence. Afterward the dazed campus turned back to the business of the classroom.

THE CROSS ADMINISTRATION Since Courtney Smith had previously announced his intention to retire at the end of the academic year, a selection committee was already at work choosing his successor. By the end of April the committee announced the choice of Robert Cross, president of

Hunter College, who had been a popular member of the department of history at Swarthmore during the fifties. Although he was the first non-Rhodes scholar picked for the office since Swain, Cross's academic credentials were impeccable. Clearly there was to be no change in the fundamental academic emphasis inherited from Aydelotte.

In his first two years as president, Robert Cross was not able to overcome all the suspicions and disaffections still lingering on the campus, but he did manage to instill confidence to the degree that almost all the various factions around the campus now trust the administration more, at least, than they trust one another.

The general faculty confidence in the administration was ensured when Charles Gilbert, of the political science faculty, the chairman of the original CEP, was named to the new office of provost— effectively dean of the faculty. Cross also took such pains to ensure that younger faculty and radical faculty were represented in committee appointments that the radical bloc voted with the conservatives last year to leave the appointing power in his hands, especially since recent faculty elections, by whichever procedure, have been extraordinary for the extent to which they have favored recognizably "establishment" figures such as department chairmen.

Now that coed dormitories are in operation, the remaining constraints on students are curricular requirements imposed by the faculty, so the faculty, rather than the administration, are the targets. Tenure, hiring policy, degree requirements, grading systems, and departmental autonomy have all been under a mild attack from the students, who look to the administration for sympathy and possible political leverage.

While this relative confidence in the administration has been refreshing, it could still prove temporary, and Cross has tried hard to find a system of college governance that doesn't put the administration in the middle, especially on the questions involving traditional faculty prerogatives. He tried to promote a new College Council and had one committee or another at work on this from the time he arrived on campus, but without success. The faculty is naturally jealous of its powers and is not disposed to let its standards of academic excellence suffer the same kind of erosion that befell the Quaker-originated social rules. The black students are also distrustful of any arrangement that might jeopardize their own hard-won special provisions. It is hard to see how any workable College Council could be put together that would satisfy all constituencies.

The most singular problem that Cross had to handle arose in March 1971 when an FBI office was broken into in the nearby town of Media, Pennsylvania. Contents of the files were taken and subsequently released to the press, bit by bit. Nobody at Swarthmore had anything to do with the theft, but because of the locality of the office the college figured prominently in the papers which were released. The documents mostly reflected FBI ineptitude and misinformation, even in the cases of the very few students and faculty in which specific interest had been shown. The most distressing development was the evidence that some college employees with access to personal information about students and faculty were accustomed to cooperate freely with the FBI whenever information was requested. There was little to be done about past indiscretions, since the authenticity of the documents could not be established. To avoid further occurrences of this type, Cross promptly issued a stern statement to all members of the college community prescribing, as a condition of continued membership, "intelligent restraint" in dealing with future outside requests for information. He quickly put together a special committee to spell out the policy details of the obligations of the college, and of its employees, to preserve the privacy of the college community as far as possible. Later he made a strong public statement condemning indiscriminate surveillance of college campuses. Outside the college these responses predictably angered those citizens who feel that the FBI can do no wrong. Within the college the new policy should assure that college handling of inquiries from any outside person or agency will be formal, responsible, and more reserved than it has been.

In most other respects, paradoxically, the Cross administration has distinguished itself by steady efforts to loosen things up, to promote informality and accessibility. This policy has done much to diminish the long-term level of college tension.

Another marked characteristic of this administration has been a strong affirmation of the college's new institutional encouragement of the arts. President and Mrs. Cross have both proved to be enthusiastic personal supporters of the arts. Under Cross's leadership the college has undertaken to build a new music building, to be the first building on campus intended from the beginning for an artistic discipline.

In October 1971 Cross began the third year of his presidency with the unexpected announcement that it would be his last: "I have concluded that being president is not my forte." Initial campus reactions were surprise, disappointment, and chagrin, but these were followed quickly by a general expectation that the choice of his successor would probably be an especially definitive decision in determining the whole educational policy of the college for some years to come.

THE SEARCH FOR A SUCCESSOR The board of managers underlined its intention to renew its statutory responsibility for naming a new president, specifying that the selection committee should forward to the board a list of at least five nominees for final consideration. A subsequent clarification was needed to assure outraged students and faculty that the recommendations of the committee would be given proper weight and that the views and interests of all members of the college community would be taken into account in the final decision.

The tripartite selection committee includes five students, five faculty members,[10] and five members of the board, sharing equal responsibilities. Interviewing committees visiting potential candidates on other campuses have commonly consisted of a student, a faculty member, and a board member.

The committee, endeavoring to make its deliberations as public and open as the nature of the task would permit, has introduced a set of open forums where prospective candidates could be introduced to members of the college community and subjected to public questioning. Since the selection process is still under way at this writing, it is too early to judge what the net effect of the forums will be, but it is already evident that most of the misgivings with which faculty traditionalists viewed this development have given way to delight and satisfaction.

THE PROSPECTS FOR CHANGE The college can probably accommodate itself to a lot more innovations of this kind, and is perhaps more apt to do so now that the earlier strident and insistent pressures for change have abated somewhat. For several years the campus was in the throes of a mystique of *change* which insisted that change per se was imperative and overdue. During the height of this movement the view was widely held that all society was to be rebuilt from the ground up, starting with the university, particularly Swarthmore. Traditional

---

[10] Among the five faculty representatives on the committee, chosen freely by the faculty in secret-ballot proportional representation (P.R.) elections, are two top college officials: Provost Gilbert and Vice President Cratsley. This would appear to be an unusually clear and spontaneous expression of faculty confidence in the present administration.

academic disciplines represented fragmentation of knowledge, experience, and life and were to be abandoned. Grades and examinations had to go because they were destructive of cooperation and community spirit.

The older faculty were not much swayed by this kind of thing, but many of the idealistic younger faculty found it very inspiring. In spring 1970 the department of philosophy sponsored a course called "Phil. 10—Methods of Inquiry," a general critique of disciplinary approaches taught by a dozen or so younger faculty members (mostly members of the New University Conference) from assorted departments. Phil. 10 had a sizable enrollment and a very large attendance.

Later in the same semester, many of the Phil. 10 students and a few of the faculty formed an extracurricular association called Tensor, based on a philosophy of "holism" and intended to be one of the instruments of change.

Because activist-minded Swarthmore students were already wrapped up in Tensor activities at the time of Cambodia–Kent State, Swarthmore's participation in the subsequent "strike" was decidedly idiosyncratic. From a non-Tensor viewpoint it seemed that Swarthmore students were ready to talk the ears off each other, off striking students at other campuses, off the world at large. Delegations were sent around to local community groups to evangelize and spread the Tensor gospel.

Though arrangements were afoot the following fall to set up a complete new core curriculum, again under the auspices of the philosophy department, momentum was fading. While the administration was still scrutinizing this idea, the whole movement quietly collapsed.

Tensor itself seems to have died completely, but some of the ex-Tensorite students and faculty are still active in something called Labor Committee, representing (as the author understands it) a nonviolent residue of the national Students for a Democratic Society after the Weathermen separated off. Labor Committee is avowedly Marxian socialist, though in a prophetic vein that is strictly *sui generis.*

Among the other younger faculty who organized Phil. 10 or otherwise led the movement for radical academic reform, a few have left in disgust, and some were let go by their departments when their appointments ran out. Most are still around and seem, without abandoning their views, to have made their peace with the limited rates of change and kinds of change that the college can sustain.[11]

Though the academic program of the college has not changed much over several decades, there has been in the past four years a drastic decline in the number of graduates going on to graduate school in academic subjects. The number going on to professional schools to study for nonacademic careers in medicine, law, education, social work, the ministry, and so on, has been holding remarkably steady at 50 ± 8 out of a graduating class of 230 ± 20. Until 1968 the number going on to graduate study in other, nonprofessional, academic areas, presumably to prepare for careers in college teaching, was also steady at about 90 ± 5. In 1968 this latter number began to drop. By 1970 it was down to 46, and there was a further drop to 27 in 1971.

This change in career direction occurred earlier and more strongly among the men. Until 1968 roughly 80 percent of all Swarthmore male graduates went on to some kind of graduate school. This was down to 45 percent in 1970, and down further to 33 percent in 1971. For the women graduates, the pre-1968 figure of 50 percent was down slightly to 40 percent in 1970, falling abruptly to 28 percent in 1971. The change in the selective service regulations in 1968 seems to have been a major factor in starting the decline among the men, but this has been followed by a general disenchantment with pure academic work which has been reinforced by the well-publicized tightness of the academic job market.

The number of seniors graduating in honors was also way down in both 1970 and 1971, but this seems to have been mainly the result of many students dropping out of honors at the time of the Cambodian "strike." The number of seniors in honors is larger

[11] The whole pattern of change at Swarthmore is nicely symbolized by a paragraph to be found in the current college catalog under the title "Tradition and Change," which begins, "A college is never static. Its purpose and policies are always changing to meet new demands and new conditions."

The paragraph has been reiterated, almost verbatim, in every catalog since 1948; it has drifted around in context depending on circumstances. In early catalogs it was included in the section on "Admissions" to warn alumni and friends that they could no longer count on their offspring being admitted automatically. In later editions it wandered into a hortatory section on "Academic Competence," still bearing the same message. Then it moved to the section entitled "The Religious Tradition," where it served to disclaim traditional Quaker constraints. Since 1968 this same paragraph, under its present title, has been attached to a brief account of the 1966 CEP and its recommendations.

than usual this year, with an even larger number anticipated next year. It will be interesting to see whether this recovery will be reflected in the numbers of graduates going on to graduate study.

The current widespread concern for the status of women in American society—the women's lib question—should place no strain on Swarthmore, for that very question has been a traditional concern here where women have always been regarded as the intellectual and social equals of men. Women faculty members, though in a minority in all departments and altogether missing from some—especially in the sciences—have served as department chairmen and division chairmen. Before Dean Susan Cobbs retired two years ago, she had served for seven years as the most important academic officer of the college. There is, at this writing, a genuine possibility that the next president will be a woman.[12]

A major defect in college policy with regard to women has been the inferior status accorded to part-time instructors, most of whom are women. The administration is now committed to extending faculty promotion-and-tenure policy to include part-time instructors, though many details remain to be resolved.

While the Quaker inheritance of coeducation is suddenly right in step with current educational fashions, it has lost its competitive advantage thereby. As long as Swarthmore was one of the few topflight schools offering genuine coeducation, the number of women applicants for admission was always greater than the number of men applicants. Since many of the better-known men's colleges have begun taking women, the number of women applying to Swarthmore has dropped sharply, so that, for the first time, admissions for men are more selective than for women, though not by a great deal.

All the other problems of American education should pass Swarthmore right by. Take the question of whether or not the conventional academically oriented curriculum is appropriate for the broad segment of population entering colleges today. Swarthmore has deliberately concentrated on a restricted clientele of bright students for whom the academic orientation has proven highly suitable for nearly 50 years. Or take the decline in government funds for research and for graduate programs. Swarthmore has

---

[12] Note added in proof: For *is* read *was*. An offer was made; at the last minute the fair lady turned us down, Vice President Cratsley will be serving as acting president for the academic year 1972–73. Meanwhile, the selection process begins again.

steadfastly refused to consider a graduate program[13] and has never relied on research grants to carry any part of any instructor's regular salary. Swarthmore's involvement in military or classified research has been nil; because of traditional Quaker concerns even the college's investment portfolio has been free of any taint of military or aerospace stocks, as well as of any connection with tobacco or alcohol.

Such relative good fortune in the institution's past policies is apt to make the faculty complacent today, which would be unfortunate. Much of the disaffection of students today seems to stem from a desire for something more personal than the academic fare that has been provided them in one form or another for a dozen years before they come to college. The young radical professors have been able to respond to that need, to supply personal leadership and personal inspiration, to share their deepest convictions their values, and sometimes even their living arrangements with students. The older professors have cultivated a rigid code of self-restraint that inhibits exactly that kind of thing lest academic objectivity be lost or lest a student be unduly influenced. One result is that the older faculty come across to today's students as stereotypes with vested interests but without convictions or deep moral feelings. Very likely the older faculty need to take a cue from the younger fellows and devote more time and patience to candid general discussions with students. At a place like Swarthmore the personal contact between faculty and students *should* be close enough for the individuals to come across as individuals. If not at Swarthmore, where else?

---

[13] A major reason for this has been simply the recognition that the college could not hope to attract graduate students of the same quality as the undergraduates. The college *does* award an occasional master's degree at the rate of about one a year. In the past decade there have been 14 master's degrees awarded, of which nine have been in astronomy and psychology, two fields in which the college has long-standing research programs of wide reputation. Of the other five degrees, three were taken by alumnae housewives as a means of academic reentry.

16. Academic Change and Crisis, Canadian Style

by Jill Conway

Traditionally the University of Toronto has looked to England for its educational ideals and institutional models. Other Canadian institutions have shared a North American concern for democracy in education, but in the cultural metropolis of Toronto elitism in education was a living part of the British heritage as late as 1960. This was apparent in two ways, each utterly unlike the competitive meritocracy which characterises elite institutions in the United States. First, the University of Toronto prided itself on being the representative, in a colonial society, of a high culture which had its roots in Oxford and Cambridge. Secondly, it was confident that as an institution it educated Ontario's and indeed Canada's social elites, though in addition it opened its doors to a large commuter population drawing upon talent at all social levels in Toronto. As the 1960s opened, the influence of Oxbridge was clearly apparent in the undergraduate curriculum of the Faculty of Arts and Science. This influence was just as strong in the institutional structure of the university: a federation of three colleges[1] with religious affiliations which served Anglicans, Roman Catholics, and Methodists, and a fourth non-denominational college which served, apparently without sense of contradiction, other Protestant, Jewish, and non-affiliated undergraduates. The structure was a heritage from Canada's Confederation era, when a group of separately founded colleges had come together, drawn into union by the aspiration to create a university of national stature.

[1] The University of Toronto is a federation of four universities, joined in affiliation with a number of professional and special college bodies, to which have been added a number of constituent undergraduate colleges as the student body has been expanded. The use of all these terms would only confound the general reader. Accordingly, *college* in this essay refers to an undergraduate institution attached in some way to the University of Toronto. *University* refers to the collectivity of the University of Toronto wherever used.

Whatever their religious orientation, the colleges shared the assumption that undergraduate education should involve spiritual growth and growth in self-awareness through genuine participation in a community of one's peers. This community was in part residential, but the majority of undergraduates were commuters who found in the colleges a religious and social centre and a vehicle for the expression of political concerns. Each college had the right to teach or refrain from teaching religious knowledge to its undergraduates; in other respects the instructional role of the colleges was slight in relation to that of the university departments. Each college had a lively tradition of student government and student involvement in disciplinary procedures. Once the federation was achieved, this tradition of a self-regulating student community was transferred to the university as a whole and student affairs were largely controlled by a universitywide Students' Administrative Council. In matters of student discipline college bodies, and upon rare occasions a universitywide council upon which faculty but no student representatives sat, exercised control. By custom this universitywide disciplinary body refrained wherever possible from exercising its jurisdiction, thereby emphasising the collegiate structure of the university and deferring to the tradition of student government.

The liveliness of this tradition in Canadian universities constitutes another striking difference between universities in Canada and the United States, where student government has never developed deep roots. Two cultural factors of immense importance account for the difference. First, and most importantly, the Canadian assumption duplicated that of the British that a student finishing high school is a mature person, ready, should he so choose, to enter the business world without further training, and therefore to be conceded to in many ways as an adult when choosing to enter college. Secondly, because of the reverence for parlimentary democracy which is central to the cultures of the British Commonwealth, experience in student government has always been deemed an essential preparation for a political career, for it is here, in the give-and-take of debate and in the ability to appeal to an electorate, that a student will learn the important parliamentary skills.

Under the federation, the Toronto undergraduate curriculum and the recruitment of faculty to teach it acquired an idiosyncratic administrative structure of almost Byzantine complexity. Academic disciplines which were accepted or established areas of scholarly endeavour at the time of the federation remained college subjects taught by separate faculties. Besides religious knowledge and theology these were classical studies, English, ethics, French and German, Near Eastern studies, and philosophy (at St. Michael's College only). Academic disciplines of more recent provenance, like anthropology or psychology, and those which seemed value-free in relation to the difficult task of developing the spiritual man or woman, like mathematics, were taught by a universitywide faculty having no college affiliation and organised in the conventional departments of the modern university. Many of the important areas of undergraduate teaching were thus separated from the colleges. Indeed a student might be enrolled in St. Michael's College (Roman Catholic) and yet receive all his instruction (apart from a mandatory study of religious knowledge) from universitywide departments with a secular approach to learning. Thus though all undergraduates were required to enroll as members of a college, the peculiarities of the university structure meant that for large numbers of students the colleges were social centres quite separate from their intellectual experience. The social sciences, for example, were all taught through universitywide departments, though the British tradition lingered in some departmental titles. Political science, economics, and sociology were taught within one vast empire wistfully given the title *political economy,* as though the very words could conjure up the spirit of Mill, Bentham, and Ricardo to preside over the burgeoning social sciences and fit them into a respectable English mold. However, the single title did not foster synthesis within the three disciplines, nor did caution in nomenclature discipline the tendency to growth in the sciences and social sciences which has been the major intellectual development of the years since the federation brought the university into being. Indeed by the crucial decade of the 1960s the academic centre of gravity of the institution had shifted from the colleges to the university departments and professional faculties, which in 1964 had between them some 1,000 full-time staff members as opposed to a college faculty of approximately 200.

Much of this change was masked at the opening of the 1960s by the extent to which the university remained committed to maintaining excellence in undergraduate education. The influence of British models was strikingly apparent in the effort put into the undergraduate honours program in the Faculty of Arts and Science.

This program provided four years of carefully organised study in a special field of concentration. These fields were so narrowly defined that at the end of four years an undergraduate studying English, for example, would be well acquainted with the whole body of English literature, but probably unaware that there were literary insights to be derived from psychology and anthropology. Besides its carefully contrived specialisation, the honours program had as its pride a system of tutorial instruction which aimed at duplicating, through the weekly meeting of a small discussion group, the Oxford don's relationship with individual undergraduates.

This system of undergraduate instruction was maintained in 1960 at a university which normally educated approximately half the student population of Ontario (some 19,355 full-time students). That feat was made possible simply by dividing the undergraduate program into two separate but avowedly unequal parts. The honours program preserved the elitism of British educational values; the general B.A. program, where many concessions were made to numbers, faced the problems of mass education. The general B.A. lecture courses purveyed knowledge in supposedly easily assimilable form for a student body assumed to be uninterested in specialised learning and attracted by the shorter three-year degree. In this way the "general education" concern of the 1950s was meshed with the financial exigencies of budgeting for the instruction of large numbers of students. Students in the general program were taught in large lecture courses, often by junior instructors, and they rarely encountered a tutorial. Thus although the distinction between the general B.A. and the honours B.A. was one which attempted to resolve the problem of maintaining elite programs in the face of increasing pressure for mass education, the extreme specialisation of the honours courses and the questionable academic quality of work in the general program made both susceptible to criticism.

FOUR FORCES FOR CHANGE At the beginning of the 1960s it was the fond hope of many established Toronto faculty that the foundation of new universities in the province of Ontario (seven were founded between 1959 and 1965) might create a hierarchy of institutions that would preserve Toronto as an elite college while newer and lesser universities provided general education for the masses. In the ensuing decade four major forces combined to blight this hope and to change the character of the institution irrevocably. The first and decisive factor was the refusal of the provincial government, and in particular its Minister of Education, William Davis,[2] to accept the idea of elitism in the allocation of tax revenues for the support of higher education. Supporting such a decision was Mr. Davis's strong personal ambition to create a system of mass education in the Province of Ontario, modeled upon the ease of access of the California or New York state system rather than upon any British tradition.

The second force for change came from the necessity to recruit new faculty from outside Canada and the Oxbridge tradition to teach the rapidly expanding numbers of students, since Canadian graduate schools did not graduate a fraction of the annual national demand for new faculty during the 1960s, a decade when student numbers in Canadian universities tripled. In addition to pressure for new faculty created by unprecedented increases in student numbers, growth in the social sciences in the 1960s took place in advance of the development of strong graduate programs in Canadian universities. This meant that development of new areas of study at Toronto (as in Canada's other universities) required the recruitment of a non-Canadian faculty which had no necessary commitment to Toronto's institutional arrangements and curricular traditions. To those for whom they were not an organic growth both the narrow specialism of the honours program and the somewhat specious generalities of the three-year degree seemed equally unsatisfactory on pedagogic grounds. Both seemed to limit innovation in teaching and to prevent the easy integration of new areas of study into the curriculum. The administrative structure of the university seemed equally cumbersome to new faculty appointed to the large university departments who had almost no awareness of the colleges except insofar as their separate existence complicated the annual process of registering students and recording their annual examination results.

To this faculty disaffection was added a third force for change, which was the growing exasperation of undergraduates both with conventional academic specialisation and with instruction through the large lecture course. For undergraduates the problem of "relevance" in the curriculum was compounded by an increasing awareness of major transformations that had occurred in Canadian society since World War II. Many of Toronto's undergraduates were English-speaking but not of English-Canadian parentage. For them, the automatic relevance of a curriculum which related Canada's development to British politics, history, and social

---

[2] Mr. Davis was to become leader of his party and Premier of the Province of Ontario in 1971.

thought could no longer be assumed. While these upwardly mobile children of immigrants did not question the university as an institution which could confer professional status and enhanced opportunity upon them, other undergraduates did. Like their peers in Europe and elsewhere in North America, young Canadians in the 1960s discovered the Third World and were more concerned with understanding their relationship with Latin America, Asia, and Africa than they were with probing the Western cultural tradition of which they were often critical. But neither of these sources of change in student interest excited the radical emotions to the degree that the fourth major source of change—the supposed Americanisation of the teaching of the social sciences in Canada—did. Student radicals critical of the United States and its world posture began to see in the recruitment of American-trained faculty the danger that Canada's cultural heritage might be obliterated by an American penetration of Canadian cultural institutions as complete and controlling as that already established in the Canadian economy. Although students with conservative political opinions were less critical than the radicals of America's role in the cold war, they were equally incensed by the threat of cultural penetration, so Americanisation was an issue that could unite the entire spectrum of political opinion. The American threat was regarded as particularly dangerous in disciplines such as economics, sociology, history, and political science which dealt with questions of value about social and political organisation. American-trained physicists, it was thought, probably represented no danger to Canadian values, but the sociologist who taught with reference only to American social structures was a cultural imperialist who must be resisted bitterly.

Ironically, many American faculty were genuine emigrants to Canada and were anxious to be converted to the very Canadian values they were thought to threaten. On the other hand many emigré Americans who were violent critics of American imperialism naïvely assumed that their task in Canada was to lead Canadians along the correct path to life, liberty, and the pursuit of happiness. This situation gave a distinctly Canadian flavour to radical student attempts to test classroom authority and gain a voice in departmental governance, for the counterculture which was being asserted was not the familiar utopian rejection of international youth culture, but a strong nationalist desire to possess and understand a national experience seen as threatened by external forces.

Radical groups were less concerned with disrupting the classroom than with dramatising and asserting the right to question both content and structure of courses which they regarded as devoting insufficient attention to the Canadian experience or as insufficiently critical of the United States. Since the Americanisation issue centred around matters of curriculum and upon the recruitment of new faculty, students were obliged to focus their discontent on university structures and governance, for it was only by influencing curriculum and recruitment that their nationalist feelings could be satisfied. On the question of student participation in governance, a spectrum of opinion quickly developed ranging from the demand for an equal voice with faculty on all governing bodies in departments, faculties, and colleges to the assertion that a student voice in all matters touching recruitment and curriculum should be institutionalised at important levels within the university. To this undergraduate concern was added the professional concern of graduate students who wanted to assert their competence to share academic judgments with faculty and also wanted to protect their own interests as against foreign candidates when new appointments were made.

INSTITUTIONAL RESPONSES The response of faculty and administration to the growing concern with Canadian culture was mixed. At the opening of the decade, President Claude Bissel decided that the most vital national function that the University of Toronto could perform was to expand its School of Graduate Studies upon a scale which would permit the education of a substantial proportion of the estimated approximately 20,000 new faculty who would be required to staff Canadian universities by 1970. This estimate underestimated the need, because full-time student numbers in Canadian universities were to triple within the decade. President Bissell's decision, supported unwaveringly throughout the 1960s, brought about a change in priorities for the allocation of institutional resources, which, by subordinating the undergraduate curriculum to the pressure of graduate work, forced a major revision of undergraduate studies. However, the decision to develop the graduate school was taken without a serious attempt to consider whether the development of a Canadian scholarly profession trained along the lines of the most efficient American graduate schools could best serve Canada's cultural needs. The professionalisation of learning, the Ph.D. system, and the conception of the graduate school as a laboratory where scholars might pursue their disinterested research free from overt social pressure were not necessarily the social changes most likely to preserve or articulate a distinctively Canadian cultural heritage. Indeed such changes might in themselves become a subtle form of Americanisation if based too uncritically upon American institutional models. Certainly they encouraged scholars in Canada as elsewhere to give their allegiance to a profession and to standards of scholarship which were internationally defined. A presidential committee appointed in 1964–65 did examine the future of Toronto's graduate school, but its approach was pragmatic and was directed toward the manner in which the university could proceed with all due speed toward the most efficient system of professional training rather than directed toward the larger question of the potential impact such a system might have on the scholarly community in Canada.

Canadian universities had hitherto prided themselves upon their exemption from American pressures to publish or perish. They had likewise regarded themselves correctly as places where the ideal of scholarship might be expressed through brilliance in teaching as much as in writing. With the adoption of an ambitious plan for graduate development and a rigorously professional notion of scholarly publication, important forces for change which undermined older attitudes were unleashed in the university. Though he had been instrumental in setting these forces in motion, President Bissell remained unaware of their significance until the closing years of the decade. Then his serious attempts to use administrative initiative to rehumanise the scholarly community foundered upon the professional identification of a faculty whose strong professional aspirations he had unwittingly encouraged.

The first attempt to initiate real changes in the quality of undergraduate experience was the appointment in 1966 of a presidential committee to examine undergraduate studies at Toronto. This committee was given the widest possible terms of reference and encouraged to contemplate sweeping changes. During its full year of deliberations it heard briefs at open meetings from interested faculty, departments, student groups, and college bodies. These protracted discussions focused undergraduate attention upon freedom of the individual student to fashion his or her own program of study, upon the curriculum changes necessary to achieve this liberty, and upon the kinds of changes in teacher-student relationships which such a freedom might imply. So far as the faculty was concerned, no clear position emerged, though those with college affiliations tended to defend the Toronto honours program with a passion that was singularly lacking in those who had only departmental ties. For departmental faculty, innovation was a pedagogic necessity because of the numbers of students they dealt with, and because of the need to devote attention to the major growth areas of graduate study.

The committee's report was presented in the fall of 1967. Its major recommendations concerned the abolition of the distinction between the general and honours programs and the development of an elective system of undergraduate study which would permit students to specialise or not as they chose and which would lead to a pass degree after three years or an honours degree after four. For students who decided not to specialise in any field, no requirements would be imposed except maintenance of the necessary academic standing to secure either a pass or an honours degree. Departments would be left free to impose prerequisites for advanced courses for those students who elected to specialise in a particular discipline. The committee also recommended a substantial reduction in the number of undergraduate hours spent in lectures, a corresponding increase in small-group instruction, and the development of new interdisciplinary courses of study which would permit the widest possible experimentation in course content and styles of teaching. With regard to the overall structure of the university, the committee recommended that the colleges be given an increased teaching function through the cross appointment to them of faculty from the university departments. In this way it was hoped that the professional impersonality of large departments which taught the biggest numbers of students (both honours and general under the old curriculum) could be broken down in the more intimate college setting.

Both faculty and student response to the idea of increased intimacy within the more human dimensions of the college communities was mixed. Students from the denominational colleges relished the freedoms of the wider secular university. Faculty from university departments whose ties were with professional peers and who looked to graduate teaching as a way of maximising professional standing were reluctant to submerge these interests in college and undergraduate affairs. Thus the only recommendations of the committee on undergraduate study to be implemented were those relating to the elective system, the abolition of the distinction between the general and honours programs, and the creation of new interdisciplinary courses.[3] These courses were administered by a standing committee of the Faculty of Arts and Science that was given the financial resources to support courses which because of their innovative nature did not find a place within the academic offerings of existing departments. Interdisciplinary course offerings tended to be of five general types: courses dealing with the theory and practice of communications, courses in comparative literature (since no such department exists at Toronto), courses treating modernisation and the problems of community (including community involvement of students and faculty), courses on scientific explanation and the place of science in society, and courses treating problems of special topical interest such as one devoted to "Understanding Quebec" or a course on "Women in the Twentieth Century." Since funds were available to encourage such non-departmental courses, recruitment of faculty (generally youthful) to the program was relatively easy since departments were reimbursed for the faculty time released. The recommendations of the committee to examine undergraduate studies concerning increased teaching functions for the colleges were ignored because no faculty or organised student support emerged for them. Finally, those relating to reduced lecture time and increased group instruction encountered the intractable obstacle of faculty conservatism, buttressed, by 1967, by financial pressures against innovation.

FINANCIAL PRESSURES The source of these financial pressures was the provincial government. In 1966 the decision was reached that the provinces would take over from the federal government the entire responsibility for the financing of education. This decision, made largely because of the understandable desire of the province of Quebec to gain complete control over public money expended on its educational system, had serious repercussions throughout Canada. In Ontario, the decision permitted the provincial government to launch a system of unit financing. The purpose of the unit-financing scheme, which took effect in 1967–68, was to provide a supposedly objective mechanism for determining the share of the total government operating grant for higher education allocated to each Ontario university. The provincial government therefore set out to devise

3 Part of the abandonment of the distinction between the honours and general programs was the decision to remove the requirement for courses in religious studies as a necessary part of an undergraduate degree.

a formula which would permit it to determine the basic operating cost per student enrolled for each university. Different categories of student enrollment obviously involved differential costs: medical students are more costly to educate than undergraduates in general science; graduate students, in general, are more costly than undergraduates. The government's formula was "weighted" to take into account these disparities in cost, then the revenue derived from fees was subtracted from the basic unit, and the remaining sum constituted the amount of the government operating grant per student enrolled for the ensuing financial year.

To reserve for the 14 provincial universities the maximum autonomy within the rigidities of this system, the provincial government made its operating grants with no restrictions on the manner in which they could be spent, so there remained some freedom of choice within individual institutions about priorities for expenditures. However, two general consequences of the formula system were inescapable: universities could only increase their operating revenue by expanding enrollment, and the most financially rewarding type of expansion was at the graduate level. At the University of Toronto, another implication of the formula system was its failure to support adequately the expenditures of denominational colleges. Thus any hope of revitalising the teaching functions of the colleges was stillborn. Instead, the financial future of an institution, which was dependent on government funding for 66 percent of its operating costs and 85 percent of further capital expenditures, seemed to lie with continued emphasis on graduate study. This emphasis was particularly vital for the University of Toronto because in 1967–68, the year the formula system came into effect, it had reached the limits of undergraduate enrollment on its main campus in the centre of Toronto. It could thus expect growth in undergraduate numbers only at its two suburban colleges located on the eastern and western rims of the city, where space was available for continued expansion.[4] The decision to build upward on the downtown campus, thereby accommodating vastly increased student numbers, was one which would have required abandonment of the existing collegiate structure of the university, and in any event capital grants from the provincial government for further construction were not likely to be forthcoming while so

[4] The enrollment on the downtown campus in 1967–68 was 20,709 full-time students. The total enrollment of the entire university in that year was 38,108 students.

much of the plant of the province's seven new universities remained incomplete.

The implications of this situation were clear for the future development of the University of Toronto. Thenceforth new programs could be initiated only through the termination of existing ones, and more systematic planning would be necessary if the university as a whole were to gain any noticeable advantage from its freedom to allocate its annual operating budget as it chose. Under these circumstances the university needed some decision-making body with the time and resources to devote to planning, and whose legitimacy within the university community would secure assent to academic and financial decisions which would now touch on the welfare of the whole institution. Presidential initiative again set in train the search for new legitimacy in governance. In 1965, troubled by what seemed to be a false distinction between the responsibility of the university senate for academic matters and the responsibility of the board of governors for financial matters, President Bissell urged the formation of a special President's Council which would bring together members of the board of governors, ex officio members (senior academic and administrative officers of the university), and five (eventually seven) elected members of academic staff. During the summer of 1966, in response to the creation of the President's Council, both the Association of Teaching Staff and the Students' Administrative Council presented briefs outlining the major reforms of the university's governing structure which they considered necessary. The faculty position centered on revision of the University of Toronto Act which would permit faculty representation on the board. A faculty voice on the board was felt to be essential because in exercising its discretion about the expenditure of operating revenue the board of necessity determined the percentage of annual increases which would be allocated for increases in faculty salaries. In addition, since the board represented the university to the provincial government, it was felt that a strong faculty voice there was the best method of ensuring that faculty needs were considered in the annual calculations of the university's basic operating cost per student enrolled.

The student position was the more radical one; it called for increased student representation at all levels of university government, and in particular on any university committees charged with proposals for the reform of the university's governing structure. A major theme of the student brief was its insistence upon openness in all deliberations touching the governance of the university, and indeed in the meetings of all governing bodies of departments, academic divisions, and colleges. This concern with open discussions of all matters of financial or academic policy was derived from three major interests of student radicals. First, open deliberations seemed essential to them if accurate information was to be acquired concerning the supposed Americanisation of the university. Secondly, effective participation in university committees depended upon access to all the information relevant to decision making. Thirdly, those radicals who drew, however indirectly, on the Maoist idea of cultural revolution felt that open discussions of university policy were the first steps toward making the university truly responsible to "the people." An essential difference between the University of Toronto and American university environments of equivalent size was the extent to which radical student emotions were directed to political activity through the existing structures of student government. Thus the college government and the universitywide Students' Administrative Council were centres of political power from which radical students could work to effect changes in university governance. While this structure held up, radical student opinion was less concerned with disrupting the operation of the university than with effective use of political initiatives. For this reason the entire mood and tone of the debate about governance was more reasoned and less violent than its counterpart in the United States. Canadian students were no more able than Americans to concede intellectual authority to an older generation, but the tone of the refusal was less vindictive and abusive than that heard to the south. By 1969–70, however, when the structures of student government failed to contain extreme radical opinion, the first occupation of the university administrative building occurred, to be followed the next year by systematic disruption of the meetings of the Council of the Faculty of Arts and Science.

Though many American undergraduates and a larger number of American graduate students attend the University of Toronto, student leadership remained predominantly Canadian. The deep anti-Americanism of Ontario (Tory Upper Canadian) culture kept student government in the hands of native-born activists at the undergraduate level, though American and British radicals did play their part in the less effective Graduate Students' Council. Canadian student activists came from every college community and every religious and ethnic background. The sons and daughters of establishment Anglicanism and privilege joined with angry radicals from big-city high schools and rebels against traditional Catholic piety to project their discontents against the university. Only the right-wing (though sadly misnamed) Edmund Burke society drew on a clearly definable constituency, attracting members from East European families who were emigrés from communism, and the devout children of pious families from small Ontario towns. Such a right-wing group, though vocal and often more violent than its radical opponents, did not swing enough political weight on the campus to make a significant impact in the debate on governance.

In contrast to student radicals, the Toronto faculty—radical, conservative, or conventionally liberal—were not politically organised when the issue of governance became critical in the mid-sixties. Attendance at meetings of the Association of Teaching Staff was often dishearteningly low. Strong feelings had been excited about salary negotiations and about participation in the deliberations of the board of governors, but the faculty at large was either slow to grasp the issues involved in revising the governing structures of the university or reluctant to devote valuable time and energy to what soon became endlessly repetitive discussion. When the question of governance became critical in the mid-sixties, there was general faculty hostility to the board which, questions of salary aside, had more to do with the manner of selecting board members than with a long history of radicalising faculty-board confrontations. Under the University of Toronto Act[5] members of the board were appointed by the lieutenant governor of the province upon the advice of the government in power. The board was thus widely held to be composed of a group of men from established Ontario families whose appointment was in the nature of a recognition of political services having very little to do with their concern for, or competence in, academic matters.

While this estimation of the social composition of the board was correct, it obscured the real concern of many members with the university. The very political nature of their appointments

---

[5] The University of Toronto Act of 1906 was revised in 1947. The 1969 Commission on University Government suggested the first major revision since that date.

meant that board members were little disposed to intervene in the day-to-day running of the university, and with the increasing dependence of the university upon public funds, the board's financial discretion had been more and more severely limited. The formula system ruled out the use of personal political influence in securing university grants, and the calculation of the basic unit of operating cost required expertise in the technical subject of educational finance rather than the general financial skills of the successful businessman. These hard financial facts persuaded board members that a review of their functions was necessary, though as a group they could not have been less likely to respond to ideological winds of change. A minority of faculty, concerned for the independence of the university, opposed a major review of the board's functions, rightly holding an obsolescent board to be a greater protection against outside interference than a revitalised one with increased supervisory functions. However, a majority of faculty were strong supporters of radical change in the board's composition because of the need for an effective negotiator with the provincial government, and because the board's financial jurisdiction would become critical in the near future when financial pressures could force the termination of some academic programs in the interests of introducing or expanding others. Since in the past, on salary questions, the board had shown a disposition to listen to, but not to heed, faculty representations, the majority of the Association of Teaching Staff were convinced that an effective faculty voice in these matters could only be secured by substantial representation on the board.

In this context of organised student opinion, faculty disarray, and reluctant board consent, resolutions were passed through both senate and board by August of 1968 calling for the formation of a special committee to examine the whole governing structure of the university. The committee was to be chaired by President Bissell and to be composed of two members drawn from each of four constitutencies — board, faculty, students, and administrative officers of the university. The method of selection suggested was that of nomination from the constituted authorities in each constituency. Thus the board was to name its members, the Association of Teaching Staff was to name its members (to be appointed by the president), the Students' Administrative Council would name its members, and the university administrators would be named by the president. Immediately, the legitimacy of selection through constituted authorities and the nature of the constituencies to be represented were questioned by both faculty and students in a manner which revealed profound tensions within the university. The Students' Administrative Council, more than ready to nominate its representatives on the committee, was anxious to secure a composition more amenable to student interests than the one proposed. It therefore suggested the appointment of an eight-member parity faculty-student body upon which the president and representatives of the board of governors could sit as ex-officio non-voting members. The response of the Association of Teaching Staff was more complex, and indicated a wider disaffection with constituted authority throughout the university than its former political apathy might have suggested. In a crowded meeting held in October 1968, addressed by both President Bissell and a representative of the Students' Administrative Council, the faculty rejected the proposed committee in favour of one composed of four faculty members elected by vote of the entire faculty of the university, four students, the president of the university, non-voting representatives of the board and senate, and a chairman from outside the academic community. The Association of Teaching Staff underlined its rejection of the board by making its participation in the proposed committee conditional upon the agreement of the board that it would submit the committee's report to the provincial government "without change and without delay." It further emphasised, by insisting upon a democratic election of faculty representatives to the committee, that the majority of faculty felt the existing administrative structure of the university did not represent them and did not necessarily function to express their interests.

In this context of mutual mistrust, agreement was secured from board and senate to participate in a committee composed along the lines of the faculty-student proposals. This committee, though technically a committee advisory to the president, became in popular opinion an independent commission of the university community, with eight of its nine voting members representative of students and faculty. The student election returned members from the centres of political activism in the student community, the social sciences. The four students elected were from the disciplines of history, political science, Latin American studies, and the general arts program. The democratic process operated among the faculty to select four representatives who all held senior administrative posts within the university, though their rank proved to be no guarantee of conservatism on the question of governance. Two held important posts in the college community, and two had administrative responsibilities in the faculties (medicine and engineering).

Given the presence of four senior administrators on the commission, it was natural that it should approach community building for the university through some adaptation of its existing administrative structures, rather than through any radical new concept of the boundaries of responsibility for a given curriculum or learning process, though it was in some freeing of curriculum from departmental hegemony that the interests of students and junior faculty might have coincided. Given the concern of radical students with the emotional basis of community, it was also inevitable that the commission would not give serious thought to the interdisciplinary nature of most growth areas in knowledge, and to the real need to reexamine on intellectual grounds the accepted departmental units of academic responsibility within the faculties and schools of the university. The central problem to which the commission addressed itself during its nine months of discussions was, therefore, the precise manner in which existing structures could be modified to produce the degree of participation in shaping the learning process that radical students felt to be the basis for a community of feeling between students, faculty, and non-academic members of the university. It might have been possible to secure some common ground between faculty and students concerning a restructuring of the university upon grounds which faculty could accept as meaningful to them as scholars, or on grounds which faculty could see as strengthening their power to influence a university more and more subject to government financial control. But there was little to appeal to them in the recommendations of a commission which merely undertook to give students and faculty equal positions in decision making about academic and financial matters within the existing pattern of departments, faculties, and colleges, while offering the timeworn device of strengthened executive power to resolve all cases of potential conflict between faculty and students. Confronted with a version of reform which strengthened deans, chairmen, and other executive officers, junior faculty, already restive at the degree of executive control over their careers, united with senior faculty motivated by their desire to preserve professional prerogatives in near-united opposition to the implementation of the recommendations.

The assumption of four senior administrators, the executive head of the university, and four students not yet acquainted with the realities of academic politics that all the major executive offices in the university could be held by men who had the confidence of both their faculty and students was touching and, no doubt, predictable. More startling was the unanimous endorsement by the commission of the principle of parity faculty-student representation on all governing bodies of the university. Since the final deliberations of the commission were *in camera,* the reasons for this unanimity can only be a matter of conjecture, but several specifically Canadian factors probably weighed heavily in favour of the students' arguments for parity. In the University of Toronto context college administrators (two faculty representatives held senior college posts) are accustomed to a high degree of student participation in governance, and therefore less disposed to question the extension of parity to academic matters. For other senior administrators interested in academic reform, responsible student representatives could be seen as potential allies against a recalcitrant and conservative faculty. There was above all the large question of ensuring continued Canadian control of an institution recruited extensively outside Canada in the previous decade. Faculty representatives on the commission who were unwilling to concede to nativism in faculty recruitment could safely accede to it in student participation in governance, for the students spoke with the authentic voice of a resurgent Canadian populism.

RESPONSES TO THE RECOMMENDATIONS Whatever the motives of faculty representatives on the commission a substantial majority of the faculty proceeded to repudiate them and to work for the political organisation of the faculty to oppose the implementation of the commission's recommendations after their publication in October 1969. Even the proposal to abolish the board of governors and substitute for it a unicameral Governing Council with sole authority to reach final decisions on all academic and financial matters incurred faculty opposition. The new council was to be composed of equal numbers of faculty, students, and representatives of the public together with six ex officio executive officers of the university. Whereas faculty had been used to controlling all decisions on academic matters through the senate, they would, in the commission's proposed council, have only a minority voice. This, again, was a structural change which brought the great majority of faculty into vociferous opposition. Two groups alone appeared ready to welcome such innovations: faculty whose major responsibilities were within the colleges and a sprinkling of radicals who expected an ideal community to emerge from the sharing of all authority with students on equal terms.

However predictable was the majority faculty response to change of the kind envisaged by the Commission on University Government, the nine months of its deliberations had developed expectations of a utopian kind among students, and not merely among those of a radical bent. The idea of a community held together through legitimate authority had strong roots in Ontario's Tory tradition, and it therefore appealed to students of all ranges of political opinion. The proposals for parity between faculty and students on all university deliberative bodies became the symbol for the utopian belief that a new and emotionally satisfying educational experience could be contrived within a few months by a simple political device. Though there were some *enragé* radicals bent on using the situation to humiliate faculty, to deride authority, or to further special ideological ends, the very manner in which the commission had been formed, the length of its deliberations, and the unanimity of its recommendations suggested that the new order might come without too much turmoil.

The 1960s therefore drew to a close at Toronto in a situation which boded ill for the 1970s. A politicised faculty was virtually united in opposition to a student body for which parity with faculty in university government had become the focus of utopian longing for community. This preoccupation with parity brought with it a new development in student politics; for the first time, the formal structure of student government appeared inadequate to express radical student aspirations on the campus. Nor was there a possibility of presidential initiative in reconciling the opposing blocs of faculty and student opinion. In endorsing the recommendations of the Commission on University Government, the president had taken from genuine conviction a position from which there could be no retreat. There were signs also, as the academic year 1969–70 drew to a close, that the concern of the students for community might take new and potentially disruptive forms. Early in the spring term the first occupation of the administration building occurred. The threatened closing of a volunteer day-care centre organised by supporters of the women's liberation movement in a building which was university property sparked the sit-in led by a woman faculty member (one of the few faculty to participate in the occupation). The sit-in took place in a senate chamber graced by the slogan "Babies of the world unite! You have nothing to lose but your sitters." Beneath the banner a remarkably orderly crowd discussed with passionate concern the problem of reorganising society to ensure social justice for the "under two's." The particular dispute was resolved by the president's decision that the university should accept financial responsibility for the day-care centre for the forthcoming year. However, the wide support of the sit-in by students who had no formal connection with the women's liberation movement suggested that restructuring the community was a major student concern.

There was ample evidence just one block to the north of the university of the drive to create a utopian educational community. This was Rochdale College, an impressive but somewhat tattered monument to the ideal of cooperative community building as expressed in the 1960s. Rochdale was a cooperative residence completely separate from the University of Toronto, opened in 1968 by students and faculty inspired by utopian ideas about building a truly "liberating" educational community and able to secure government support for the construction of their building. Rochdale was to be the pioneer community from which the new lifestyle would emerge to redeem the "straight" university just down the road. By 1970 it was facing bankruptcy, unable to meet the interest on the loans which had financed its construction. In disciplinary terms it had been a blessing in disguise for the University of Toronto, because Rochdale, rather than the university campus, had been the centre for experimenting with lifestyles likely to outrage the mores of respectable Toronto or to bring penalties from the law. By 1970, however, it was clear that the Rochdale venture was not going to provide the model for building a new community of scholars and that the cooperative educational efforts of its members had not resulted in a learning experience any more "relevant" or dynamic than that offered a block to the south in the conventional university. Thus as the 1960s drew to a close, the energies of seekers after community, student and faculty alike, formerly channeled into the Rochdale endeavour, were once more concentrated on restructuring the University of Toronto. By 1970 this was an institution which had lost much of its flexibility during the acrimonious debate over the report of the Commission on University Government, while financial and administrative pressures made it imperative to move toward some new governing structure.

During 1970–71 the discussion on governance was shaped by the need to move the debate from the university community to the less sheltered setting of the Provincial Legislature, geographically located within a stone's throw of the university but in all other respects a world away. The basis for a single university recommendation on the form of government to be created by new legislation was secured by a University-Wide Committee composed of some 150 members which met in three-day sessions as the year 1969–70 drew to a close. In accordance with student desires for a more inclusive university community the membership of this committee was drawn from five constituencies: elected representatives of faculty, academic administrators, students, non-academic staff, and appointed representatives of the alumni. By a series of compromises this body achieved a set of recommendations which brought the idea of an egalitarian campus community into uneasy harmony with the professional concerns of the faculty. The reluctant consensus of the committee was embodied in the recommendation that the new governing structure of the university should be a unicameral body carrying out the functions of both board of governors and senate. Six different constituencies were to be represented in the 72-member Governing Council together with the president of the university and the chancellor, who were to hold their places ex officio. Elected faculty representatives were to hold 21 places on the council, elected student representatives 14, elected representatives of non-academic staff 6, and alumni representatives 10. The community at large was to be represented by 14 members appointed by the lieutenant governor on the advice of the provincial government, and three additional appointees were to be nominated by the president from among his senior administrative officers. The University-Wide Committee brought its deliberations to a close by appointing a subcommittee empowered to "assist" the provincial government in writing a draft of a new University of Toronto bill to be enacted as soon as possible. In forming this subcommittee, the University-Wide Committee revealed its mistaken assumption that its recommendations would determine the form of new legislation which the government might introduce. The same sense of termination of the discussion on governance was conveyed when President Bissell announced his decision to retire at the close of the 1970–71 academic year so that the introduction of a new governing structure could be accompanied by the inauguration of a new university administration.

The assumption that the debate was concluded, however, overlooked the political factors which were to come into play when the
question of the form of the new governing structure was moved
from the university to the Provincial Legislature. Immediately
the transfer occurred, it became clear that arguments about the
legitimate basis of community had more weight with Ontario's
elected representatives than those concerning the fostering of
intellectual excellence. Two ˙specific political considerations were
at least as compelling in influencing the form of the bill as the
views already expressed by the university community. The political
factor which was of the first importance was that the government
ensure that a university which derived 80 percent of its revenues
from the public purse should be seen to be subject to adequate
public control in expending those funds. Hence, while accepting
unicameralism as the wish of the university community, the
government of Ontario insisted that 50 percent of the members
of this single governing body be representatives of the lay community appointed on the advice of the government. A second
consideration of a more general kind was the particular political
climate of Canada in 1971. This was one in which it was in the
interests of all parties to appear in tune with the aspirations of
youth and as spokesmen for systems of government instantly
responsive to the wishes of the people. To question the promise
of youth was to question Canada's future (a dangerous occupation
for a politician), and to appear in favour of entrenching privilege
or an undemocratic authority was to move counter to the current
of the times. Worse still was to defend the status quo in Canadian
universities, which had been the subject of attack throughout the
decade as institutions which had failed in the task of defending
Canada's beleaguered cultural heritage. In national politics, Prime
Minister Trudeau had carried his Liberal party to political victory
by cultivating the public image of the trendy swinger, and in 1971
no Canadian politician worth his salt could afford to ignore the
success of this strategy. In Ontario the government-sponsored
University of Toronto bill was introduced during a legislative
session in which a bill to lower the voting age to 18 was to receive
the support of all parties. This meant that debate concerning the
representation to be accorded to faculty and students on the Governing Council of the University of Toronto was conducted in a
political atmosphere of extreme solicitude for youthful opinion.
In the committee of the Legislature which examined the bill, re-

newed student requests for parity with the faculty on the Governing Council encountered a receptive hearing while faculty submissions urging a preponderant faculty voice on the council were listened to in pained disbelief.

Behind the question of lay representation and behind the need to court youthful voters there was a third issue politically more explosive though more amorphous and difficult to debate. This was the issue of Americanisation, which arouses deep feelings at all levels of Canadian society. In the committee the faculty were therefore seen as non-Canadian while the students were welcomed as genuine exponents of a populist voice of the people. Despite the receptive hearing accorded to students by representatives of all parties during the legislative hearings, the Minister of the newly created Department of University Affairs used the government's majority in the Legislature to secure legislation which kept intact the proportions of faculty and student representation recommended by the University-Wide Committee, explaining that the government did not wish to legislate for the university a degree of student participation in governance which faculty were clearly not ready to accept. However, the provisions regulating membership on public bodies in Ontario made it possible for the government to write into its legislation the provision that all members of the Governing Council of the university must be Canadian citizens, and to specify that no non-Canadian could hold the office of president.

In its final form the bill was designed to make both academic and financial policies of the university constantly subject to review and scrutiny by representatives of the public of the province of Ontario. The bill provided for a Governing Council of 50 members: 16 appointed representatives of the public, 12 elected representatives of the faculty, 8 elected student representatives, 2 elected representatives of the administrative staff, 8 elected representatives of the alumni, the president and the chancellor holding office ex officio, and 2 presidential appointees from among the senior administrative officers of the university. Thus for the first time in the university's history, decisions on academic matters were no longer the exclusive prerogative of the faculty, while it remained open to question whether the quality of community life within the university would be enhanced under a governing structure so directly susceptible to external pressure.

Whatever the outcome of the new governing structure, which was to be subject to review within two years from its introduction, it was unquestionable that the university had been transformed within the space of a decade. Its reliance upon an Oxbridge past had vanished along with any hint of elitism in curriculum. The tradition of student government had flourished during the decade, and student concern with the preservation of a distinctly Canadian culture had culminated in bringing about student participation in the final decision-making bodies of the university. The major questions of academic and financial policy which had troubled the university during the 1960s remained unresolved, and only the future could reveal whether the somewhat drastic surgery performed on the university's body politic would strengthen or weaken it in coming to terms with them. What time could not reveal was whether the energies exhausted in four years of repetitive debate on questions of governance and faculty-student parity could have been more creatively committed by both students and faculty to innovation in teaching and research.

17. The Wesleyan Story: The Importance of Moral Capital

by Burton R. Clark

The Wesleyan University of 1972 is a small place of complex character. A settled institution of ivy heritage and New England tradition, it changed sufficiently in the years after World War II that it is now widely considered progressive as well as stable, of first-rank academic quality as well as of solid virtue. Quiet self-alteration has made the college seem unproblematic throughout nearly all the recent years, not exciting but noteworthy as a model of how to adapt gently in an evermore turbulent environment.

In 1969, the college became front-page news as a small campus in serious trouble, with a stream of articles and accounts telling of militant black students clashing with whites, and how the campus was thrown into turmoil by demands, sit-ins, fights, and fires. Whispers could be heard in college administrators' circles about "the Wesleyan problem." Had the college gone too far too fast in admitting blacks? Had it been too permissive in facing strident student demands? Had Wesleyan stumbled into crisis? Were there any lessons to be learned from its experience?

In order to interpret specific events and changes, we must, even in a brief essay, attend seriously to the historical development and the resulting identity of the college. Recent happenings can then be seen in context, assigned meaning—as they are by the knowledgeable actors in the situation—in relation to the flow and style of the institution. The context of events at Wesleyan is one where the advantages of substantial conventional capital, in the form of high income and competent staff, have been joined by the advantages of moral capital, an accumulated strong self-belief formed around a legacy of moral understanding. To trace the development of these dominant features, we begin with a glance at Wesleyan's earlier history and then portray the critical change in the character of the institution in the last quarter century.

In the distant retrospect of a later century, there was little that was unusual about Wesleyan University in its early years, for foremost were the practices and rhetoric of the search for survival so common among the private small colleges of the United States. Begun in 1831 by a group of Methodist clergymen full of determination but lacking in money, the college survived repeated financial and administrative crises while struggling to find an identity that would offer some security. Forced to muddle through for decades, the college stubbornly refused to die. Time and again at Wesleyan, as during the depression of the 1870s (Peterson, 1964, pp. 58–59), a small number of committed faculty, trustees, and churchmen rooted themselves in a logic of sentiments, keeping open an organization that any economic calculus would have sent to the grave. Their style involved a rhetoric of sacrifice: "the work of the college has been confined by the narrowness of its means . . ."; we have been "neglected and forgotten by the church . . ."; "[the] heroic professors [have] submitted to personal sacrifices . . ."; and "among the faithful and self-sacrificing friends of this institution, when it was poor and hungry and weak, must be recorded the honorable names of . . ." (*Semi-Centennial . . . ,* 1881, pp. 14, 17, 19). The early Wesleyan style also involved the common religious college dilemma of autonomy and dependence, in relation to the formal church of the parent denomination. At times the college drifted away from the church, as administrators sought self-determination, the faculty greater freedom in teaching, or the students more fun and games. At other times the college moved toward the church, to reassert religious values, obtain more money, or strengthen the traditional constituency.

In the early Wesleyan, the elders were also fond of preaching to the young, from the set lectures of the fixed curriculum to the discourse to the graduating class on *Early Piety: The Basis of Elevated Character* (Olin, 1851). The intent to elevate character within a closely guarded community generated a counterforce that Wesleyan shared with other colleges: the students revolted from time to time. Under a severely paternalistic president known for his "correct views," who was bound "to do my duty" (Peterson, 1964, p. 115), Wesleyan in the 1880s was a center of smoldering resentment that erupted finally, in 1887, when a day set aside for student hell-raising got out of hand and events escalated into a mass egging of the president (ibid., p. 117).

Wesleyan also underwent the general evolution of the time. By the turn of the century, one could speak of Wesleyan and the other surviving New England colleges—after the changes of the 1870s, 1880s, and 1890s—as having modified greatly their control and atmosphere. Wesleyan's faculty had moved toward the concept of academic freedom made popular in the new universities of the American scene. The students had moved toward freedom in the classroom under the elective system and toward more control of their lives outside the classroom in the subculture of sports and fraternities. All the basic features of the New England college were there, with an occasional idiosyncracy such as the move into coeducation in 1872, a deviation corrected when the college returned in 1912 to the maleness of Amherst, Williams, and Bowdoin.

And so it went in the early decades of the twentieth century. The college was a solid WASP institution which occupied a respectable place in the little-Ivy triad along with Amherst and Williams. Moderation and tradition were the names of the place. The religious commitment eased toward a respectable nonsectarianism. Standards were stiffened gradually but never too severely. Although a university in name, the institution remained a liberal arts college that concentrated on undergraduate education. The student body grew from about 300 in 1910 to 700 in 1940. Student life centered in residential fraternities. Either boy met girl at the weekend mixer for which the girls were imported from women's colleges, or the men traveled to where the girls were. There were no deep financial crises, no faculty upheavals, no abrupt transformations, no major unique efforts.

Clearly, just before World War II Wesleyan was a college with a defined social role that had evolved slowly over decades, with no distinctive thrust. Its evolved role, however, was no mean asset. Interpreted in the light of later development, the college had established a base camp solid in the aura of tradition and the loyalty of established alumni. The tradition included moral uplift in the character of the young, a generalized theme upon which a man with a mission, one incorporating old-fashioned virtues, could resonate a special effort to climb higher in both quality and morality. After the war came the shift to mission, with purpose first sharpened and more strongly defined from within, then embodied in new practices and structures, and finally felt as a spirit on the campus.

THE AIMS AND MEANS OF CHANGE Major change in the college was engineered during a presidency that spanned nearly a quarter of a century, from 1943 to 1966—

that of Victor Butterfield. Butterfield had vision and the capacity to persist in the hard work of implementing it. He also happened upon several conditions that greatly facilitated the work of institutional change.

Butterfield based himself in tradition by stressing that the college would remain small, independent, and nonsectarian. On that foundation, he mounted an effort to seek "distinction for quality" and suggested that there be no compromise with this principle (Butterfield, 1955, p. 1). At the same time, however, Butterfield wanted an institution of great moral concern, one rooted deeply in a Christian humanism. A liberal college should have "faith," he persistently maintained, faith based on intellectual understanding and expressed, not through exhortation, evangelical appeal, or compulsion, but rather through the personal example of men of "full and coherent conviction . . . willing to share their insights and opinions" or men who, feeling that their most cherished values are highly personal and private, will simply "let their light so shine" (ibid, p. 11). A sufficient number of such people would mean a "working spirit" of the whole that would be "by all odds the most important method of keeping the Christian tradition alive and vital and of giving it concrete and perpetually renewed meaning" (ibid, p. 12). Butterfield's aims, then, were a combination of high academic quality and modernized Christian tradition.

Among the means of achieving these aims, the most important in Butterfield's view was the recruitment and retention of appropriate faculty. The faculty should be a heady mixture of academic talent and moral concern, characteristics that seemed increasingly antithetical within academic circles. The ideal faculty member would be both a ranking scholar and a saint among men. Fully aware that faculty selection was the main tool of institutional change, Butterfield kept himself deeply involved in recruitment. Right up to near the end of his term, long past the time when a man of lesser commitment would have retired to quieter activity in his office, Butterfield was still on the road looking for faculty or interviewing candidates on their visits to the departments and divisions of the colleges. His efforts became legendary, told in stories of how he wined and dined and talked the evening through with a scholar, encountered by design or chance anywhere in his travels, whose character and intellect seemed to him appropriate for the mission of the college.

Butterfield was fortunate, particularly in his early years in office, that many faculty openings occurred through retirement, wartime turnover, and institutional expansion. The men he recruited were often so impressive that they could not all be retained against the lure of an important university professorship or an inviting career in academic administration. A young Nathan Pusey was already on the scene in classics and was put to work shaping a freshman humanities program. David C. McClelland was brought into the psychology department in 1945, and the following year saw the arrival of Norman O. Brown in classics, Carl E. Schorske in history, and Steven K. Bailey in government—the latter to join two nationally known political scientists, Sigmund Neumann and E. E. Schattschneider, already on the faculty. Such appointments were evidence enough that Butterfield had a sharp eye for academic talent, men of high intellect and moral concern who could share in some degree his vision of what Wesleyan could become. The degree to which the faculty quickly became a Butterfield selected group, quantitatively, was also impressive. One observer has calculated that "by the postwar period [about 1950] he had brought in fifty-four [72 percent] of the seventy-five members of the faculty" (Hefferlin, 1969, p. 48). In the later years of his term, the faculty was almost entirely composed of men added during his presidency.

The considerable enlargement of the faculty was made possible by a vast increase in financial resources. Here the story approaches the unbelievable, as several trustees responsible for investment policy struck gold several times over. The purchase of an educational publishing firm which produced the *Weekly Reader,* read by millions of schoolchildren, proved so enormously profitable that good taste, invading competition, and the concern of the Internal Revenue Service over the nonprofit status of the college dictated a move to other investments. So the trustees sold the firm at great profit to Xerox Corporation, accepting in exchange Xerox stock that promptly took off on a success story of its own. The result of this and a few other bonanzas was that Wesleyan became, on a per capita basis, the richest college in the land. In 1962, its endowment was about $60 million, compared with about $30 million at Swarthmore—a well-financed college—and $5.5 million at poverty-stricken Reed. By 1966, its endowment had climbed to over $150 million, a truly fantastic sum for a small college. The institution had little difficulty in paying competitive salaries and financing expensive experiments as well as general expansion. It can even be said that for a few years the college had too much money.

The money and the faculty gave Butterfield and his senior colleagues the means of supporting and staffing a number of new programs and special units, among them a broad humanities course required of all freshman, a Public Affairs Center (1955) incorporating within it the social science departments, and a Center for Advanced Studies (1959) that appointed visiting scholars and men of affairs (Herbert Read, C. P. Snow, Daniel Patrick Moynihan, Richard Goodwin) and later became a Center for the Humanities. Departments grew in size and competence; some could even effectively staff graduate programs through the Ph.D. The campus experimented with subcolleges; in 1960 it had one in letters, one in social studies, and one in quantitative studies.

As at other colleges, the traditions of student life were stubborn and difficult to overcome. As late as 1955, the faculty felt that the fraternity system was "the most important single non-curricular force on the campus in the formation and development of student values" and were concerned that the fraternities remained anti-intellectual (*Report of the Educational Policy Committee. . . ,* 1955, pp. 61–62). But slowly student life swung toward the academic and the intellectual, even in the late 1960s toward the radical and the nonconforming. Membership in fraternities declined from about 85 percent of the student body in 1955 to about 35 percent in 1970. With students perceiving the fraternities as "an archaic, dying and confining institution" and the college offering attractive alternative housing, the number of surviving frats declined from 11 to 7 between 1968 and 1970 (Surgeon, 1970, p. 74). The students were coming predominantly (70 percent) from public high schools, and as the college became known as a liberal institution, even the students drawn from prep schools were more likely to be liberal or radical than conservative. In a survey of the class of 1972, only one in five would define himself politically as a conservative, while three in five held the campus middle ground as liberal, and one in five saw himself as radical (ibid., pp. 4–6, 43–45).

If the beginning of the Butterfield era was a move from passive role to active mission, the middle years were a time of embodiment of mission in structure, practice, and belief. There had been a particular leader, a special effort, a set of new practices, and, finally, what seemed to be a unified institutional character in which men believed deeply. There was a modest organizational saga, a story of special accomplishment that was rooted in historical fact but also romanticized into a sentimental belief.[1] There was a rhetoric of normative concern that mixed with a rhetoric of innovation. There was special meaning given to such terms as "liberal arts university" and "the little university" and a belief that Wesleyan, a small college, would experimentally and innovatively grow toward the commitments of a first-rate university but always with small scale, the liberal arts, and moral concern as primary values. Already in the early 1960s, one of the best historians of American higher education was describing Wesleyan as "moving toward a new integration of collegiate and university purpose" (Rudolph, 1962, p. 492).

The distinctive air of deep normative concern coupled with an attitude of innovation resonated well with the perspective of the Danforth Foundation, where the same sentiment of needed reform in American education, based on a Christian humanism, had taken philanthropic roots. Butterfield became a key figure in Danforth affairs; Kenneth Underwood, whom Butterfield brought in as professor of social ethics and public affairs and later made head of the Center for Public Affairs, was for years closely connected with the Danforth group; and others on campus have been participants in Danforth seminars or have received Danforth awards for excellence in teaching. The convergence of values here between a college and a value-focused foundation was as natural as it was considerable. In the language of academic clichés, Danforthites set the moral tone of Wesleyan and were "swinging religionists" committed to reform and willing to work in reform efforts with completely secular men. Perhaps the most visible agent of this spirit in the late 1960s was John Maguire in religion, a man of charismatic tendency who left in 1970, taking a small cadre of faculty and recent graduates with him, to head up the troubled, experimental Old Westbury (see essay by John Dunn in this volume).

In the 1960s, Wesleyan contained a definite strain between well-rounded amateurism and professional competence, a tension that can be observed everywhere among the liberal arts colleges that have continued to take seriously the traditional view of liberal education as general and interdisciplinary in nature while at the same time attempting to meet the interests of faculty and students

[1] On the buildup of sagas in college, see Burton R. Clark, *The Distinctive College: Antioch, Reed and Swarthmore* (1970).

in competence in the specialized disciplines. Wesleyan's strong embodiment of a generalized moral concern, on the traditional side, and its upgrading to university-level scholarship, on the side of modern specialization, has ensured that the tension would be real. The high-caliber scholars whom Butterfield and his associates brought to the campus were not all perfectly balanced on the twin commitments of scholarship and morality. Predictably, prestigious faculty members would more often tilt toward the values of scholarship than toward those of general education and service to one's fellow man, and these sharp, high-priced people pressed to bring in men of their own type in making junior appointments from top graduate schools. Such men rejected the strand of Butterfield's thought that equated liberal arts with nonspecialization and became impatient with both the latter-day Christian humanists and the traditional "Mr. Chips type" in the faculty who, full of warm sentiment about "little Wesleyan," held to undergraduate liberal education to the detriment of scholarly competence. The specialist-scholars, pushing beyond Butterfield's dream, generated a move in the 1960s to evolve from "the Academy to the University" ("The New University," 1961).

All was not sweetness and light, of course, since institutional tension, in practice, spells prolonged argument and even steady anger over the other man's foolish views. The spending of all that money in new centers and various experimental structures caused some friction and had some fracturing effect on unity. Then, too, the president had almost inevitably worn himself out, and in his last years in office others had to steady the college. Some toll was there, paid in the energies of men and in the coherence and dynamism of the institution.

But even within the ranks of the specialists, who at many universities are the nonloyal cosmopolitans ready to exit for the better offer, there were men devoted to the welfare of others and, convinced that Wesleyan had great if not unmatched virtues, were completely committed to the institution; for example, Robert A. Rosenbaum, who had served for years in top administrative positions, Earl D. Hanson in biology, and William J. Barber in economics. Compared with other colleges and universities, many men were paid well in the coin of belief and morality as well as in that of salary and academic status. It was in this relatively healthy condition that the college moved into the special days of the late 1960s.

In 1965, Wesleyan committed itself to admitting black students. In 1965–66, the admissions procedure brought in a small number of blacks, a group that suffered high attrition in the freshman year. An exceedingly vigorous effort under Jack Hoy, the director of admissions, brought a large jump during the next several years, to the point where, in 1969–70, blacks and Puerto Ricans numbered about 20 percent of the freshman class and 12 percent of the total student body of 1,400. This effort, in a small private college, was considerably in excess of what was occurring at the time in even many urban public colleges and universities, let alone in private institutions. For example, the Wesleyan enrollment of blacks alone in 1969–70 was about 10 percent, compared to 5 percent or less at Berkeley and Buffalo as well as at Columbia, Harvard, and Yale. Clearly, some internal adjustments would be necessary, perhaps some special tutoring for those blacks who were underschooled, but in the beginning there was little to draw upon by way of relevant experience at other colleges and hence adjustments had to be worked out as emerging problems revealed the failures of anticipation. At the same time, black students throughout the country were moving to militancy, with black separatism much on their minds.

In 1968–69, Wesleyan broke out with a rash of trouble. Black students were hearing racist slurs that they were no longer willing to dismiss as the highjinks of upper-class party boys in a few fraternities or as the hopeless stupidities of ultraconservatives in the town. Some were frustrated and angered by the problems set by inadequate scholastic preparation and by the misunderstandings generated by the linguistic and other cultural differences that separate lower-class blacks from upper-middle-class whites. The black students began, with an outspoken statement in the fall term, to react collectively to personal and institutional "insensitivities," the latter including the absence of adult blacks on campus. A few months later, they moved to a specific demand that classes be cancelled for a day of education on Malcolm X and Martin Luther King; and, when the faculty voted a refusal, the black students orderly occupied for one day the main classroom building. The students proceeded during the spring term with more specific demands in which the central issue was the establishment of an Afro-American Institute that would help to bring black visitors to campus and to infuse black faculty into the normal departments. In the fall of the following year (1969–70), the troubles escalated in the form of specific and dramatic acts of violence and illegal activity: after a fight, the room of a white student was set on fire; shots were fired at a black administrator; many burglaries were occurring in the dormitories, and several blacks were arrested for armed robbery in the town. At one point, on the occasion of a homecoming weekend, the administration obtained an injunction against disruption by the blacks, a move that helped the college get peacefully through the weekend but, by stirring further resentment, helped cause continuing problems. The college now had significantly gotten the attention of the mass media and had gained national reputation as a college in trouble, signified notably by a long article in the Sunday magazine section of the *New York Times,* entitled "The Two Nations at Wesleyan University" (Margolis, 1970). The *Times* article, sure to excite alumni, donors, and parents of current and prospective students, spoke of white anger and fears, of increasing suspicion on both sides, and concluded on the note that "white students and black students do not even talk to each other" (ibid., p. 64). When white and black students together wrote a letter objecting to the article, the *Times* reporter replied that they were wrong and that "the racial polarization at Wesleyan is genuine and runs very deep" (*New York Times Magazine,* 1970).

During the same period, white radicalism had also heated up, centered in 1968–69 on student demands that military recruiters be barred from campus. Out of the growing concern about the Vietnam war, some white students developed a confrontation with a Navy recruiter. A joint faculty-student committee was set to work on the issue and came up with a quick report, complete with majority and minority recommendations. The faculty thereupon voted that Wesleyan should not bar any recruiters from campus; the students muddied the waters with a vote, on three alternatives, that was subject to varying interpretation. The faculty position prevailed, but the issue lingered.

Then, in the spring of 1969–70, the concerns of white students and black students came together in the three issues of Cambodia, Kent State, and the New Haven trial of Bobby Seale and other Black Panthers, and the campus took part in the strike action of students that stretched from coast to coast. In the fall of 1970–71, the campus returned to a peaceful state, punctured once by an isolated bombing of a campus building, and it remained that way throughout the academic year.

Before and during the months of trouble, the campus had been working on various adjustments. Under sponsorship of the blacks, the college instituted a black repertory theater and a black arts festival as well as two courses in black history and culture. In the course of several years, more than 20 blacks were appointed to the faculty and a black associate provost was added to the administration. In response to the demands of early 1969, an Afro-American Institute was established and a historic John Wesley House was converted into a Malcolm X House. The college for several summers sent some blacks to compensatory education programs at other colleges, and when this effort seemed not to work, the campus turned to voluntary tutorials staffed by upperclassmen and teachers for anyone requesting help. Course work could be spread out over five years. Perhaps most important was that in such a small college black students came to know with whom they could and could not work, person by person in the faculty, administration, and student body. As initial institutional naiveté was replaced by the hard realities of implementing a change, specific programs and specific individuals broke through what the blacks had seen as a solid structure of institutional racism. One could even make a case, as it has been made at the college, that the basic changes in structure and relationship were well under way by 1969–70, when, in several months of bad luck, a number of isolated incidents involving a few individuals snowballed into heightened group tension.

The trouble and strain were certainly enough to make the most dedicated supporters of the heavy admission of minorities doubt at times that the college had moved wisely in this effort. The resisters had much to point to in complaining that academic standards were eroding at a pace commensurate with the decline in law and order and sanctioned their general complaint with specific labeling of some departments as "gut departments for blacks." But the supporters would not retreat. Here interpersonal ties and regard for the institution had a part. Men of quite different persuasion on the specific issue were not only equally committed to the general institutional welfare but also equally committed to be fair to one another and to the individual student. There were outstanding examples of personal caring, as when a faculty member quietly took out a mortgage on his house to bail out of jail a student whose values were completely antithetical to his own. The college held its basic unity and continued the effort to work out the necessary new adjustment.

Meeting the demands of blacks and coping with the wishes of

white radicals were not the only items on the institutional agenda in the late 1960s. There was also a major self-study centered on other issues and some administrative reorganization. Upon Butterfield's retirement, Edwin D. Etherington was lured from the presidency of the New York Stock Exchange to become head of the college, and he immediately initiated a policy study. The study committee took up women's education and recommended the addition of undergraduate women. It also took up graduate education and the roles of the Public Affairs Center and the Center for Advanced Studies and recommended that the college proceed carefully into additional graduate programs, that the Center for Public Affairs be rejuvenated as a center for multidisciplinary work in the social sciences, and that the Center for Advanced Studies be replaced by a Center for the Humanities. The advanced learning programs, even when leading to the Ph.D., were to be interdisciplinary as much as possible, and the two interdisciplinary centers were to revolve around faculty and students rather than visiting fellows. The study group also examined the college's efforts in teacher education and recommended changes oriented to urban schools and community colleges.

Efforts to implement these recommendations began in 1968–69. On undergraduate education for women, the college accepted transfer students in 1968–69 and in 1969–70 and began admitting women as freshmen in 1970–71, toward the goal of having, by 1974, 700 women in a student body of 1,700. A woman was appointed as an associate provost. In advanced training, history and psychology became defined as the departments headed next for Ph.D. programs, beyond the five already there (biology, chemistry, mathematics, physics, and world music), and the new Humanities Center came into being. Teacher education was reconstituted as proposed.

Under Etherington, the college made several changes in structure and procedure designed to improve communication and make administration more effective at three levels. A student-faculty senate was created with legislative and advisory powers. The central administration was reshaped to give the president more time for long-run planning, changing the direct involvement of his office in many campus affairs that had been a hallmark of Butterfield's personal style. At the level of the board of trustees, the college added faculty members and students to trustee committees, and blacks, women, and younger alumni to the board itself. "Participatory governance" was clearly making some headway at Wesleyan.

In February of 1970, Etherington resigned to run for political office. The chancellor, Robert Rosenbaum, filled in as acting president for a few months, and then Colin Campbell, who had come to the college with Etherington as executive vice-president, was selected as the next president. Young and vigorous, tested on the firing line during the days and nights of tension, Campbell has won widespread respect and support on the campus.

As Campbell began his presidency in 1970–71, the view was growing that Wesleyan was overextended. The effort to implement the commitment to the education of blacks, with its attendant strains, together with the various other efforts reviewed above finally seemed too much at one time, especially as the financial problems of colleges hit even Wesleyan. The strains of 1968–1970 thus led the college toward a hard look at priorities. Out of that examination, by the sping of 1971, there was forthcoming an unambiguous reassertion of the primacy of undergraduate liberal education. In the language of the new president: "we have faced the obligation to make hard choices in order to preserve our future"; "in reexamining the purposes for which Wesleyan stands, we have seen with renewed clarity the centrality of our commitment to excellence in undergraduate education"; "we must hone and harden our innovations to survive in a world of realities, a world of limited resources which we, no less than others, ourselves inhabit"; "survival at Wesleyan must continue to mean survival to innovate and excel" (*Remarks. . . ,* 1971). The president went on to openly rank programs according to their importance to the undergraduate curriculum, giving first priority to core under-graduate programs and financial aid for undergraduates, the latter notably to support substantial numbers of minority-group students. He assigned second rank to the existing advanced work in some departments and the interdisciplinary Humanities Center; and he offered lowest priority to certain activities which "we do not view as central or significantly in support of undergraduate education here," e.g., the Wesleyan Press and the Master of Arts in Teaching program (ibid., pp. 5–6). The press was put under review, the M.A.T. program began a phasing out. A number of major decisions were yet on the agenda, the president added, but he concluded that "in the end the University will be leaner, stronger, healthier and better focused on its primary objectives as the result of today's challenges" (ibid., p. 6).

THE IMPOR-
TANCE OF
MORAL
CAPITAL
Wesleyan is witness to the value of moral capital in a college. It underwent considerable stress in its days of trouble, paying a fair price for its rapid affirmative action in admitting blacks and the pulling and hauling that followed as one unforeseen change after another in internal structure and procedure was debated and then effected. The price paid would have been much higher, however, if the context had been one, observable elsewhere, in which inter-personal trust and institutional belief were in short supply. Under those conditions, campus conflict can all too readily exhaust the meager fund of trust and overwhelm frail belief in the goodness of the place. The result is a plunge below the threshold of goodwill and affirmative belief, setting in motion the vicious circle of suspiciousness and recrimination that polarizes a campus. In contrast, Wesleyan's character offered reserves that could be spent in a crisis to recover from deep stress before the dynamics of the vicious circle set in. As is evident elsewhere, a college which strongly believes in itself can withstand stresses, shocks, and even shortages of resources and carry on so effectively that it is widely heralded as a success.[2] Wesleyan is a notable instance of self-belief within which the personal morality of many on campus interlocks with an institutional morality. In the 1968–1970 crisis the college had to draw critically on its moral accounts rather than its budgetary ones. Since those funds were considerable, the odds on recovery from the injuries of stress were high. Hence many at the college could not only believe in 1971 that the action on minorities was morally right and the troubles worth it but also feel that the institution was in good health and not vulnerable to repeated strain.

The effects of institutional crisis, then, are determined considerably by the institution's character as it enters into a period of stress. Perhaps what is true for individuals is true for institutions: a crisis, even severe illness, is not always a bad thing. The outcome depends upon the reserves of character and the predispositions that determine the capacity to cope. In the character and the coping of the institution we will find structure and procedure

[2] See the sections on Antioch and Reed in Burton R. Clark, op. cit. (1970) and the account of recent intense conflict at Antioch by Gerald Grant in this volume.

playing a part. But organizations of higher education are much dependent on normative rather than utilitarian or coercive bonds and we must also look to the role of ideas and values. The Wesleyan experience suggests the fascinating possibility that belief and concern remain the core of the healthy institution of higher learning.

References

Butterfield, Victor L.: *The Faith of a Liberal College,* the President's Annual Report to the Board of Trustees, Wesleyan University, Middletown, Conn., 1955.

Clark, Burton R.: *The Distinctive College: Antioch, Reed and Swarthmore,* Aldine Publishing Company, Chicago, 1970.

Hefferlin, J. B. Lon: *Dynamics of Academic Reform,* Jossey-Bass, Inc., San Francisco, 1969.

Margolis, Richard J.: "The Two Nations at Wesleyan University," *The New York Times Magazine,* Jan. 18, 1970.

"The New University," statement prepared by a group of Wesleyan faculty members, Feb. 18, 1961.

The New York Times Magazine, Mar. 8, 1970.

Olin, Stephen: *Early Piety: The Basis of Elevated Character,* a discourse to the graduating class of Wesleyan University, August 1850, Lane & Scott, New York, 1851.

Peterson, George E.: *The New England College in the Age of the University,* Amherst College Press, Amherst, Mass., 1964.

Remarks by Colin C. Campbell, President, Wesleyan University, alumni luncheon, June 5, 1971. (Mimeographed.)

Report of the Educational Policy Committee to the Faculty of Wesleyan University, Wesleyan University, Middletown, Conn., 1955.

Rudolph, Frederick: *The American College and University,* Alfred A. Knopf, Inc., New York, 1962.

Semi-Centennial of Wesleyan University, 1881. (No publisher indicated.)

Surgeon, George P.: *Political Attitudes at Wesleyan,* unpublished student paper, December 1970. (Mimeographed.)

18. The Champagne University in the Beer State: Notes on Wisconsin's Crisis

by Philip G. Altbach

The explosion which caused more than $1 million in damage to several University of Wisconsin buildings and killed a postdoctoral fellow in physics on August 24, 1970, was only the most dramatic of a series of crises that have occurred on the Madison campus since 1966. The combination of a large cosmopolitan student population, a distinguished graduate school, and a tradition of radical student activism has proved to be a potent mixture. The growth of militant student activism in the mid-sixties coincided with a growing conservatism in the state. These factors, combined with a fiscal and enrollment crisis in the latter part of the decade, proved to be more than the traditional governance of the university could handle effectively. The focus of this chapter is on why students, faculty, administration, and regents failed to deal effectively with the unprecedented challenges of the sixties.[1]

IN PROFILE Understanding the historical, academic, and social context of the University of Wisconsin is critical to understanding its current problems. It is a large state university with four major campuses and seven two-year campuses, and it enrolls 61,546 students. The Madison campus, heart of the institution, has 31,132 students and 2,300 faculty. During the presidency of Fred Harvey Harrington (1962–1970), growth was a watchword and no one at the top levels of the administration foresaw the retrenchment now evident in higher education. President Harrington not only expanded enroll-

---

[1] Many of the issues discussed in this paper are elaborated in Altbach, Laufer, and McVey (1971). I am indebted to Matt Pommer, Durward Long, R. S. Laufer, Sheila McVey, David Riesman, and Verne Stadtman for their comments on an earlier draft. Since this essay was written in 1971, the University of Wisconsin has merged with the Wisconsin State University system. The important issues raised by that merger are not considered here.

ments but also diversified the university into its present parts and added many new programs, some of which were based on "soft" (grant) funds. One cost of this rapid growth was the partial disappearance of the academic community (due to expansion and diversification of the faculty); another was deteriorating relations with the state government, which was only rarely consulted during the university's scramble for federal funds during the 1960s. The growth of the university also meant that academic governance became more complicated, and this contributed to the institution's difficulty in responding to crisis.

The University of Wisconsin is a large university with a substantial commitment to graduate education, but it is located in a relatively poor state. Expensive graduate programs and the size and quality of the institution generally place a substantial burden on the state's taxpayers. The university arouses a mixture of respect for its unquestioned quality and resentment at its high cost. When student agitation combined with a losing football team for several years, the resentment of the public took the upper hand. As one local legislator put it, "Wisconsin is a beer state and cannot afford a champagne university." The fact that the president of the university earns more than the governor and that many professors earn more than senior state officials does not help matters.

The university commands statewide attention. The main campus and the state capitol are only a mile apart at either end of State Street, a thoroughfare which has been the scene of many demonstrations and some "trashing" in the past few years. Indeed, the usual route for demonstrations is from the campus to the capitol, and on at least one occasion students invaded the legislative chambers and held lawmakers captive for several hours.

The national crisis of higher education has impinged directly on the University of Wisconsin. This is most dramatically seen in fiscal difficulties and leveling off of enrollments. During the regime of President Harrington, a quite successful effort was made to attract federal and other outside funds and to quickly expand both enrollments and new programs. Relatively little thought was given then to the long-term effects of the sources of funds or of the new academic programs. Thus, when outside funding declined, the university found itself in trouble with regard to some of its "soft" programs, particularly in the medical school. At the same time, extremely high out-of-state tuitions and the State Legislature's quota on non-Wisconsin undergraduates have decreased their proportion in the student body. The leveling off of the birthrate has meant that in-state students have not filled the gap. As a result, in 1970 the Madison campus enrollment actually dropped for the first time since World War II, and the budget, which is in part linked to enrollments, suffered.

The financial and enrollments crisis is related to the political difficulties of the University of Wisconsin. President Harrington's effort to build a "national" university resulted in his neglect of the Legislature and important segments of Wisconsin public opinion. Had Harrington involved the Legislature in the planning of the university during the early 1960s and in general treated individual legislators with more respect, the university might have fared better in a period of belt tightening. Recurring student demonstrations and violence strengthened the Legislature's notion that the faculty and administration were unable to "deal with" the situation and further eroded the influence of the university.

ROLES OF THE CONSTITUEN-CIES There is no question but that many of the problems which have recently affected the University of Wisconsin are due to national forces and events. Nevertheless, elements within the institution — students, faculty, administration, and regents — have been critical both to the crisis and to the response which the institution has made to it.

Students Students at the University of Wisconsin have a long tradition of activism and social involvement.[2] The Progressive movement in the early years of the twentieth century relied on student support, and many of its political conventions were held on campus. Madison was a center of student activism in the 1930s and was one of the bastions of student radicalism during the apathetic 1950s.

The student "movement," however, has undergone substantial changes in recent years. Although students are very much concerned with broad social issues, especially the Vietnam war, they

[2] For a discussion of the history of student activism at the University of Wisconsin, see Shlomo Swirsky, "Four Decades of Student Activism at the University of Wisconsin" in Altbach, Laufer, & McVey (1971). The best overall discussion of the history of the University of Wisconsin is Merle Curti and Vernon Carstenson, *The University of Wisconsin: A History, 1848–1925* (1949). The book deals in detail with student affairs as well as with broader university issues.

are increasingly dissatisfied with the academic environment of the Madison campus (Mankoff, 1970). Many undergraduate students have been concerned about large classes, about what they perceive as overly rigid course and other requirements, and, perhaps more importantly, about a university administration which they feel is unresponsive. Various campus surveys conducted in recent years indicate that the proportion of dissatisfied students has increased dramatically. For example, it is clear that distrust of the university administration has increased during the various crises on campus (Lyons, 1971, p. 49).

The growth of a "counterculture" with its emphasis on rock music, drugs, and a general alienation from many of the values of the existing society has intensified the intellectual and social distance between students and the university. The organized student left, after a short period of attempting to organize around issues of university reform (in 1968), has withdrawn from those efforts except for attacks on the institution for its complicity with the Vietnam war or other involvement with the military-industrial complex. Even the Wisconsin Student Association (WSA), the elected student government, has moved away from concern with academic reform—largely as a response to the meager results it felt it achieved through previous involvement in student-faculty committees on various issues. This general dissatisfaction, while not the direct cause of any demonstrations, underlies much student militancy on campus.

Although it is certainly true that the Madison faculty and administration have not given up any of their basic power to the students, in the past few years students (usually token) have been placed on virtually all the many Madison campus committees. In addition, the university has moved slowly to liberalize regulations concerning dormitories and other aspects of nonacademic life and has, despite hesitation from some regents and many alumni, moved away from the idea of *in loco parentis.* Undergraduates, however, generally have not been impressed with this gradual involvement and liberalization. A current mass exodus from university-owned dormitories, which has caused something of a fiscal crisis for their management, is an indication of the growing detachment of many students from the whole institutional environment. It is significant that students have, by and large, not been impressed with the fairly modest curricular changes that have been made recently in the College of Letters and Sciences. In the 1970–71 academic year, for example, the language requirements for most B.A. degrees were modified, the pass-fail system was extended, and the grading system was somewhat changed. The overwhelming response from articulate student opinion was to consider these changes "tokenism." Even those relatively moderate students who served on the various curriculum committees which proposed more sweeping changes were dissatisfied with the final outcome.

It is always true that a majority of students are fairly happy with their academic experience and cause few problems for the authorities. However, available studies, combined with general observation, indicate that the minority of increasingly articulate dissatisfied students is growing rapidly. And on a campus of 31,000 students, even a small percentage of dissatisfied students can organize a significant demonstration and have an impact. The constituency for militant activism during times of crisis in Madison is quite large, especially when police or national guardsmen are brought on campus or the administration is perceived by many students to have acted badly. Rallies of close to 10,000 young people are not uncommon during crises, and at least 300 militant students are constantly active on and around the campus. In addition, Madison has become a center for a large "nonstudent" youth community of University of Wisconsin dropouts and others who come to the area. This community supports a thriving counterculture in and around the now famous Mifflin Street area which has been the scene of many confrontations with the police. The youth culture reflects on the image of the university and is a ready recruiting ground for participants in all types of militant demonstrations.

Graduate students, often ignored in discussions of student activism, have been a particularly important element in crises at the University of Wisconsin.[3] Traditionally, graduate students have been deeply involved in their academic pursuits and socialized to their roles as future professors. Even radical graduate students — and the Madison campus has been a center for such students for several decades — have maintained a commitment to the university and to academic careers. This situation has changed dramatically in recent years, and as a result graduate students have become quite important in the crisis at the University of Wisconsin.

The changing self-perception and growing activism of graduate

---

[3] See Altbach (1970). This article deals in general with the problems of graduate students and discusses the University of Wisconsin situation in particular in some detail.

students has a number of causes. Certainly, the overproduction of Ph.D.'s which became evident in 1970 in many fields and the resulting difficulty experienced by many new Ph.D.'s in finding employment had led to dissatisfaction and a decreasing professional commitment. It must be remembered that the graduates of universities like Wisconsin only a few years ago were not only assured jobs, but could expect initial appointments at fairly prestigious universities. Now they are lucky to find any employment at all in some fields. The counterculture has also encroached upon graduate student ranks, and there has been a growing rejection of the entire academic career pattern. Radical graduate students, who only a few years ago felt that their major commitment was to conduct "radical" research, increasingly reject research altogether; they no longer wish to associate with "prestigious" universities, but prefer working-class students in junior and community colleges. And, of course, the broader political crisis in the country that affects undergraduates also has its implications for graduate students. All these factors, and more, have produced a new generation of graduate students—one which many professors find it difficult to understand or work with.

Graduate students have been active in a number of departments —sociology, history, English, mathematics, and several others in the College of Letters and Sciences—in efforts to institute reforms such as changes in preliminary examinations and involvement of students in departmental affairs. These efforts have been largely unsuccessful, although a few departments have made some modest changes. In most departments, with the partial exceptions of those cited above, reform efforts have been sporadic and both undergraduate and graduate students have been unwilling to spend time on committees and in other undramatic work needed to formulate and implement change. In addition the faculty, for the most part, has been fairly intransigent, and many personal animosities have developed, often to the disadvantage of the graduate students, who depend on faculty members for academic progress and ultimately for their degrees.

The most important manifestation of graduate-student discontent is the Teaching Assistants Association.[4] The TAA was established in 1966 by a small group of around 50 of the more than 1,600 graduate students who are employed by the university as teaching

[4] The history and ideology of the TAA are discussed in Zorn (1971).

assistants (TAs), usually in large undergraduate courses. It has been estimated that 68 percent of freshman and sophomore undergraduate teaching is done by TAs *(Report of the Committee . . . ,* 1968). The TAA grew because of many teaching assistants' discontent over working conditions, lack of involvement in course planning, poor remuneration, and threats by the State Legislature to cut out-of-state graduate enrollment and to eliminate the out-of-state tuition scholarships which were automatically granted to TAs. These threats, although never carried out, provided impetus for the TAA, and by February of 1969 the TAA claimed a majority of teaching assistants as members and demanded to engage in collective bargaining with the university.

In a still controversial decision, Madison campus Chancellor H. Edwin Young agreed to bargain with the TAA over a contract, and negotiations began in the fall of 1969. The talks continued for four months, and the TAA, feeling that the administration was uninterested in reaching a settlement and also fearing the loss of many members because of its failure to produce "results," first suspended negotiations and then called a strike. This strike, which took place in March of 1970, shortly before the Cambodia–Kent State crisis on campus, effectively halted most teaching in the humanities and social sciences for more than a week and affected other parts of the campus as well. Student support for the strike dwindled, and many of the undergraduates who had stayed out of classes returned. At the same time, many TAs who were out on strike simply could not afford an extended period with no income. The TAA was forced to agree basically to the prestrike contract offer of the university. However, the contract was unprecedented in Wisconsin history. The TAA gained a substantial measure of job security for its members, and also a delineation of working conditions, class size, and other matters. The university made a commitment to joint TA-student-faculty educational planning but did not spell out mechanisms for implementation. While not meeting the original demands of the TAA, the settlement provided teaching assistants with more power and security than they previously had.

The TAA has exhibited a combination of the traditional trade-union approach to bread-and-butter issues and more militant concern for social and academic reform. Much of the leadership of the TAA is radical, although the rank and file is probably more interested in the specific gains which the association has won. For the first time, graduate students have been willing to risk the enmity of senior faculty in order to build a union, thus indicating that the commitment to an academic career and to the traditional subservient role of the graduate student is no longer as widespread as it once was.[5] One result of the existence of the TAA has been a marked deterioration of relations in some departments between graduate students and faculty, and a number of departments are talking seriously of abolishing the teaching-assistant system completely. As this chapter is being written (in the summer of 1971), negotiations between the Madison campus administration and the TAA are taking place for a new contract. With a widespread feeling among faculty against the TAA, due especially to the large number of grievances which the TAA has filed against many departments, and an apparent drop in support for the TAA among some teaching assistants, the outcome of these negotiations is very much in doubt.

In summary, a change has occurred in the student population at the University of Wisconsin, or at least among major segments of that population. Increasing alienation from the academic system and perhaps from the entire employment structure of the society are evident. The pressure of national and international affairs, and especially the Indochina war, has radicalized many students. Finally, the impact of the counterculture, as yet generally unanalyzed, has made itself felt in increased alienation. It is clear that not only the cosmopolitan students from New York and Chicago, long the scapegoats for campus unrest at Madison, but young people from urban and rural middle-class Wisconsin families are participating in the student movement and are part of the counterculture in increasingly large numbers.[6]

Faculty Perhaps more than any other element of the university, the faculty has been deeply affected by the events of the past few years. As a major university in the United States, the Madison campus has traditionally attracted a research-oriented, articulate, and generally competent faculty. It has a first-rate faculty despite the fact that it ranks 10th in the Big Ten and 154th among American universi-

---

[5] An interesting sidelight on the TAA is the fact that several of the association's leaders have left graduate school to become full-time organizers for such unions as the teamsters' and the hospital workers'. Thus it may well be that participation in campus unionism provides its own career line.

[6] See Mankoff (1970) for an elaboration of this point. See also Mankoff & Flacks (1971).

ties in salaries. The excellence of Wisconsin's faculty is related to what is generally known as the "Wisconsin Idea." This ethos combines the notion of academic autonomy for departments and for individual faculty members, a very large measure of faculty self-government under the very broad aegis of the regents, and a commitment to making the university relevant to all elements of the state's population (and by implication in the fifties and sixties to the nation as well). The "Wisconsin Idea" dates to the Progressive era, when the university was intimately involved with the state government and built its reputation for both relevance and scholarly achievement.

In the past few years faculty autonomy has come under major attack, and neither faculty nor administration has been able to restore the balance in terms of morale, power, prestige, or, importantly, salaries. The faculty has lost much of its internal autonomy to the regents and, to a degree, to the administration. Its prestige in the state has been substantially diminished in part because of its "inability" to deal with student radicals. And in a period of financial stringency, highly paid professors who, according to the press and some legislators, spend little time teaching, are the subject of controversy.

The faculty more than doubled during the presidency of Fred Harvey Harrington, and academic programs on the Madison campus burgeoned with the addition of many institutes, centers, and other programs. To some extent, younger academics, particularly in the social sciences and humanities, who did not share many of the values of their senior colleagues entered the system. Traditional means of faculty governance came under attack from both internal and external sources. Regents attacked the faculty for not being harsh enough to student protesters and for failing to maintain "order" on the campus, while students criticized the faculty for its conservatism.

The basis of academic governance has traditionally rested in the senior faculty, who controlled the important University Committee, the nine-man executive committee which is the "voice" of the faculty to the administration and to other audiences as well. The University Committee, aided by a complex array of other committees dominated by the senior faculty, governed the Madison campus with substantial autonomy and little challenge for decades. In the past, the highest faculty governing body was the entire Madison campus faculty. The regular monthly faculty meetings were attended generally by a small group of faculty especially concerned with specific questions on the agenda or who were members of various committees. This situation changed as the faculty became more heterogeneous and as dramatic crises meant the calling of faculty meetings to which more than 1,000 came. These factors led to the establishment, in 1970, of a faculty senate of 200 members which now operates in place of the all-campus faculty meetings. While the senate has had the effect of strengthening the power of the senior faculty and especially the University Committee, which sets the agenda and has a major voice in the conduct of meetings, most of the various factions on the faculty, from radicals to extreme conservatives, are represented.

The politics and structure of the Madison campus faculty do not differ greatly from those of other major academic institutions. Until the mid-1950s, the faculty constituted a fairly close community with strong loyalty to the institution. In a "cosmopolitan" research-oriented university, the ruling elements of the faculty were more local-oriented and perhaps less interested than many of their colleagues in research and nationally visible scholarship.[7] Junior faculty either used the university as a stepping-stone to other jobs or were willing to leave the day-to-day decision making to their senior colleagues. The regents were content to leave the actual running of the campus to the faculty and its complicated committee structure. The community of interest between research-minded faculty, who were willing to leave the governance of the institution to others, and those who actually did the decision making was close.

The situation on campus has changed, and the faculty no longer constitutes a homogeneous community. Its response to crisis generally has been without coherent direction and has, in fact, contributed to the institution's malaise. In a period marked by an overproduction of doctorates, student discontent, and demands for better undergraduate teaching, the traditional research orientation of the Madison faculty has come under attack. As was recently indicated by a national survey of faculty sponsored by the Carnegie Commission, faculty members are notably conservative on issues of university reform and change, with the senior faculty holding the most conservative positions (Lipset, 1970, pp. 85–118). Certainly the Wisconsin experience supports these national findings. The faculty, especially its senior members, has not been willing to relinquish

---

[7] In this respect, the University of Wisconsin conforms to the paradigm developed by Gouldner's articles (1957–1958).

any real power that professors have over the educational process and over their own professional lives. The usual faculty response to crisis is to appoint a committee to study the matter and, with few exceptions, do little to change the status quo. This response is increasingly rejected by both students and regents, who demand that solutions be implemented. The faculty, in part with superior knowledge of the intricacies of academic governance and a commitment to Wisconsin's traditional values and in part as a result of its own vested interests, has refrained from suggesting major changes.

The politics of the Madison campus faculty are significant and, in a sense, surprising. Despite the existence of a few defined "factions," there has been little of the bitter infighting or protracted factionalism among the faculty that has been evident at Berkeley or to some extent at Harvard. Despite some of the fears of some regents and a few administrators, the organized faculty left, grouped around the very small and generally ineffective New University Conference chapter, has little strength and almost no direction. The United Faculty, a union with a membership of some 200 which is loosely affiliated with the American Federation of Teachers, has experienced some growth, but is not a force on the campus. An ad hoc group of liberal faculty, largely drawn from the social science and humanities departments, comes together for common action during crises but has little in common at other times. The mainstream of the faculty is mildly liberal in politics but traditional on matters of academic governance.

Despite the lack of political activism among the faculty, there is some discontent. Many junior faculty are unhappy with their lack of power in policy making and with the general direction of the institution. Worsening conditions on campus in terms of salaries, teaching conditions, self-image, and autonomy have demoralized many faculty, and there has been a substantial exodus from a number of departments, notably in the College of Letters and Sciences. Unlike Berkeley, Wisconsin does not seem to have a great deal of holding power in periods of stress.

Administrators Most administrators have been University of Wisconsin faculty members or have taken their academic training at UW. They are usually selected by search-and-screen committees dominated by senior faculty members. For the most part, Wisconsin administrators are professors who have chosen to follow the "local" academic career pattern and who have given up scholarly productivity to devote themselves to academic administration. While styles of administration differ, the close advisers and/or immediate staff of the chancellor are senior faculty and very few younger individuals are involved in the top level of academic administration.

Many administrators, particularly since 1965, feel that they are "protecting" the institution from the ravages of Wisconsin's legislators. This feeling has also been expressed by the board of regents, who are in closest touch with the opinions of legislators and perhaps with public opinion. The administration also seems to feel that it is protecting the faculty and, in a sense, the students from harsh treatment by state authorities. This state of mind, somewhat justified, has led the top levels of leadership in the university to increasingly conservative public statements and policies in an effort to placate public opinion. Administrative policy seeks to assure the public that the university will remain calm or at least that disruption will be dealt with effectively.

On the Madison campus, the profusion of schools, colleges, programs, and other agencies makes efficient administration difficult, and the implementation of reform is next to impossible because of the complicated decision-making structure and often overlapping jurisdictions. And at the bottom of the system are the academic departments. The departments have substantial autonomy and tend to be organizationally conservative and quite jealous of their own prerogatives. Reform plans are often bogged down when they reach the departmental structure.[8]

From 1967 to 1970, student agitation and its implications occupied a major portion of the time of academic administrators. In the 1970–71 academic year, severe budget cuts and an impending merger of the University of Wisconsin and the Wisconsin State University (WSU) system were imposed on the administration by the state government.[9] In its internal functioning, the administration is severely limited by the immensely complicated system of faculty governance and the innate conservatism of the senior facul-

[8] See Dressel, Johnson, & Marcus (1970) for a more detailed discussion of the nature and functions of academic departments in large universities.

[9] Wisconsin has three separate systems of higher education. The oldest and most prestigious, the University of Wisconsin system, is based on the Madison campus but now has branches in various parts of the state. The Wisconsin State University system, founded in 1964, now enrolls 64,214 students on nine campuses throughout the state. The emphasis of the WSU is on undergraduate education, and the basis of the system is a series of former teachers colleges upgraded in the past decades to liberal arts colleges and recently to universities with some graduate programs. The final components of the state's higher education network are the vocational and technical colleges.

ty and most of the departments. The university is unable to implement change from the top because of internal governance; at the same time, it no longer has funds to ensure expansion and improvement from the bottom because of budget cuts. Thus administrators live from crisis to crisis with little scope for creativity and with growing frustration.[10]

Given these constraints, it is not surprising that the administration has not responded very creatively to any of the crises which it has faced in the past five years. Internal and external pressures, in addition to the general "establishment" orientation of the administration which is ensured by its recruitment and background, has meant that crises have been met by short-term compromises or, more often, by outside force. The general pressures of Madison campus academic administration, the continual balancing of political forces, and the inability to make much headway on educational improvement or reform has caused many administrators to resign. But the nature of decision making and the general orientation of senior faculty who have taken on administrative posts have remained fairly constant.

Regents   The board of regents[11] consists of nine individuals appointed by the governor for nine-year terms, plus the superintendent of public instruction. As a result of the appointments of Gov. Warren Knowles, a Republican who served during the bulk of the 1960s, the board has recently developed strong conservative majorities. The composition of the board of regents, as Gregory Nigosian has pointed out, reflects a cross section of the Wisconsin establishment. Most regents are college-trained, usually at the University of Wisconsin; almost all are Wisconsin-born and have strong ties to the state.[12]

---

[10] The problems of academic administrators are reflected in Altbach, Laufer, & McVey (1971). See especially chapters by Dean of Education Donald McCarty, Vice Chancellor Durward Long of the Center System, and ex-Vice Chancellor for Administration Robert Atwell.

[11] There is very little written about or by the University of Wisconsin board of regents. For two commentaries, from rather different perspectives, see DeBardeleben (1969, pp. 69–91) and Gelatt (1969). Both authors served on the board of regents, and Mr. Gelatt still holds office. See also Nigosian (1971).

[12] Nigosian (1971). The Wisconsin situation conforms generally to the national characteristics of members of academic governing boards which were reported in Harnett (1970). One slight variation noted by Nigosian is the local origins and involvements of the Wisconsin regents.

The board members have taken an increasingly "activist" role (Pommer, 1970, pp. 27–28). Until the major disruptions of the mid-1960s, the regents traditionally (with some exceptions during earlier periods of the university's history, for example in the late 1920s) left direct policy making and administration to the faculty and its administrative officers. Recently, because the faculty has been perceived to have failed to maintain order on campus, the regents have intervened directly in academic affairs.

According to law, the regents have final authority over the university and its staff and are empowered to use this authority in almost any way they wish. At regental initiative, a committee to reexamine the tenure system was established in 1971. The regents have also used "study committees" on drugs, student and faculty discipline, buildings, and other subjects to stress their authority and initiative. When these study committees have arrived at conclusions different from those of the faculty, in most cases the regents' opinion has prevailed. This increased involvement and broadened jurisdiction is looked upon with great fear and mistrust by the faculty and administration. Recently the regents have more deeply involved themselves in faculty affairs by refusing to grant a salary increase to sociology professor Maurice Zeitlin because of their displeasure with his controversial public statements and his antiwar activities. Only after a major campaign by the faculty were the regents forced to back down on this issue, perhaps indicating that a united stance by the faculty still influences those with formal power in the university. The point, however, was made, and it is likely that faculty will be more careful in the future to avoid the ire of the regents. As the regents are quite sensitive to the political climate in the state, it is possible that the incumbent Republican regents will moderate their positions in deference to a liberal Democratic governor and the Democratically controlled State Assembly.

President Harrington did not involve the regents in his administration, except at the very broadest level, and as a result they seemed to have been somewhat unaware of some of the new directions in which the university was moving. The Madison campus administration has traditionally attempted, with a good deal of success, to obscure its work so that outside forces could not effectively control it. The regents, the Coordinating Council on Higher Education—a state agency which is responsible for the allocation of funds to the various public universities and colleges—and the

Legislature itself have all been somewhat unclear about the nature of the university's budget and other aspects of its functioning. As outside sources of funding disappear and the university must turn increasingly to the state, it is not surprising that both the regents and state authorities should wish for greater accountability and control.

WISCONSIN'S CRISES

Madison's crises began two years after the Berkeley student "revolt." The first disruptive protest took place in 1966 and was concerned with the Vietnam war. The focus was twofold: opposition to the university's cooperation with the selective service system and opposition to job recruiting by the Dow Chemical Company, manufacturers of napalm. When students occupied a part of the engineering campus in an effort to prevent Dow interviews, the police were called. A number of students were arrested, but no physical confrontation took place and little damage was done. In a move which effectively defused a volatile situation, Chancellor Robben Fleming paid the bail of the arrested students with a personal check for more than $1,000. His action was praised by the faculty and moderate students. But he was criticized by many legislators and some members of the board of regents, who felt that he had given in to radical students. He resigned shortly after this incident in order to assume the presidency of the University of Michigan.

The first large-scale disruption of academic life took place in the fall of 1967—again over the issue of job interviews by the Dow Chemical Company.[13] Chancellor William Sewell, a liberal sociologist, following a previous faculty resolution that normal university processes should be followed under all circumstances, called the police to eject students from the Commerce Building, where the interviews were taking place. Tear gas was used, about 50 students were injured, substantial numbers were arrested, and several were suspended from the university. In the following days massive student demonstrations were held to protest "police brutality," and what had started as a small disruption by leftist activists became a major campus strike that effectively stopped most classes in the College of Letters and Sciences for several days. Although students were upset about the war, they were mobilized largely on the basis

[13] For a more detailed discussion of the Dow crisis, see Long (1970) and Sklar (1970).

of the issue of "cops on campus," and, in fact, efforts by the United Front—Students for a Democratic Society and other radical groups—leadership failed to provide a greater degree of ideological commitment from the majority of student protesters.

The faculty met in emergency session to discuss the crisis and, when asked for a vote of confidence in the administration, backed the chancellor by less than 50 votes out of a total of more than 1,000 cast. For the first time, it was clear that the faculty was divided on a major public issue. During the crisis, the Republican-dominated State Legislature passed by a vote of 94 to 5, a resolution which demanded that the regents "reevaluate administrative policies of excessive permissiveness in handling student demonstrators." Other antiuniversity bills were introduced in the following weeks, and while only a few passed, the lesson to university administrators, and particularly to the board of regents, was clear.

Thirteen Black Demands

The next major crisis on the Madison campus came in February 1969 over the issues raised by "13 black demands." Following the annual week-long Wisconsin Student Association–sponsored symposium devoted to the race question, black students submitted 13 demands to the university administration. Essentially, they asked for the creation of an Afro-American studies department mainly under student control, the establishment of a Black Cultural Center, the admission of 15 black students expelled several months earlier from Oshkosh State University, and a substantial increase in the number of black students at the university.[14] There are only about 800 black students on the Madison campus.

With the support of all of the white radical student groups, the black students called a strike and engaged in militant demonstrations. Initially, the strike did not generate widespread support, so the strikers moved to forcibly prevent students from entering classroom buildings. The administration responded by calling city police to keep academic buildings open. The calling of police had the same effect at the University of Wisconsin as it did at many other universities: the strike won substantially more support. Because of continued disruptions and sporadic acts of vandalism by students, the National Guard was called in on the morning of February 13, 1969. With the National Guard on campus, student support for the

---

[14] For a more detailed discussion of the black demands crisis, focusing mainly on student response, see Lyons & Lyons (1971).

strike escalated, and most classes in the College of Letters and Sciences were effectively halted. After a few more days of sporadic demonstrations, some vandalism, and virtual occupation of the university by troops and police, student support for the strike waned, and it was eventually called off by the organizers.

The immediate results of the black demands strike more or less paralleled those of the Dow demonstrations the previous year. The faculty met in an emergency meeting and, after heated discussion, voted to support the administration's position of not negotiating or giving in to any of the demands. At the same time, several committees were established which promised to examine the question of a black studies department and related issues. On the initiative of the regents, several student leaders were suspended or expelled and a formal investigation of the university was undertaken by the Legislature. The student movement, so powerful during the crisis, all but disappeared, and the cooperation between white and black militants, based on white support for the demands and the tactics of the blacks, came to an end.

This crisis, however, produced greater change than the Dow demonstrations did, perhaps because minority-group protest seemed more legitimate to the university community than antiwar demonstrations. An Afro-American studies department was established in the College of Letters and Sciences about a year later, and an Afro-American Center opened on campus within a semester after the crisis. While the department's structure did not satisfy the demands of the black students for control, it did constitute a substantial university response to the challenge, due in part to the support of Dean Leon Epstein of the College of Letters and Sciences. Although there was some opposition to the concept of a black studies department from conservative faculty, the compromise departmental structure which finally emerged met with no major opposition.

Spring of 1970 The most recent major campus crisis, related to the Cambodia invasion in the spring of 1970, was national in scope, although it also had some specific local ingredients. The national agitation over Cambodia–Kent State was preceded at Wisconsin, in March, by a strike of the Teaching Assistants Association over contract demands. This strike was generally peaceful and involved no outside police on campus. It lasted for several weeks and effectively disrupted undergraduate classes in the College of Letters and Sciences for more than a week. The strike stemmed from long-standing discontent among teaching assistants, noted earlier, and had major undergraduate support. This support was based in part on the general dissatisfaction of many undergraduates with their education and also on the stress that the TAA placed on undergraduate participation in educational planning. When this aspect of the TAA's demands was not included in the final contract, there was some discouragement among undergraduates.

Within weeks of the TAA strike, the Cambodian incursion took place. The reaction on the Madison campus was swift and brought academic life to a halt for the rest of the semester. The Teaching Assistants Association and a large part of the faculty were mobilized in general sympathy with the students. For the first time in a number of years, the isolation of liberal elements of the faculty from the student movement was broken, if only for a short time.

The scenario of protest was similar to that of earlier incidents described above. A student strike, followed by militant demonstrations, some property damage, and trashing in the local business area led to the calling of the National Guard by the university officials who otherwise did not speak publicly on the crisis. Classes in many parts of the university, especially in the College of Letters and Sciences, were cancelled for almost a week. Several schools, including law and nursing, suspended classes for varying periods of time. With the exception, perhaps, of the engineering and agriculture campuses, the university did not function normally for well over a week. The combination of the TAA strike and the Cambodia –Kent State crisis meant that during the final six weeks of the spring semester of 1970 there was a major disruption of the academic program of the university. But Wisconsin did not officially close or, with the exception of some revisions in grading patterns, officially change its schedule.

The faculty response to the situation was significant. Close to 300 professors—out of a total faculty of some 2,300—signed a statement opposing the United States government's actions, calling for the university to close, and indicating that they would not conduct "business as usual" during the crisis. While not quite a strike statement, this was the most radical response taken by UW faculty members during the various crises. Indeed, the faculty, meeting as a "committee of the whole" shortly after the signing of the statement, voted to close down the university, thus indicating the depth of its members' feelings. Some 1,200 members attended the meeting, and the resolution passed by a large majority. The university administration, however, did not follow the wishes of the faculty majority, kept the university open, and refused to convene another faculty meeting until the crisis was over and the end of the semester was at hand. The administration, no doubt, breathed a sigh of relief that the Legislature was not in session at the time and thus no dramatic outcry was heard and no investigation launched.

The Cambodia–Kent State crisis had some lasting impact. For one thing, the board of regents, after threatening to "tighten up" discipline for some time, finally set up new procedures to mete out swift justice to student offenders and to bypass the slow processes of the previous faculty-run discipline system. It is significant that the state attorney general was instrumental in devising these new procedures, thus indicating the increased interest of the state government in university affairs. This "incursion" of the regents into what has traditionally been a function of the faculty is but one example of the increasingly activist role of the regents.

Many faculty members, particularly younger and more liberal ones, were deeply disillusioned by the crisis and the response of the university to it. Wisconsin, with its strong tradition of faculty self-government, had long counted on the ethos of "faculty power" to keep top-quality professors in Madison when other institutions offered higher salaries and better conditions. Thus the tradition of faculty control and perhaps the stability of the faculty were dealt a blow by recent regent actions. The student reaction is more difficult to gauge, but it is at least possible that the atmosphere which was created by the whole experience of the Cambodia–Kent State crisis, made the bombing of the Army Mathematics Research Center (AMRC) which occurred only a few months later more acceptable to many nonrevolutionary students.

The Fatal Bombing The bombing of the Army Mathematics Research Center not only was one of the most dramatic events of recent years at Wisconsin; it also had implications for the country at large. While it is fairly clear that the actual bombing was not connected to the "movement" on campus, two of the four individuals who allegedly participated in the event were University of Wisconsin students and ex-members of the staff of the *Daily Cardinal,* the student newspaper. The reaction of politically minded students on campus was mixed generally, revealing deep sorrow at the loss of life but at the same time showing satisfaction that one of the key issues of the student left, the continued existence of the AMRC, was "solved" by the bombing. (Of course, the question was not in reality solved, since the AMRC has simply moved to other quarters and continues to function.) The general campus reaction was one of shock and helplessness that has not yet disappeared.

The bombing threw the movement into tactical disarray. Activists have found it difficult to deal with the bombing even in terms of "revolutionary" strategy, while the large majority of students, including many of those sympathetic to the movement, were outraged by it. Many within the student left disagreed with the action on both tactical and moral grounds. As of this writing, the campus left has not recovered—there have been no successful mass demonstrations, and the active political groups do not seem to be functioning effectively. There is no question but that the bombing contributed to the political inactivity of the 1970–71 academic year on the Madison campus and perhaps nationally because of the demoralization and tactical confusion it caused. Many students felt that the bombing was the "logical" outcome of the confrontation politics of the sixties. Yet the bombing was morally unjustifiable and politically ineffective. Thus many students withdrew from the movement feeling the lack of a clear direction.

The faculty was both outraged and demoralized. There was little that its members could do to prevent another bombing. Faculty opposition to student radicals, already strong, probably increased. The administration and the regents merely increased their tendency toward a "law and order" posture in the face of campus problems. For the first time, city police were brought on campus to patrol on a regular basis, and contingency plans for various kinds of disruptions were made.

IMPACTS ON THE INSTITUTION The University of Wisconsin has been severely constrained and influenced by various forces, both from within and from without, in its handling of the events of the 1960s. Perhaps the most dramatic and well-publicized pressure on the university in terms of its response to crises has been the political situation in the state, as expressed by the press, the Legislature, and, to an extent, the board of regents. Chancellor Fleming's restrained yet effective handling of the 1966 crisis engendered criticism from "hard line" elements. That criticism made it clear that the University of Wisconsin probably does not have the option that the University of Chicago used so effectively in handling student disruption—simply waiting until the demonstrators left the occupied building or ended their demonstrations and then applying harsh academic discipline. Pressures from the state and the regents force the Madison campus administration to act quickly, even if the action means that the National Guard will be called or that the student movement will be strengthened. Thus the responses to crisis available to the University of Wisconsin administration are almost inevitably limited from the outset to "confrontation politics."

Another element of the academic equation at Madison is the rather poor communications between the administration and both students and segments of the faculty. Due in part to the personality of Madison campus Chancellor H. Edwin Young, who has preferred to conduct his administration in a fairly anonymous manner, in part to the bureaucratized structure of the administration, and in part to the broadly antiestablishment posture of the student movement, there has been a notable lack of communications. Even the Wisconsin Student Association, the elected student government which under normal conditions could be "co-opted" into some kind of relationship with the administration, has become relatively intransigent. The structure of the faculty emphasizes the views of senior professors with a substantial commitment to the institution, and this has meant that younger academics, as well as those with somewhat unorthodox views, are not often in direct communication with members of the administration. Because of the communications "gap" and increasingly wide differences of interests and style, the administration and to some extent the senior faculty are out of touch with student opinion and with the views held by those at the bottom of the academic ladder. This situation has created tension and sharply limited the vision of the administration in dealing with campus problems.

The usual means of academic response to crisis is to appoint a committee to look into the problem. The committee's report, which usually comes only after long deliberation and often too late to deal with the situation in question, is then debated, amended, and perhaps passed by the faculty, approved by the administration in most cases, perhaps ratified (and sometimes rejected) by the regents, and finally implemented (if approved) by the administration in collaboration with elements of the faculty. In the years since 1966, perhaps a dozen ad hoc committees have been appointed by the faculty to deal with various issues facing the campus. Committees have made reports and recommendations on the involvement of

students in university governance, the response to disruption, interview and placement policy, the advisability of the establishment
of a black studies department, the ROTC program, curriculum
reform in the College of Letters and Sciences, and the role of the
teaching assistant. Some recommendations have been adopted and
implemented, while others have been shelved or perhaps rejected
at various stages of consideration. It is impossible to analyze each
of the committees which deliberated on the various crises, but the
processes they followed are lengthy and their failure rate is quite
high. The Wisconsin Student Association, which has had the responsibility of appointing the (usually) token student representatives to those committees, has responded to the failure to achieve
results by refusing to appoint students to many of the committees.[15]

The decline of a sense of community among the faculty and the
appearance of a small but vocal minority of young militant professors have impelled the administration, the regents, and some senior
faculty to search for means of disciplining faculty members quickly.
The traditional means of nonretention of junior staff and withholding of salary raises and other harassment of tenured professors
were not sufficiently fast or public for legislators, regents, or others
anxious to mete out swift punishment for those who violate academic norms. As a result of regental initiative, the University Committee drafted a code of faculty discipline and a structure for admin-
istering punishment for violators. After lengthy debate and some
modification in the senate, this code passed and is now (June 1971)
being considered by the regents.

On several occasions, the regents have directly involved themselves in the "solutions" to campus problems. Two issues are illustrative in this regard: The regents revamped the disciplinary procedures in order to ensure that students charged with violations
of university regulations would be dealt with promptly, an action
which was in violation of careful faculty legislation in an area which
has traditionally been under faculty control. The regents have also
involved themselves in the affairs of student housing. They have
on several occasions liberalized dormitory regulations with regard
to women's hours, while at the same time they vetoed a faculty-
approved request for coeducational dormitories. In these actions,

---

[15] It is worth noting that the WSA has itself suffered something of an eclipse
in recent years. Participation in student elections has declined, and there is
little interest in student government on campus.

the regents acted partly in response to various outside pressures—public opinion, student demands, or other pressures.

Most of the university community's response to crises has been without great conviction. It seems that most academics would prefer to be left alone to pursue their work without being involved in the university's crisis. The various changes, such as modifications in the curriculum, the creation of a black studies program, and increased student involvement in governance, have been far from radical, and most have not been fully implemented. Many students do not think that they deal adequately with the major issues which students and others raise. Yet the University of Wisconsin has begun to implement some reforms as the result of pressure from students, regents, and the Legislature. If there is any lesson to be learned from the university's response to crises, it is that confrontation politics and threats do bring a sense of urgency to the reform process.

LITTLE CHANGE IN SIGHT There is no doubt that the University of Wisconsin has been subject to the very serious pressures facing American higher education generally in the past decade. Despite this fact, it is clear that the university has not basically responded to many of the challenges which face it. The symptoms of failure are evident: a faculty senate was organized in 1969–70 with neither the consultation nor the participation of students despite the fact that at other universities, such as Columbia, students were involved in similar changes in governance; despite a great deal of deliberation and some conflict, no basic reforms in the curriculum have been made and the administrative structure has remained unchanged, although there are some indications that this situation may be changing. The university has not been able to move far or fast enough to meet demands on it from undergraduate or graduate students, from teaching assistants, or occasionally from junior faculty. While it is very likely that some student demands should, on their merits, be rejected, the University of Wisconsin has met almost none, regardless of merit.

Those in charge of the University of Wisconsin—the regents and the senior faculty–administrators—are certainly not evil men. They are not even, for the most part, incompetent. They are simply locked into an academic system which was formed over a period of almost 50 years and which was solidified during the "boom" period of the fifties. This system has served the interests of the senior faculty quite well and has permitted the University of Wisconsin to grow and to maintain if not expand its national prestige. But this situation has changed, and it is clear that neither the increasingly radical and dissatisfied students nor the financially strapped state government will continue to support the "traditional" means of academic governance and orientation of the university.

The political future of the university is unclear. In February of 1971, Governor Lucey, in his budget message to the Legislature, called for an amalgamation of the University of Wisconsin system and the Wisconsin State University system under one board of regents. Such a shift, which the Governor claims will save $4 million in administrative costs, would have major implications for the Madison campus if implemented and would probably mean financial disaster. The availability of funds under the new Democratic administration in the state is also unclear, and the prospects seem very dim indeed. Thus the University of Wisconsin enters the 1970s without direction and in a state of substantial crisis. Budgetary crises have forced administrators to spend much of their time belt tightening while students demand that more attention be given to undergraduate instruction and other expensive proposals. What is more, the will to adapt to what are clearly new situations does not seem to be dramatically evident.

References

Altbach, Philip G.: "Commitment and Powerlessness on the American Campus: The Case of the Graduate Student," *Liberal Education*, vol. 56, pp. 562–582, December 1970.

Altbach, Philip G., Robert S. Laufer, and Shiela McVey (eds.): *The University of Wisconsin: Multiversity in Crisis*, Jossey-Bass, Inc., San Francisco, 1971.

Curti, Merle, and Vernon Carstenson: *The University of Wisconsin: A History, 1848–1925*, 2 vols., The University of Wisconsin Press, Madison, 1949.

DeBardeleben, Arthur: "The University's External Constituency," in W. Metzger et al., *Dimensions of Academic Freedom*, The University of Illinois Press, Urbana, 1969.

Dressel, Paul, F. C. Johnson, and P. M. Marcus: *The Confidence Crisis. An Analysis of University Departments*, Jossey-Bass, Inc., San Francisco, 1970.

Gelatt, Charles: *The Regents: Rulers or Rubber Stamps?,* Board of Regents of the University of Wisconsin, Madison, 1969.

Gouldner, Alvin W.: "Cosmopolitans and Locals: Toward an Analysis of Latent Social Roles, I and II," *Administrative Science Quarterly,* vol. 2, pp. 281–306, 444–480, 1957–1958.

Harnett, Rodney: *The New College Trustee: Some Predictions for the 1970's,* Educational Testing Service, Princeton, N.J., 1970.

Lipset, S. M.: "The Politics of Academia," in D. C. Nichols (ed.), *Perspectives on Campus Tensions.* American Council on Education, Washington, 1970, pp. 85–118.

Long, Durward: "Wisconsin: Changing Styles of Administrative Response," in J. Foster and D. Long (eds.), *Protest!,* William Morrow & Company, Inc., New York, 1970, pp. 246–270.

Lyons, Morgan: "Campus Reactions to Student Protest," unpublished Ph.D. dissertation, University of Wisconsin, Department of Sociology, 1971.

Lyons, Morgan and Judith Lyons: "Black Student Power: Protest and Reaction on Campus," in P. G. Altbach, R. S. Laufer, and S. McVey (eds.), *The University of Wisconsin: Multiversity in Crisis,* Jossey-Bass, Inc., San Francisco, 1971.

Mankoff, Milton: "The Political Socialization of Student Radicals and Militants in the Wisconsin Student Movement during the 1960's," unpublished Ph.D. dissertation, University of Wisconsin, 1970.

Mankoff, Milton and Richard Flacks: "The Changing Social Base of the American Student Movement," *Annals of the American Academy of Political and Social Science,* vol. 395, pp. 54–67, May 1971.

Nigosian, Gregory: "The Regents," in P. G. Altbach, R. S. Laufer, and S. McVey (eds.), *The University of Wisconsin: Multiversity in Crisis,* Jossey-Bass, Inc., San Francisco, 1971.

Pommer, Matt: "Regent Rule at Wisconsin," *Change,* vol. 2, pp. 27–28, September–October 1970.

Report of the Committee on the Teaching Assistant System, University of Wisconsin, Madison, 1968.

Sklar, Bernard: "Faculty Culture and Community Conflict: A Historical, Political, and Sociological Analysis of the October 18, 1967 Dow Demonstrations at University of Wisconsin," unpublished Ph.D. dissertation, University of Chicago, 1970.

Swirsky, Shlomo: "Four Decades of Student Activism at the University of Wisconsin," in P. G. Altbach, R. S. Laufer, and S. McVey (eds.), *The*

University of Wisconsin: Multiversity in Crisis, Jossey-Bass, Inc., San Francisco, 1971.

Zorn, Steven: "Unions on Campus: The TAA," in P. G. Altbach, R. S. Laufer, and S. McVey (eds.), *The University of Wisconsin: Multiversity in Crisis,* Jossey-Bass, Inc., San Francisco, 1971.

19. *Commentary and Epilogue*

by *David Riesman*

THE
COMPLEXITIES
OF THE
SUBJECT

The authors of these reports were given an almost impossible assignment, namely, to try to capture the specific flavor of the institutions they were writing about and at the same time to try to say how the institution had been affected by the campus turmoil of the late 1960s—and all this in brief compass. Furthermore, they were writing about living people in ongoing institutions—in a number of cases their own. Few nonradical academicians (and all the contributors except John Walsh of *Science* are academicians) enjoy writing harsh things about either their own institutions or those that have given them entrée, however acerb they may be in private discourse. There is a further problem, which has often haunted me in my own research on higher education: Many colleges and universities are precariously situated in terms of public and private support; hence it follows that praise may be turned into a public relations asset while criticism may damage the institution in its competition for scarce resources. Though one's principal aim may be understanding rather than amelioration or transformation of particular institutions, this human

NOTE: I am indebted to the Institute for Advanced Study for the opportunity during a year's leave of absence from Harvard to work on problems of higher education, and to the Carnegie and Ford foundations for further support of that work. A number of my coauthors made helpful suggestions concerning this commentary: Jill Conway, Zelda Gamson, Gerald Grant, Algo D. Henderson, and Marshall Meyer; also the following: John H. Bunzel, Victor L. Butterfield, J. W. Garbarino, Lyman Glenny, Edwin Harwood, Everett C. Hughes, Richard M. Hunt, Seymour Martin Lipset, Walter Metzger, Cushing Strout, Vartan Gregorian, Robert Blackburn, Christopher Jencks, Barry Munitz, Moses Rischin, John Silber, and Lewis Mayhew.

concern with their vulnerability may shade both how one interprets and how one reports events.[1]

Survey data collected over many years indicate that, as everyone knows, professors are more liberal than the general population; and as most people know, social scientists are generally the most liberal of these and some are even radical; and as fewer people know, distinguished academicians are, holding other things constant, more likely to be toward the Left of the political spectrum than their less well-known contemporaries. Contributors to this volume are for the most part drawn from this segment of the academic profession, either from the social sciences, including history, or in several instances (David R. Goddard, Algo D. Henderson) from careers in administration. Doubtless, for each of the institutions represented here, one could have found quite a different account; for some, such as San Francisco State College and Berkeley, there already exists a whole library of exegesis. Accident played its inevitable part in determining which institutions are included in the volume; a number of important private ones (e.g., Columbia, Chicago, Cornell) are missing; and among state institutions many different and additional choices might of course have been made. Not a single Southern institution is represented here, white or black, unless Federal City College in Washington, D.C. is considered Southern; nor is any Catholic campus, whether more or less stressful, included; nor any community college. The immense range of four-year public colleges, many of which have experienced great disruption, is represented here only by the examples of San Francisco State, CCNY, and Old Westbury. Proportionately, the volume emphasizes private higher education, which enrolls a dwindling minority (less than 30 percent) of students, and the more visible and selective state universities.

In spite of this somewhat haphazard selection, however, the essays do reflect emerging changes at many different kinds of academic institutions. Not only do the major universities influence the whole field of higher education by the models they set, but also indirectly through the faculty they prepare to teach in less eminent places—perhaps particularly today, when many Ph.D.'s from lead-

---

[1] In general, of course, liberals hesitate to tell some truths which may give aid and comfort to reactionaries (reactionaries exercise an analogous censorship). Reactionaries rarely depend on the evidence provided by liberal or radical critics, and the latter, by overprotectiveness, undermine their credibility among the uncommitted, while preserving their standing vis-à-vis each other.

ing institutions are glad to get a job even in a community college. (Sometimes, the administrators of the latter are understandably afraid that such "overqualified" Ph.D.'s will be snobbish, will not know how to teach their students, and will become disgruntled and restless.) In a few visits to new commuter colleges, I have met a number of avant-garde young faculty who have gotten or who are finishing their doctorates at places like Berkeley, San Diego, Columbia, Pennsylvania, and are now teaching lower-middle-class and working-class students, the first generation in their families to attend college. Sometimes the faculty seek to persuade their students to spend their energies expanding their consciousness or, more rarely, engaging in protests rather than to work hard and to rely on meritocratic standards to enter middle-level professions and careers. This two-step flow of influence from the leading centers is facilitated by the smattering of upper-middle-class students in the commuter colleges and of course by the mass media, by the messages of rock music, and by the drug culture. Indeed, it is conceivable that students in major universities have been returning to a more serious if not scholarly orientation even while more hedonistic orientations continue to spread in some of the more local institutions, particularly on the East and West Coasts.[2]

"EXPLAINING" CAMPUS UNREST   Some marginal and indirect evidence concerning the "downward" spread of avant-garde ideas is provided in a study by the research staff of the American Council on Education. In their essay, "Campus Unrest, 1970–71: Was It Really All That Quiet?" Alan Bayer and Alexander Astin contend that, while there was much less attention on the part of the media to campus disruption in the

---

[2] In "The Blueing of America," Peter and Brigitte Berger (1971) contend that the counterculture in its cultural and political forms leads to the circulation of elites: the hedonistic children of the affluent will be downwardly mobile and make room at the top for the upwardly mobile children of the working class, who remain unaffected by self-doubt and the cult of sensibility and aesthetic experience, even though they may acquire some of the newer tastes in clothing and music. However, since most first-generation students lack the family backing, the verbal ease, and the personal charisma that would take them to their destination in the absence of meritocratic selectivity and hard work, it may be that in some measure the democratization of aristocratic insouciance will permit the upper-middle-class children to remain only marginally mobile downward, because the ambition of the lower middle class has in some measure been undermined. Whether a large industrial society can hold together under such conditions is another story.

academic year 1970–71, this mainly reflected the lesser turmoil on the more visible and selective campuses, whereas the less selective ones were often experiencing their first disruptions.[3] What characterizes America, however, in contrast to many other industrialized societies is the lack of a single metropolitan center from which political and cultural movements spread to the provinces. Consider how the books and essays written about the events of May 1968 in France focused almost entirely on Paris, so that only rarely could one discover what was happening at Grenoble or Marseilles or Toulouse, which was in any case usually seen simply as an offshoot of Paris. Similarly in Japan, Tokyo—along with the ancillary university center of Kyoto—has been the center from which movements radiated outward.

Often quite self-consciously, the student movements around the world draw on the ideologies and even more on the tactics developed elsewhere. Just as some Columbia activists of 1968 turned up to see what they could do at Harvard in the spring of 1969, so students in Paris in May 1968 were well aware of Columbia's building occupations of the previous April. In a book of penetrating observations on universities in Western Europe, Japan, and the United States, Christopher Driver (1971) suggests that the troubled universities in different countries had in common in the late 1960s a fantastic expansion of sheer numbers in the preceding decade (the University of Chicago being a notable exception). Yet such an explanation is unsatisfactory. As Jill Conway observes in her report on the University of Toronto, Canadian universities expanded threefold while American universities were doubling in numbers; but Toronto is less, rather than more, troubled than its American counterparts; and Canada (Simon Fraser University and Sir George Williams University excepted) has had generally less turmoil than the United

---

[3] Whereas quantitatively the level of disruptions remained high, the change in locale may have had qualitative consequences not captured by the survey report. See Bayer and Astin (1971). Correspondingly, it is no longer possible to predict the likelihood of campus unrest by looking for collections of the kinds of students described by Kenneth Keniston, Richard Flacks, Seymour Martin Lipset, and many others: affluent, children of the professional upper middle class, often Jewish and generally agnostic, majoring in the social sciences and humanities, etc.—of course, one would have to add black militants (many of the leaders of whom are understandably upper-middle-class blacks) to this panorama. As illustrated by the explosion of radical Catholicism, activists today may come from students whose parents are conservative, even fundamentalist. See for discussion Lipset (1971, Chap. 3), and Meyer (forthcoming).

States. The demographic tide of children born after the Second World War who entered college in the 1960s did not have an impact so much on account of sheer numerical surge as on account of the subsets of "critical masses" who were recruited into strategic locales and who could be mobilized or subject to contagion there. The commuter colleges could expand dramatically without encountering major disturbances (with exceptions among community colleges such as Merritt College in Oakland or the College of San Mateo, also in California). But when residential Wesleyan moved in three years from a handful of black students to 10 or 12 percent of blacks —many from the ghettos—the combination of upper-middle-class guilty, antagonistic, or simply tactless whites and underprepared lower-status blacks had an explosive potential.[4] Furthermore, the expansion of undergraduate enrollments was accompanied by a much greater expansion of graduate enrollments, so that in many colleges and universities in the sixties, one could find faculties the majority of whose members had been appointed in the last three years. Many faculty members in the liberal arts had as little orientation to the particular institution where they were beginning their teaching careers as did some of the newly recruited black students.

The reports in this volume may be useful if they curb the temptation to explain campus unrest in terms of one or two social or psychological variables. Historical events are connected with each other by Rube Goldbergian transmissions. Soon after student and faculty civil rights activists discovered what Nathan Glazer in the Scranton Commission report has termed "the Berkeley invention," namely, the particular organizational tactics first employed by the Free Speech Movement (FSM), the litany was advanced that students were demonstrating because they were dissatisfied with the impersonality of the institution, the irrelevance of the curriculum, and so on.[5] But on-the-spot studies showed that activist students tended to be less dissatisfied with the curriculum than their more acquiescent fellows.[6] Yet litanies, like other ideas, have consequences, and notions about the sources of student discontent led to educational reforms and, more common-

---

[4] For an account of the complex symbiosis between activist black students and uneasy white faculty, especially in the humanities, see Strout (1970, p. 45*n*).

[5] See Glazer (1970, Chaps. 3–5).

[6] See, e.g., Somers (1965, pp. 549–550).

ly, relaxations in requirements on many of the campuses considered here. Japanese and European student radicals are often astonished when they visit American colleges and universities to see how overdrawn in their terms is the concept of "the student as nigger." They seldom find the overcrowded libraries and nearly impossible access to professors of the universities of Rome or Tokyo, nor the difficulty in changing fields and faculties that a British or French student can experience. What matters, of course, are expectations, the way in which conditions are mediated and interpreted by ideology, and in America expectations are different. It is of America that Margaret Mead (1970) has written that adults are immigrants in the country of the young. The American upper-middle-class father seems more eager to be regarded by his children as a "good guy" than his social-class counterparts elsewhere. Senior faculty members are generally parents as well as teachers, and in both capacities are often insecure concerning the legitimacy of their own values and of the institutions or procedures in which their values have been articulated and embedded.

As I have already suggested, student activism in the United States in recent years would have been far less significant if it had not had support of a practical and moral sort provided by faculty members. Sample surveys conducted by the American Council on Education (ACE) established that in protests of the late sixties, faculty were involved in planning over half; in 1967–68, faculty bodies in two-thirds of the cases passed resolutions approving of the protests.[7]

It is common on the campus and off to hear it said today that it was students who discovered the immorality and horror of the Vietnam War, of racial oppression, as well as the dangers to the

---

[7] Boruch (1969, pp. 21, 50); see the discussion in Lipset (1971, Chap. 6). As a member of the Advisory Committee of the ACE Study of Campus Unrest, I had an opportunity to examine data accumulated from the student press during the late 1960s which supported and illustrated the data gathered by survey research. What the survey data do not make clear is what sort of protest with what sort of tactics got faculty support either ahead of time or retroactively. Very few faculty either planned or favored violence. However, faculty often found it difficult to condemn violence when practiced by "their" side. Many supporters of Senator Joseph McCarthy used to say that they approved of his anti-Communist aims but disapproved of his tactics; in some cases, I was inclined to think that what they secretly admired were precisely the tactics with their stamp of virility and toughness. Occasionally, I have had the same uneasy sense vis-à-vis faculty members who would deplore student tactics while praising student idealism. Some were understandably fearful for their own or their family's safety.

environment of unchecked production of people and goods. This is untrue. The concern with the threat of nuclear annihilation goes back to the atomic scientists and their allies after Hiroshima; awareness of the dangers of the Cold War was nurtured by scholars, diplomats, and journalists; American (as distinguished from French) recognition of the dangers of war in Vietnam, beginning around 1954, was confined to a small minority of intellectuals, foreign correspondents, and government officials and consultants and was so confined until 1965 when, as Zelda Gamson describes in her essay on Michigan, the first teach-in was invented. That teach-in was an uneasy compromise, principally among faculty, of propaganda and educational aims. Only as the method spread and became employed for other causes did it come to resemble a teach-out to prospective converts in and out of the colleges, an organizational weapon as often in the hands of students as of faculty. Even so, at the University of Texas and many other places the teach-in sought to inform and illuminate, frequently seeking to represent a broader spectrum of opinion than the range among the organizers themselves.

Of course, when ground troops moved into South Vietnam and the draft expanded, male students faced often intolerable moral and practical dilemmas which older faculty escaped.[8] What has been characteristic of the student movements in America as elsewhere has not been a greater alertness to evil but a greater willingness to take risks in its extirpation. Perhaps especially in the middle class, the young are less well-defended against idealism than are their elders by cynicism and skepticism; the young are more apt to respond with unchecked indignation to what they see as cruelty and unfairness, and to maintain a more idealistic belief that, by heroic exertion and sacrifice, the unconditional surrender of evil can be assured. Much as a young blue-collar worker might enthusiastically support George Wallace whereas his parents remain committed to bread-and-butter unionism and the Democratic Party, so the college-student children of liberal or socialist parents might join the Venceremos Brigade in Cuba or seek to stop troop trains in Oakland, California.[9]

---

[8] On the efforts of young women to identify with these preoccupations, see Thorne (1972).

[9] Correspondingly, young people may more quickly respond by nihilism and despair when their idealistic or compassionate impulses are frustrated. See the reflections of James Q. Wilson (1972, pp. 50–54).

If one focuses, as I want principally to do in this commentary, on the educational concomitants and consequences of the more directly political events described in these reports, the teach-in assumes a symbolic importance of another sort. Aimed at action and at mobilization, it combined the informational with the evangelical and often in my observation had the quality of a revival meeting. Some of the campuses reported on in this volume devoted special days to discussions of the war or racism or university complicity, etc., in which faculty members often took the lead in declarations of penitence on the ground that their work and life had been irrelevant or blind to the evils now revealed to them.[10] While sharpening the boundary between the pure and the corrupt, the later, more dramaturgical teach-ins illustrated the antagonism of many faculty as well as students to the boundaries separating the campus and the society, between one's proper field as an academician and one's obligations as a citizen between one's existential concerns and one's day-to-day routines. Thus, the later, less educational campus teach-ins resemble the efforts at the annual meetings of professional societies to mobilize these also as cadres against the war, against racism or sexism, against arguably complicitous or irrelevant research.

Awareness of the vocational hazards of teaching has perhaps increased recently.[11] The ambiguities of being a mentor, an influence on the aspirations, moral preoccupations, and sacrificial impulses of the young, can haunt the sensitive teacher who does not want to crowd others with his own moral imperatives. However, some young faculty who appear blithe about the dangers of indoctrination refuse to believe that they themselves are any different from their students or have any particular weight other than that of an articulate fellow-student. They want to deny the existence of what is for them a disagreeable boundary of status, expertise, and chronology. Their innocence

---

[10] Benjamin DeMott (1970, p. 55; 1972, pp. 24–29) of Amherst College has a special talent for describing the evangelical climate of such occasions on his own campus.

[11] With variation among fields and contexts, these resemble the hazards of psychotherapy. Cf. Wheelis (1958, Chap. 7).

allows them often to be quite deracinating vis-à-vis "square," inarticulate, and shy students.[12]

We know from Carnegie Commission surveys and other data how variously and differentially the academic disciplines have been agitated, with sociology and philosophy at one extreme of involvement and engineering, agriculture, and education at the other. Harder to assess are the day-to-day consequences of what might be called the teach-in style, seen in the classroom at retail rather than in the auditorium at wholesale. Neil J. Smelser remarks in his report on Berkeley in this volume that the curriculum has been relatively unaffected by recent turmoil. This might be so in the formal sense, but the tone of many classes may have changed underneath the labels; the reading lists may have changed; and the balance of authority and control between teachers and students may have changed. One would have to look closely at all these aspects to discover subtle changes.

However, the intense interest of many able undergraduates in entering medical or law schools has brought renewed seriousness, or at least competitiveness, to preprofessional courses and programs. Similarly, the disappearance of the boom market for Ph.D.'s has led some young, alienated faculty to stick within their departmental boundaries and to continue serious work as the road to job security. All this could be happening at Berkeley even while what I have termed the teach-in style may still be spreading in non-preprofessional fields from major university centers to some of the less cosmopolitan campuses. On the other hand, in the major centers too, the renewed legitimacy given to emphasis on teaching as against research and consulting may have encouraged some faculty members not to bother with trivial though publishable research when they can find institutional support for a conscientious concern for teaching and advising.

Such a judgment on the part of faculty depends both on the local context of the institution and the life cycle of individuals. It is a risk to the latter if they come to their first college teach-

---

[12] There is an older literature, going back a long way, contending that faculty have negligible influence on students. For a critique of this conclusion see Riesman (1958*b*, pp. 732–739). For a young teacher to persuade himself that he carries no special mandate is a limited protection from the feelings of inadequacy most of us periodically have about our work.

ing job with only the negative identity that they are not going to be researchers and that they are not going to distinguish themselves from their students—indeed that they are going to love them more than anybody else. At Antioch and Old Westbury and at other innovative colleges, where some faculty members have self-righteously rejected "publish or perish," they may find that in the absence of all curricular requirements they are now simply working in a personality market where the implicit mandate is to "teach or perish," a situation in which one can perish even faster and with fewer alternatives. If they have many talents and great energies, they may survive and have other options; if they have more modest gifts, their institutions may be stuck with them because they have been so devoted—and so invisible. Many men and women who were students in the late sixties and prepared themselves for college teaching in the climate of those years at institutions of the sort represented in this volume may be slowly moving into that obscure position.

A NEW IVORY TOWER? The Free Speech Movement at Berkeley grew out of the civil rights movement and the effort to mobilize students for that concern in the Bay Area. Originally it sought only the right to free political expression of that concern on university premises. The FSM initially had no educational aims, and the attacks on the alleged impersonality and inadequacy of the educational process were mainly a propagandistic afterthought—a useful one in unsettling faculty and curtailing institutional authority. Increasingly, however, as campus protests spread, their focus became intramural. Many activists, faculty as well as students, attacked the university as symbol or stand-in for the corrupt society. Or they sought to make the university behave more nobly or righteously than other social institutions.

One result was the creation of a new sort of ivory tower which differed from its surrounding locality in its ethnic composition as well as its preoccupations. Old Westbury can serve as an example here too, which brought to Nassau County—which is overwhelmingly white—a student body of whom more than half are intended to be nonwhite (with similar proportions among faculty and staff). Livingston College of Rutgers University in New Brunswick, New Jersey, has, so to speak, imported a large slice of inner-city Newark to its somewhat isolated campus. Similarly, Antioch's New Directions program brings inner-city blacks to rural and small-town southwestern Ohio. To be sure, there is an extramural thrust to all these efforts, a desire to grapple with the race question in society at large, and of course many of those involved in the effort may also be tutoring in inner-city schools or otherwise working beyond the ivory tower. But the desire to purify one's own institution has been an essential element of a great deal of activism, often with the consequence of increasing group isolation and conflict within the walls, even while hoping for a greater sense of community. Benson Snyder's account of a particular confrontation at MIT poignantly illustrates the antagonism among people who differed on the tactics or locale of opposition to the Vietnam war. Jill Conway's account of the effort to establish a kind of communal governance structure at the University of Toronto reveals the quixotic hopes of many students and some faculty that increased participation would bring collegiality, whereas in fact it brought animosity.

Of course, animosity was sometimes the aim, however concealed. Most of the writers of these reports tend to accept the definitions of the agenda provided by white campus radicals or black militants, that is, that they are attacking the war or racism as the case may be, for instance by blocking military or Dow recruiters or demanding that the university get rid of its investments in companies doing business in white-controlled Africa. I would myself think that on the larger, more radicalized campuses, many activists have been geologists prospecting for emotion-laden issues on which to mobilize and to attack within the somewhat protected university precinct. Politicians generally proceed in this way, by prospecting for issues. Saul Alinsky learned to do it; so did Joe McCarthy.

Only a few activists wanted to destroy the universities—rather they sought to use them as bases for mobilization or hoped to purify them as models for and contrasts to the corrupt society. But what economists might call the externalities of the effort have often been harmful to universities, pure or impure. Fighting the war in the university precinct, even when it did not polarize colleague groups who might not differ on the war but on the tactics of opposing it, tended to diminish the support for universities among private and public constituencies. Many academicians and a very large number of students considered these costs worth paying (and of course such costs are always borne unevenly, often by nonparticipants). The same may be said of the struggle for racial justice which made use of the universities, whether in their extramural reach or their intramural collectivity.

One easily gets the impression that all higher education has suffered because of the backlash against campus turmoil, and against the symbolic crusades mounted from the campus in favor of new values and lifestyles. Yet quite apart from campus unrest, higher education was bound to lose the momentum of its great leap forward in the 1950s and early 1960s, else it would have consumed the national product for salaries and the national forests for journal articles. All public education has had to compete with new welfare and other demands and to do so when its promises of miraculous benefits to individuals and society have lost much credibility. Nevertheless, many private universities have been able to maintain the support of leading donors among their alumni in the face of considerable resentment about what has happened at their institutions. A certain patrician liberalism and self-abnegation may often be involved here; I recall attending a meeting of major Harvard College philanthropists in 1969–70, where the suggestion that the Admissions Committee should screen applicants for radicalism was dismissed as shameful and vulgar. Indeed, the children of some eminent alumni have been among the radical student leaders. Even so, I have been surprised at the continuation of support in dollar terms even when numbers of alumni have been turned off. Of course it does not follow that the private institutions will not go bankrupt, since their costs have escalated so rapidly, sometimes reflecting increased obligations incurred as a result of turmoil.[13]

In the state-controlled sector of higher education, the public disenchantment, along with continuing demands for undergraduate education from young people and their parents, has led in some states to the regional universities' and the community colleges' gaining ground relatively speaking over the major state universities. Probably not many people even in Wisconsin remember black students' protests at Oshkosh, where a number of the black students were expelled, while probably few have forgotten violence and repeated protests at the University of Wisconsin in Madison, the

[13] See Cheit (1971).

state capital. That university has suffered drastic restrictions in what was once a generous freedom to recruit out-of-state students; and the merger of the University of Wisconsin system with the state university system, mentioned in Philip G. Altbach's essay, illustrates the symbolic, if only partial, loss of hegemony by the Madison campus. (Similarly, the University of North Carolina in Chapel Hill has been made part of a statewide amalgam.) The granting of university status to some of the California state colleges, long opposed by the University of California, may be seen not only as justified elevation of the former to reflect the actual distinction of San Diego State, San Jose State, and San Francisco State, but also as an effort to pull Berkeley down. Rutgers likewise suffers from the rivalry of the advancing state colleges, as well as from the pressure to provide local services at its Newark and Camden campuses. And if the University of Michigan as described by Zelda Gamson remains preeminent in the state, she also makes clear that money to meet the demands of the Black Action Movement must come partly out of departmental budgets, perhaps impairing the research function on behalf of the functions of undergraduate teaching and community service.

Another form of leveling is the effort in many states to increase the teaching loads at the state universities, making them more comparable to those in state and community colleges.[14] The student and faculty Left, who often see research as a form of counterinsurgency and who are ideologically egalitarian and hostile to distinctions, are glad to join the Philistine Right in this attack on the privileges of the research-oriented professor and the major university he inhabits. A major privilege is the right to choose one's own workload and, within collegial limits, whom and how much one teaches. Contrary to legend, professors in research-oriented institutions prefer to combine teaching with research, often including undergraduate teaching.[15] At a confer-

---

[14] Because of its constitutional status, the University of Michigan could legally resist the legislative requirement of a minimum teaching load, but through appropriations, pressure has been put on to increase the minimum from six to ten hours. To be sure, Good Soldier Schweiks as we are, faculty members have been able to reinterpret such legislation, for example, by having student conferences count as a class, to minimize the impact. Quite possibly, the result of such legislation may be a diminution of the quality and intensity of teaching while total hours on the job rise only nominally.

[15] See Parsons and Platt (1968, pp. 497–523), and other writings by Parsons and Platt; see also Fulton and Trow (1972).

ence cosponsored by the Western Interstate Commission for Higher Education and the Center for Research and Development, John Silber (1971, p. 40) has declared:

The slogan, "Give us the old-fashioned teacher," may disguise the intent of colleges and universities to hire professors who are so incompetent or lacking in energy that they cannot survive as writers or be in demand as consultants to major corporations. . . .

No doubt, few institutions are purposely seeking incompetent professors, but it seems correct to declare that the reintroduction of high teaching loads and the effort to get rid of research and consulting are efforts to reduce the prestige of some professors, and perhaps to elevate other candidates for worthiness (ibid.). In the same symposium, Walter P. Metzger (1971, pp. 79–80) argues that a profession grounded in research "clings tenaciously to qualitative judgments by peers; a didactic profession more readily submits to judgment by pupils, parents, and lay authorities." Metzger implies that a research-oriented profession is prepared to take its chances with an unlimited supply of competitors, because in principle there is no limit to the amount of research that can be done (though there is surely a limit to the amount of funding for it) and its standards of quality are more evident to peers, while a purely pedagogic profession may resort to unionism to limit the supply of teachers, since the touchstones of distinguished teaching are far less evident and reliable than those of research.[16]

[16] A few years ago I was asked by the Danforth Foundation to review its program of Harbison Awards for Gifted Teaching, which gave me a chance to examine evaluations by students, colleagues, and visiting Danforth observers. When it comes to these nominations of outstanding teachers who are evocative for undergraduates and at the same time hold them up to high standards, it is possible to arrive at reasonably consensual judgments based on multiple evaluations even while being aware of the lack of comparability among students, institutions, and observers—and of the danger that ratings can be manipulated one way or the other by cliques. Of course, not all Harbison Awards have been noncontroversial. It would be still more difficult to arrive at agreement concerning the ordinary run of teaching, neither the most distinguished nor the most dilapidated. Obviously, this is not to argue that judgments concerning research are self-evident!

However, Christopher Jencks (Jencks et al., forthcoming, Chap. 6, footnote 22) observes that school teachers have not really tried to limit entry into teaching, remarking, "Education courses and teachers' colleges have been widely available and virtually free." The insistence on degrees has not been intended to limit the supply of teachers but to raise their status.

The rise of faculty unionism seems to me one of the most profound of ongoing transformations, but it is an issue barely dealt with in these pages. My interest here is primarily in the intramural educational consequences of unionization and not in the possible extramural political consequences.[17] Nathan Glazer's chapter on CCNY suggests that the grievance machinery and the embedded union tradition that supports it make it difficult to allow dismissal of any faculty member who can make a case for staying on.[18] The teaching assistants who struck at the University of Wisconsin were torn, as Altbach observes, between their desire for more control over the educational process and their concern with more traditional bread-and-butter union issues; in the bargaining, apparently, the educational issues tended to disappear, although the educational impact of the strike did not, for a good many faculty decided that they really were not as dependent on TAs as they had thought, and because of this attitude and legislative reaction, the actual number of TAs has been drastically reduced.[19]

The essay by Algo Henderson discusses the ideological passions behind the strike by members of the American Federation of Teachers at San Francisco State College. Through the medium of a strike, a minority of faculty sought to put the leverage of the Bay Area labor movement behind the nonnegotiable demands of

[17] What the latter may be like in the future is adumbrated by the conflict between the local union at Nassau County Community College on Long Island and the local fiscal authorities who found great public support in their effort to require the faculty to increase their teaching loads and in resisting union demands for salary increases. See also the discussion by Jesse Pitts of the short-lived strike by an AAUP union newly formed at Oakland University in Michigan, in *Change* (Pitts, 1972).

[18] During the late 1960s I kept being reminded of Mary McCarthy's *The Groves of Academe,* a novel out of an earlier academic era in which a faculty member in a liberal college who knows he is about to be let go claims to be a Communist. On such matters there are of course enormous differences among departments in a single institution as well as among institutions the country over; today in a tighter faculty market and an altered national mood, there may be less interest in and tolerance for nontenured faculty radicals.

[19] Marshall Meyer's essay on Harvard discusses the efforts in the spring of 1972 to secure sole bargaining rights for the Harvard Graduate Student and Teaching Fellow Union, and the Union's brief work stoppage. There was some division between those concerned principally with economic issues of tuition rebates, rates of pay, etc., and those whose preoccupations were primarily with issues of societal, and to a lesser degree university, reform. Yet so-called economic issues are seldom purely that, as they often involve questions as to the extent of mutual consultation and the degree of esteem implicit in financial formulae.

the Third World Liberation Front; labor support was muted, faculty support was partial, and the strike eventually failed.[20] On the whole, there have not been strong union movements at the more distinguished state universities; at Berkeley, as Neil Smelser reports, membership in the AFT (seldom in any case the chosen instrument at leading universities) is negligible.[21] However, what has happened at Rutgers, as described in Richard McCormick's essay, may be indicative of developments at other major state universities, for the Rutgers faculty has made the American Association of University Professors its bargaining agent, separating itself in this way from the AFL-CIO and also from the local New Jersey union of the state college faculties. Both at Oakland University and at Rutgers, faculty members fear statewide leveling tendencies; they hope to be able to lobby in the state capital to maintain their position vis-à-vis the rest of public higher education in the state. The growth in the power of state coordinating commissions of higher education and of gubernatorial budgetary intelligence reflects the increase in centralized control which makes many faculty members feel as if they were being deprived of professional autonomy and treated like employees of the highway or tax departments. The move to unionize may then reflect a resentful acceptance of the lot of the middling civil servant.

For the last three years I have spoken at the annual Institute for College and University Presidents, which is run as on-the-job training for recently installed incumbents by the American Council on Education. At each of these week-long sessions, discussions of the impact of unionization have been a major feature of the agenda. Private colleges with an annual operating revenue of $1 million or more are subject to the National Labor Relations Board, but most of the presidents from small private colleges do not regard union-

---

[20] For a quite different account by a former San Francisco State College faculty member, see Bunzel (1971); and for still another account, focusing on the strike, see Goldman (1970, pp. 271–292). While AFT intervention added legitimacy to the students' cause, it eventually weakened militancy because the AFL-CIO Council sanctioned the strike for its economic, not its political, aims; radical students, however, could not appear to reject an alliance with labor, no matter how reformist the latter.

[21] Since Neil Smelser wrote, there has been a strong movement at Berkeley to develop a Faculty Association which could send representatives to lobby in Sacramento and could fight, union style, against the economic pinch increasingly being felt. So far, the movement is in the hands of moderate faculty (including Smelser).

ization as a likely immediate prospect, although there have been strong moves to form unions in some of the Jesuit colleges. The presidents of state colleges who have had experiences with unions seem to believe that they make encouragement of innovative teaching more difficult by handicapping any individuated "merit" treatment of faculty. In their more cynical moments, which are rare, the presidents can even imagine bargaining with a union delegate to grant a salary increase in return for the union's not pressing the case of a particularly unpopular faculty member who claims his academic freedom has been violated.[22] Commonly, presidents find that a union tends eventually to weaken the power of the Faculty Senate, even though during a transition period they may have to deal simultaneously with both the union and the senate. While different unions have different priorities and ideological flavors, all tend to develop an adversary relation with the institution, muting the possibility of leadership even by department chairmen (sometimes treated as management, sometimes as labor); administrators soon recognize that whatever they say may be held against them in bargaining sessions or in grievance procedures, thus formalizing the lack of trust that may itself have helped precipitate formation of the union.

Despite such general consequences, the impact of unionization will vary greatly depending on the size and nature of the bargaining unit. Many units include librarians, counselors, and other professional but nonacademic staff; but what about part-time faculty, research associates, and agricultural extension agents? There have been arguments as to whether law-school faculty members properly belong in the same bargaining unit as liberal-arts-college faculty; and then should the unit be systemwide in a state college system?[23] However these questions are decided, there is no doubt that voting in the bargaining unit will be on the basis of "one man, one

[22] More likely in a unionized faculty shop there would be peer pressure on individual faculty members to refrain from publicly irritating behavior during the course of delicate bargaining sessions at the state capital. To be sure, such pressures would be present in some measure even without a union. But the demands of union solidarity may encourage some faculty to go along with the union rather than, for example, to demonstrate to protesting students that they are *for* the students. For comparison of British and American styles of solidarity of work groups, see Burrage (1972, pp. 141–162).

[23] I owe some sensitivity to these questions to conversation and correspondence with Walter Metzger; also, to the work of Joseph W. Garbarino (e.g., Garbarino, forthcoming).

vote," which will tend to weaken the relative power of senior faculty.

In talking with department chairmen and others in the City University of New York system and several other unionized campuses, I have had the impression that procedures for assessment of faculty, for tenure, and for the handling of grievances make it extremely difficult, at times nearly impossible, to raise the level of faculty quality. As in other walks of life, to be a strong union member may provide a kind of political insurance. The presence of the union adds to the ever-present pressure for "fairness" in promotion, making it difficult to promote talented people unusually quickly since this would create invidious distinctions. But there has not been enough experience with faculty unionization at different levels of academic quality to make any assured judgments as to the consequences.[24] Yet it seems to me that for effective functioning, a college faculty needs to combine the individualism one associates with artists and free-floating intellectuals, with the cooperative-competitive collegiality, not of a submarine crew, but of a research group, a private medical clinic, or the partners in an elite law firm. When it comes to the most intricate and individualistic sorts of academic work, whether in research or in teaching, persuasive control by one's peers becomes much more important than either formal control by a bargaining contract or hierarchical control by "management."[25] Trusted academic leadership is also necessary, once the group in question grows beyond the

[24] Faculty vitality, as well as voice, may be increased by unionization in community colleges, where administrative despotism, not peer pressure, has been the faculty's problem. See discussion in Blackburn (1972, pp. 40–44). Blackburn observes that English academics are unionized without reducing the status of Cambridge and Oxford; plainly, the impact of unionization depends on the total context.

[25] These essays make clear how seldom a faculty group will censure one of its own members. I am a fairly regular reader of the AAUP *Bulletin,* where one can find ample instances of protecting colleagues against administrative or regental interference, and none of holding them to standards or canons of a more informal sort vis-à-vis their students and colleagues. To be sure, if a faculty member appeals to the AAUP against his or her own institution, the informal negotiations that often ensue may take account of the faculty member's own sense of collegial and institutional responsibility. And of course departments and other academic units do seek to enforce minimal codes on their individual members; however, the academic professions possess nothing like the guild cohesiveness that unevenly characterizes the medical profession.

limited span of control of a peer group without official leaders. Burton Clark's account of the combination of morality and morale with high academic standards at Wesleyan in the Victor Butterfield era illustrates the kind of persuasive control through the colleague group and through a leader that can sometimes operate in an institution not of giant scale nor of exorbitantly diversified constituencies.

If the present trend toward centralized state control of budgets and policies of all public universities continues, it seems quite possible that the great public institutions will become unionized while the well-endowed, humanely administered, selective private colleges and universities such as Wesleyan or others discussed in this volume will not. This may depend on whether private-college pay increases can keep ahead of inflation, whether faculty will continue to feel that they are treated as professionals and not made to punch metaphorical timeclocks, and whether faculty politics can continue to maintain some consensual quality and some support for the tenured elders, who are generally more resistant to unionization. In that case, it seems to me that a small number of private colleges and universities might be able far to outstrip their distinguished public competitors, once unionization has embraced the latter. Even if the general position of private higher education continues to decline, some venturesome faculty may be tempted to leave the relative security of public higher education for the greater freedom of a few private institutions.[26]

The relation of unionization to professionalism among teachers

---

[26] John Livingston (forthcoming), dean of Sacramento State University, argues cogently for granting instant tenure in his article, "Tenure, Anyone?" He believes that tenure decisions lead to competitiveness and lack of collegial solidarity without greatly improving faculty quality, since in most institutions not many people are ever let go, and since the second or tenure decision on someone is not likely to be better than the first or hiring decision. He might possibly have a better case if no institution failed to grant instant tenure and hence left open the possibility that it could recruit new faculty to fill its upper ranks and thus respond to targets of intellectual opportunity. But since for the foreseeable future at least some of the eminent private institutions will continue to have tenure and to grant it rather sparingly, some faculty may be attracted precisely to such institutions by the chance to live in a bracing, if also competitive, intellectual and academic climate, in which at least occasionally good work and workers are encouraged by promotion and by the hope of keeping good academic company. (On the miseries of seeking such company, see Thomas Cottle's "The Pains of Permanence" [Cottle, forthcoming].)

is partly a semantic and partly a substantive controversy.[27]
Some radical faculty seek unionization precisely as an attack on
professionalism, which they regard as private and elitist. As
union members, they can declare that they are not privileged and
precious eggheads; while, given the present lack of enthusiasm
for the union movement in the Left in America, they may not think
of themselves as the vanguard of the proletariat, they may still
not have completely buried the intellectuals' romance with labor.
Yet many must in their own imaginations envisage that their
freedoms will not be curbed, so that they can have a feeling of
worker solidarity without the corresponding constraints.

Yet there *is* a kind of collegial solidarity which unionization in
the present academic climate will obtain for faculty, and that is
to provide them with a forum from which students are automatically excluded. There is irony here, since many, especially of the
younger faculty who see joining a union as ideologically virtuous,
are also those faculty members who proclaim that they are oriented
to students rather than to the academic guilds. In governance discussions, they would certainly have voted to include students in any
of the sorts of assemblies, based on the premise of codetermination,
that faculty-student representatives voted for at Toronto and
obtained at Princeton, Wesleyan, and many other places.[28] Faculty
members today are feeling cumulative pressures on their autonomy—from state legislatures, coordinating commissions, HEW

[27] Cf., e.g., Dreeben (1972, pp. 326–337). In one sense of the term *professionalism,* several college presidents have observed to me that a union bargaining
agent is more businesslike and matter-of-fact than a talky and rhetorical group
of faculty members. To be sure, when there are competing unions for different
cadres on the same campus, union bargaining may become as superheated as
any faculty senate.

[28] At many universities even now, as Philip Altbach complains about Wisconsin,
senior faculty do not include students in their intramural discussions about
promotions to their own tenure ranks. Hence in institutions which are partially
participative, senior faculty may have their (only occasional) club meeting,
but junior faculty are never present unless students are also present, whether
as representatives or observers or part of the general town meeting. The
second version of the College at Old Westbury began its efforts to govern itself
by including not only students but spouses and staff; in such a potpourri of
communal claimants, junior faculty might particularly be grateful that a union
provides a legitimate caucus where they can talk with each other in private.
Studies suggest that feelings of alienation rest as much on belief in one's
own powerlessness as on unsatisfactory or meaningless work or embittered
personal relations. Cf., for an illuminating comparison of America and France,
Seaman (1972, pp. 385–402).

officials, and other outside authorities—and the presence of students, no matter how generally welcome, may add to a cumulative feeling of being surrounded.[29]

It is understandable that nothing is said in these pages about the unionization of students, that is, student bodies in general rather than teaching assistants, and there is not much to say as yet, since the movement is only incipient. However, the increasing separation of student government from any official role on the campus tilts some activist students toward unionizing, and so does a glimpse of possible power as a lobby. The State University of New York Student Association maintains legal counsel in Albany, and University of California students have a lobbyist in Sacramento, who on fiscal matters will work with the chancellors and regents for budgetary increases, while battling independently ‚for student rights on other issues.

Though radical students sometimes like to see themselves as workers, as potential producers being groomed for slots all too useful to a worthless Establishment, students in fact are primarily a consumer group and as such unlikely to attain in higher education the bargaining power that faculty as a producer group can exert through a union. Most students are apt to be apathetic concerning the quality of teaching, and hard to mobilize systematically against faculty as distinct from administrative power.[30]

[29] The essay on the University of Pennsylvania by Goddard and Koons declares that students behave quite as well on committees as faculty do (although there has been some leakage of confidential information), but what is left out of such an observation is the sheer impact of numbers, both in terms of delaying decisions and of diluting ties between junior and senior faculty—often, although not invariably, because the junior faculty are apt to identify with students. The Trow-Lipset survey done for the Carnegie Commission shows how wide the generation gap is among faculty on such questions as participatory democracy. Furthermore, whereas faculty, and especially senior, institutionally oriented faculty, are inclined to try to decide matters among themselves by consensus, resisting settling issues by narrow majority votes, students and the faculty who side with them have no such restraints and are bent on winning, except in those occasional instances where they regard their group as a commune and insist on unanimity. See, for a penetrating discussion of these differences in orientation, Stinchcombe (1971).

[30] In my observation, some faculty members of the New Left are so committed to spontaneity that they often do not meet their classes or office hours or get their papers corrected and returned—an exercise which in any case they might be inclined to deprecate. But activist students have been quite unwilling to bring pressure against such goofing off. It is hard for them not to be tolerant of spontaneity; to criticize would put them in the position of being called uptight, and would perhaps confess a greater concern with the curriculum and

**THE
LIMITS OF
PRESIDENTIAL
POWER**

In some institutions, the budgetary stringencies of recent years have increased presidential power by depriving individual faculty members and departments of any flexibility and requiring them to argue at the president's court even to maintain present levels of expenditure. Nevertheless, as I reflect on the essays in this volume, it seems to me that the college presidents who figure herein have lost power, and probably influence as well, in the last few years. In the public sector, statewide coordination, for better as well as for worse, has begun to curb the entrepreneurial zeal of presidential tycoons seeking new prestigeful graduate and professional programs in order to overtake and surpass their local and national rivals. The sharp drop in the rate of increase of federal funding (except in the biomedical area) has tended to make presidents more dependent on local sources of support; the president who can depend on many diverse sources of support may feel a somewhat greater freedom than one who is almost wholly dependent on the good will of the local legislature or a particular body of trustees and philanthropists. But few presidents can afford an eye single toward external sources of support. The growth of the demand for intramural participation, coupled with the naïve notion that if people would only communicate they would understand each other better, compels presidents, like other people, to spend much more time in meetings and in informal conversations with students, faculty, and staff.[31] Thus the presidents' agenda of intramural and extramural public relations and "relating" leaves little time for significant intervention in educational issues except insofar as they have a chance to tilt decisions by their leverage on the

---

with adult responsibility than their ideology allows. However, this might change, and a Ralph Nader–type consumerism could well spread among the students, indeed intensifying faculty pressures for unionization as, among other things, protection against harassment from students.

Furthermore, I am inclined to think that a strike by a liberal, unionized faculty could be severely damaged if black and other nonwhite students complained that they were not being taught, and that they could not afford this. And I believe that when the first highly visible faculty strike is broken, as will almost surely occur, current enthusiasm for unionization may be somewhat curbed.

[31] The trustee-faculty-student search committees that now involve themselves in the selection of presidents are often looking for someone who they feel can relate to them and be accessible—although as a character trait this accessibility may also imply openness rather than hauteur vis-à-vis the institution's enemies. However, financial perils may in other cases impel a search for presentable but hard-driving managerial types.

various committees or commissions, with their appropriately balanced tickets, whose ensuing reports seem so often (as in the accounts in this volume) bypassed by events.

One of the few presidents in office throughout the period is James Dixon of Antioch; he is an exception also to the general rule that if the president loses the support of his faculty, he is almost certain to lose his office, even if he retains the support of other constituencies. (The other exception is S. I. Hayakawa of San Francisco State College, who, however, unlike Dixon, has been an inactive and uninvolved president, though very visible and photogenic off campus, whom the trustees cannot fire because of the symbolic role he played, and who for most faculty is now no more than a symbolic presence.[32]) For a time, Dixon was able to rely on an alliance which is seldom recognized and is generally tacit, between innovative administrators and more or less radical undergraduates, in opposition to scholarly faculty. Kingman Brewster, Jr., of Yale, has perhaps been the most dramatically adept at this kind of administrative jujitsu. But Gerald Grant's report on the Antioch "systems" suggests that Dixon's ability is more intricate still, depending as it does on moving so fast in so many places that his critics cannot quite keep up with him. His virtuosity is enhanced by his position as heir to a tradition of innovation; consider by contrast the situation of the new incumbent at City College, Robert Marshak, whose energetic ingenuity must combat highly paid unionized (and often politically entrenched and mutually contentious) faculty, and among other polarized city and state supporters and adversaries, an antagonistic vocal alumni body.[33]

It is hardly news that during the late 1960s college presidents in the more exposed institutions had to be extraordinarily resilient and adept simply to stay in place. Privately, many complained that they did not enter on academic careers to become tacticians in the proper combination of force and public relations. In some instances, as with President Goheen at Princeton, they presided with sense and sensibility over the happy or resigned abdication of adults from noncurricular areas and the diminution (in Princeton's case, quite modest) of requirements in curriculum.

---

[32] What I say here is based on my own, perhaps mistaken impression, and not on the Algo D. Henderson essay.

[33] For a sensitive account of City College under stress, see Kriegel (1972).

But they could and often did play a modest educational role in facilitating the new departments and programs that reflected the era: Afro-American studies in many places, war-peace studies in a few, ecological or environmental studies in a good many, and women's studies beginning more recently than many of these essays could take account of. I regard these instances as illustrations of a more general observation, namely, that most academic innovation which involves new allocations of resources (rather than, for example, alterations in the reading list or mode of teaching of particular courses) depends on administrative initiative and often on outside support as well. Some of these changes, such as the coalescence of environmental studies into a program, have been made without the spur and fireworks of confrontation politics; and there the leadership of presidents and deans has generally been necessary to pilot a new organization through the veto groups built into academic life by departmental and collegewide decision-making processes. But with Afro-American studies, the president may have been just carried along in a mass meeting, like other stray individuals, whatever logistical and budgetary tangles were left for him to resolve afterwards.

These processes are illustrated at the University of Michigan, where Robben Fleming, more happily situated than formerly at the University of Wisconsin, could coax and compel departments in effect to tithe themselves so as to provide the funding to meet the goal of 10 percent black enrollment which was the nonnegotiable demand of the Black Action Movement; the anarchic departments could not and would not have done this on their own. Correspondingly (although it does not appear directly in these pages), the president or other chief administrator could carry out the mandate of finding places for black, Spanish-speaking, or, presently, women faculty and administrators, bribing departments with funds in some cases, cajoling or even coercing them in others.[34] It is with the presidents that HEW representatives

---

[34] As administrators have discovered to their dismay, not all black, Spanish-speaking or even women candidates will satisfy the constituencies they are supposed to represent. An Argentinian at home in the literature and history of the American Southwest will scarcely placate a group of Chicano and Chicana students, nor will a Chicana administrator satisfy Chicano students or faculty; a Dominican is not likely to satisfy the expectations of Boricuan (Puerto Rican) students. Appointment to a Black Studies program of a black from Martinique or Jamaica or Nigeria may be regarded as an insult by North

hammer out what the affirmative action program of the institution should be to meet the goals (de facto quotas) agreed upon for hiring approved minorities, including women. (By the newest HEW regulations, these include Eastern and Southern European ethnic groups such as Italians and Poles; there is as yet no goal for white male Southerners, who occasionally believe themselves discriminated against in Yankee institutions, nor for other possibly aggrieved cadres who have not yet invented their ethnicity.)

A handful of American colleges, going far beyond what any government official would conceivably suggest, has sought to explore what could be accomplished by multiracial recruitments at all levels, even when the immediate locale is predominantly white. Livingston College of Rutgers, as already mentioned, has pursued this path, as has the Third College of the University of California at San Diego. The second version of the College at Old Westbury, going beyond the guidelines established by the first, has set itself a formula for recruiting students and faculty of 30 percent black, 30 percent Spanish-speaking (principally Puerto Rican), 30 percent white, 10 percent "other," and 50 percent women.[35] This is in Nassau County, with a black population of 4.8 percent; however, there are enough prospective black and Puerto Rican students in the county so that Old Westbury need not recruit in New York City to fulfill its demographic aims. But it is the only public four-year college in the county (the State University at Stony Brook is in neighboring Suffolk County), and the community colleges are beginning to turn out students, predominantly white, who will want to transfer for further work to four-year institutions. Old Westbury is now so small that the incongruence of its student mix to the local potential commuter-student body has not yet been

---

American black students. And women who are regarded as insufficiently militant as women, may be viewed as a placebo by an activist Women's Liberation group. Old Westbury has faced conflicts over this whole range of issues.

[35] Earl Lane (1972, p. 22), in "The 'New' Old Westbury," gives the actual mix in 1971–72: "Of the 496 full-time and 69 part-time students last year, just under 40 percent were black; 19 percent were Puerto Rican or Spanish-speaking; the median age was 29. . . ." The sex ratio is not given. Of 57 faculty members for 1972–73, there are 34 men and 23 women; 22.5 are white, 19 are black, and 12 are Spanish-speaking, with 3 "others" all of Chinese origin, including a Chinese woman raised in Trinidad and educated in Glasgow, who is acting academic vice-president (information from President John D. Maguire).

made a political issue. In being willing to take the risk of such an issue developing, the president, John Maguire, may not have carried with him from Wesleyan his sense of the latter's fortunate endowments, private protections, and residential exclusiveness, but he has proceeded with a rare intrepidity.[36]

CHANGES IN CAMPUS CLIMATES: RACIAL INTEGRATION When racial and ethnic mixtures of this sort are talked and argued about, the case is generally made for and against without reference to social class or what in *The Academic Revolution* (1968*a*) Jencks and I speak of as cultural class. Thus it is often declared that it is good for white students to be exposed to black students, especially if the former have been suffering from a homogeneous suburban environment. But this is said without reference to the cultural class of either group, which means sometimes that affluent upper-middle-class white students provide the surround for entering inner-city black proletarians, as apparently happened at Wesleyan, Antioch, the first Old Westbury, and Livingston College at Rutgers. White students and faculty at these institutions would often talk about sharing "*the* black experience" as if there were only one and it was exotic, deprived, and militant. Some of the most antiwhite blacks lived up to this white image; many black leaders were in fact upper-middle class themselves, with guilts vis-à-vis less fortunate blacks comparable to those of upper-middle-class white radicals who sought to act as if proletarian. The educational outcome for the large mass of newly arrived black students has been at best mixed; often it has been traumatic. The radical pedagogic experimenters at Federal City College were teaching some extremely square and vocationally oriented older black students who wanted a "regular" four-year college and not an experiment. (I recall an older black woman who worked a full shift at Bethesda Naval Hospital and who, in the first year of the college, said to me that she wanted to learn chemistry, not some kind of unified science. She also resented black militants who had closed the college to celebrate a visit from black athletes who had acted defiantly in the Mexico City Olympics.) For such students, a college degree was their platform to become upwardly mobile in the larger society, and the platform would be impaired if the college's degree was discredited by inflated grades (or pass–no credit grading) or by an undistin-

---

[36] For a recognition by two innovation-minded sociologists that administrators tend to be more supportive of innovation and of students' interests than are faculty, see Fashing and Deutsch (1971, Chap. 8, especially pp. 264–271).

guished or unscholarly faculty. Their chances would also be harmed, to recur to an earlier metaphor, if the whites involved in the greening of America should, as some blacks at Old Westbury put it, try to persuade everybody to seek degrees in GG, "Grooving on the Grass."[37] To be sure, many of these black students found sufficient support to see them through, in spite of the unstructured and often disorienting milieu into which they were drawn, out of white and sometimes also black guilt, fear, public relations, hopefulness, and idealism.

The short-run educational impact on white students of the recruiting of nonwhite students seems to be problematic. Even from the suburbs today, many affluent white students do not go to college with an innocent and sheltered outlook on sex or race; the age of political and cultural consent, like the age of puberty, has been dropping pretty steadily. Yet there is innocence, or repression, about the matter of class, and many whites believe themselves asked to cross the race line when in fact they are being asked also to cross a class line, thus complicating matters more than either side initially realizes. To the degree that blacks have become separatist, white students have tended, whatever their desires, to be exposed to the stereotyped spokesmen and not to individuals; fortunately in this respect, only a minority of black students is generally enrolled in black studies departments, and probably only a minority of these departments is wholly separatist on the student and faculty levels, so there is at least classroom acquaintance among white and black students, even if there is minimal social contact.[38] It might be an arguable proposition that white students presently learn as much about life in the inner city through tutoring and field work projects as they do from spasmodic

[37] I recall a discussion with a group of entering black students at a new state college who, jumping to the defense of apparent underdogs, had been readily mobilized to support several faculty members (whom they themselves declared to be terrible teachers) whose contracts had not been renewed. I pointed out to the black students that some of the white affluent students who had led the protest depended on the platform of their family, their charm and vivacity, and their connections, to give them such place as they might seek when they were through with college, whereas the blacks, all of them on scholarship, would depend on the standing of the college itself; it was their principal springboard. Were they not being overly generous in supporting faculty members who by their own account had neither scholarly repute nor ability as teachers?

[38] It seems a reasonable inference from these essays that political contact has also been minimal in recent years. While white radicals at Michigan supported the Black Action Movement and strike, they felt used by the black students,

contacts with fellow students who are black or Spanish-speaking. Indeed, in all the discourse concerning the advantage of a heterogeneous student body, the assumption is often implicit that there is no such thing as vicarious learning, and that direct personal experience raises no questions of mediation or interpretation. Undoubtedly, black students often resent being put in the position of being Exhibit A, for what appear to be sentimental, overly sympathetic, and inquisitive whites.[39]

CHANGES IN CAMPUS CLIMATES: RESIDENCE The antagonism to what is called elitism and selectivity as well as the desire (if less commonly the practice) for seeking heterogeneity of acquaintance has meant that fraternities and sororities are everywhere in trouble on the liberal campus. David Goddard and Linda Koons in their profile of the University of Pennsylvania have nothing at all to say in favor of these enclaves. At Princeton, some clubs still have "Bicker"; some are completely nonselective; most have become coed; the majority of students do not join—and only alumni mourn. Roughly half the Wesleyan fraternities have now expired despite the leadership they took in battles against discrimination. Faculty members in general, except for the few home-guarders who are alumni both of a college and of its fraternity row, are either hostile or at best indifferent to that system, but seldom raise the question as to what will take the place of these delegitimated enclaves. However, some faculty members and administrators have attempted to develop subcolleges, such as the colleges of Wesleyan or the Residential College of Michigan, as cocurricular substitutes for the fraternity system that might contribute to the intellectual life rather than provide a buffer against it.[40] Princeton also has moved to create several alternatives to both the traditional dormitories and the

---

and the latter blamed them for the incidents of violence and disruption. Black militants have rarely joined white radicals in antiwar activities, and even less on ecological issues or feminist ones.

[39] I recall the story of a black Radcliffe student who had been quizzed by a liberal white tutor as to why she was not majoring in the Afro-American Studies department, but preferred instead to concentrate in something as unrelated to "the community" as European literature.

[40] Some evidence that this hope of the planners of the Residential College has not been fulfilled is presented in Newcomb, Brown, et al. (1971, pp. 99–142). The Residential College began in 1967, when the counterculture was also gain-

traditional fraternities or eating clubs. The Yale Colleges and Harvard Houses were, among other things, earlier efforts in the same direction.

The almost claustrophobic desire of vocal students to be entirely on their own makes all such efforts problematic. It seems to me highly unlikely that in an era when class and family boundaries are being torn down, fraternities and sororities can thrive. For some students in the natural sciences, laboratory groups, like geologists on field trips, can provide a quasifraternity. Student journalism and broadcasting, like some athletic teams, can serve in the same way. The same is true of some volunteer groups, such as those engaged in tutoring or working in a mental hospital. For a few students during recent years, political groups have served as coed substitutes for fraternities and sororities, dispensing, of course, with the despised formalities of dating.[41] However, the combination of sexual and task subordination of women in such groups was one of the sources of the women's liberation movement, and possibly of the contemporary pattern in which many of the leading activists on campus, as at Princeton and Harvard presently, are women. Both on and off campus, some women do meet together for consciousness-raising, sharing of experience, and mutual support. However, for many students of both sexes nothing has taken the place of the fraternities and sororities (which in the great state universities never enrolled more than a minority). Reading these essays, one gets the picture of a good deal of anomie and loneliness, even on the small campus, such as Wesleyan or Antioch or Swarthmore. Whereas in an earlier day intelligent, upper-middle-class college students repressed their miseries to the point of their remaining unconscious, today many students would regard themselves as callous and superficial if they lacked a balance of coolness and Angst.

---

ing strength; it is obviously difficult to separate the trajectory of the College from what was happening in the cultural milieu influencing its students and faculty.

[41] Marshall Meyer points out in his essay on Harvard that there is a sizable cadre of talented political leaders drawn from Harvard, MIT, and other student and nonstudent populations in the Boston-Cambridge area who have been engaged in organizing and planning for the life of several student generations. Entry into this "fraternity" is based on belief and good works, but of course these too may be grounds for exclusiveness.

Most of the institutions represented herein mix together students who are more and less cosmopolitan and sophisticated. Whether in coresidential dormitories or in such off-campus locales as the Mifflin Street area in Madison, Wisconsin, peer pressures on square or provincial or socially and sexually inexperienced young people can be extreme. I do not think many of our contributors prepared themselves for their task by staying in dormitories or off-campus residences, which tend to be governed by what I have come to term physiological democracy—a procedure which grants hegemony whether in a meeting or in a residence to those who need the least sleep, have the loudest voices (usually male) and electronic accoutrements, and often have the fewest scruples.[42]

The abdication of the adults from any monitoring of campus residences occurred with extraordinary speed in the last few years, and has affected not only those colleges which enroll students from sophisticated permissive families but also colleges quite without selectivity, including many denominational institutions which were once extremely strict. It is interesting to speculate as to why this happened so quickly and in so many places outside cosmopolitan centers. Not only have very few faculty members been willing to live in residence halls, but virtually none have been willing to mix their pedagogic roles with the disagreeable chore of policing dormitory life. Young faculty are generally married and seldom need to reside in the dormitories, in whatever capacity, to save money, forcing dependence on upper-division resident assistants (RAs) for minimal counseling and supervision. It is a rare young adult who can say no to another young adult (including nonstudent "guests") with any conviction. It may be

---

[42] The account of the University of Pennsylvania mentions the hospitality of the college to Jewish students at a time when other Ivy League institutions were less welcoming. It seems to me at least arguable that Philadelphia Main Line families were willing, if not eager, to allow their offspring to attend the University because they could be protected by the fraternity-sorority system from extravagant contact with deprecated groups. Similarly, in some of the great state universities, such as Berkeley, recruitment of local First Families could occur because the latter were assured that their children, especially their girls, would not make unsuitable marriages because the Greek-letter institutions would serve as matchmakers and chaperones. In this way, exclusiveness made it possible for these universities to be democratic in social composition in the sense that they could include students from the very top of the social pyramid as well as from the middle and some lower levels. However, in some Southern universities fraternities mobilized to oppose entry of black students; more recently in a few stag colleges, some fraternities opposed coeducation.

that parents are so petrified of the danger of their children becoming drug addicts that the issue of their sexuality looms less
large, particularly since for young women the pill and other
contraceptives can lessen some of the dangers.[43] Furthermore,
many parents have already given their children such virtual
freedom at home that they cannot look to the colleges as protectors
of traditional virtue, nor can the colleges impose restraints more
severe than the students experienced at home.[44] In addition,
many young people enjoy the feeling of maturity that comes from
being entirely on their own, and they have ample evidence for their
conviction that they can manage their lives better than most
adults can.

It seems clear to me from Paul Sigmund's account of Princeton
that abandonment of parietal regulations, as well as of the ban
on automobiles, whatever its other motives, was part of a package
deal to defuse student discontent that could be mobilized for
larger political ends. Likewise, the panicky speed with which single-
sex colleges have gone coed in recent years has often occurred
from similarly mixed motives of faculty preference, student
pressure, and administrative desperation. Many men's colleges
(and secondary schools) have gone coed with little consideration
for the actual educational opportunities they were offering to
women students, although in other cases (Dartmouth, Princeton,
Williams, and Wesleyan), a good deal of thought was given to the
situation that women would find on campus. (To be sure, curric-

[43] The unplanned pregnancies (and corresponding need for abortions) which
occur among college women may be evidence both for the hegemony of the cult
of spontaneity and also for a residual innocence among young women who prefer to be surprised by sexual intercourse rather than to plan ahead for it.

A good deal has been said about the so-called incest taboo, where men and
women live on the same floor and share the same facilities. The one ethno-
graphic study I am familiar with suggests that not all floors are alike in this
respect; at one state university, extramural dating was characteristic of several
floors, while on another floor intramural convenience — always the preference
of the men — prevailed. See DeLamater (1971).

[44] Commuter colleges are now attracting some well-to-do upper-middle-class
students who would once have wanted to get away to a residential college in
order to be on their own; they may now prefer to save money for a trip to Europe or elsewhere by living at home and enrolling in the local college. Sometimes they can then form an audience for young, hip faculty who regard their
college as mission territory.

Conversely, the interest-hungry mortgages on their now overbuilt dormitories lead many state and private institutions to make virtually any concession
that will bring students back into rent-paying residence.

ular differences between the best men's and women's colleges are minimal, although the latter probably have marginally higher standards, especially now that young men are tending to move away from the sciences into the "softer" fields.) Even so, opening up formerly stag enclosures to women often took insufficient account of what the new women recruits would find in the way of models, mentors, and support in an unfamiliar clime.[45]

CHANGES IN CAMPUS CLIMATES: CURRICULUM As I have implied throughout these remarks, what tends to get lost from view in many of these changes are judgments of the subtle educational costs and benefits. Despite the mounting pressure at all levels of education for accountability, these costs and benefits are extraordinarily difficult to assess, let alone to predict. In our own affairs, we academicians proceed by a guesswork that we criticize in other aspects of our national life; even many social scientists among us talk about "the students" when what we are actually relying on is anecdotage about particular individuals or impressions from looking at the faces and figures in a classroom. A number of the institutions represented in this volume have offices of institutional research, but my general observation is that the work of these offices is rarely studied by

[45] For further discussion of the judgment that the educational problems of men and women undergraduates are not quite symmetrical, see Jencks and Riesman (1968a, Chap. 7); also Riesman (1970, pp. 52–63). I believe that there are some young women who are sufficiently shy and diffident so that they may flourish better at some point in their development in a single-sex setting where what Matina Horner (1970, pp. 45–74) has termed their fear of success may be somewhat muted. I would be sorry if the rush to coeducation, often based on the specious argument that it is "more natural," should eliminate all single-sex institutions except the Service Academies, or go so far that anyone who expresses a preference for a single-sex institution is thought at once to be unwholesomely deviant. Perhaps the women's liberation movement has come along just in time to preserve a few women's institutions. I should add, however, that as a faculty member I much prefer to teach in coeducational milieux. I prefer classes in which there is heterogeneity of age as well as of sex, and I particularly welcome the contribution of older women returning to the university to complete or continue their educations. In my observation, this heterogeneity tends to diminish stereotyping across the generation gap, particularly since the adults who do return to college do so for the most part as eager volunteers and not, like so many students in their late teens, as reluctant semicaptives.

In "The Tyranny of Structurelessness" Jo Freeman remarks on the mishaps and manipulations that can occur in women's groups out of the contemporary fears of formality, of the public holding of power, or of the charge of elitism. See Freeman (1972, pp. 151–164).

faculty members, although administrators may make use of it. The snobbery of many professors in the liberal arts toward studies of their own institutions reflects the fact that the study of education has until recently been associated with schools of education which have had such a low status in the university—the status of sociology has sometimes not been much higher—and these reputations are not wholly undeserved. However, there is another kind of effort, more episodic than institutional research, but often more consequential, namely, the kind of investigation Paul Mangelsdorf, Jr., describes, which the Commission on Educational Policy launched at Swarthmore in 1966.[46]

In general, the self-studies recommended greater curricular flexibility, minimizing prerequisites and required courses. Some, however, sought greater coherence, for all or for selected student volunteers. Thus, Wesleyan created thematic subcolleges which would also offer faculty an opportunity for collegial interdisciplinary work.

The University of Michigan's Residential College similarly emerged from long committee planning with a core curriculum. Several years ago, however, that core, under fierce attack from students and some faculty, was abandoned. In recent years, every one of the institutions discussed in this book greatly loosened its requirements and offered a greater variety of careers and pacing to its undergraduates. The University of Toronto, in Jill Conway's account, liquidated its Honours Program and its clear Oxbridge-style distinction between a Pass and an Honours Degree, which at Toronto meant that on top of the 13 grades of the Ontario school system, the Honours Program was a four-year course as against the ordinary three-year course.[47] It would take extraordinarily careful and detailed institutional research to assess the educational

---

[46] See the Commission on Educational Policy (1967); and discussion of the self-studies at Berkeley, Toronto, Wesleyan, and elsewhere, in Ladd (1970). Mangelsdorf observes that Swarthmore called off classes for a week to discuss the committee reports, setting a precedent Swarthmore students could use for demanding further "days" when classes must be suspended for campuswide discussion of an urgent topic. I wonder if any college anywhere now has compulsory chapel as a diurnal forum where everyone automatically meets.

[47] In the idiom of educational reform in the United States, the idea that superior students should take longer seems odd; a number of colleges in the 1960s offered a three-year option for especially bright students, whereas at present many institutions offer the three-year option less selectively to any students who can show that they have met minimal requirements for the degree.

consequences for different levels of students of these curricular loosenings. Undoubtedly they helped create a freer academic market within institutions, reducing the tariff barriers of departmental majors, serried prerequisites, and other ways of routing student customers. But the uses students made of these choices and the ways faculty responded to the heightened need to lure customers differed very much among institutions. At Antioch, Gerald Grant describes the freshman classrooms as virtually deserted after the institution of the wholly nonrequired first-year program. At Federal City College, the faculty judgment that the pass–no credit grading system left many students floundering or wandering about the streets led to efforts, apparently not very effective, to limit the number of terms a student could stay at the college without making any academic progress.[48]

In his essay on Princeton, Paul E. Sigmund writes of a return to greater academic seriousness in the academic year 1970–71. Other essays in the volume indicate also that many students are presently studying more and protesting less. Many activists themselves declare that their confrontation politics were a failure. Actually, they won many campus victories, but newer demands kept outstripping these; and where these demands were extramural, such as stopping the war or ending racism, confrontation only strengthened the Nixon Administration.[49] Furthermore, since the Movement has proceeded from the universities to the liberal arts colleges and from these to the high schools, a good many students now arrive as freshmen with a fair amount of political experience, less easily manipulated or mobilized. In addition, the decline in the pressure from the draft was something of a pacifier on the campus,

[48] See Irene Tinker's essay, page 99. Even where there are grades, faculty often do not use failing grades, but allow students to take "incompletes" or give them an "R" for repeat. There is at present no structured freshman program at FCC.

[49] Thomas J. Cottle has described how activist students, bitterly opposed to Humphrey in the 1968 election, had had second thoughts when he was actually defeated by Nixon, and discovered some sympathy for parents and other deprecated liberal adults so compromised as to have supported Humphrey. See Cottle (1971, Chap. 10).

I believe there is ample data from studies of public opinion to support my judgment in the text concerning student antiwar protests, which allowed the Administration to campaign against disruption even among those voters who were themselves opposed to the war. I know the argument is not a simple one, involving as it does various constituencies and short-run versus long-run consequences of disruption; see, e.g., Rosenberg, Verba, and Converse (1970).

although many Americans (myself included) saw this as a Nixon tactic to continue the war with minimum American objection, since most of the victims are now Southeast Asians. The job market served similarly to make it appear that one could not automatically move into a good job if one neglected one's university work, and the depressed market for faculty may also have had a sobering effect on a good many of the faculty exhorters whose moral support for student activism had been such an important factor in the past.

As with any movement that gathers disciples rapidly, the purity of original ideologies and motivations becomes muted as new, less committed adherents join, often in the case of campus activism going along for the dramaturgical ride and for the human solidarity, or even as a substitute for freshman mixers and computer dating. The counterculture as a primarily unpolitical movement was seen by many New Left students as an antagonist, leading possible constituencies to withdraw and making them unavailable as recruits. Yet the counterculture also served—as some activists recognized—to spread some messages far beyond the elite students and the elite colleges; I have talked to a few Harvard activists who saw marijuana, dress codes, and rock music as the leverage to delegitimize authority in schools and colleges and then in society in general. Moreover, it goes without saying that there is not a single counterculture, but a diversity of subcultures to which the label (from Theodore Roszak's book) has been applied. For some, the counterculture meant an effort to adumbrate a new and more humane society in small, self-reliant enclaves. Others in the university context felt that in rejecting what they saw as the rationalism, the competitiveness, the game-playing, the impersonality of their universities, they were making a declaration of intent vis-à-vis American institutions in general and the evils, such as imperialism and other kinds of destructiveness, thought inherent in these institutions. Thus some students fighting for a less structured curricular mold, or for the entry into the curriculum of courses facilitating a greater expressiveness, could feel that they were participating in a larger political crusade.

That crusade, like the student movement in general, of course far transcends North American developments. As many people have pointed out, its origins go back a very long way to a strand of antinomianism in Western thought, to romantic and Bohemian movements of the nineteenth and early twentieth centuries, to periodic revivals of religious enthusiasm in our own American history. In the United States, the civil rights movement preceded the flourishing of the counterculture. Its leaders, including the FSM leaders at Berkeley, were by today's standards square and academically nonantagonistic students. For some of their successors the counterculture became more important than the civil rights movement itself, even though the counterculture has found in the myth of the Negro folk a specifically American counterpart to non-American myths of workers or peasants.[50]

At Federal City College, Jimmy Garrett (previously one of the driving leaders of the Black Student Union at San Francisco State) and his disciples contended that "decolonialization of the mind" was more important than upward mobility into a rancid white world. They did not ask their students; they told them. This was in fact a rare case where in recent years an effort has been made to create a controlled rather than an elective curriculum. More commonly in recent years, reexamination of undergraduate programs such as occurred at Wesleyan, Swarthmore, and Stanford (as well as many other institutions) led away from requirements and in the direction of a greater range of electives, including student-initiated courses, arrangements for Independent Study on and off campus, hand-crafted majors, etc. Evaluation of the impact of these changes is generally lacking. As with Michigan's Residential College, it is hard to sort out the educational consequences from everything else that has happened in the institution and in the society at large. And this sorting out is seldom done in terms of specific cadres of students. For example, Independent Study, introduced in recent years into most of the institutions discussed in these essays, seems to have worked well only where self-reliant students could count on a good deal of supervision from faculty. These faculty had to deal with the psychological hazards faced by students who tackled too large a project or who feared to test their adequacy in areas of uncertain competence. For some students doing Independent Study, lack of self-confidence is the main psychological problem; for others, it is narcissism and the belief that one already really knows everything important, so why bother to demonstrate it?

---

[50] Some of the most beleaguered and isolated college students of the late 1960s have been square, middle-class blacks who were forced by white as well as black attitudes to accept black proletarian styles as the truly authentic ones and to deny their own family-based traditions. Cf. Donald, Jr. (1970, pp. 153–204).

I have already mentioned how the change in political and cultural climates in the major universities has helped give a somewhat greater legitimacy to teaching as against competing faculty activities, especially for newly emerging Ph.D.'s, but also for some senior faculty who have become converts to the new vogue of caring about students. There is generally some correlation between the vocation one seeks and one's competence in it; nevertheless, many faculty who are eager to teach have had negligible on-the-job training vis-à-vis the different kinds of students they encounter. Thus it seems possible that, just as many idealistic psychiatrists and therapists suffer from therapeutic despair when their patients seldom get better (or if they do, not on account of anything the therapist is aware of having done), so I have observed a good many young faculty suffering from pedagogic despair when their concern for students and their devotion to teaching turn out to be ineffective.

DISTRACTION AND OVER-EXTENSION At one time or another, I have visited all the institutions included in this volume, except CCNY, and I have some limited feeling for their pedagogic climates. In all of them, administrators and some faculty members are distracted from the task of learning more about pedagogic problems because of all the other assignments flowing from the political concerns of students and faculty regarding the society and the institution. For many, perhaps the majority, these distractions may have taken the place of earlier ones, now sometimes outdated, such as playing bridge or golf. At the same time, many faculty and some students have had to try to think through what had been easy assumptions as to who can teach what to whom at what point in the development of teacher and taught. The hope for or insistence upon "relevance" has offered opportunity to reassess the aims of education in some settings, while symbolizing it in others through formless rap sessions or faddish demands for response to extramural crusades.

Since life is short and resources scarce, concededly humane goals compete with each other, and the more responsive institutions described in these essays seem overextended. Their administrations are asked to be omnicompetent in the sense of responding to policy questions that would tax a city or state government. The University of Pennsylvania, in the account of David Goddard and Linda Koons, is not only stretched to become a more national institution with a more distinguished faculty and an abler student body in the Wharton School and the liberal arts, but it is also compelled from within and without to make itself responsible for housing and civic benefit in its West Philadelphia neighborhood. Both aspirations require vast amounts of money, and it goes without saying that raising such sums absorbs immense executive energy. MIT is asked by some students and faculty to alter its highly competitive scholarly climate so as to evoke greater spontaneity and joy in learning from students and everyone else. But at the same time, it is under pressure to divest itself of research which antiwar students and faculty consider impure in source or topic. One result of this latter effort is to diminish the overhead from which money for educational reform might become available. Some members of the San Francisco State College (now University) faculty, observing that the California Master Plan of 1960 had made them more selective and reduced their proportion of black students from 11 percent to 4 percent, concluded that they must compete with the community colleges for black and Spanish-speaking students without relinquishing their long campaign against the University of California's near-monopoly of doctoral programs; they want all the educational missions, and not only those assigned them by the Master Plan. Of course, this puts it too simply: some faculty want one mission, some another, and the institution pressing against its budget and its sources of public support finds it hard to restrain these aspirations and the euphoria as to what can realistically be accomplished. The College at Old Westbury conducts simultaneously experiments in race relations, curricular structure, and participatory governance—a mélange so overwhelming that it will be impossible if there are failures to attribute them to any single source.

In some of these institutions, as would seem true at Antioch and Old Westbury, undergraduates appear to have in effect a second major (as Gerald Grant would put it) in political science as they involve themselves in struggles over governance with faculty, administrators, trustees, and each other.[51]

[51] In talking several years ago with a student member of Antioch's Administrative Council, which supervises practically everything on the campus, I suggested that he might be better advised to postpone his committee work, on which he will be embarked for the rest of his life, and use his undergraduate years to acquire those skills for which college provides the best opportunity, including, in addition to curricular skills, learning to play an instrument, a lifelong sport, and so on; his characteristic response was that he had learned more through his Council membership than he could have through his courses. I

I believe that if faculty members and administrators would be more modest in their aims and focus more narrowly on explicit educational issues, they might find a way of responding to the kinds of conflicts reported in these essays, even though they might have to temper their educational responses in the light of momentary political urgencies. Let me take the Princeton Plan as an illustration. This ten-day fall recess to allow students to campaign for candidates was voted by faculty at Princeton after Cambodia, and Paul E. Sigmund's essay describes both that occasion and how during the academic year just past the faculty first reversed itself and then voted it once more for the fall of 1972. When the proposal came before the Harvard faculty in May 1970, it was defeated. Marshall Meyer's essay suggests some of the divisions among the radicals at Harvard that may have been one factor in this defeat. My own opposition was principally on educational grounds. Both with students and with faculty colleagues, I contended that students needed to be disabused of the notion that the adult population was just waiting in readiness to hear their wisdom when they should appear in October without previous contact and conversation. We would be derelict, I thought, in our role as teachers if we allowed students to believe that they could do a great deal to affect the political process by a Stakhanovite burst of activity in October; what was required was steady, year-round work in the precincts, at the local level. I urged antiwar activists to spend summers in their home towns canvassing with the local minister, the newspaper editor, members of the Chamber of Commerce, and other groups who might put pressure on the local congressman. (In several of the Harvard residential Houses, undergraduates wrote to the alumni of the particular House, seeking to enlist them in the antiwar effort in their local bailiwicks.) A good many went to Washington, D.C., to lobby with congressmen as well as to protest; some worked in the congressional campaign of Father Robert Drinan, S.J., that summer and fall. Only a few

---

did not think the Antioch curriculum so dreary as to justify this eager anticipation of the inescapable tasks of most professional committeeprone adults. But I would not lay this down as a universal rule. Some students can indeed combine educative campus political work with many other sorts of learning, and I have no doubt that students can contribute to their institutions. The question remains as to whether there are not some undergraduates who are being too generous to their successors since, despite current talk about lifetime learning, they may not so easily have the chance again to do supervised laboratory work or supervised field work or to wander in the stacks of a great library.

threw themselves into such work full time, postponing their academic obligations or taking their chances with these.

In an intense discussion with a group of seniors in the Social Studies Program, the majority of my faculty colleagues and I insisted that students should not ask for or receive academic amnesty from their General Examinations, although they might properly ask for postponement of these (and hence their baccalaureate degrees) until the fall. Some students argued that because we on the faculty were also antiwar activists, we should make the students' own activities easier by dispensing with requirements altogether; we took the position that the students had to live, like ourselves, in a world where obligations had to be balanced against each other, and that in fact most of them in this particular highly selective honors program were exquisitely capable of combining examinations along with everything else. This position, dubbed by one of my colleagues as "Riesman's theory of cold showers and virtue," rested on the assumption that special political privileges for students were politically as well as pedagogically unwise. But the line we had taken was reversed by the general faculty the following day, which in effect granted amnesty for the remainder of the term.[52] A few days later, when we had voted down the Princeton Plan, a colleague upbraided me for my opposition to it, saying that it cost nothing to give this to students as in effect a political tranquilizer; they would be off campus—whether on the beaches or canvassing—and there would be a let-up in disruption.[53]

It does not require a particularly hallucinatory imagination, in

[52] Because Harvard was then in the Reading Period, when most classes were not meeting, the campus strike was somewhat perfunctory and there was less "restructuring" than Neil J. Smelser's paper reports from Berkeley or than occurred or was attempted elsewhere.

[53] This colleague is a natural scientist, sober and conscientious in the affairs of his own department. It is one of the limitations of the unavoidably brief essays in this volume that they cannot discuss except in the largest terms the interesting differences among academic fields in reaction to campus turmoil. In my observation, natural scientists have often appeared to believe that their own turf is protected by the high tariffs of their fields' intrinsic difficulty and quasi-cumulative nature. Regarding much of the rest of the campus, not entirely without justification, as an intellectual slum, they may feel that failure to punish disrupters is not likely to affect them, or they may vote, as the Harvard faculty did, to allow partial student control of the new Afro-American Studies department, since such a concession is hardly likely to affect what happens in astronomy or microbiology. This observation is of course only partial; natural scientists are frequently extremely idealistic, and some have been

the light of the essays in this volume, to want to close a campus in a time of troubles, as CCNY was closed after the black and Puerto Rican students had occupied the South Campus, in fear of the brigades that could be brought in from nearby Harlem. But to close a campus seems to me a desperate last resort, antieducational per se; and to seek to pacify students by a measure that may mislead them either as to where the faculty stand or where they should stand seems to me antieducational also.[54]

THE UNIVERSITY AS PRECINCT In arguing out these issues with students and faculty members, I was repeatedly reminded that for many, the college was their only viable precinct, particularly so when their own residential base was a long distance from the campus. Anyone who has done even a bit of canvassing knows how arduous it is, and indeed how frustrating is most political work outside the solidarity and support of a collegiate base. In contrast, the more liberal campuses have offered an enclave of tolerance and even support similar to that furnished the IRA in the "no-go" areas of Londonderry. The faculty liberals and left-leaning Democrats have a very hard time curbing their own extremists (something which is also true on the Right). A small, somewhat isolated college like Antioch in Yellow Springs, or a large university like Wisconsin, Michigan, or Berkeley, in a (mostly) college town creates an atmosphere which has been compared to that of a mining camp or shipboard in sealing many denizens off from intercourse with middle-majority Americans. Such settings are conducive to militancy since inhabitants are not subject to the restraints that come from living among kinfolk and others who hold divergent opinions.[55] I have found it very difficult on my own and on other liberal campuses to persuade

---

willing to pay the price in reduced funding—and even in heavier teaching loads—of the generosities and dispensations they have urged on their institutions.

[54] J. K. Zawodny, professor of political science at the University of Pennsylvania, has described to me in conversation the extraordinary sacrifices made by the Polish Underground during the Nazi occupation to keep academic life going in extreme situations: professors of classical culture were treated with as much care as if they had been ballistics experts; classes met on schedules varied to limit risk, yet fiercely held onto; students would risk their own lives to protect those of their instructors.

[55] The analogy drawn here between campus climates and unions (including night-work printers) prone to extremism and militancy particularly reflects the work of Clark Kerr and S. M. Lipset.

students and faculty that there has not existed a strong adult antiwar majority in America (and up until 1966–67, not even a student antiwar majority), since almost "everybody" they knew was in agreement with them on the war. And those who did agree that they were in a minority (particularly so in condemning the war on moral rather than pragmatic grounds), and that the war's continuation did not simply represent a collusion on the part of the President, his civilian hawk advisers, Dow Chemical, and the Pentagon, then jumped to the conclusion that the American people were rotten from top to bottom, with violence or withdrawal the only possible responses.

By 1968, there had been mobilized an antiwar majority on most liberal campuses, among students, faculty, and administrators, and it exercised moral hegemony over the wavering as well as over the residual, mostly silent hawks. But those who regarded the war as an error were not in agreement with those who regarded it as an outrage. In many of these essays, perhaps particularly Benson Snyder's on MIT, one can see how easily the antiwar majority became unstuck over issues as to the nature of the war and how best to fight it, whether intramurally or extramurally, whether with nonviolence or with disruption and violence, whether with reasoned discourse or revival meetings, whether with traditional campaigning or putting bodies on the line.[56] Often, the question of how to respond to war-related disruption took priority over the war itself.[57] The legalism and forensic display of campus judicial proceedings could often drain the electrical energies of participants to such an extent as to stop all discussion of the war and to produce a virtual blackout of many other activities.

To be sure, for a small number of student and faculty activists,

[56] It is a truism of radical politics that the opponents with whom one is most involved and against whom one is most ferocious are those marginally to the Left or Right and that the tactical issues around which these splinters divide come to symbolize profound ideological (and often personal) chasms.

[57] The game of trying to get police called onto campus often provided a scenario more salient than the war. Since most Americans are not Quakers, I believe that one needs fail-safe mechanisms to prevent the exploitation of other people's tolerance and decency, or their arousal to vigilantism in response. Thus I have never understood why there should be such fierce moral (as against pragmatic) repugnance to calling the police. See my contribution to a *New York Times* symposium on this subject (Riesman, 1968); see, however, Marshall Meyer's discussion concerning the belief that universities should be sanctuaries not only in the realm of ideas but also in the realm of actions in support of political ideas (Meyer, 1971, pp. 263–266).

this halting of what they termed campus business as usual was just the point. They wanted the campus to testify in and out of season to the evils of society, to become more socially committed to the extirpation of evil, and to set a model of institutional citizenship for the whole society. Far from seeing universities as public utilities, capable of offering individuals the option of taking different directions in their search for commitment, this approach treats the universities as sacred, as the vessels of a secular faith. Some measure of institutional charisma seems to me unavoidable; no doubt those who run public utilities with conscientiousness also regard them with a certain devotion. The question is what aspect of the university will be regarded as in some measure sacred. I regard the traditional university functions of scholarship and of the conservation and transmission of knowledge as a quasi-religious charge. A university should be more than a collection of professional guilds struggling with each other, as Clark Kerr once put it, over parking. But neither faculty nor students should, in my opinion, be asked to join an intentional community or a secularized religious order which, however, lacks the traditional disciplines and asceticisms of an order. At Federal City College, the effort of some faculty—white as well as black—was to turn blackness itself into a religion—although for Jimmy Garrett and his followers, no public college could ever be black enough, so that they hived off to form a separate community for urban missionary purposes.[58] The quest at Federal City College to become "blacker than thou" shunted aside the College's responsibility as a public utility for the majority of its upwardly mobile students. In effect, they were being asked to make for their cause the sacrifices generally asked only of the already arrived and well-off, for whom dedication to a cause may supplement a career and interrupt it but only rarely derail it, and who in any case possess an abundance of options.

UNDER-GRADUATE EDUCATIONAL REFORM With great unevenness the country over, predominantly white colleges are struggling to respond to new cadres of black and Spanish-speaking students, some of whom (like many at Federal

[58] Compare the group of faculty and students who split off from Reed College to found the Portland Learning Community, which in turn, as Gerald Grant mentions, linked up with Antioch for credential purposes. See the account of that community by David French (1971). Mr. French does not mention the community by name; see also Abrams and Price (1971).

City College) are older high school dropouts. Compensatory efforts on the part of faculty often misfire. Students sometimes feel humiliated when placed in remedial programs, even when college credit is given for them; but when placed in regular classes, they may sometimes feel shy and overwhelmed. For white faculty, black (and Spanish-speaking) students presently provide the most visible group of students whom they are aware of not reaching, sometimes leading to desperate efforts to appear relevant to these students, to talk their supposed language—well-intentioned reactions often felt to be patronizing or counterfeit. For some students, a black-controlled black studies department may provide a kind of decompression chamber, offering, until one is prepared to cope with integrated classes, nurturance not regarded as counterfeit. But this has been a strategy only for a minority of students.[59] And white and black faculty members alike, as for instance at Old Westbury, are sometimes finding that they cannot teach these students even if they want to, and are recruiting faculty from high schools or elsewhere to help with the task. If I am right that faculty in the kinds of institutions represented in this volume have tended to teach somewhere above the median level of their students, one might hope that the effort to reach and respond to nonwhite students would carry over to those less visible or threatening white students who have also been incomprehending or unresponsive.[60]

---

[59] See the discussion by Thomas F. Slaughter, Jr., (1972) of Douglass College of Rutgers of the dissatisfaction and tensions within Black Studies programs between the more activist and the more academically oriented black students and between these students in turn and the marginal black faculty and staff of the programs.

[60] Some of the more effective remedial programs are those that take place in the summer before college entry, when less prepared students can become oriented to the campus and to each other. Similarly, in a de facto black college like Federal City College, some of the psychological problems may be somewhat attenuated, since black students are not exposed to humiliation in the presence of large numbers of better-prepared whites, and perhaps find it a bit easier to take their time with difficult subjects. (However, even if whites are not physically present, they may be psychologically present, just as men are present in the imaginations of students in women's colleges.)

Federal City College lost an opportunity to provide a model for the entry or reentry into higher education of Vietnam veterans, who are so much worse off than the veterans of World War II who had a more generous GI Bill of Rights, and who were welcomed even in the most overcrowded colleges. Irene Tinker mentions the way in which white and black antiwar faculty refused to cooperate with the Army in a plan for teaching veterans, even

The need to respond to the black presence on the predominantly white campus may be an element in some of the curricular changes that have occurred, in addition to the creation of black studies programs and departments. Pass-fail or pass–no credit grading may among other things be seen as a way of succoring marginal students; a certain grade inflation may come about because if one passes such students, one may feel bound to give honor grades to those who do more than pass. But in general, in reading these essays, I have concluded that there is little if any correlation between the degree of political turmoil on campus, whether over questions of race or of war or other issues, and the educational and curricular venturesomeness of recent years. For example, the two specifically educational consequences that ensued after the FSM explosion at Berkeley were, as Smelser's paper mentions, the Tussman Experimental College and the Muscatine Report.[61] Tussman could not find enough Berkeley faculty to keep his College going, in part because senior faculty were not interested in this kind of lower-division collegial enterprise. To be sure, longevity is not the only test of a new pedagogic venture; indeed, Tussman's own enterprise reflected his experience at the Experimental College begun by Alexander Meiklejohn at the University of Wisconsin in the 1920s, which lasted only a short while. No remembered experiment ever wholly dies.[62] Perhaps the same consolation exists for the program of student-initiated courses that began at Berkeley following the Muscatine Report, support for which diminished after an effort to test the limits of tolerance and of "student power" vis-à-vis the regents by recruiting Eldridge Cleaver for one of these courses. Perhaps some of the materials and modes of teaching developed in these experimental courses have been absorbed into the regular curriculum. But from Smelser one would conclude that for the most part the departmentally orga-

---

before their release, at Army bases around Washington. On a brief visit to the College in the fall of 1968, I observed a similar effort to score what seemed to me a negligible point against the war at the expense of disprivileged prospective students who were not given their own choice in the matter. The issue was especially tense because at that time the war was not the most salient issue for many blacks, even when whites interpreted it for them as an exercise in racism.

[61] On Tussman, see his own book (1969); and on general problems of undergraduate education at Berkeley, see Trow (1966, pp. 17–43).

[62] Cf. Duberman (1972, pp. 30–46).

nized faculty gave short shrift to undergraduate education, while maintaining large although now declining graduate enrollments. Teaching assistants can be subsidized to interpose themselves—by no means always to student disadvantage—between the faculty and especially the lower-division undergraduates. Nevertheless there seems to be little if any effort to help the teaching assistants become less awkward instructors.

Although there have been modest reforms in graduate education in recent years, most of the discussion of educational reform in these essays does in fact concern undergraduate education only. Richard McCormick's account of Rutgers demonstrates that innovation there went into the founding of Livingston College, one of the Federated Colleges, and not into starting new postbaccalaureate programs. Pennsylvania has started subcolleges for freshmen built around a particular interdisciplinary theme. Antioch has had a new freshman program, or nonprogram. Stanford has offered undergraduates the Stanford Workshops on Political and Social Issues as well as the Grove, a residential experimental educational unit. Michigan has its undergraduate Residential College. Benson Snyder also speaks of changes in the undergraduate program at MIT, while Jill Conway describes the abandonment of the Honours Plan at Toronto. Nowhere do I recall a reference to educational change in the graduate departments of arts and sciences. Yet it is here, I believe, that change must come if we are to alter substantially the quality of undergraduate education. Even though avowedly experimental undergraduate colleges like Old Westbury I and II and the initial Federal City College have recruited some nonacademic faculty (for example, artists or poverty workers or lawyers), they must still rely for the most part on men and women with graduate training. Yet most graduate students are not prepared by their training to teach interdisciplinary courses to a wide spread of students in a liberal arts college, nor are they prepared for colleagueship in such a college. And while it has been said in many criticisms of traditionally trained faculty that they seek to re-create in their colleges the guild mentalities of a graduate school and to justify themselves only by those bright students they can send on to graduate school, it is not a great improvement if faculty come to their first college teaching job with only the negative identity that they are not going to seek an audience for their work and talents in what they would term the rat race of the academic marketplace.

It seems to me that the graduate schools now have a new incentive, in the face of the prospect of underemployment for many of their protégés, to try to do a better job of preparation for college teaching. This involves supplementing, but by no means abandoning, the tradition of research training. College teachers need to have done research; many of their students will be quite capable of research themselves, and all will need interpretations of what research signifies. But beyond his special field a college teacher needs to have a wider orbit of academic interests and capacities, and it would help if he had some awareness of the subcultures of academia, so that he will have some basis for judging the place where he lands, other than comparing it to his recollection of his own undergraduate and graduate schools. There are adumbrations of what I have in mind. For example, the Zoology Department at the University of California at Davis offers its graduate students a one-term course in the undergraduate teaching of biology and natural science, a course that includes microteaching, some work on the learning process, and the preparation of a natural science curriculum for a hypothetical liberal arts college. Some discussions of the doctor of arts degree, notably at Carnegie-Mellon University, illustrate the concerns I have set forth here.

It seems probable, however, that for the foreseeable future college teachers will have to learn on the job most of what they need to know as teachers. For some, the loosening of curricular undergraduate requirements has been a mixed blessing. If students are allowed free choice, then faculty are also freed from what in the past have been obligations to develop sequential or coherent programs; even if they did develop such programs, students might not turn up for the newly minted offerings.[63] My own education in the social sciences owes a debt to my having taught in the required social science sequence in the College of the University of Chicago, where I worked with social scientists of diverse disciplines and cognitive styles to hammer out an endlessly tinkered-with curriculum. Similarly, a newly recruited don at St. John's College in Annapolis and Santa Fe undergoes an immersion experience in the totality of a wholly required program which the don must master under the mentorship of colleagues.

[63] Wesleyan has abandoned its required freshman humanities course, although it remains a popular elective. None of the core programs in the Santa Cruz cluster colleges survive. I have already mentioned the disbanding of the core program at Michigan's Residential College. Concerning Federal City College, Irene Tinker writes, "The result of a year-long controversy [over degrees of blackness and who should control] has been to leave course content up to the individual faculty."

But it may not be a good idea for a young faculty member, immediately after finishing his dissertation, to have to shelve his specialty in a staff-taught course or program. It might make more sense to have new faculty teach advanced upper-division courses and to ask older and more established faculty to teach lower-division students, though this teaching need not be of a survey or general sort. The dichotomy often posited between general and specialized education seems to me misleading. It is sometimes fruitful for entering students to explore intensively the way some historians work, proceeding by sampling rather than by survey. To be sure, especially for the less well-prepared student, the samples may need to be given some anchoring in a general framework of intellectual and academic life, but this still does not mean that courses have to cover everything under the sun.[64] The voluntary Freshman Seminars that have been introduced at MIT and many other institutions encourage faculty to exploit their specialties in the hope that their enthusiasms will be contagious for new students; but of course what may work at MIT, with its freshman year on pass-fail, its exceptionally talented and motivated entering class, and its wide range of faculty preoccupations, might be too loose-jointed to succeed elsewhere in academia.

Correspondingly, what is required to keep up with one's field varies greatly among fields. A Shakespeare scholar is not likely to find his professional advancement hindered by the opportunity to teach the undergraduate Shakespeare course. In the humanities generally, and in the less cumulative social sciences, undergraduate teaching may be helpful, or at least not entirely distracting, for the specialized professional. However, when I participated in an MIT Colloquium on Knowledge and Values and recommended that faculty who had served for three years in an interdisciplinary undergraduate program should be given a sabbatical to renew themselves in their own disciplines, I was told by natural scientists that in their particular fields one would need at least a year to catch up if one had been away for as little as two years from full-time work in the area, so quickly did their fields advance.[65]

[64] See the admirable discussion in Bell (1966); also Riesman (1969*b*, pp. 377–388).

[65] See Commission on MIT Education (1971). The sometimes tragically short academically productive half-life of many mathematicians and natural scientists, analogous to that of star athletes and beauty queens, suggests the need for beginning, as it were, second careers even while the first career is at its most luminous — with tenure often bestowed almost immediately after winning the doctorate.

In the traditional curriculum, there is therefore some unavoidable tension between what a faculty member would feel most eager to teach and what a student would be most eager to learn. When students obtain more complete freedom of choice to do their thing, the complex understandings that bind faculty to maintain coherent departmental majors may also be loosened. Thus I have met occasional faculty in experimental liberal arts colleges where student-faculty relations are entirely contractual and individuated, who declare happily that they no longer need to keep up with their entire field since there is no longer any expectation on the part of students that they be prepared in a field; such faculty can then concentrate on their own corner of interest quite irrespective of the spread of interests among their colleagues. The honors program at Swarthmore is at the opposite extreme, because the use of outside examiners compels instructors to keep up with their own fields of knowledge in order to prepare their students to pass muster with the visitors.[66]

CONTINUITY AND CHANGE Paul Sigmund says about Princeton that as a result of the changes of recent years, "Princeton is a better place to teach, to learn, and to live." Pondering these essays, originally written a year or so earlier, in the equanimity of the Institute for Advanced Study at Princeton in the spring of 1972, I was quite inclined to agree with him about Princeton University, which, as Sigmund observes, has become a more interesting place because it is now coeducational and recruits from a wider catch basin, and also because its changes have not been discontinuous and have not produced bitter intradepartmental mistrust.[67] To be sure, Princeton faculty who teach courses which are no longer required might regard matters some-

---

As I have already suggested, devoted undergraduate teachers may sometimes face similar problems: when students make great demands on a young instructor, he may exhaust his capital investment in himself during the short trajectory of these students; of course many faculty believe themselves intellectually immortal and respond to these expectations, only to find that a new generation of students brings with it other concerns and preference for other mentors.

[66] It may be that only a college with undergraduates as distinguished as Swarthmore's can induce faculty from elsewhere to act as external examiners. Of course, most faculty members will still want to send some of their better students on to graduate school and will believe—not always accurately—that this requires maintaining a departmental major that graduate school admissions committees can recognize.

[67] The contrast with Stanford as described in John Walsh's essay is dramatic. (For a sympathetic picture of Stanford at an earlier point, cf. Michael Novak

what differently. Philip Altbach's essay on the University of Wisconsin stands in sharp contrast to Sigmund's on Princeton; Altbach sees the hopes of radicals and reformers shattered, and regression if not reaction in the process of restraining the University's aspirations, pulling back from its tradition of hospitality to out-of-state students and out-of-joint ideas. The view from San Francisco State College is not much more sanguine, although a surface peace has been restored; at Federal City College, all hope of distinction has evaporated.[68] But in general, it would seem that the older institutions reported on here have maintained their relative standing and their ability to recruit students, faculty, and resources at a level recognizably comparable to what it was in the early 1960s. This is what Neil Smelser argues vis-à-vis Berkeley; it is what a historian would expect. However, smaller cycles of change may be concealed within larger continuities. Consider Wesleyan. During his presidency, Victor Butterfield was able to recruit some extraordinary faculty who combined intellectual distinction with normative concerns. When in the middle sixties some of these men departed, and younger, more narrowly specialized men came in, eager in some cases to move into graduate education, and as the student body itself became still more academically talented than theretofore, the larger humanistic and normative concerns became somewhat attenuated. These returned with a rush in the late 1960s in the form, for instance, of a fierce preoccupation with assuring racial justice within and outside the university. But the new wave led to apparent overextension of resources, and at times to antirational and self-righteous dogmatism which back-

---

[1971, Chap. 11]). At Harvard also, as Marshall Meyer describes it, there is a greater residue of mutual mistrust and probably of apprehension among faculty.

It may possibly be of significance in understanding Princeton that there has been a well-organized and articulate conservative-libertarian group among the student body (as is also the case at the University of Toronto), whereas in most liberal colleges, including Harvard, the more moderate and conservative students have tended to be silent and to withdraw. This has then had consequences for the range of opinions likely to be comfortably voiced among faculty and administration.

[68] Irene Tinker, like some of the other authors of essays in this volume, revised her essay in the spring of 1972 to take account of changes since its original prompt preparation. But this too-delayed book could not have gone to press at all if we had to keep up with all new developments: in the late spring of 1972, President Harlan Randolph of FCC was fired by the Board of Higher Education—an action he is protesting; no successor has been named.

fired. Presently, the sense of urgency has moderated at Wesleyan, scholarship is again fully legitimated, although the special Butter-field amalgam with its relative serenity has of course not returned.

From such instances, one might well conclude that neither the hopes of the antiacademic wing of the radical movement in the late 1960s nor the fears of their opponents have proved predictive. I had thought a few years ago that the combination of increasing demands on the institutions of higher education coupled with public disenchantment would produce an immediate budgetary crisis and even the bankruptcy of many institutions (Riesman 1969*a*, pp. 363–369). Yet a Republican President has just now (June 1972) signed into law a Higher Education Act whose provi-sions for undergraduate education are exceedingly generous, even if for the time being they are likely to be insufficiently funded. The curtailment of public support for higher education has been less severe than I had anticipated. Where it has occurred—and in some states it has not occurred—it has reflected disenchantment and antagonism but also genuine fiscal dilemmas and the recogni-tion of other domestic priorities, such as the judgment that a dollar spent on a Head Start program may go further in equalizing life-chances than a dollar spent at any level of postsecondary education. Thus while it is true that higher education has lost the extraordinary momentum it had in the period from Sputnik to nearly the end of the 1960s, and while budgetary plateaus and occasional actual cuts have hurt operating programs as well as plans for expansion, it is clear that the influential publics have not concluded that higher education is a luxury but instead that it is something to which nearly everyone is entitled as a matter of right.[69]

Yet, as Martin Trow has argued in a series of articles, the process of expansion of access to higher education from massive-

---

[69] Making this decision of course says nothing about how expanding enrollments are to be financed. In this as in other areas, taxpayers would like to shift the burden elsewhere. Insistence on negligible or low tuition for public higher education would seem to signify a desire to shift the burden of educating one's own children from the moderately well-off, whose children regularly attend public institutions, to the poor, whose children seldom do, and to the very rich. Christopher Jencks and I argue this controversial position in "Social Stratification and Mass Higher Education" (1968*b*, Chap. 3, pp. 136–140). In favor of the idea of an Educational Opportunity Bank, we contend that scholarship aid in combination with income-contingent arrangements can pro-vide greater opportunity for students from really impoverished backgrounds who cannot afford to attend even free commuter colleges because of the costs

ness to near universality is likely to make the maintenance of what he terms the autonomous functions of the university more difficult.[70]

These functions are tied directly neither to undergraduate teaching nor to community service, although of course they have oblique relations to both. A few distinguished research-oriented universities have been created by short-order academic cooks especially when, as at Irvine or San Diego, they could depend on the prestige and support of an already established university. But the great majority of upwardly mobile state colleges and regional universities, though they may have embarked on doctoral programs, have not been able to overtake fewer than 50 more or less research-oriented great universities that belong to the Association of American Universities. Such gaps are now everywhere under attack as "elitist." I have already mentioned the intrastate efforts to achieve parity between the major state universities and their regional rivals.[71] The regional universities have the populist advantage of appearing closer to the people than the major state or private institutions.

But the attack on elite institutions did not come only from outside, but also from within the major universities and university colleges. That is, each institution is under pressure from within as well as from without to serve some redefinition of its traditional constituency and to be less selective with regard to topic and mission as well. The Master Plan, developed for public higher education in California in 1960, gave each set of institutions a separate mission. The plan in effect created a moat around the University of California by providing genuinely open admissions at the community college level, with the university accepting only the top one-eighth among high school seniors in the state. The focus of the University on upper-division and graduate work was to be facilitated by the use of the community college network to prepare a minority of students for transfer to the university; the majority were to be terminal or "cooled-out." Moreover, vis-à-vis the state

---

of subsistence and of income forgone; we also believe that the prevailing system forces students who are neither well-to-do nor exceptionally talented to depend either on their parents or the local public college, limiting their freedom of consumer choice in higher education.

[70] See Trow (1970; 1972).

[71] For discussion of the aspirations of the latter, see Dunham (1969) and my appended commentary.

colleges, which were allotted a more modest selectivity, the university was to maintain its virtual monopoly of doctoral programs. Today, though somewhat battered, the Master Plan still stands. The university and the state colleges admit more minority students with low scores than they did, but there is little pressure to transform Berkeley and UCLA by "Open Admissions," the way CCNY has been transformed. The Master Plan has been loosened up enough so that black and Spanish-speaking students do not feel that they are forcibly being "tracked" into the community colleges, which in any case seem to have a higher standing and morale in California than in many other parts of the country.[72] Nevertheless, the widespread sense of state pride in the eminence of Berkeley has been somewhat diluted within Berkeley itself, through self-abnegation and guilt for the supposed crime of elitism: and of course the university has been the special target of Reaganite backlash. Like other major institutions, the university of California has suffered from budgetary freezes, undermaintenance, and diminished flexibility.

That all the branches of the University of California have maintained their relative national standing in spite of these pressures reflects the fact that state pride has not completely soured into populist resentment, and that many and at times a majority of the regents have defended the university, as they regularly did in the early 1960s, before "Berkeley" became an international symbol, like "Nanterre." Yet I have found in conversations with liberal and radical faculty members and students at several branches of the university that they seldom appreciate the role of the chancellors or regents as buffers against political attack. Instead, the regents would be criticized for representing various Establishments rather than "the people," whereas it appeared to me that the wealthy cosmopolitan Northern California regents helped provide California's equivalent of patrician protection for the university, so that one could only wish there were enough such regents to go around the country over.

ACADEMIC FREEDOM: INSIDE AND OUT   In addition to selecting the top executive, I believe that the most important role of governing boards and regents is to mobilize support for the institution and to defend it against intemperate,

[72] Precisely the tracking aspect of the California arrangement and similar institutional hierarchies are attacked by Karabel (forthcoming; 1972, pp. 38–43).

incomprehending outside critics. The eagerness in many institutions to have faculty members and students represented on boards of trustees sometimes suggests an unwillingness to recognize how crucial this buffer role is.[73] Jill Conway's account of the University of Toronto's governance struggles seems to show that the Canadians are not notably wiser about who needs to be represented to whom than we are.

In this connection, Benson Snyder has observed that at MIT more information on the budget and on hiring practices is now made available, and that this has proved beneficial. What Edward Shils long ago, during the Joseph McCarthy era, called the torment of secrecy has led, in the universities as in the federal government, to a tremendous effort to find out what is going on behind closed doors with the assumption that there should be no closed doors.[74] Yet Snyder also recognizes the tremendous distractions that beset a professor at a place like MIT. He sees the leadership of the institution as distracted from educational change by the turmoil of confrontation (see p. 155 in this volume) and one can draw similar conclusions from accounts elsewhere. But the information offered for public consumption by trying to end the torment of secrecy is still another distraction. It seems conceivable to me that the use of slogans, now so endemic in the endless campus meetings, is accelerated by the need to cope with the flood of information, allowing us to deal with an issue like governance or investment policy in a catchword.

In an earlier era, colleges and universities often prospered because they were benignly misunderstood. The paying public confused science with technology and sought the benefits of the latter by benefices to the former. Some confusion may also prevail concerning the length of time that faculty are required to spend

[73] Depending on context, there are many things to be said for and against having students, faculty from the institution in question, and faculty from other institutions serve on boards of trustees; I do not intend to deal with all these issues through the brief remarks in the text. For illustration of how helpful young former students can be in educating a board of trustees, see the statements, especially by trustees from Vanderbilt and Princeton, in Armbruster (1972, pp. 3–9).

[74] Notice the insistence of the Students Administrative Council at Toronto that all meetings be open: ". . . those radicals who drew, however indirectly, on the Maoist idea of cultural revolution, felt that open discussions of university policy were the first step toward making the university truly responsible to 'the people.'" Cf. Shils (1956, p. 17).

working with doctoral candidates, some of whom require extremely close apprentice-type supervision, while others work pretty independently and send in chapters or even a whole dissertation for cursory review. In many cases, a college freshman may need more direct help and require about as much faculty time as a graduate student. Yet the great state universities have built their programs in considerable measure on the basis of FTE (full-time-equivalent) formulae that assumed, for example, that a ratio of four doctoral candidates to one faculty member was a reasonable workload as contrasted to a dozen or more lower-division students per faculty member. (However, since the FTE formulae have been used to build up the peaks of state university excellence vis-à-vis their regional or community college competitors, it might be damaging to recalculate such formulae now.)

Today, much more information is available and much protective obscurantism has been lost. If one considers in addition the provocations that especially the selective public and private universities have offered to prevailing values, it is remarkable how ineffective soured alumni, harassed trustees, and even legislators have been in actually monitoring the eminent campuses. To be sure, they can impose indirect controls, such as limiting out-of-state enrollments, or cutting out sabbaticals, or using budgetary stringencies in punitive and niggling ways. But despite excesses (as, for example, interference by regents at Texas) the major campuses have maintained relative political and cultural inviolability. If one examines the reports of Committee A of the AAUP, most of the colleges which are censured are public and small, sometimes black; UCLA with the Angela Davis case is an exception.[75] In occasional meetings with college faculties and with administrators, I have sometimes asked them what they would expect the president of the institution to—metaphorically—die for in terms of academic freedom, particularly in a public institution: should he die only for freedom of discourse, or also for pornography in the student paper or the student stage, or for incendiary obscenities, or incitements to violence by faculty? For most liberal and radical faculty and students with whom I have discussed the issue, there *is* no issue: academic freedom is a seamless web and everything short of violence that is done or said in a good cause such as opposing the war, or calling for human liberation,

---

[75] See, e.g., *AAUP Bulletin* (June 1972, pp. 115; 145–155).

must be defended down to the last trench. In response to this, I have argued that we do not live in a patrician society where the eccentricities of the privileged are defended by hierarchy, by status, and by secrecy. We live in a populist, often demagogic society, in which the protections even of lawful First Amendment privilege can become precarious. For example, if the president of a public institution in a conservative state is asked to defend an obscene cover of a student magazine, the chances are that necessary distinctions will not be made by the state or the regents and that concessions will be extracted on all fronts, including the intellectual freedom to hear all contending views, to invite anyone to the campus, and to assign any kind of reading matter in the classroom.[76] The answer I myself give to this question is the traditional one, that the institution and its membership must be prepared to support—against antilibertarians of the Left as well as the Right—the obligations and privilege of free discourse and teaching no matter what the consequences. Within this orbit, my view is absolute and I would be prepared if need be to sacrifice the institution with the inevitable harm this would bring to individuals. But I hold a less absolute view beyond the margin where one abandons discourse; the line I draw here may be narrower than the constitutionally protected rights of citizens—and there is no question that this is a difficult line to draw.[77]

Many radicals would contend that the essays and my commentary on them understate the degree of repression that has already occurred because students, faculty members, and administrators, anticipating punitive reactions by federal and state authorities, have censored or restrained their own speech and conduct or have

---

[76] John Silber (1971, p. 44), has asked: "If the collective ambition of the faculty and student body of the university is to become the most extreme faculty and student body in the country, then what financial costs, in terms of the forfeiture of public and private patronage, are they prepared to pay?" The converse of this is suggested by Samuel Eliot Morison's discussion of Harvard President Lowell's defense of academic freedom: "He not only believed in academic freedom but practiced it through trying circumstances, defending the rights of instructors to teach the truth as they saw it and in their public relations to express unpopular opinions with which he fundamentally disagreed. The knowledge that he could be depended upon to defend these rights made the members of the several faculties more responsible and cautious in their utterances than they would have been under a President likely to let them down" (Morison, 1936, p. 440).

[77] See the discussion among H. Bruce Franklin (1972, pp. 31–39), Nathan Glazer (1972, pp. 40–44), and Lewis B. Mayhew (1972, pp. 45–47) in *Change.*

suffered reprisals from administrators and boards of trustees for not doing so.[78] To some student and faculty radicals, a speech by Vice-President Agnew to a Republican luncheon is already an omen of repression, while undoubtedly there are millions of Americans who would like to see a curb on radicalism by whatever means necessary. Yet a visitor to America has the impression that talk and debate are extraordinarily free. The same impression is true for the visitor who is from an earlier era, even only one generation earlier.[79]

In the era of McCarthyism, faculty members in liberal departments in relatively liberal institutions felt a certain degree of solidarity vis-à-vis what they saw as a hostile and Philistine public.[80] Divisions within liberalism of course existed then: concerning Stalinism, concerning the Cold War, concerning attitudes toward the quality of American life. But in the country as a whole, these divisions were muted in something like a united front of rejection of both the bland and the mean aspects of Eisenhower's Middle America. Ten years later, liberal academic man was sitting pretty, courted by some agencies of the federal government and by some sophisticated corporations and attended to, if not always responded to, by a vastly larger audience of students. But of course, the same national developments that shattered the country also shattered the liberal academic coalition, that is to

[78] A number of observers have suggested that the killings at Kent State and Jackson State also served to inhibit the student movement as individuals recognized that they faced not only the risks of arrest or possible beating, but the actual danger that they or other people would be killed. (Cf., however, Adamek and Lewis [1972] indicating that participants and observers in the Kent State shootings became more prepared to believe in the need for violent revolutionary change.) Undoubtedly, the explosion which killed a graduate student in the mathematics building at the University of Wisconsin led a number of students to pull back from the brink of violence, a reaction that in some measure supports Kenneth Keniston's argument in *Young Radicals: Notes on Committed Youth* (1968) concerning the genuine hatred for violence of many activist students.

[79] Indeed, in an article on the Radical Right written in 1955, Nathan Glazer and I would seem to have overestimated the future of the Right Wing potential in this country. The fact that history has perhaps temporarily taken another course, however, does not incontrovertibly establish that we were mistaken at that time. See Riesman and Glazer (1955).

[80] For detailed discussion, see Lazarsfeld and Thielens (1958). See also my discussion of the role of the local and the student press in arousing apprehension or creating reassurance among faculty with politically sensitive views in Riesman (1958a, pp. 3–8).

say, the escalation of the Vietnam War and the escalation and movement to the North of the racial struggle. For college-age young men (and young women sympathizers) the Vietnam War has been a personal as well as a public issue: one which has seemed to justify their despair, to haunt their courage, to offer them such options as overprivileged deferment, jail, or expatriation. Moreover, for white students and faculty, it has been the Vietnam War which has served to discredit political authority and liberal politics. The "search and destroy" missions relentlessly demolishing Vietnamese life have had their nonviolent but tortured psychic counterpart among university people (and of course many others too) who, turning from the judgment that America must be the greatest country, to one of equal vanity, that it must be the worst, have sought to search out and destroy the illusions about America and about Western civilization in which many in the older generation were nourished. Correspondingly, the fear of being thought a fascist or a racist has become at least as inhibiting a thought on some campuses as the fear in an earlier era of being thought a communist or a "nigger-lover." Black students, too, and their many white sympathizers, have been purging themselves of illusions concerning American race relations. In 1944, Gunnar Myrdal saw Americans as caught in a dilemma between their ideals of equality and their practices of racism. A quarter-century later, what he saw as a dilemma is commonly regarded as at best white hypocrisy, compartmentalization, and escapism; at worst, it is outright racism. His energetic, nonfatalistic hopefulness is gone.

Correspondingly, the earlier relative solidarity of liberal faculty has been shattered by divided reactions to the internal consequences of these extramural events. Zelda Gamson's essay describes the precarious way in which Michigan's liberal coalition held onto itself in spite of divisions as to how to respond, for example, to the demands of the Black Action Movement and its white supporters. Marshall Meyer's essay on Harvard mainly describes divisions among the students, not among the faculty; but among the latter there have been wide divisions, illustrated by divergent reactions to the harassment of Professor Richard Herrnstein.[81] Indeed, on some campuses where equanimity now

---

[81] Herrnstein's article on IQ (1971) came under almost continuous attack from SDS and its affiliates (and of course also from many other critics) during fall and winter 1971–72: his classes were invaded and he was relentlessly pursued; some Harvard faculty came to his personal defense publicly, but many stayed on the sidelines or found reasons in the article or the context to disap-

seems to prevail, it may reflect not only the relative decline of confrontational energies, but also an unwillingness of more traditionally liberal faculty members and administrators directly to challenge the political and moral boundary lines of the confrontationally inclined Left or even, direct confrontation aside, the moral hegemony established among most of us by the great polemical traditions of the Left at least since the French Revolution. In the American egalitarian ethos, as I have argued, selectivity, hierarchy, and secrecy lack standing in court either judicially or in the feelings we academics have about ourselves.

At Antioch, Old Westbury, and Toronto, the question as to who is in charge, or who is to participate and how has often taken priority over the question of what is to be done, though of course it is hard to separate the two. At Antioch, at Old Westbury, and at Federal City College, judging by these essays, arguments over educational policy and over the kinds and limits of experimentation created fissures, somewhat along generational lines, between older liberal scholars and younger activist experimenters. Because CCNY has depended more on high selectivity of student intake for its distinction than on the quality of its faculty, its faculty members, as Nathan Glazer describes them, are polarized in responding to Open Admissions; many doubt whether traditional standards can be adhered to when it comes to conferring the baccalaureate when those standards have been breached at the point of entry.[82] Similarly, when some faculty members invite HEW investigators onto the campus either to examine specific instances of alleged discrimination or to press for an Affirmative Action plan, it becomes clear that solidarity against government intervention has almost completely vanished, at least when what many liberal and radical faculty consider good causes are at stake.

prove of Herrnstein and hence to mitigate their reprobation of the SDS tactics — reminiscent of the way in which during the era of Joe McCarthy many people slid toward the anti-Communist Right wing by almost imperceptible gradations. The Commencement Issue of the Harvard *Crimson* (1972, pp. 18–19), provides a review of the issues and episodes and an interview with Herrnstein by Peter Shapiro.

[82] The union activists of the Professional Staff Congress of CCNY give no external sign that they may be apprehensive concerning the willingness of taxpayers to pay extremely high salaries to faculty members who are actually doing remedial work of a high-school level. Even if one contends, as I would, that this work is more demanding than most college teaching and requires exemplary tact and patience, the disparities in salary structure both within public higher education and between higher education and the public schools may prove difficult to sustain in a time of statewide budgetary rationalization.

Yet it would be rash to say that student activism is in a period of permanent decline. It takes very few students to change a campus climate. Less than a handful of students at the University of Pennsylvania created an impression of mass student enthusiasm for Martin Meyerson as a candidate for president. Zelda Gamson writes that no more than 30 students at the University of Michigan have been the core of radical activity. And of course even fewer terrorists can cause enormous havoc. Moreover, the wounding divisions within academic liberalism have not been healed.

But what should perhaps give modest grounds for hope is a certain muting of the external hostility directed toward the campus. I am impressed by the generosity and tolerance there are for institutions which are costly and seemingly or actually radical. They may no longer be the secular cathedrals of our time, but they still encompass some of our local and national pride. Alumni, donors, legislators, and government officials have been willing to come to their aid to minimize the looming insolvencies—if sometimes with too little too late—and influential adults continue to realize that there are elements of self-transcendence involved in university life.

I feel less sanguinity about the question as to what we academics will do with the degrees of freedom the society still allows us. I feel fairly sure that there can be no return to the relatively unquestioned assumptions of the immediate post-Sputnik era in higher education. Though we may be seeing a temporary pedagogic Thermidor on some campuses, I believe with Martin Trow that higher education has been permanently altered by the entry of new near-universal constituencies at the student level and new types of recruits for faculty, administrative, and staff positions. There is a much freer market for new forms of education, for both new and old clientele, a greater transiency as to the timing or phasing of higher education, meshing with a greater fluidity of values and commitments in the society at large. (Many Carnegie Commission Reports and documents have been saying just that, and indeed contributing their mite to the fluidity, to the refusal to take former boundaries for granted.) My own observations, in some measure supported by these essays, have been that many of the new reforms have not been working well—and that there has been little serious evaluation of them either at the institutions in question or comparatively. Thus, like other institutions, higher education would seem to be stumbling backward into an uncertain and opaque future. I still believe, as I argued in *The Lonely Crowd,* that we need to live simultaneously on two levels: one being the pragmatic day-to-day enterprise of tolerable survival, and the other some vision of what our common enterprise might be like in a quite conceivable but rather different future — a vision by which we can marginally guide and judge our day-to-day procedures.

References

AAUP Bulletin, vol. 63, pp. 115, 145–55, June 1972.

Abrams, Janet F., and Charlton R. Price: "The Learning Community, Portland, Oregon: A Report to the Carnegie Corporation of New York," December 1971.

Adamek, Raymond J., and Jerry M. Lewis: "Social Control, Violence, and Radicalization: The Kent State Case," paper delivered at the American Sociological Association meeting, New Orleans, August 1972.

Armbruster, Robert: "From the Boardroom: Young Trustees Speak," *Alma Mater,* vol. 39, pp. 3–9, May–June 1972.

Bayer, Alan E., and Alexander Astin: "Campus Unrest, 1970–71: Was It Really All That Quiet?" *Educational Record,* vol. 52, pp. 301–313, Fall 1971.

Bell, Daniel: *The Reforming of General Education: The Columbia College Experience and Its National Setting,* Columbia University Press, New York, 1966.

Berger, Peter L., and Brigitte Berger: "The Blueing of America," *The New Republic,* vol. 164, pp. 20–23, April 3, 1971.

Blackburn, Robert T.: *Tenure: Aspects of Job Security on the Changing Campus,* Southern Regional Education Board, Atlanta, July 1972.

Boruch, Robert F.: "The Faculty Role in Campus Unrest," American Council on Education, Research Reports, vol. 4, no. 5, Washington, 1969.

Bunzel, John H.: "The Faculty Strike at San Francisco State College," *AAUP Bulletin,* vol. 57, Autumn 1971.

Burrage, Michael: "Democracy and the Mystery of the Crafts: Observations on Work Relationships in America and Britain," *Daedalus,* vol. 101, pp. 141–162, Fall 1972.

Cheit, Earl F.: *The New Depression in Higher Education: A Study of Financial Conditions in 41 Colleges and Universities,* McGraw-Hill Book Company, New York, 1971.

Commission on Educational Policy: *Critique of a College,* Swarthmore College, November 1967.

Commission on MIT Education: *Report of Colloquium on Knowledge and Values,* Massachusetts Institute of Technology, Cambridge, May 27, 1971.

Cottle, Thomas J.: "Thank God for the Simple People," *Time's Children: Impressions of Youth,* Little, Brown and Company, Boston, 1971.

Cottle, Thomas J.: "The Pains of Permanence," in Bardwell Smith (ed.), *The Tenure Debate.* Jossey-Bass Publishers, Inc., San Francisco, 1972.

DeLamater, John: "Boys and Girls Together: The Incest Taboo in a Coed Community," unpublished paper, Department of Sociology, University of Wisconsin, Madison, 1971.

DeMott, Benjamin: "Seven Days in May," *Change,* vol. 2, no. 5, pp. 55–68, September–October 1970.

DeMott, Benjamin: "Letter to an Unhappy Alumnus," *Change,* vol. 4, no. 6, pp. 24–29, Summer 1972.

Donald, Cleveland, Jr.: "Cornell: Confrontation in Black and White," in Cushing Strout and David I. Grossvogel (eds.), *Divided We Stand: Reflections on the Crisis at Cornell,* Doubleday & Company, Inc., New York, 1970, pp. 153–204.

Dreeben, Robert: "Reflections on Teacher Militancy and Unionization," *Sociology of Education,* vol. 45, pp. 326–337, Summer 1972.

Driver, Christopher: *The Exploding University,* Hodder Stoughton, Ltd., London, 1971.

Duberman, Martin: "Black Mountain: Reflections on a Pioneer Living-Learning Community," *Change,* vol. 4, no. 6, pp. 30–46, Summer 1972.

Dunham E. Alden: *Colleges of the Forgotten Americans: A Profile of State Colleges and Regional Universities,* McGraw-Hill Book Company, New York, 1969.

Fashing, Joseph, and Steven E. Deutsch: *Academics in Retreat: The Politics of Educational Innovation.* The University of New Mexico Press, Albuquerque, 1971.

Franklin, H. Bruce: "The Real Issues of My Case," *Change,* vol. 4, no. 5, pp. 31–39, June 1972.

Freeman, Jo: "The Tyranny of Structurelessness," *Berkeley Journal of Sociology,* vol. XVII, pp. 151–164, 1972–73.

French, David: "After the Fall: What This Country Needs is a Good *Counter* 'Counter-Culture' Culture," *New York Times Magazine,* October 3, 1971, pp. 20–21+ .

Fulton, Oliver, and Martin Trow: "Research Activities in American Higher Education," University of Edinburgh, Center for Research in Educational Sciences, May 1972.

Garbarino, Joseph W.: "Creeping Unionism and the Faculty Labor Market," in Margaret S. Gordon (ed.), *Higher Education and the Labor Market*, McGraw-Hill Book Company, New York, forthcoming.

Glazer, Nathan: *Remembering the Answers: Essays on the American Student Revolt*, Basic Books, New York, 1970.

Glazer, Nathan: "Why a Faculty Cannot Afford a Franklin," *Change*, vol. 4, no. 5, pp. 40–44, June 1972.

Goldman, Ralph M.: "San Francisco State: The Technology of Confrontation," in Julian Foster and Durward Long (eds.), *Protest! Student Activism in America*, William Morrow, New York, 1970.

Harvard Crimson, vol. 103, pp. 18–19, June 15, 1972.

Herrnstein, Richard: "IQ," *Atlantic Monthly*, vol. 228, pp. 43–58+, September 1971.

Horner, Matina S.: "Femininity and Successful Achievement: A Basic Inconsistency," in Judith M. Bardwick, Elizabeth Douvan, Matina S. Horner, and David Gutmann, *Feminine Personality and Conflict*, Wadsworth Publishing Company, Inc., Belmont, Calif., 1970.

Jencks, Christopher, and David Riesman: "Feminism, Masculinism, and Coeducation," *The Academic Revolution*, Doubleday & Company, Inc., New York, 1968a.

Jencks, Christopher, and David Riesman: "Social Stratification and Mass Higher Education," in *The Academic Revolution*, Doubleday & Company, Inc., New York, 1968b.

Jencks, Christopher, et al.: *Inequality: A Reassessment of the Effect of Family and Schooling in America*. Basic Books Inc., Publishers, New York, forthcoming.

Karabel, Jerome: "Open Admissions; Toward Meritocracy or Equality?" *Change*, vol. 4, pp. 38–43, May 1972.

Karabel, Jerome: "Community Colleges and Social Stratification," *Harvard Educational Review*, forthcoming.

Keniston, Kenneth: *Young Radicals: Notes on Committed Youth*, Harcourt, Brace, & World, Inc., New York, 1968.

Kriegel, Leonard: "Surviving the Apocalypse: Teaching at City College," *Change*, vol. 4, no. 6, pp. 54–62, Summer 1972.

Ladd, Dwight R.: *Change in Educational Policy: Self-Studies in Selected Colleges and Universities*, McGraw-Hill Book Company, New York, 1970.

Lane, Earl: "The 'New' Old Westbury," *Change*, vol. 4, September 1972.

Lazarsfeld, Paul F., and Wagner Thielens, Jr.: *The Academic Mind: Social Scientists in a Time of Crisis* (with a field report by David

Riesman), The Free Press of Glencoe, Inc., New York, 1958.

Lipset, Seymour M.: *Rebellion in the University,* Little, Brown and Company, Boston, 1971.

Livingston, John: "Tenure, Anyone?", in Bardwell Smith (ed.). *The Tenure Debate,* Jossey-Bass Publishers, Inc., San Francisco, 1972.

Mayew, Lewis B.: "Dissent: A Campus View," *Change,* vol. 4, no. 5, pp. 45–47, June 1972.

Mead, Margaret: *Culture and Commitment,* Natural History Press, New York, 1970.

Metzger, Walter P.: "The Academic Profession and Its Public Critics," in Robert A. Altman and Carolyn M. Byerly (eds.), *The Public Challenge and the Campus Response,* Center for Research and Development in Higher Education, University of California, Berkeley; and Western Interstate Commission for Higher Education, Boulder, Colo., 1971, pp. 71–87.

Meyer, Marshall W.: "Harvard Students in the Midst of Crisis," *Sociology of Education,* vol. 44, pp. 245–269, Summer 1971; also "Harvard Students in the Midst of Crisis: A Note on the Sources of Leftism," *Sociology of Education,* vol. 45, forthcoming.

Morison, Samuel: *Three Centuries of Harvard,* Harvard University Press, Cambridge, Mass. 1936.

Newcomb, Theodore, Donald Brown, et al.: "The University of Michigan's Residential College," in Paul L. Dressel (ed.), *The New Colleges: Toward an Appraisal,* Jossey-Bass Publishers, Inc., San Francisco. 1971, pp. 99–142.

Novak, Michael: "Green Shoots of Counter Culture," in *Politics: Realism and Imagination,* Herder and Herder, Inc., New York, 1971.

Parsons, Talcott, and Gerald M. Platt: "Considerations on the American Academic System" *Minerva,* vol. 6, pp. 497–523, 1968.

Pitts, Jesse: "Strike at Oakland University," *Change,* vol. 3, no. 1, pp.16–19, February 1972.

Riesman, David: "The Local Press and Academic Freedom," *Political Research: Organization and Design,* vol. 1, no. 3, pp. 3–8, January 1958a.

Riesman, David: "Review of the Jacob Report," *American Sociological Review,* vol. 23, pp. 732–739, 1958b.

Riesman, David: "America Moves to the Right," *New York Times Magazine,* Oct. 27, 1968, p. 34ff.

Riesman, David: "The Collision Course of Higher Education," *Journal of College Student Personnel,* vol. 10, pp. 363–369, November 1969a.

Riesman, David: "The Search for Alternative Models in Education," *The American Scholar*, vol. 38, pp. 377–388, 1969*b*.

Riesman, David: "Observations on Contemporary College Students—Especially Women," *Interchange*, vol. 1, no. 1, pp. 52–63, April 1970.

Riesman, David, and Nathan Glazer: "The Intellectuals and the Discontented Classes," *Partisan Review*, Winter 1955; reprinted with a further commentary in Daniel Bell (ed.), *The Radical Right*, Doubleday & Company, Inc., New York, 1963, pp. 105–159.

Rosenberg, Milton J., Sidney Verba, and Philip E. Converse, *Vietnam and the Silent Majority: The Dove's Guide*, Harper & Row, New York, 1970.

Seaman, Melvin: "Alienation in Pre-Crisis France," *American Sociological Review*, vol. 37, pp. 385–402, 1972.

Shils, Edward: *The Torment of Secrecy: The Background and Consequences of American Security Policies*, The Free Press of Glencoe, Ill., Chicago, 1956.

Silber, John: "Campus Reform: From Within or Without," in Robert A. Altman and Carolyn M. Byerly (eds.), *The Public Challenge and the Campus Response*, Center for Research and Development in Higher Education, University of California, Berkeley; and Western Interstate Commission for Higher Education, Boulder, Colo., 1971, pp. 39–49.

Slaughter, Thomas F., Jr.: in Rhoda L. Goldstein, June Albert, and Thomas F. Slaughter, Jr., "The Status of Black Studies Programs at American Colleges and Universities," paper prepared for presentation at the American Sociology Association meetings, New Orleans, August 29, 1972.

Somers, Robert H.: "The Mainsprings of the Rebellion: A Survey of Berkeley Students in November 1964," in S. M. Lipset and Sheldon S. Wolin (eds.), *The Berkeley Student Revolt: Facts and Interpretations*, Doubleday Anchor Books, New York, 1965, pp. 549–550.

Stinchcombe, Arthur: "Orientation to the Department of Sociology," address to sociology graduate students, University of California, Berkeley, October 1971. (Mimeographed.)

Strout, Cushing: "A Personal Narrative of a Rude Awakening," in Cushing Strout and David I. Grossvogel (eds.), *Divided We Stand: Reflections on the Crisis at Cornell*, Doubleday & Company, Inc., New York, 1970, p. 45*n*.

Thorne, Barrie: "Girls Who Say 'Yes' to Guys Who Say 'No': Women and the Draft Resistance Movement," paper presented at the meeting of the American Sociological Association, New Orleans, 1972.

Trow, Martin: "The Undergraduate Dilemma in Large State Universities," *Universities Quarterly*, vol. 21, pp. 17–43, December 1966.

Trow, Martin: "Reflections on the Transition from Mass to Universal Higher Education," *Daedalus,* Winter, 1970.

Trow, Martin: "Admissions and the Crisis in American Higher Education," in W. Todd Furniss (ed.), *Higher Education for Everybody?,* American Council on Education, Washington, D. C., 1970.

Trow, Martin: "The Expansion and Transformation of Higher Education," *The International Review of Education,* vol. 18, February–March 1972.

Tussman, Joseph: *Experiment at Berkeley,* Oxford University Press, London, 1969.

Wheelis, Allen: "The Vocational Hazards of Psychoanalysis," in *The Quest for Identity,* W. W. Norton & Company, Inc., New York, 1958.

Wilson, James Q.: "Liberalism versus Liberal Education," *Commentary,* vol. 53, pp. 50–54, June 1972.

Acknowledgments

Many people contributed to *Academic Transformation* in indispensable ways. As typists, reviewers, informants, and advisers, they have rendered services for which we are very thankful. We want particularly to thank the authors for the care and insight with which they prepared the essays that give this volume its substance. We also appreciate their patience with our many questions and with some of the delays we encountered in putting the book together. We want also to thank Martha Glazier and Lynn Pease for rendering invaluable assistance in the preparation of the manuscript for Chapter 19 and for tracking down references and generally coordinating the often hectic Cambridge-centered activities of the editors. We wish also to thank Terry Y. Allen and Karen Seriguchi for their copy editing, proofreading, reference-closing, and vital assistance at Berkeley.

David Riesman
Verne A. Stadtman

Index